Northern Duty,
Southern Heart

ALSO BY H. LEON GREENE
AND FROM MCFARLAND

*The Confederate Yellow Fever Conspiracy: The Germ Warfare
Plot of Luke Pryor Blackburn, 1864–1865* (2019)

Northern Duty, Southern Heart

George Proctor Kane's Civil War

H. Leon Greene

McFarland & Company, Inc., Publishers
Jefferson, North Carolina

ISBN (print) 978-1-4766-8961-6
ISBN (ebook) 978-1-4766-4795-1

Library of Congress and British Library
cataloguing data are available

Library of Congress Control Number 2023013504

© 2023 H. Leon Greene. All rights reserved

*No part of this book may be reproduced or transmitted in any form
or by any means, electronic or mechanical, including photocopying
or recording, or by any information storage and retrieval system,
without permission in writing from the publisher.*

Front cover: George Proctor Kane (Tanner & Vanness, Photographers);
background map of Baltimore, 1860 (Johns Hopkins)

Printed in the United States of America

*McFarland & Company, Inc., Publishers
Box 611, Jefferson, North Carolina 28640
www.mcfarlandpub.com*

Acknowledgments

The author would like to thank the following people for their invaluable help with this project:

Colleen Puterbaugh—James O. Hall Research Center, Surratt Museum, Clinton, Maryland, for help in finding archival documents.

Laurie Verge—Surratt Museum, for encouragement.

Roger Norton—Lincoln Discussion Symposium, for encouragement.

Micah Connor—Reference Assistant; Sandra Glascock—Special Collections Archivist; Francis O'Neill—Senior Reference Librarian; Hannah Lane—Visitor Services; Mallory Herberger—Special Collections Archivist; Leslie Eames—Imaging Services, Maryland Center for History and Culture, for research assistance.

Paul Espinosa—Curator, George Peabody Library, Johns Hopkins Sheridan Libraries, for research assistance.

Tara Wink—Historical Librarian and Archivist, Historical Section, Health Sciences and Human Services Library, University of Maryland, for assistance in locating archival documents.

*Our decisions and goals
both lead us and follow us.*

Table of Contents

Acknowledgments — v
Illustrations — viii
Introduction — 1

1. Kane's Formative Years — 3
2. Kane's Early Career — 5
3. Kane's Connection to Baltimore Theatres and the John Wilkes Booth Family — 16
4. Baltimore Militias — 27
5. The Hibernian Society of Baltimore — 33
6. Baltimore Fire Departments — 38
7. Gangs of Baltimore and the Baltimore Elections — 44
8. Baltimore Police — 57
9. Slavery in Maryland and Baltimore — 69
10. The Baltimore Plot — 72
11. The Baltimore Riot — 108
12. Kane's Arrest — 146
13. Fort McHenry — 166
14. Forts Hamilton, Lafayette and Columbus — 170
15. Fort Warren — 184
16. Kane's Confederate Activity After Release from Prison — 196
17. Return to Baltimore — 218
18. A Late Turn as Mayor — 227

Epilogue — 238
Appendix — 241
Chapter Notes — 251
Bibliography — 275
Index — 279

Illustrations

1. Kane's Homes and Businesses—Map ... 4
2. Merchants' Exchange Building—Drawing ... 7
3. Merchants' Exchange Building—Photo ... 8
4. Location of the Merchants' Exchange Building—Map ... 8
5. George Kane—Carte de Viste ... 10
6. Rockdale Mill—Map ... 13
7. Location of Baltimore Theatres—Map ... 16
8. Location of Baltimore Hotels—Map ... 17
9. Arnold's Olympic Theatre—Drawing ... 17
10. Holliday Theatre—Photo ... 19
11. Newspaper Ad for Charles Street Theatre ... 20
12. Kane and Booth Home Locations—Map ... 21
13. Booth Home—Drawing ... 21
14. Playbill from Baltimore Museum and Gallery of Fine Arts ... 22–23
15. Newspaper Ad for Benefit at Holliday Theatre ... 25
16. Barnum's City Hotel—Drawing ... 36
17. Fire Companies—Map ... 39
18. Gangs of Baltimore—Map ... 46
19. "Plug Uglies Riot in Baltimore" ... 47
20. "Plug Uglies, Political Argument on Railroad Train" ... 48
21. "At the Polls" ... 52
22. Lincoln's Inaugural Train Route—Map ... 72
23. Proposed and Actual Train Route from Philadelphia to Washington, D.C.—Maps ... 73–74
24. Northern Central Railroad Line—Map ... 76
25. Philadelphia, Wilmington, and Baltimore Railroad Line—Map ... 77
26. Barnum's City Hotel—Photo ... 80
27. Downtown Baltimore, Site of Conspiratorial Activity—Map ... 81

28. Baltimore Railroad Stations—Map	89
29. Railroad Stations–1858—Drawings	90–91
30. President Street Railroad Station—Photo	91
31. Camden Street Railroad Station—Drawing	92
32. Lincoln's Route Through Baltimore—Map	93
33. Calvert Street Railroad Station—Drawing and Photo	94–95
34. Lincoln's "Passage Through Baltimore"	100
35. Crowd at Baltimore Awaiting President-Elect Lincoln's Arrival	103
36. "First Blood"	117
37. Page from Eutaw House Hotel Register	120
38. Rail Lines around Baltimore and Washington—Map	136
39. Broadside from Bradley T. Johnson	142
40. George Kane—Tintype	143
41. George Kane—Drawings	144–45
42. Kane's Arrest	147
43. Kane's Alleged Arsenal	154
44. Indictment Against Kane	159
45. Union Civil War Prisons—Forts McHenry, Lafayette, Hamilton, Columbus, Warren—Map	163
46. New York Prisons—Forts Columbus, Lafayette, Hamilton—Map	164
47. Fort Lafayette, Casemate #2	173
48. The Canadian Confederacy—Map	199
49. George Kane—Painting	236

Introduction

George Proctor Kane (1817–1878) was an enigma in his time. Born in Baltimore and a lifelong Baltimorean until the Civil War, Kane was raised in an environment where one could find sympathizers for both the North and the South. Maryland was a border state, and as such it contained many elements: urban and rural, industrial and agrarian, slave-emancipating and slave-holding. Baltimore was both a city of immigrants and a city intolerant of immigrants. Kane dealt with these opposing factions throughout his entire life.

Kane himself was an image of contradictions and conflicts. While he unequivocally held Southern proclivities, he performed tasks for the city of Baltimore and the state of Maryland that some would characterize as Northern functions. Two major events would define his life as the Civil War approached. Kane was responsible for protecting President-Elect Abraham Lincoln during his passage through Baltimore on his grand journey from Springfield, Illinois, to the inauguration in Washington, D.C., in February 1861. Lincoln's trip through the rough streets of this hostile city might just end his life. Kane had to guarantee that it didn't. Only a few weeks later, Lincoln found it necessary to call up troops as the Civil War loomed. Kane was also assigned the job of escorting the Massachusetts Sixth Regiment through these same volatile streets as it traveled to defend Washington, D.C., and protecting the citizens of Baltimore during the April 1861 event later called the "Pratt Street Riot." How did he manage to contain two opposing pulls on his psyche—his obligation to enforce laws in the North, and his emotional identity with the South?

George Kane's story must be told because his life embodied conflicts that persist today. He made difficult choices, many of which we might condemn, but we can honor select facets of a man's character without respecting everything that he represented. Such a man's life can instruct us in both how to act and how not to act. Abraham Lincoln himself addressed this issue when, speaking about Stonewall Jackson, the famous Confederate military officer, said that Jackson was "one who, though contending against us in a guilty cause, was, nevertheless, a gallant man. Let us forget his sins over his fresh made grave."[1]

While we must not embellish the character of someone who fought for the Confederacy under the guise of his devotion to "states' rights," to some falsely noble pursuit of a "lost cause," or to the protection of "Southern chivalry," we should discuss Kane's life and acknowledge his virtues, as well as his faults, without elevating him to sainthood. We should interpret history in a context appropriate to the past, sensitive to the present, and aware of its implications for the future. Kane was a good man—brave, honorable, true, honest, and courageous—who found himself using his gifts and attributes for the wrong cause.

George Proctor Kane was deeply flawed, as we all are, but his position in Baltimore in the mid–1800s led him to become a man who—in part—accomplished great things. He was a complex personality thrust into a most difficult time. He had to deal with the politics of a border state. His loyalty was to the South, but he functioned in Maryland, where Northern sentiments and laws had to be obeyed and enforced. It was a dichotomy that he was forced to navigate. This story tells of a man who had a Northern duty, but a Southern heart.

George Proctor Kane served Baltimore during the 19th century in many capacities. As a port collector, he was responsible for collecting the taxes that accrued to the government. As a businessman, he promoted the well-being of the economy of Baltimore. As a member of the militia, he protected the city from external threats. As a firefighter, he risked his life for others' safety. As a civic philanthropist, he supported the immigrant, the poor, and the uneducated. As a chief of police, he cleaned the city of its mob rule. As a sheriff, he enforced the laws. As a mayor, he directed the city toward growth.

But in the midst of these civic duties and responsibilities, Kane became Baltimore's whipping boy. He was arrested for his sentiments, not for any overt acts of lawlessness that he had yet committed. While he indeed participated in the arson of railroad bridges, he performed these acts as part of his duty to protect the citizens of Baltimore from riots. Keeping Northern troops from passing through Baltimore's streets prevented inevitable conflicts that would likely have resulted in many deaths. His actions were approved—probably even ordered—by the mayor of Baltimore and the governor of Maryland. In fact, Kane was imprisoned because of what he *might do*, not because of what he *had done*. He was denied a lawyer. He was denied habeas corpus. He languished in prison for 17 months without a trial. This story chronicles the contradictions embodied by a man who lived during this time.

1

Kane's Formative Years

George Proctor Kane was born in Baltimore on Conway Street on August 4, 1817, to John M. Kane (1790–1822); his mother's name has been lost to history.[1] John Kane was a Presbyterian from Londonderry, Northern Ireland, who immigrated to the United States in 1798. He was a member of the military in the 27th Regiment that fought at the Battle of North Point in the War of 1812. The elder Kane, who was wounded in that battle, died in 1822 at age 36, when George P. Kane was only about five years old. George had one older brother, John K. Kane,[2] who was born in 1809 and died in 1840,[3] who would have been only about 13 at the time of their father's death.[4] George's and John K.'s father was in the grocery business in Baltimore, the store first located at the southwest corner of Light Street and Pratt Street, at the edge of the shipping basin (today called the Inner Harbor), approximately where the PNC (Pittsburgh National Corporation) Bank now sits at One East Pratt Street. This commercial part of downtown was also the business center of Baltimore in the early 1800s.

The Kanes lived first at 72 South Charles Street; they moved to 10 Pratt Street (corner of Pratt and Light Streets) between 1814 and 1816, just prior to George's birth (Appendix). In about 1817 the family briefly moved to Conway Street near Hanover Street (where George was born) before taking residence on the west side of Aisquith Street, between Comet and Douglas Streets, a home described in tax records as a two-story frame dwelling, no doubt a very modest structure.[5]

After the death of the elder Kane, George's older brother John K. apparently assumed the management of the family grocery business, though he was still a teenager. Documents from this era show that Kane and Polk Grocers, located at 5 Light Street at the wharf, was run by John K. Kane, who lived on Aisquith Street near Pitt Street,[6] likely the same dwelling described by his father as north of Comet, south of Douglas, on the west side of Aisquith Street, since these locations are within yards of each other.[7] By 1833, John K. Kane had moved to Sharp Street.[8] George at this time would have been about 16 years old. The first commercial listing for George Kane had him as a "wholesale grocer,"[9] and the next year as a "commission merchant,"[10] located where his father and brother previously had their grain and grocery business at 5 Light Street near the wharf.

Little is known of George Kane's youth, except that he received his schooling in Baltimore. In his early years he worked as a clerk for John Gill, a local notary public, and also served a clerkship at a local commission house.[11] After the death of his brother in 1840, George at age 23 took on additional duties within the family

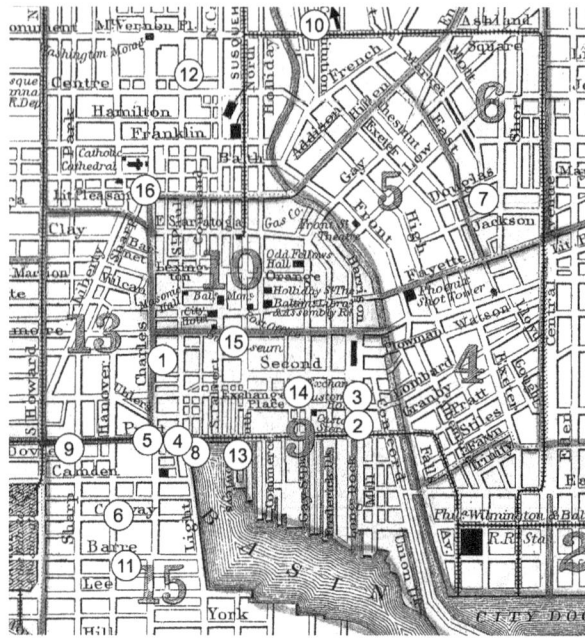

Figure 1. Locations of Kane's homes and businesses. (Appendix 1) Adapted from Samuel Augustus Mitchell, Jr.'s 1872 "Plan of Baltimore."

Kane's Homes and Businesses:
1. 72 S. Charles
2. 35 Market Space
3. 12 Market Space
4. Pratt at Light Street
5. 10 Pratt Street
6. Conway near Hanover
7. Aisquith, N. of Comet, S. of Hanover, W. Side
8. 5 Light Street Wharf
9. 51 S. Sharp Street
10. York Road, near first tollgate
11. 64 Barre
12. 163 St. Paul Street (615 today*)
13. 3 Bowley's Wharf
14. Exchange Buildings
15. 8 German Street
16. 87 N. Charles (333 today*)

*Street numbers changed in 1887.

business, including the sale of grain and groceries and the running of the commission merchant enterprise. It might explain how he became reasonably well-to-do relatively early in his life. By 1849, George's commission merchant business would be moved to 3 Bowly's Wharf[12] with a partner named Michael Stewart, as Stewart and Kane Commission Merchants.

Kane next lived at 64 Barre Street (near Hanover),[13] (Figure 1) though the 1851 directory had him living on Belvidere Road.[14] By 1860 Kane had moved to York Road, "near the first toll gate,"[15] an area popular with Baltimore businessmen. One history records, "The surface is rolling and beautifully diversified, the soil fertile and well cultivated. Most of the land is owned by the wealthy merchants of Baltimore City, and there is probably no district in in [sic] America that has so many beautiful country places."[16] Traveling from this home to downtown, even in this idyllic location, could be a dangerous proposition, as Kane discovered in August 1859. A newspaper report about Kane revealed, "He was riding on the York Road, and while descending a hill his horse stumbled and fell, throwing him violently on the road. He was badly bruised about the limbs and body, but fortunately sustained no other injury."[17] The first tollgate on York Road was situated in an area known as Friendship, slightly south of what was then called Waverly Avenue. Today York Road begins in Baltimore as Greenmount Avenue, and the neighborhood of Waverly still exists, though old Waverly Avenue has been replaced by what is now approximately 32nd Street. The first York Road tollgate would have been close to current Greenmount Avenue between 30th and 31st Streets.

2

Kane's Early Career

Politics and Employment

The political Kane was originally a Whig, though he later became a Democrat. Kane first participated in the Young Men's National Whig Convention in Baltimore, attended by 15,000–20,000 persons. He was one of the Assistant Marshals of the parade held on May 4, 1840, supporting Whig William Henry Harrison ("Old Tippecanoe") for President.[1] There were 94 Assistant Marshals in this parade, including future Baltimore Mayor George William Brown, who would factor heavily in Kane's political future.

Kane next worked for Henry Clay's Whig presidential campaign in 1844, with Kane serving as Grand Marshal in a parade of the Young Men's National Whig Convention in Baltimore on May 1, 1844. Kane's connection to Whig President Zachary Taylor yielded him the post of Port Collector of Customs for Baltimore (actually located in nearby Canton), replacing William H. Marriott.[2] Kane began his duties on June 1, 1849, and Whig President Millard Fillmore reappointed him; he served from 1849 to 1853. Kane's appointment to this title was widely accepted as purely a political move. That position also made him officially the "Superintendent of Lights and Buoys" in 1850.[3]

In his role as Port Collector, Kane acted for the benefit of the public health of Baltimore when in April 1852 he made the public warehouses at Lazaretto Point, opposite Fort McHenry, available to house passengers with "ship fever" (now known to be epidemic typhus) from the ship *Jane Henderson*. The First Branch of the Baltimore City Council (there were two Branches to Baltimore's City Council in the 1800s) allocated funds to house patients there and to provide physician and nursing care, in addition to necessary supplies.[4]

In 1852, controversy arose over Kane's tenure as the Port Collector. Though still a Whig himself, Kane found opposition within his own party for his continuation in that position, and a committee sought to have him ousted.[5] Part of the objection to Kane's performance of his duties was his refusal to remove some 50 Democratic employees of the Port and replace them with Whigs.[6] Kane believed that these employees—even though Democrats—were essential to the function of the Port of Baltimore and he stood his ground, refusing to replace them with political appointees from his own party. As a young politician, Kane proved himself to be unmovable from stances he felt to be right.

Other charges led the committee to go to Washington to implore the President to get rid of Kane. President Millard Fillmore demanded that any charges against Kane be presented in writing, a request that delayed the process until the Whig Convention was held in Baltimore in April 1852. Because of the delay (and Whigs could not even agree on their support for Fillmore), the Convention chose to drop the charges and the request for Kane's removal. Kane remained in his position as Port Collector until 1853, when Phillip Francis Thomas succeeded him.[7] In spite of the controversy surrounding Kane's last few months on the job, reports said that Kane "won the respect of the mercantile community, and retires with the kind wishes of the public generally."[8] In this position, Kane proved himself to be a man of principle, not bending to pressure from his own political party to distribute political spoils to party faithfuls.

Kane became a Democrat in 1852, and with the election of Democrat Franklin Pierce, he was selected as a member of the Baltimore citizens' committee to welcome Pierce to Baltimore on July 11, 1853.[9]

By the 1850s Kane was a rather well-to-do Baltimorean by any standard. Today we would likely classify him as a member of the upper middle class; his fortunes did not reach the atmospheric heights of upper-class Baltimore that included Johns Hopkins, John S. Gittings, or John W. Garrett, but Kane certainly rose in prominence through his family grocery and commission merchant business.

Kane invested widely and wisely in property in Baltimore and Maryland, and in October 1853 he purchased a plot of land dubbed "Lavender Hill," located on the Harford Turnpike in an area then called Harkersville, but now called Parkville. Kane's property there was a desirable location six miles from the center of Baltimore, and it had over 41 acres of land, a house with 26 rooms, a stable, and other structures. It sold for $63 per acre. At the same time, Kane purchased the adjacent lot containing over 21 acres for $48 per acre.[10] Kane turned around and sold both properties in October 1854, when they were described as a 63-acre estate.[11] By 1861 Kane's wealth was estimated to be $24,500 (approximately $735,000 today), compared to Mayor George William Brown's $27,825. The average member of Baltimore's First Branch of the City Council had an estate of $14,916 (with a median of $7,633). The Second Branch member's average estate was $15,889 (with a median of $10,950).[12]

The incomes from his businesses were initially modest, and his pay as Port Collector was likewise nominal. However, Kane and his brother and father before him had apparently successfully leveraged the family business into a sizable fortune. The family was involved in the grocery, grain, and commission merchant businesses, thriving in the Inner Harbor of Baltimore, and George inherited these activities. These family businesses ultimately had become very lucrative.

Business and Civic Involvement

As his business ventures expanded, Kane became a co-owner of the Baltimore Merchants' Exchange, which began with its incorporation on January 25, 1816, as the "Baltimore Exchange Company," with William Patterson as Chairman and 11 others as members. Construction proceeded from 1816 to 1820. The building was the grand design of architects Benjamin Henry Latrobe and John Maximilian Maurice Godefroy, incorporating materials specifically chosen to be aesthetically attractive on the Baltimore scene. It opened on June 1, 1820. The location in the center of Baltimore's business district was only one block from the wharves and about two blocks from the Kane grocery and commission merchant businesses. Located in the center of Exchange Place, a grouping of buildings bounded by Gay Street, Second Street, Lombard Street, and South Street, it was the shape of an "H" with a large double dome, with an upper and a lower level, in the center of the crossbar. At one time it was the largest domed structure in the United States, towering 115 feet above the floor. The building itself was four stories high, including a vaulted basement. Not exactly symmetrical, portions of the west wing of the "H" were only two stories high, though the original design had both wings of equal size. A large rotunda dominated the center of the building, and it was here that many major social and political events in Baltimore were held. (Figures 2–4)

The Exchange at various times housed not only the Merchants' Exchange Company itself, where Baltimore merchants and ship owners gathered daily for business, but also the Exchange Hotel, the stock market, the Branch Bank of the United States (later the Merchants' National Bank of Baltimore), the Customs House, a

Figure 2. Merchants' Exchange Building, located at the northwest corner of Lombard and Gay Streets. The drawing depicts the structure as originally designed. From the Maryland Center for History and Culture.

SECOND
MARYLAND BLDG.
RIALTO BUILD'G
Offices HALL
INS. OFF.
3RD. NATION'L BANK
WARE HO.
12
S. HOLIDAY
EXCHANGE ALLEY
MONEY ORDER DEPT. P.O.
11
POST OFFICE
THE MERCHANTS NAT'L BANK
U.S. CUSTOM HOUSE
Dome 85'
EXCHANGE
PLACE
LIQUOR WARE HO.
SPICE W. HO.
PORK LARD & HAM
COMMERCIAL BLDG.

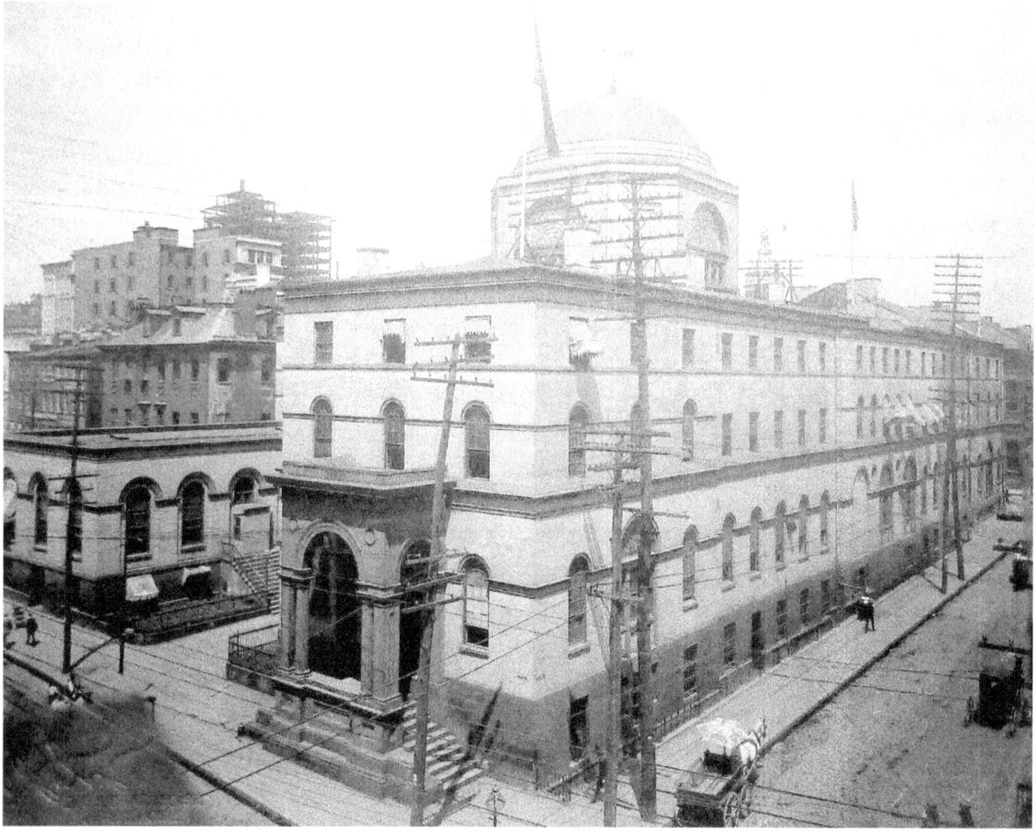

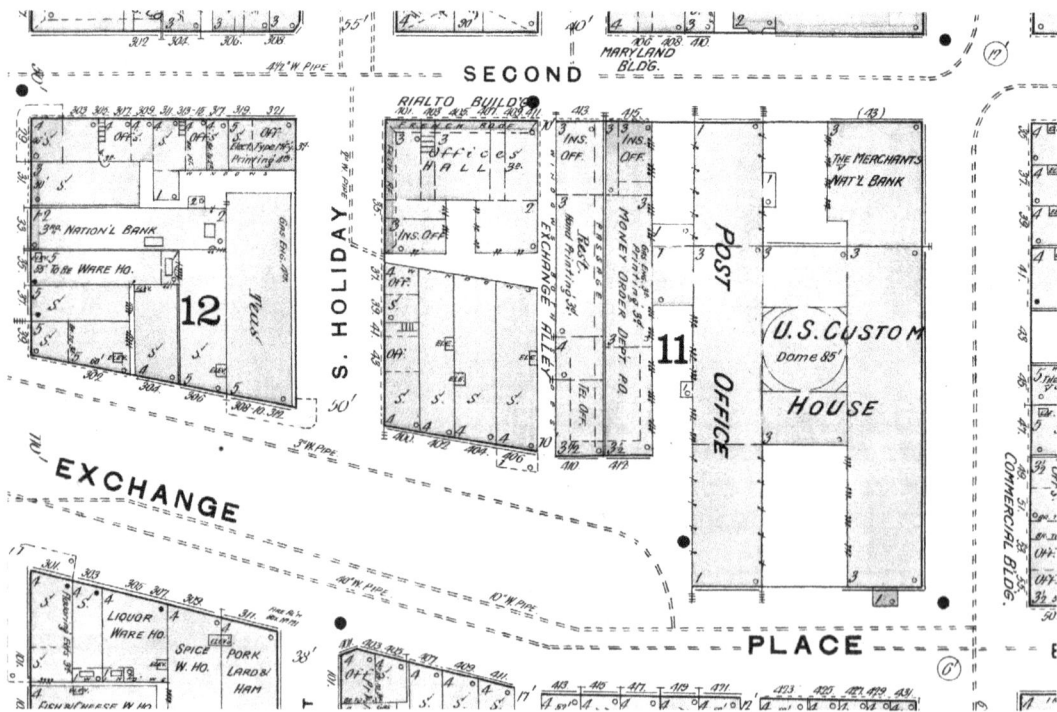

courthouse, a post office, a reading room, Baltimore's City Hall, and an apartment. Many offices, especially in the basement, provided space for businessmen, "brokers, attorneys, and counting-houses." The original cost of the structure was $270,000. Improvements were made continuously, costing $150,000, and when George Kane became the Port Collector, the size of the Customs House itself was greatly expanded.

While the concept of a central location for the conduct of business in Baltimore was good in principle, in fact it did poorly financially. In 1825 the Exchange members authorized the sale of the property, excepting the hall and reading room. They offered the building to the city of Baltimore for a mere $90,000, a third of its construction cost. The city refused to act upon the offer, and years later, in May 1851, George Kane and a group of investors purchased the Exchange Building, excluding the Customs House and the Merchants' National Bank, for $90,000.[13]

In January 1856 the United States government purchased the Exchange Building for $267,000, after buying the east wing, occupied by the Customs House, for $110,000. The payment was divided into two portions: $200,000 was given immediately to Kane and his Merchants' Exchange Company; another $67,000 was withheld until certain improvements were made to the structure.[14]

A new Exchange Building would later be constructed directly to the west of the old Merchants' Exchange Building (subsequently referred to simply as the Post Office and Customs House), under the auspices of a new "Baltimore Exchange Building Company" or—more succinctly—the "Exchange Company." George Kane and many of his friends and colleagues—including John C. Brune, Henry M. Warfield, John W. Garrett, Johns Hopkins, Robert A. Dobbin, and Hugh Jenkins (as Chairman of the Board)—were designated as "Commissioners" (totaling 34) who owned stock.[15] The Maryland Legislature granted them the right to form this company in March 1858, with Kane as its president.[16] In March 1859 the Corn and Flour Exchange (alternately called simply the Corn Exchange) was split from the new Exchange Company, and a separate facility was built on Bowly's Wharf for this purpose. Kane had many partners in this venture, as well.[17] The new Exchange Building was finally completed in August 1859. Here the newly formed Board of Trade met and functioned to promote businesses in Baltimore. Over 500 firms counted themselves as members.

Kane attempted to improve the civic environment as he constructed these various buildings connected with his businesses. As he was building his new Exchange Building, he included the placement of a fountain in the north yard of the Post Office, both for its aesthetic qualities and for the use of thirsty passersby. Kane applied to the City Council to grant free use of water for this drinking hydrant and artistic fountain, arguing that it was both a useful resource and a

Opposite, top: Figure 3. Merchants' Exchange Building, photographed from the corner of Lombard Street and Gay Street, looking northwest, ca. 1900. From the Maryland Center for History and Culture. *Opposite bottom:* Figure 4. The new Exchange Building was built directly west of the old Merchants' Exchange, which housed the Post Office and the Custom House. From the Library of Congress.

beautification to the city. The city refused, and the fountain and hydrant were thereafter abandoned.[18]

Fires remained a threat to all manner of buildings in Baltimore during this era. In September 1858 the Customs House suffered a serious fire caused by a lantern candle igniting papers in one of the offices. George Kane himself physically fought the fire with the Mechanical Fire Company. Though damage to the building itself was only $5,000, the loss of records and documents was formidable. The fire was ruled to be an accident, and no criminal charges were placed against the workmen who inadvertently started the fire, but the building was not insured.[19]

The Merchants' Exchange Building endured until the early 1900s. The demolition of the Exchange and the excavation for the new Customs House on that site began in 1901–1902. The new Customs House was itself also considered to be an architectural landmark.

Kane's first foray into city politics (Figure 5) came when he ran for sheriff of Baltimore City in 1848, his major opponent being Charles F. Cloud, a Democrat; John Mitchell was another Democratic candidate. At this time Kane was a Whig, though the party officially didn't endorse Kane as their candidate (they endorsed no one; candidates James Hance and Captain A. P. Shutt were also Whigs). Cloud barely beat Kane, 9,086 to 8,919, with 3,644 votes being cast for the other candidates.

Kane was drawn back into politics in 1856 when he ran for the First Branch of the Baltimore City Council. He sought to represent the Fifteenth Ward in a special election on January 2, 1856, following the death of previously elected Levi Taylor. It's unclear how much of the initiative for this candidacy was Kane's and how much was the idea of his friends. He ran as an Independent, unaffiliated with any of the major political parties of the time. Joseph Simms, a member of the Know-Nothing party, opposed Kane. Democrats had no candidate, though they supported Kane, who was described as "an Independent anti-know-nothing

Figure 5. George P. Kane, Baltimore—date unknown. From Richard Berglund and Kenny Driscoll.

Whig." Kane's attempt to enter politics this time was also unsuccessful; he lost, 624 to 469. The contest was notable for the mid–1850s because "[t]he election passed off quietly, being attended with no unusual excitement, and no violence."[20]

Even the Whigs themselves had differing opinions of Kane and some of his friends. Kane was alleged to be a member of "'a Court House clique, composed of a set of very unprincipled men, selfish, immoral & tyrannical,' and whose gambling and 'hard drink[ing]' scandalized them."[21]

Political parties in the 1830s through the 1860s were complex. Much shifting of names, allegiances, and policies occurred. Though Kane had run as an independent earlier in the year, he was a participant in the 1856 Old Line Whig State Convention in Baltimore. The first order of business was for the group to declare "[t]hat no person shall be considered a member of this convention who is a member of the Democratic or American [Know-Nothing] parties, and that every person who remains in this meeting and participates in its action shall be regarded as thereby declaring that he does not belong to either of said parties."[22] Kane became the representative for Baltimore City to this convention, so at this time he was allied with the Whigs.

Nevertheless, upon the election of Democrats James Buchanan and John C. Breckinridge as President and Vice-President in 1856, Kane joined in the Democratic festivities in Baltimore in early 1857 prior to their inauguration in March. Kane was a member of the "Committee of Reception on the Part of the Wards," representing the Fifteenth Baltimore Ward.[23] Following this display of support for the new President, Buchanan offered Kane a lucrative position as United States Appraiser General, allegedly "tendered by the President as a compliment to the 'Old Line Whigs' of the city and State." It's unclear why Kane declined the position, since he had been Collector of the Port of Baltimore under Whig President Millard Fillmore.[24]

Kane's position and the honor accorded to him by his fellow man did not protect him completely from adversity, though many of his problems were neither targeted nor politically motivated. An unoccupied brick building he owned on Spring Street near Monument Street burned and was entirely destroyed in October 1857. At least five nearby houses were also damaged, and the fire was attributed to "incendiarism,"[25] today called "arson." Slightly more than three months later Kane had his pocket picked while he stood observing a fire on Hanover Street. Newspapers reported that Kane lost "$10 and some papers."[26]

Furthermore, Kane was not immune to political infighting and bad publicity. As Inspector of the Third Division of the Maryland Militia, he was required to maintain its military readiness. Maryland Governor Thomas W. Ligon had ordered Kane to supply the Third Division with bullets—"cartridges"—for use in any potential contingency, which Ligon had termed "to prepare certain ammunition and military stores that were absolutely essential to the due performance of his solemn duty." Kane bought the supplies as ordered. Kane's detractors claimed either that the bullets were not used, or that at least their whereabouts could not be ascertained, implying either that he had submitted a fraudulent request for reimbursement for the purchase of these supplies (totaling $273.90), or that he had misappropriated them. Kane objected strenuously, reporting that indeed the bullets had not been used, but that they had been stored for future use "with the consent of the Governor," as requested by Governor Ligon himself. The bullets needed to be deposited somewhere they could not be easily stolen from and in a place where they would be immediately available for use in future emergencies. He declared that the military supplies still remained where he had stored them, and that he had informed the Governor of their whereabouts. Kane took exception to the charges that he had misappropriated funds, saying that he was "aggrieved at the publication of the aforesaid report, in which it is represented that he has received money from the contingent fund for which he has never accounted." Kane chided the committee that had accused him, saying that it was "reflecting so seriously upon him." He emphasized that many people had received small reimbursements from Ligon's funds, and that it seemed to him that he was being singled out for particular scrutiny, and ended by saying that he was "humbly representing the injustice that has thus been done to him, and requesting that the same may be duly repaired and corrected."[27] Perhaps Kane was looking forward to some day when he might need to rely upon his good name as he sought political office, or maybe he was simply defending his reputation.

Kane again revealed his Southern leanings in 1858 when he joined many of his Baltimore friends in supporting the admission of Kansas Territory as a state in the Union under the principles of the Lecompton Constitution, which allowed slavery and prohibited free Blacks from living in the proposed state. Little did these men know that their association around pro-slavery issues would in just a few short years cause them to be arrested and imprisoned together for 17 months.[28]

George Kane rose in prominence in Baltimore throughout the 1850s. The "Sons of the Defenders of Baltimore in 1814" was a group forming in 1857 to commemorate the heroic defense of the city against the British in the War of 1812. The Battle of North Point had begun on September 12, 1814, and was a part of the larger Battle of Baltimore, in which Francis Scott Key wrote "The Star-Spangled Banner." In 1857, Kane was instrumental in the organization of this group that sought to revive the celebration of the Battle of North Point and to build a monument to its memory. It is celebrated today as "Defenders' Day," and the monument ultimately erected to honor this event is the Battle Monument, located on North Calvert Street between East Fayette and East Lexington Streets. At the first meeting of this group at the old City Hall, they had no structure and no President. Kane's reputation was solid, and the attendees asked him to chair the meeting.[29] The group soon took the name of "Sons of the Old Defenders," and Kane was one of the five men who constituted the Financial Committee. One week later he became one of four men from the Third District (there were five districts) to represent the organization.[30] He then became one of two Vice-Presidents of the organization.[31]

Family Life

Kane married Anna ("Annie," "Ann") C. Griffith (1824–1882), daughter of John (1790–1861) and Mary (1795–1853) Griffith of Dorchester County, Maryland. The date of their marriage is unknown. Dorchester County is located on the Eastern Shore of Maryland, a farming region with strong leanings toward the Southern politics of the time, even though it was the birthplace of Harriet Tubman, the famed facilitator for the Underground Railroad that freed many slaves. It was also the home of Patty Cannon, infamous slave trader, reflecting the regional political schizophrenia of the time.

By the mid-1850s George and Anna Kane were prominent in the social scene in Baltimore. Firefighting companies frequently had social gatherings that the Kanes attended.[32]

In 1858 one of the factories along the Jones Falls River was auctioned, and Kane was the successful bidder. Named the "Rockdale Factory" or the "Rockdale Mill," covering about 25 acres, it was one of the flour mills in the area of what was to be the Hampden neighborhood of Baltimore, about two miles north of the city limits (Figure 6). This area was the center for production of cotton fabric, cotton duck, and cotton canvas, as well as flour. The property had an "EXTENSIVE GRIST MILL, GEARING, MACHINERY, BUILDINGS AND LANDS THERETO ATTACHED."[33] The factories were initially powered by water-driven wheels, but large steam engines eventually replaced this power source in the late 1850s.[34] George Kane won the auction of this property on May 12, 1858, paying $8,500, the terms being one-third cash and another third paid each at 6 and 12 months.[35]

Not all was smooth thereafter regarding this property; in December 1858, Kane accused the city of Baltimore of damaging a dam and therefore the flour mill on the property. The Jones Falls River was the source of some of the water used by the city of Baltimore. This river flowed along the property of Samuel D. Tonge, the prior

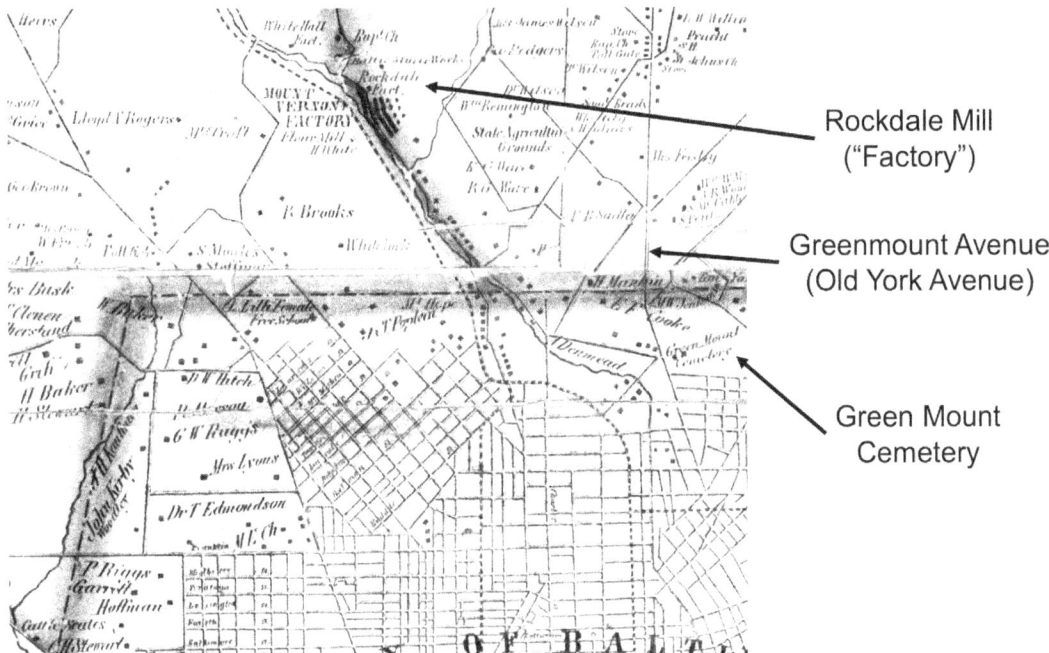

Figure 6. Rockdale Mill (called "Rockdale Fact." [meaning "Factory"] on the map). Kane purchased the Rockdale Mill, located in the Hampden area north of Baltimore City, one center of cotton fabric manufacturing in Maryland. From the Sheridan Libraries, Johns Hopkins University, Baltimore, Maryland.

owner of the Rockdale Mills. The city, under the Act of 1853, chapter 376, titled "An Act to supply the city of Baltimore with pure water," had condemned portions of the Jones Falls River bed to secure the supply of water to the city. Tonge was reimbursed for the land taken by the power of eminent domain, but he continued to use the dam and sluice gate for water power for the mill. After transfer of the property to Kane following its auction, Kane claimed that the city of Baltimore, under the direction of James S. Suter, the water engineer,

> entered upon the dam belonging to the mill, then in possession and use of the complainant [Kane], and forcibly and violently, and against his will and consent, opened and destroyed the sluice-gate in the dam, and thereby let off and discharged the water from the mill-dam, so that the mill can no longer be used, as before, for the manufacture of flour; and further, that since the sluice was opened and destroyed, the engineer has commenced and is now prosecuting the actual destruction of the whole of the dam, cutting away the wood-work and blowing up the abutments, so that when its destruction shall be completed it will be incapable of being rebuilt, as before, the present abutments being natural rocks of immense size, which cannot be replaced by any artificial structure.[36]

Kane and his lawyers argued that the use of the water as power for the gristmills to grind the wheat into flour did not affect either the quantity or quality of the water available for the city of Baltimore downstream. He also argued that other mills—both cotton and flour—used the water from the Jones Falls River in the same manner and that they did not affect the water available to Baltimore, either, but that Kane alone had been singled out for restriction of the use of water power from this river. The courts eventually ruled in Kane's favor.[37]

This property also suffered the effects of a fire in 1859. An "incendiary" ("arsonist") gained access to the building and started a fire. The Baltimore City fire departments responded after an alarm was sounded, but they discovered that the location was outside the city limits, where they were not allowed to go. One building with its contents burned completely. The arsonist had started the fire in the upper story of the building, which had not been used for some time; factory workers had been using only the first floor. High winds caused the flames to spread rapidly, and very little could be salvaged from the building. Even the machinery in the building was completely destroyed. Being four stories high with the walls constructed of stone, only the shell of the walls remained after the fire burned through the building. Kane estimated that the loss was about $14,000, with insurance covering only about $8,250.

Kane also purchased real estate near the new Exchange Company. In June 1858 he bought a lot next to the Post Office/Customs complex, extending from Exchange Place to Second Street and having two three-story brick buildings on it. For this property he paid $25,000.[38]

Kane's real estate dealings occasionally created controversy. In February 1859 he argued through letters in the *Baltimore Sun* about the siting of a new post office. Kane preferred the Merchants' Exchange, while U.S. Representative J. Morrison Harris preferred the site of the old First Presbyterian Church, at the corner of North and Fayette Streets. Heated exchanges, charges, and countercharges went back and forth in the news media, and Kane finally prevailed when he revealed that Harris was not only a member of the church that the congregation was trying to sell, but also the attorney promoting its sale.[39] Kane ended the communication with the newspapers about Representative Harris with an uncharacteristically terse statement: "I have done with Mr. Harris." The Post Office and Court House remained located at the Merchants' Exchange for years. In later years the United States Court House and the Baltimore City Hall would be built at that intersection of North and Fayette.

There were scores of charitable institutions in Baltimore, and George Kane and his wife supported many. The Baltimore Association for the Improvement of the Condition of the Poor was one such organization. Baltimore was divided into 20 wards, and Kane was one of the managers of this charity for the Ninth Ward.[40] This organization dispensed charity regardless of the religious creed of the recipient, and it required all able-bodied men to work as they could. By the end of George Kane's life, this group was helping over 17,000 persons, distributing food, fuel for heating, and other provisions, costing $20,200 per year. However, the Constitution of the Association forbade giving money to its beneficiaries: "Its object and design is to discourage indiscriminate alm-giving, street begging, pauperism and idleness; and to elevate the moral and physical condition of the indigent, and so far as compatible with these objects, the relief of their necessities."[41]

3

Kane's Connection to Baltimore Theatres and the John Wilkes Booth Family

George Kane's early life was intimately connected to the theatrical scene in Baltimore. He supported many thespian projects, including the funding and maintenance of buildings and theatres, companies, and actors and actresses themselves. Baltimore's many theatres (Figure 7) were mostly located near each other and in close proximity to the major hotels (Figure 8), which themselves would later play a key role in Kane's activities in Baltimore. The history of the stage in Baltimore thus includes significant input from George Kane.

The Charles Street Theatre (Figure 9), where John Wilkes Booth had his debut, began as the Howard Athenaeum, or "Howard Athenaeum and Gallery of Arts," opening on June 12, 1848, seating about 800–1,000 playgoers. It originally existed under the direction of Charles Howard and John Hill Hewitt, the managing

Major Baltimore Theatres:
1. Charles Street, later called Arnold's Olympic
2. Adelphi
3. Holliday Street
4. Front Street
5. Ford's
6. Academy of Music

Figure 7. Location of theatres in Baltimore. Adapted from Samuel Augustus Mitchell, Jr.'s 1872 "Plan of Baltimore."

Baltimore Hotels:
1. Barnum's Hotel
2. Guy's Hotel
3. Maltby House
4. Sherwood Hotel
5. Exchange Hotel
6. Hall's House
7. Eutaw House
8. Fountain Inn
9. St. Clair Hotel
10. Howard House
11. Mann's Hotel

Top: Figure 8. Location of hotels in Baltimore. Adapted from Samuel Augustus Mitchell, Jr.'s 1872 "Plan of Baltimore." *Bottom:* Figure 9. Arnold's Olympic Theatre, also known as: the Howard Athenaeum, the Howard Athenaeum and Gallery of Fine Arts, the Olympic Theatre, Arnold's Olympic, the Charles Street Theatre, and Owens' Charles Street Theatre. From the Maryland Center for History and Culture.

company being John Hill Hewitt, John K. Randall, George P. Kane, and Charles Howard.[1] So Kane was a principal in the early days of the theatre where John Wilkes Booth started his professional career on August 14, 1855. It was renamed Arnold's Olympic Theatre in the spring of 1853. Edwin Booth, John Wilkes's older brother, was a member of the Thespian Association who worked at Arnold's Olympic Theatre. After a renovation in the summer of 1853, the venue reopened on September 12, 1853, under the direction of John E. Owens. Located in the upper floors of a building at the northeast corner of Baltimore and Charles Streets (where today the Two North Charles Street Building stands), and originally leased and run by Joseph K. Randall, the theatre was then soon transferred to the direction of the Kemble Company of Baltimore, some of whose prominent members and owners were William Key Howard, George Proctor Kane, William R. Travers, William Sperry, and others. Once more, Kane was a principal in this venture beginning two years before John Wilkes Booth played there. The theatre was once again reopened as the Charles Street Theatre in December 1853. In late 1854 John E. Owens assumed full management of this theatre, often also called the Owens' Charles Street Theatre. However, on June 10, 1855, Owens ended his association with this venue.

The Charles Street Theatre itself would have a rather short life. Prices of admission averaged $0.25–3.00. Its financial survival came into question when it was advertised as being for rent beginning in June 1855.[2] It reopened in July 1855 and struggled along through December with intermittent productions, one of which was John Wilkes Booth's debut on August 14. Following further changes in management, the Charles Street Theatre ceased to exist as such by September 1856.[3]

Another famous theatre in Baltimore that Kane influenced was the Holliday Theatre (Figure 10), sometimes lovingly called "Old Drury," located at the northeast corner of Holliday Street and West Fayette Street, directly across the street from City Hall.[4] By the turn of the 1840s its owners had encountered difficult financial times; the Holliday was sold and leased multiple times through 1854, when benefits were held to try to prevent the theatre from dying. George Kane joined with S. Teackle Wallis, Reverdy Johnson, Johns Hopkins, William Frick, Nathaniel Williams, and others in April 1855 to sponsor a fundraiser held on May 4.[5] It was unsuccessful in preserving the ownership of the theatre, the structure being sold again in 1856, and then repeatedly sold and leased through 1917.

Another more enduring Baltimore theatre was the Front Street Theatre, located at the northwest corner of Front Street and Low Street. John Wilkes Booth only performed at the Charles Street and Holliday Theatres, while his father Junius Brutus Booth played the Adelphi, the Holliday, and the Front Street, often alternating from one site to another.

The "Mud Theatre," also called the "Adelphi Theatre" or "National Theatre," saw George Kane's influence, as well—here he had a brief stint as an actor. Some called him a "bit actor," meaning that he did not have any key roles in the plays. Contemporary historians claimed that Kane was "well-received" as an actor in his own right,[6] but detailed reviews of his acting skills have been lost to history. Kane would later act on other stages as well, and Junius Brutus Booth also played at the Adelphi, so it is reasonable to think that Kane and the senior Booth might have met at this

3. Kane's Connection to Baltimore Theatres and the Booth Family 19

Figure 10. Holliday Theatre, ca. 1917. 100 North Holliday Street. From the Maryland Center for History and Culture.

location. Kane would be but one of many American actors who metamorphosed into politicians in later life.

Questions repeatedly arise about any connections between George Kane and John Wilkes Booth. Their exact relationship and status of their friendship remains obscure.

The Booth family had a 159-acre farm in Belair (Harford County), Maryland, about 25 miles from the center of Baltimore. Junius built an expansive home there in 1851, dubbed "Tudor Hall." Junius was an alcoholic and at times appeared to be mentally deranged, but he was widely acknowledged as a great actor—a "tragedian" he was called. He was one of the most famous actors of his time. In 1842, the Booths also had a Baltimore residence on the east side of High Street, north of Gay, a location only about five to six blocks from their more well-known home, a row house at 62 North Exeter Street, which they purchased in 1845.[7] This latter house was close to downtown Baltimore (near where the shot tower now stands), between Gay and Fayette, and where the post office now sits, on a portion of Exeter Street that no longer exists.[8] Here they divided their time, staying in Baltimore city mostly during the cold winter months and living in Belair in Harford County during the warmer months. The early Kane home on the west side of Aisquith Street north of Comet Street was only about four blocks from the Booth home on Exeter.

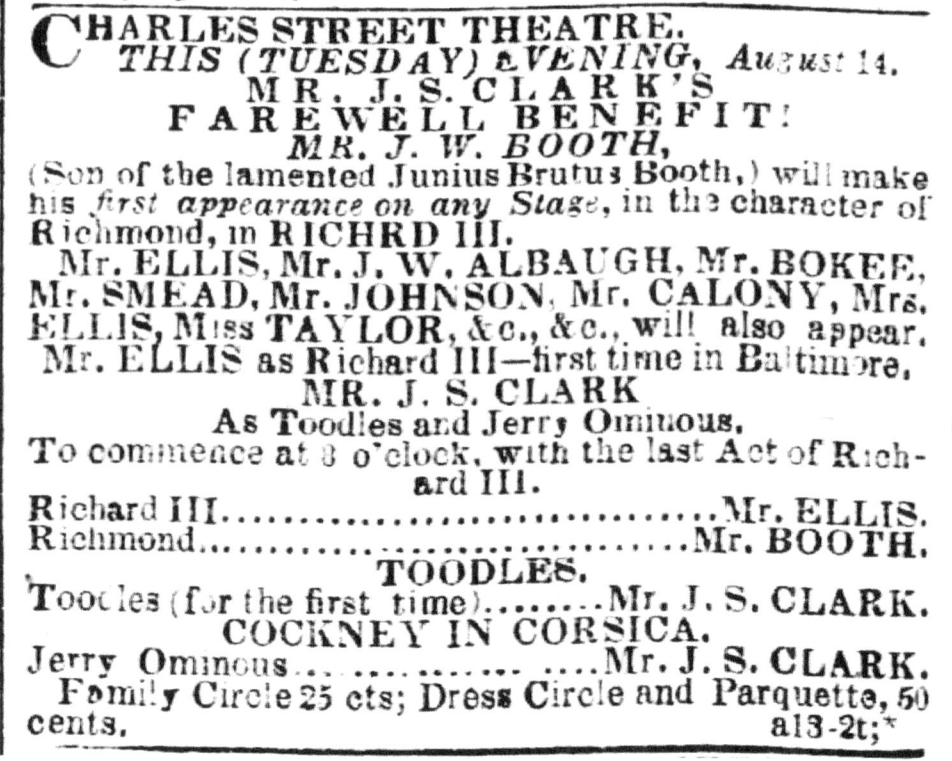

Figure 11. Newspaper ad for John Wilkes Booth's first theatrical performance. From the *Baltimore Sun*.

John Wilkes attended many schools in the Baltimore area, though his first education was in a one-room schoolhouse located across the road from the Booth farm in Belair.[9] His first schooling in a larger public setting was at the Belair Academy in Harford County (also called the Harford County Academy) in about 1846 when he would have been approximately eight years old. Booth also briefly attended schools in Baltimore city close to the family's Exeter Street home.[10]

John Wilkes Booth began his professional acting career on August 14, 1855, at the Charles Street Theatre in Baltimore as the Earl of Richmond in a Colley Cibber adaptation of *Richard III*. He was only 17 years old. A note in the August 13, 1855, *Baltimore Sun* read,

> CHARLES STREET THEATRE.—*Mr. J. S. Clarke's Farewell Benefit* previous to his departure for Philadelphia, where he is engaged for one year, will take place at the above theatre on to-morrow evening. A great feature of the evening will be the *debut* of a son of the late Junius Booth, who is said to possess much of his father's genius. Mr. Clarke will play Toodles for the first time, with other entertainments, forming a great bill.[11]

John Sleeper Clarke was actually a childhood friend of Booth's, and would marry Booth's sister Asia in 1859. The debut play in which Booth performed was a benefit for Clarke (Figure 11). Benefit performances were common in the mid-1800s. Proceeds went to actors, actresses, theatre owners, and even behind-the-scenes stagehands.

3. Kane's Connection to Baltimore Theatres and the Booth Family   21

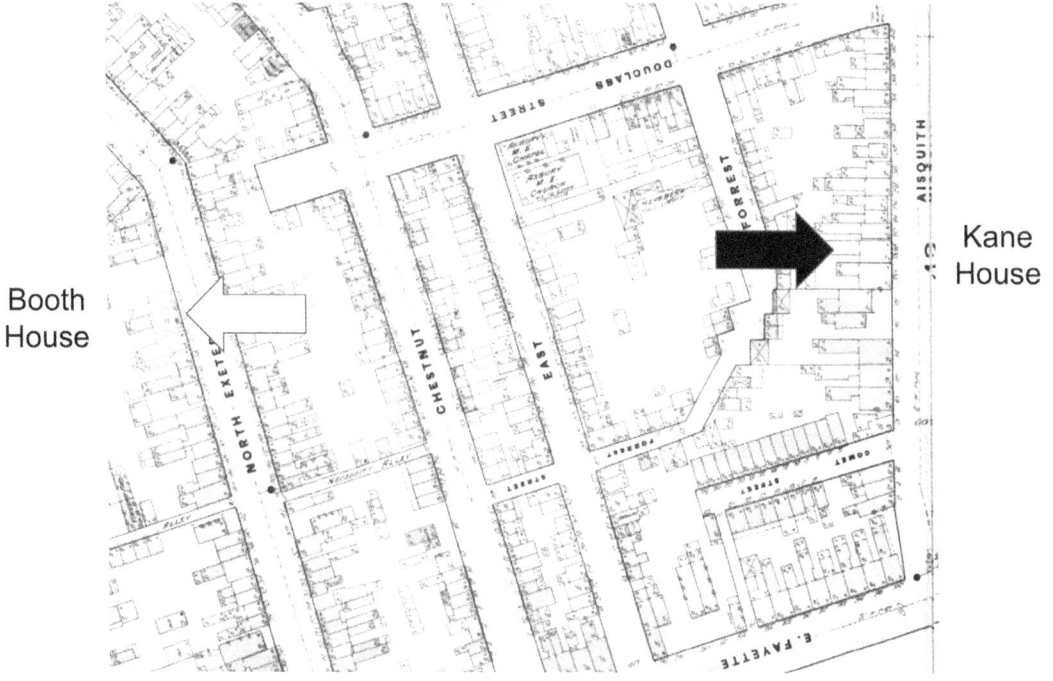

Top: Figure 12. Location of the Kane household and the Booth household in Baltimore. The Kane household had been on the west side of Aisquith, between Comet and Douglas Streets (black arrow); the Booth household was at 62 North Exeter Street (yellow arrow). Adapted from Papenfuse: Atlases and Maps of Baltimore City and County, 1876–1915. *Bottom:* Figure 13. Drawing of the Booth family home on Exeter Street. From *Frank Leslie's Popular Monthly.*

The next day, the *Sun* declared,

CHARLES STREET THEATRE.—Mr. J. S. Clarke, the favorite comedian, bids farewell to his Baltimore friends this evening on the occasion of his benefit, when he will present a most excellent entertainment. Mr. John Booth, son of the great tragedian, will make his first appearance on any stage, and a number of favorites will also appear.

The same day another announcement said,

BOOTH! BOOTH!
The debut of a son of the late
Junius Brutus Booth,
which takes place at the
Charles Street Theatre to-night,
is now the
"Town Talk."[12]

After this performance in 1855 at the Charles Street Theatre, Booth would not act professionally for another two years, working with a Philadelphia theatre company in 1857 and then subsequently in Richmond, Virginia, in 1858. Booth had strong ties to the Baltimore area, and his friendships there would cast his lot for the future.

George Proctor Kane thus had many opportunities to interact with the Booth family in their common Baltimore lives. Some historians believe that George Kane and John Wilkes Booth were actually close personal friends, though the evidence for this friendship is both circumstantial and contradictory. It is certainly likely that the Kane and Booth families were at least acquaintances during the years 1845–1865, though Kane was about 21 years older than Booth. The Kanes' and the Booths' paths definitely crossed, but the extent of their friendship must remain speculation. Nevertheless, many possibilities exist for a personal connection between Booth and Kane.

Both were Baltimoreans. Their family homes were quite close (Figure 12), only a few streets apart. The Booths resided on Exeter Street (Figure 13), at least by 1845. The Kane family had left the neighborhood in about 1832. Nevertheless, neighborhood ties were quite

MUCH ADO ABOUT NOTHING!

Benedick,		Mr. J. E. MURDOCH		
Don Claudio,	D. P. BOWERS	Verges,	- - - -	EDWIN
Don John,	- - - ELLIS	Seacoal,	- - -	GEORGE
Don Pedro,	- - WARWICK	Sexton,	- - -	THOMAS
Dogberry,	- - - PORTER	Beatrice,	-	Mrs. D. P. BOWERS
Priest,	- - - SMEAD	Hero,	- -	Miss PORTER
Leonato,	- - - LINGARD	Ursula,	- -	Mrs. ALTEMUS
Borachio,	- - - BONIFACE	Margaret,	- -	Mrs. SPENCER
Conrad,	- - - BARRY			

FAVORITE DANCE,   Miss **EVELINE**

Comic Song,   -   Master **DE MOTT**

Above and opposite: Figure 14. Playbill from February 11, 1851, at the Baltimore Museum and Gallery of the Fine Arts with both "Edwin" and "George" listed as actors. The above image is an enlargement of a section of the opposite image. Another playbill from the Baltimore Museum and Gallery of the Fine Arts from May 29, 1851, had a "George" and an "Edwin" listed as actors in the same play. Edwin Booth was known to have performed the previous night (May 28) at the Holliday Street Theatre as Richmond in *Richard III*. Dozens of such playbills exist in the 1850–1851 era with different plays and events that feature both an "Edwin" and a "George." From the Sheridan Libraries and the Milton S. Eisenhower Library, Johns Hopkins University, Baltimore, Maryland.

strong in Baltimore, and it is possible that the Kanes would have frequently visited their old neighborhood after moving away and might have interacted with the Booths there.

As a native of the Baltimore area, Booth frequently returned there during his adult life. His had many connections in the city. Many of Booth's visits to Baltimore are recorded, but likely many are not. For example, he was documented to have been in Baltimore one day after the April 19, 1861, Baltimore riot. It is highly probable that Booth and Kane, both famous in their own rights, crossed paths often.

Kane's interest in the theatre was the most likely means by which they would have interacted. Kane's connection to the theatre, initially as an actor and later as a patron, brought him near the Booth family. Junius Brutus Booth, Sr., was a regular actor in Baltimore, an owner and co-owner of theatres, and an organizer of plays in the city. Kane at one point was active in the Holliday Theatre and was part owner of the Howard Athenaeum Theatre, later called the Charles Street Theatre, where John Wilkes first acted. Kane himself acted primarily at the Adelphi Theatre. Kane's acting career would likely have ended before John Wilkes Booth began his time on stage at the Charles Street Theatre, when Kane would have been about 38 and the younger Booth only 17. However, Kane remained active in theatre projects into the late 1850s, and likely connected with the Booth family through this theatre connection.

Kane undoubtedly communicated with the Booths both during Kane's brief stint as an actor, and later while Kane was part owner of a theatre and investor in theatrical companies. Playbills from the era of 1850–1852 would frequently list actors by only their first names. Apparently producers believed that actors were so famous they did not need to list their last names for the local Baltimoreans to recognize them. Dozens of playbills from the 1850–1851 era list "George" and "Edwin" as actors in the same plays (Figure 14). While the playbills could be referring to actors named "George" other than George Kane, or "Edwin" other than Edwin Booth (for example, Edwin Forrest), the listings at least raise the suspicion that Kane and the elder Booth sibling actually appeared on stage together.[13]

Another playbill from the Baltimore Museum and Gallery of the Fine Arts from May 29, 1851, had a "George" and an "Edwin" listed as actors in the same play. Edwin Booth was known to have performed the previous night (May 28) at the Holliday Street Theatre as Richmond in *Richard III*. Dozens of such playbills exist in the 1850–1851 era with different plays and events that feature both an "Edwin" and a "George."[14]

Kane often participated in projects to raise funds for various causes in Baltimore: benefits for military groups, fund-raisers for the Hibernian Society, and occasionally benefits for actors and theatres. One advertisement (Figure 15) in February 1852 had Kane as a member of the committee to raise funds for Mr. T. J. Barton, a local supporter of the arts in Baltimore. This notice shows that Kane was connected to Junius Brutus Booth and no doubt interacted with the elder Booth in this capacity.

As a well-known businessman, Kane would have had many connections within the city, some of which might have involved the Booths, who were themselves prominent.

Kane's police work might have brought him face-to-face with the Booths, who at times were described as heavy imbibers and likely had many occasions to interact with the law (although Junius died in 1852).

Even less certain was a possible connection between John Wilkes Booth and Kane on July 26, 1864, at the Parker Hotel in Boston.[15] It is known that Booth met with four other men at that location on that date, the four other men likely using aliases. One A. J. Bursted (or Rursted) was from Baltimore, and some historians

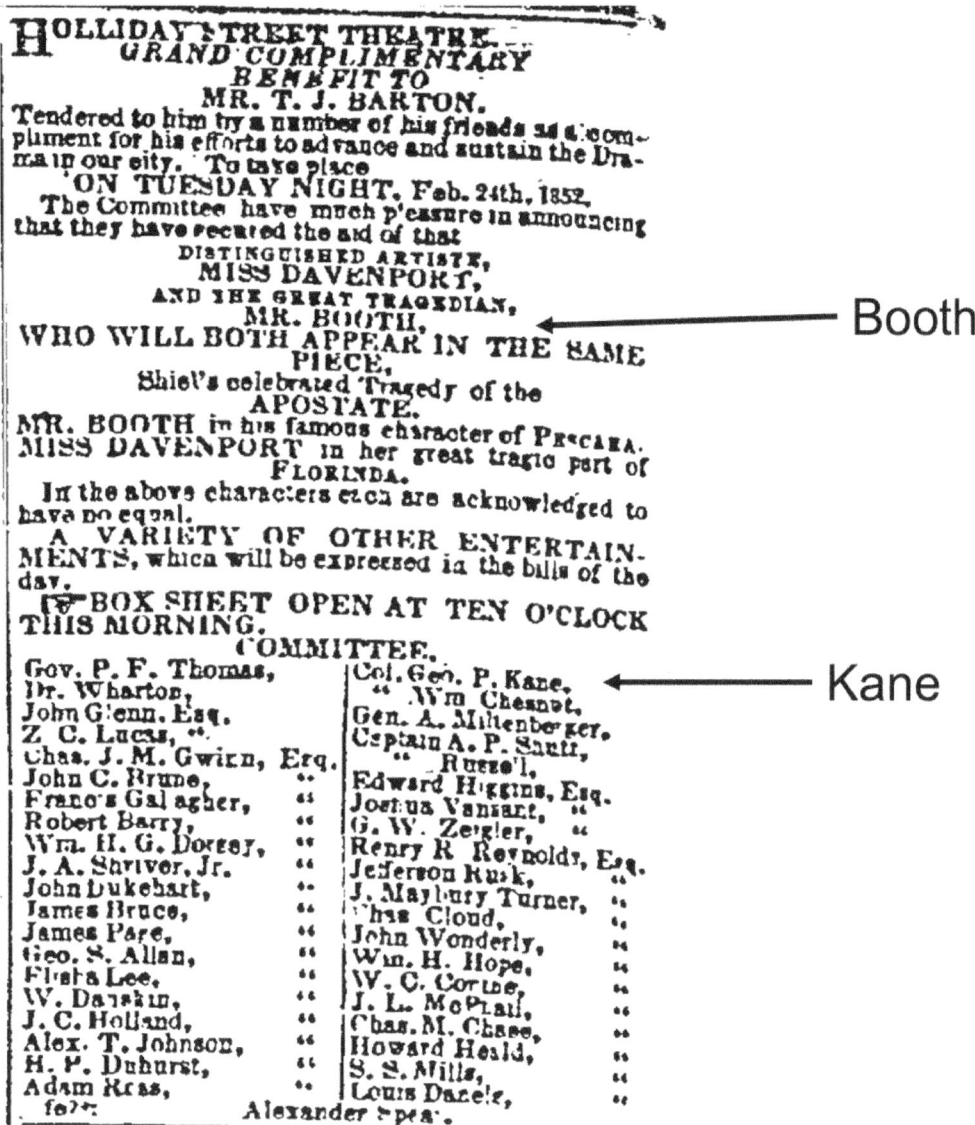

Figure 15. Kane and Junius Brutus Booth, Senior, were both members of the same benefit activity. From the *Baltimore Sun*.

believe that he was George Kane. Others think that this "Bursted" was Patrick C. Martin, who was also from Baltimore. The evidence for either identification is pure speculation, however, based solely upon Kane's and Martin's connections to Baltimore.

The most concrete evidence for any friendship between Kane and Booth was Booth's statement made in March 1862 in New York at Mary Provost's Theatre at 485 Broadway.[16] As those present for a rehearsal were discussing political events, someone mentioned Marshal Kane's arrest in Baltimore in June 1861, and everyone there knew that Kane was still imprisoned at Fort Warren in Boston. Someone said that the person who had ordered Kane's arrest should be shot. Booth allegedly said, "Yes, sir, you are right! I know George P. Kane, he is my friend, and the man who could drag him from the bosom of his family for no crime whatever, but a mere suspicion that he may commit one some time, deserves a dog's death!"[17] Booth's words, demeanor, and the intensity of his emotion seemed to indicate that he did indeed have a close personal connection with Kane.[18] However, later reports in 1864 told of Booth's request to have a letter of introduction to Kane, one that he allegedly obtained from Patrick C. Martin in Canada. These two assertions are contradictory.[19] It is possible that the letter actually contained incriminating information about Booth's plans to assassinate President Abraham Lincoln, even requesting Kane's help, and the stated need for an introduction to Kane was a subterfuge. Kane later admitted to receiving this letter from Booth, but his description of its contents varied from what Booth had requested of Martin. The veracity of Martin's letter to George Kane, and its precise contents, remain a mystery even until today. Kane at that time additionally denied ever having known Booth, a statement that would seem quite implausible, given the circumstances of both of their backgrounds in Baltimore. However, at the time that Kane denied knowing Booth, Lincoln's assassination had already occurred, and everyone was trying to distance himself from the President's murderer.

The conclusion must be that Kane and Booth were acquaintances, but there is no evidence that Kane was Booth's co-conspirator in the assassination. Their acquaintance was simply the maelstrom of social interaction that was Baltimore society and politics in the 19th century.

4

Baltimore Militias

Maryland militias began during the Revolutionary War and continued through the War of 1812; in Maryland in the 1820s there were five divisions. During the early 19th century, all able-bodied white males in Baltimore between the ages of 21 and 45 were subject to militia duty (with many exceptions—various government officials, "professors and tutors in colleges, schoolmasters, practicing physicians, drivers of mail stages, ferrymen, ministers of the gospel, Quakers, Menonists, and Tunkers").[1] Men aged 18 to 21 could join the militia with the consent of "parents, guardian, master or mistress."[2]

By 1823, the training and parades consumed only five days per year; this schedule in reality provided very little opportunity for citizen soldiers to learn what was necessary to function effectively. Their meetings usually involved marksmanship and target practice, marching and parade formation, and often a social gathering on the same day as the training. However, militia membership occasionally involved hard work, and being called to duty could expose the citizen soldier to activity that might put limb and life at risk.

Militias consolidated in 1833 as the Baltimore Regiment, under the leadership of Major General George H. Steuart. Each county and each division of the city of Baltimore was supposed to have at least one militia. Furthermore,

> Every uniformed and drafted company is required to meet annually on the 2nd Saturday of May for inspection; and for drill, in their respective battalions, squadrons, regiments, or brigades, on the third Saturday of September. Members of volunteer uniformed companies are required to meet, in addition to these two days, as many days not exceeding six, as the majority of the company shall determine.[3]

Militias generally had a large degree of independence: men elected their own officers; they chose their uniforms; they selected which military unit they joined (subject to the acceptance of the unit itself), and they often established their own criteria for membership. In this sense, the militia company was in part a social club. Often the company reflected an element of the class structure within a city. Great pride was taken in the marching, the drilling, the marksmanship, and the uniforms worn. While the militias often comprised the higher class of white male citizens, the fire companies attracted the middle and lower classes, though many men belonged to one of each. Some companies reflected a specific immigrant population—Irish or German, for example, in Baltimore.

Not everything about belonging to a militia was positive, however. Rules were rather strict for such things as attendance at drills, wearing of uniforms, training, participation in parades, behavior and discipline, and conduct toward one another and toward officers. Fines were assessed for many different reasons. Court martials were convened for more serious infractions, though rarely did breaking the rules lead to jail or prison time. The fines were assessed for such things as neglecting or refusing duty, missing a drill, absence from a parade, insubordination toward an officer, refusal to obey an order, improper wearing of a uniform or appearing at certain functions without a uniform, tardiness, drunkenness, disobedience, disorderly conduct, abusive language, quarrelling, misuse of weapons or selling or destroying arms, etc. Such fines tended to dissuade many of the poorer class from continuing membership in a militia company. Furthermore, membership required the loss of working time for the five days per year that drills were held, and attendance at parades and social functions also meant that only the richer members of society could afford to participate. Though all able-bodied white males were required to belong to a militia for at least seven years, it's unclear how strictly that requirement was enforced, and certainly the poorer members of Baltimore's citizenry would not continue service after their compulsory time had been completed. Over time, the fines for breaking the rules were relaxed, and the exceptions for participation were expanded—to politicians and office-holders, teachers, doctors, clergy, judges and clerks of the court, police, professors, stage drivers, marine pilots, post office workers, jail and prison workers, etc.

Many of the militias' functions were performed voluntarily, though they received certain equipment and supplies from the government and would petition the local and state legislatures for reimbursements for expenses. Weapons—when available—were provided by the state. State funds were also allocated for ammunition. Usually the weapons and ammunition were stored in a local armory. Some expenses were covered by governmental support. For example, in 1853 the city treasury of Baltimore funded each qualifying militia at the level of a $200 yearly stipend, "[p]rovided that the company making application … has complied, during the preceding year, with the requirements of an act entitled 'An act for the encouragement of volunteer corps of the city of Baltimore.'" An additional $500 was allocated to be

> supplied for the sole maintenance of his [the commander's] company; and be it further provided that the companies receiving the foregoing sum shall be subject to call for duty at any time by the Mayor if, in his wisdom, he may deem the same necessary; the same to be performed without any additional compensation.[4]

The Act establishing payment to these militias specified certain qualifications that had to be met for funding: officers were to be elected; companies of artillery or cavalry needed at least 20 members; companies of infantry or riflemen required at least 30 members; attendance at parades was mandatory, but other standards were generally left to the discretion of the individual militias. These militias were not necessarily organized to work closely together, but they were a repository of variably trained men for the defense of the city.

Over time, militias acquired a duty to preserve peace in the cities, apart from duties related to repelling invasions of foreign powers, similar to the National Guard today. While militias marched, drilled, held practice skirmishes, performed target practice, and remained prepared for the repulsion of any real enemies, they also assumed other duties. Compulsory militias eventually gave way to volunteer militias. They often marched and dressed elegantly and therefore were frequently sought for patriotic parades. They increasingly served as social clubs where men of stature (and those seeking stature) gathered for camaraderie, partying, and drinking. They were social centers for neighborhoods and ethnic groups (often immigrants). Their halls and meeting places were sites for anniversary celebrations, birthday parties, funerals, picnics, balls, excursions, field trips, marksmanship contests, lectures or readings, honoring of holidays, and other social functions. They sponsored charitable events that served local communities. Being an officer in such a club was a great honor, and such positions often led to political service and elected office. Schools and churches benefited from these militias. Some educational institutions and orphanages were entirely supported by these types of clubs. At times they were intimately connected to other organizations.[5]

Militias followed the military tactics and discipline of the United States Army. Most militias had uniforms, though a few went without. The militias, in general, were referred to as the Uniform Voluntary Companies. The uniforms varied dramatically among the militias, and their dress was a distinguishing feature of each unit and often a source of pride.

Kane was affiliated with many of the militias. Members of the militia would often have multiple titles, both in the individual militia itself and in the overall structure of the divisions, brigades, and regiments. Kane was briefly Ensign, Third Lieutenant, and Acting Quartermaster in the Independent Greys.[6] On January 7, 1841, he was elected to be a lifetime member of the Greys, and on November 5, 1841, he was promoted to another regiment.[7] Kane was a Captain in the Independent Light Dragoons in 1842,[8] and he was also Captain and Commander of the Montgomery Guards in the 1850s.[9] (Appendix, Tables 1–3)

Today it can be difficult to determine who belonged to what militia because members of one would often lend their good names to serve on the social committees of another. It was common for a dignitary such as Kane to belong to, or support, multiple militias, often in honorary capacities as a sponsor, a "reference," a manager of a social function, a committee member or chair, or an organizer of social events. Kane's name was often seen in Baltimore newspapers in the 1840s and 1850s on committees (often as "Manager") of the Baltimore National Blues, the Wells and McComas Riflemen, the Montgomery Guards, the Chesapeake Riflemen,[10] the Independent Greys,[11] the Shields Guards, and others.[12] Furthermore, a man often belonged sequentially to different militias. Kane frequently promoted the Eagle Artillery, the Independent Greys, the Chesapeake Riflemen, and other militias, or the various fire companies such as the Independent, the New Market Fire Company, the Deptford, the Mechanical, etc.[13]

After being a member of the Independent Greys and the Independent Light Dragoons, Kane joined the Eagle Artillery,[14] where he entered as Ensign. He was later Commander of the Second Regiment[15] and later became Captain.[16] The Eagle Artillery was granted permission in early 1844 to construct a gun house or armory for the storage of their weapons on Market Street in Fells Point.[17] However, it was not actually officially incorporated until February 1846, under the leadership of George P. Kane, Francis Waggner, John R. Kenly, Emilius Adams, Daniel McCahn, and others.[18] The Eagle Artillery encountered some trouble in March 1846 when the Baltimore City Council rescinded their previous offer of housing for the militia in the Fells Point area. Kane officially resigned as commanding officer on March 12, 1846.[19] On March 21, the Eagle Artillery posted a notice in the *Baltimore Sun* announcing their displeasure with the City Council at "being ejected from the house we now occupy."[20] In this notice they told how they had been in existence for nearly a half-century (though only recently officially incorporated), and that some members had been functioning for over a quarter-century for the protection of the city of Baltimore and the State of Maryland.

By 1846, militias in Maryland in general were struggling. These militias all met in a convention to address their concerns that the militias were not adequately manned, equipped, or supplied to address any emergency that might arise that needed their military power. They called their own organization "deplorable," and they decried the high percentage of "gray hairs of aged citizens" who might be called upon to defend the city or state. They petitioned the General Assembly of Maryland for funds to augment their strength, but they were denied, causing them all to resign their commissions. They cited lack of trained officers, troops, armament and organization as reasons for their resignations. They claimed that there were less than 600 workable military weapons in the entire city, and supplies and stores were equally deficient. The communication was signed by officers of the National Blues, Junior Artillery, Eagle Artillery (including Captain George P. Kane), Baltimore City Guards, Independent Blues, Baltimore Invincibles, Fifth Cavalry Regiment, Light Dragoons, 53rd Regiment, German Yeagers, Chesapeake Riflemen, First Light Division, and the German Guards.[21]

However, these militias soon re-formed. The pressure of the Mexican War prompted those officers who had resigned to reverse their actions and resume their former commissions. Kane was reinstated as Commander of the Eagle Artillery in May 1846 (at which time he was still Captain). He was appointed by Maryland Governor Thomas George Pratt as Lieutenant Colonel of the Second Regiment, Artillery, in the Third Division of the Maryland Militia in June 1846.[22] Later he would be advanced to Colonel. Kane's moniker "Colonel" originated here, and it would be repeated for the rest of his life.[23] One only needs to look at the references to Kane in contemporary newspapers to realize that his title of "Colonel" existed at least a decade before the Civil War. He listed himself in the 1851 Matchett Baltimore Directory as "Colonel Kane,"[24] though he was more commonly known in later years as "Marshal," referring to his position as the marshal, or chief, of police in Baltimore City, which he took in 1860. Many Civil War newspapers later incorrectly assumed that the "Colonel" in his name referred to a rank in the Confederate Army. It didn't. Kane was never officially a member of the Confederate uniformed military, though he performed many duties for them.

Kane remained the Commander of the Eagle Artillery until the summer of 1850, when he was succeeded by Captain C. C. Phillips.[25] The Eagle Artillery was a subdivision of the First Maryland Regiment of Light Artillery, First Light Brigade,[26] so Kane's title applied to that military unit, as well.

Kane retired as the Commander of the Montgomery Guards in June 1855. The members of the Guards issued a memorial:

> WHEREAS, GEORGE P. KANE, late Commander of the Montgomery Guards, has tendered his resignation as such commander, and the membership deeming it due and proper that some evidence of the high esteem and regard in which he has always been held by the Company should be in some manner expressed; therefore, before, be it
>
> *Resolved by the Montgomery Guards*. That, in parting with their late commander, they tender their earnest and sincere regret at the separation which is thus occasioned; the sterling qualities of head and heart so often manifested by him in his intercourse with the Company have created in the breasts of every member a true and lasting feeling of regard and esteem which cannot be lessened; and although he is no longer at their head, yet his gentlemanly and soldierlike deportment will always be remembered with admiration, while it increases their regret at the necessity which has induced his resignation.
>
> *Resolved*, That we tender to him our sincere and heartfelt wishes for his future prosperity and success through life.
>
> JOHN STACK,
> JOHN HUGHES,
> P. J. O'CONNELL
> Committee on behalf of the Corps[27]

The Governor of Maryland generally ordered the militias to drill and called them to duty as necessary. In Baltimore, where elections in the 1850s took on the form of riots, militias occasionally were called to supplement the police and to keep the peace, with at least one famous conflict between the Mayor of Baltimore and the Governor of Maryland over who had the jurisdiction to call the militias at all. In the fall of 1857, Governor Thomas Watkins Ligon ordered Major General George H. Steuart, who commanded the First Light Division, Maryland Volunteers, and Major General John Spear Smith, who commanded the Third Division, Maryland Militia, to preserve the peace of the city. George Kane was the Inspector of the Third Division, which included the Third and the Fourteenth Brigades. (Kane had also been elected Colonel in the First Rifle Regiment, replacing the resigning Colonel Robert A. McAllister[28]; however, he declined the position because of pressing business engagements.[29])

The Independent Greys, like many other militias, declined in activity and attendance over the years. In March 1858 they found themselves needing to reorganize. Kane was still a member, and after General James M. Anderson was elected President and Philip A. Egerton was elected Vice President, a committee canvassed the city for men willing to become "active members" again. They found about 40 such men, and the Greys were thus reconstituted.[30]

As the verbal hostilities accelerated before the start of the Civil War, the militia commanders realized that they once again might realize a useful military function. Furthermore, their recruitment accelerated, and they formed more useful alliances with each other. No longer just social clubs, they realized that they might actually need to go into battle. The Maryland Guards had formed in 1855, and in 1859 a new version emerged that also called itself the Maryland Guard (alternatively designated the Maryland Guard Battalion or the Old Maryland Guard). It was formed to aid civilian authorities in enforcing the Reform Acts that revamped the police, the courts, and the election process. By December 1859 the Maryland Guard had enlisted 226 Baltimore men into its ranks. New enlistees agreed to serve for at least three months, and they actually paid to join and to maintain membership, rather than being paid. It cost 50 cents to join and 25 cents per month to remain a member. The unit patterned itself after the French Zouaves, an elite band of men whose uniforms were striking and whose drill and marching skills were unequalled.[31] Almost simultaneously the 53rd Maryland Militia (also called the 53rd Infantry or 53rd Regiment) was formed and expanded. By February 14, 1860, the Maryland Guard had merged with the 53rd. Many, if not most, of the Maryland Guard contingent of the 53rd became soldiers for the Confederacy after the Civil War erupted. Maryland soldiers fighting with the South were mostly from the southern and eastern parts of Maryland.

Kane's Eagle Artillery would find itself under attack by the federal government in June 1861, when the Union forces seized arms from them, as well as from other militias and other sites in Baltimore,[32] presumably because of their Southern-leaning tendencies. Over the years thereafter, the militias declined in importance to Baltimore's social and military scene.

5

The Hibernian Society of Baltimore

The Hibernian Society of Baltimore was formed to aid Irish immigrants. "Hibernian" is a term that is virtually equivalent to "Irish," and is often—though somewhat incorrectly, depending upon the era—associated with the Catholic Church. "Hibernia" was the traditional Latin name for the island of Ireland. Initially named the Benevolent Hibernian Society, and organized in 1803, the group would change its name in 1816 to the Hibernian Society of Baltimore. It was officially founded on March 18, 1816, but not incorporated in Baltimore until February 1818. It would be re-incorporated on March 17, 1853, with the articles of incorporation being approved in 1854.[1]

On August 16, 1803, a small band of Irishmen gathered in Bryden's Tavern in the Fountain Inn at 5 Light Street in Baltimore. There they discussed the plight of the Irish immigrants to the United States, Baltimore in particular. Their meeting had been announced in notices placed in the *American Patriot and Fells Point Advertiser*, the *Baltimore Federal Gazette*, and the *Baltimore Telegraphe and Daily Advertiser*[2]: "Emigrants are daily arriving from Ireland; many of them are in a friendless and forlorn condition, deprived of health and an asylum."[3]

Dr. John Campbell White, an Irishman who had trained in medicine in both Ireland and England, became the first President of the Hibernian Society. White was a Presbyterian who had immigrated to Baltimore after the 1798 Irish rebellion. As a member of the Society of United Irishmen, he participated in the failed attempt to separate from Britain in 1798, forcing him to flee to the United States. White would remain President of the Hibernian Society until 1815, when John O'Donnell took over; John Oliver succeeded him in 1818. Though the Hibernian founders were Presbyterian, the Society was ecumenical and welcomed members from all religions. Presbyterianism was often associated with an anti–Catholic sentiment, but this organization remained relatively free of any religious bias in its early years. It welcomed Catholic participation.

Other cities also had their Hibernian Societies (Boston's began in 1737), so the name including "…of Baltimore" distinguished the Maryland group from others. The Society was dedicated to the aid and assistance of arriving Irish immigrants, and for decades two or more members of the Society met ships arriving in the Baltimore port, being a proactive effort to help newly arrived poor or destitute Irishmen to settle there. Needy Irishmen were eligible for aid from the Hibernians if at least two members of the Hibernian group certified their poverty and signed a petition stating such. Applicants who were accepted could receive direct financial aid from the treasury of the organization. In addition, these emissaries would always question the arriving Irishmen to ensure that they had been treated well on their journey across the ocean. They ministered to the sick among the new arrivals; Dr. John White, being a physician, was ideal for this task.

Early records of the Society have been lost; extant documents begin on March 11, 1816. Newspaper accounts from before that date reveal yearly meetings at which conviviality, good food, drinks, and almost endless toasting seemed to be the main activities of the evening. The dues were $5 per year. At the first annual gathering on St. Patrick's Day, March 17, 1804, no less than 31 toasts were raised, from one to "George Washington," to "Lately Imported Patriots," to "Canals, Rivers and Highways," to "The Fair of America, 'may their minds be as highly adorned as their bodies,'" and to "Fair Daughters of Erin, 'may they never smile on the enemies of their country.'"[4] The toasts became more obtuse with increasing numbers of previous toasts and as the volume of consumed alcohol rose.

The Society met at least quarterly, including its highlight annual meeting on St. Patrick's Day. The yearly event was suspended only once between its founding and the Civil War, missing the 1861 gathering: "in view of the unhappy and unsettled condition of the political affairs of the country, the usual dinner will be dispensed with."[5] Baltimore Hibernians supported both the militia named the Hibernian Corps of Union Greens and the Hibernian Infantry.

The Society also founded and supported the John Oliver Hibernian Free School. John Oliver became President of the Society in 1818 and died in 1823, leaving $20,000 for the establishment of a free educational institution for both boys and girls. Intended to support the education of poor children who had at least one Irish parent, the school also accepted poor children from other backgrounds as long as space and finances were available. Attendance was not limited by the religious background of any applicant, supporting the ecumenical approach of the Hibernians. The school opened on April 5, 1824, and by 1825 it had 185 boys and 170 girls in attendance. In 1827 it moved to the 200 block of North Street, later called Guilford Avenue, where it remained for decades. By the late 1820s and in the 1830s the Irish population became more Catholic, and contention between Catholics and Protestants began to increase in general. George Proctor Kane himself came from an Irish Presbyterian immigrant family, and he was a member of the Hibernian Society for more than 40 years, joining on March 16, 1838, with Hugh Jenkins as his sponsor. In 1845–1849 the great famine swept through Ireland. The famine and the attendant diseases worsened by malnutrition caused the deaths of nearly one-quarter of Ireland's 8,000,000 population. The British government appointed Kane as its representative in Baltimore to act as an intermediary to purchase and send grain to the starving in Ireland.[6] As a grain merchant by trade, Kane directed the delivery of food supplies, both to the home country of Ireland and to immigrants in the United States. He coordinated the food and ships headed toward Ireland. The famine itself concentrated the efforts of the Hibernian Society to provide relief from the starvation being experienced in Ireland. Furthermore, as the famine worsened, more immigrants came to the United

States and Baltimore, and the need for aid and assistance there also increased. In Baltimore the surge in Irish immigration—much of it by then Catholic—fostered anti–Catholic sentiment within the city of Baltimore. Gangs in Baltimore in particular targeted the Irish (and the Germans, as well) with their tactics of intimidation.[7]

Meetings in the 1840s were usually held quarterly at Boyle's Tavern, an alehouse and oyster bar at 7–10 North Liberty Street, run by Edward C. Boyle. Anniversary celebrations of St. Patrick's Day were commonly sighted at James McCormick's Saloon, also an oyster bar, in the basement of the Law Buildings on St. Paul Street.

Kane was addressed as "Colonel Kane" at the Hibernian Society meetings as early as 1850. After Kane's arrest in June 1861 and his imprisonment, his name disappeared from the minutes of the Society until March 7, 1870, when he resumed his activity with the Hibernians. Kane later served as an officer in the Hibernian Society, and from March 1872 to June 1878 as its President.[8]

The Hibernian Society celebrated its educational involvement every year at its grand St. Patrick's Day banquet. Their annual dinner topped the week's festivities, and the members spared no expense to provide a grand feast. For example, the 1859 celebration was held at the New Assembly Rooms at the northeast corner of Hanover and Lombard Streets, catered by the famous William Guy of the Monument House. This location was a meeting hall often rented by Baltimore organizations for their posh gatherings. Kane occupied a prominent place at this gala. Food was lavish, and toasts were almost unending.[9] The main educational function of the Society seemed to be lost at this yearly gathering where fine food and drinks with multiple toasts dominated the festivities.

The Hibernian Society was no small part of the Baltimore landscape, and its activities amassed large crowds. When William Smith O'Brien arrived in Baltimore for a celebration in March 1859, a crowd of an estimated 8,000 people greeted him at the train station. O'Brien was an Irish Nationalist Member of Parliament, "The Champion of Irish Liberty," a member of the Young Ireland movement, and he had years before been exiled from Ireland. Throngs accompanied him through the streets of Baltimore, and both the Hibernian Society and the Irish Social and Benevolent Society feted him at gatherings within the city, all centered that year at Barnum's City Hotel (Figure 16),[10] which was an elegant meeting place for Southerners, as well as for major events of Baltimore society, including the Hibernians.

Indeed, many of the organizations in Baltimore during this era seemed to exist solely for their Grand Balls held in celebration of various and sundry events. Grand Balls were part of the militias, fire departments, and other civic groups, all competing for the most elegant event of the year. It was common for there to be listed 30–50 prominent citizens of Baltimore as "organizers," "managers," "sponsors," or "committee members." "Elaborate fare" was commonly cited as an inducement for attendance. Each and every ball was to be conducted "in a manner never equalled in this city, if, indeed, in the country."[11] Rarely was a newspaper printed that did not have two to four announcements of these "Grand Balls." Baltimore's dignitaries all lent their good names to these worthy causes. For example, the "Anniversary Festival of the Hibernian Society of Baltimore," held on March 17, 1851, at the Eutaw House, another grand venue, was a celebrated affair:

Figure 16. Artist's depiction of Barnum's City Hotel, where the Hibernians often met. From the Maryland Center for History and Culture.

> The members of the Hibernian Society of Baltimore, on Monday evening, after fulfilling the important duties devolving on them as managers and superintendents of the Oliver Hibernian Free School, repaired in a body to the Eutaw house, to partake of their anniversary dinner, where they were joined by a number of distinguished invited guests, with others of our citizens who never fail to be present at these social reunions—so famed as they are for "a feast of reason and flow of soul."[12]

This particular night in 1851 saw those innumerable toasts, beginning with 13 "regular toasts of the Society" given by distinguished guests, then followed by toasts and songs from "volunteers" numbering over 75. Toasts were given both to and from Colonel Kane, who was regaled as "Our respected Collector—the citizen and soldier—in all positions he has never been found wanting." Kane himself toasted "Our Shipwrights—The architects of Baltimore clippers—we have among us a fit representative in the person of Andrew Flannegan."[13]

Kane noted years later in March 1876, in his role as President of the Hibernian Society, that the needs of Irish immigrants had increased over the decades. He said that the "state of destitution" was unparalleled at that time, compared to prior eras. Virtually every hour he received calls for assistance from immigrants and others. The situation was so dire that he recommended, and his suggestion was followed, that the annual Hibernian banquet be canceled and the money ordinarily used for this function be given to the poor.[14] It was only the second time in the history of the Hibernian Society of Baltimore that they declined to meet.

Kane's presidency of the Hibernian Society was punctuated by his illnesses at the end of his life. He is recorded as being absent from meetings from September 1877 through June 1878, with one notation on March 18, 1878, saying that he was "in the South on account of sickness."[15] His obituary eulogy was posted in the Society's records on June 24, 1878.

At his death, the Hibernians honored Kane in a resolution, citing his "sterling worth," noting that "his purse, his service and his influence were ever ready in the cause of charity." They lauded his "loftiness of purpose, exalted courage and such purity of action that envy itself could not detect a stain on his character." They noted that "[i]n private life the strength and dignity of his manhood were crowned with the truest social virtues and robed with the gentlest social graces." They called his death a "public calamity."[16] Kane was indeed a Hibernian, through and through.

6

Baltimore Fire Departments

The history of the Baltimore Fire Department is intimately connected to the social, legal, and political scenes of the mid–1800s. The fire companies, the gangs, the militias, the police, and the political structure were all tightly connected. George Kane was an active participant in the development of Baltimore's fire department.

Baltimore's first fire department began in 1747.[1] Initial city regulations demanded that all residents with a chimney provide a ladder of sufficient height to reach the top of the roof; furthermore, a fine was levied if the occupants of the building allowed "their chimney to take fire so as to blaze out at the top."[2] The first two fire companies were the Union (that owned the fire engine "Tick-Tack") and the Mechanical (that owned the fire engine "Dutchman"), followed by the formation of the Friendship Company in 1785. Volunteers manned all of these fire companies. Baltimore residents were encouraged:

    1. to put lights in their windows in the event of a fire (to help the fire companies see while responding to the scene, since there were not yet any street lights in the city),
    2. to have two leather buckets for the water brigade (to be marked with the family's name and sent immediately to the scene of a fire), and
    3. to have the companies designate men to organize the response to a fire, including making lanes for the passage of fire buckets and appointing men to "take charge of property to be removed in time of fire."[3]

Firefighting was a community activity, and all able-bodied persons participated. Gradually, through meetings of the fire companies, they organized their volunteer efforts, and eight fire districts were created. Wells and pumps were added around the town, and additional regulations were passed to ensure safety. Membership and participation in a fire company's activities became both a civic duty and a social marker of good citizenship.

Initially, Baltimore men of stature, including prominent business and political celebrities, joined the fire departments as a civic duty. These men were willing to leave their comfortable homes at all times of day and night to battle fires in the city, an ever-present danger in this era when most buildings were constructed of wood. A testament to the frequent and ravaging destruction of fires was the sheer number of fire insurance companies doing business in Baltimore during the 1830s–1850s.

By 1829 there were 14 fire companies, 29 engines, about 16,000 feet of hose, and 2,000 members who were loosely joined in the "Baltimore United Fire Department."

6. Baltimore Fire Departments 39

Many fire companies existed in very close proximity to each other, often only one or two blocks separating their stations (Figure 17). Their locations magnified the competition between them. Nevertheless, standards for hose size allowed different companies to work together when absolutely necessary. Individual companies even provided support and relief for families whose members had been injured in the line of duty.

However, rivalries began, and competition among the various fire companies accelerated during the 1830s–1840s. Baltimore Mayor William Steuart started the conversation about improving the quality of the fire departments when he wrote in January 1832 that "there are some irregularities among them which should be corrected."[4] His words were an understatement. Fire companies were just beginning to exert their influence, contributing to the overall rowdiness of the city, and these companies would soon become the centers of disruptive behavior, the focus of gang activity, and the inducers of riots. Though Steuart had not witnessed this degree of lawlessness among the fire departments in 1832, it was soon coming.

The fire companies quickly burst out of control. Though many—if not most—of their members were upright citizens, lawless toughs began to infiltrate their ranks. Because belonging to a fire company carried with it a degree of honor and pride, the companies quickly became competitors. Rivalries grew, and competition among the various departments likewise appeared. Some of it could have been useful—contests to see which company could arrive at a fire scene first, even though districts where

Figure 17. Approximate locations of fire companies in Baltimore. *Note: Many Baltimore directories and Scharf's descriptions listed the Deptford, the Franklin, and the Columbian Fire Companies at the same address: "NE Corner of Market [now Broadway] and Fleet Streets." Adapted from Samuel Augustus Mitchell, Jr.'s 1872 "Plan of Baltimore."

a company had jurisdiction were strictly defined. Battles occasionally erupted to determine which company could connect to water sources. Fights between members of companies arriving at the same scene were common. At the height of the problem, fire companies even tried to burn down each other's station houses. Destruction of firefighting apparatus became routine, and when the firefighters themselves (often inebriated) were not engaging in the riots they had started, the "runners" did the fighting for them. It became common for men and boys to attach themselves to the fire equipment as it was being returned to the station after a fire, and these "hangers-on" would pick fights with rival companies (or with other street gangs) after the fire had been extinguished and the legitimate firefighters had completed their task. Though the combatants often were not true members of the fire company, that company's reputation would be sullied by these antics. Gangs themselves would eventually attach to the fire companies more permanently.

The Baltimore Association of Firemen was established in 1831, followed by a more formal organization of the Baltimore United Fire Department in 1833. Both groups attempted to curb the violence that was accelerating at fire scenes. In 1833 the United Fire Department established a series of rules or Articles of Association.[5] This system divided Baltimore into seven districts. Firefighters were issued badges with "B.U.F.D." ("Baltimore United Fire Department") inscribed with the name of the fire company and a number given to the individual fireman.

Operational rules often can be viewed as a response to some deficiency or problem within an organization. One only needs to read the evolving rules of the fire departments to understand the problems that the system of multiple fire companies had generated:

1. Fire alarm bells at the engine houses were to be used only for active fires. Rules forbade the use of the bells for any other purpose, to avoid false fire alarms.

2. No company could "retain" a fireplug unless ready to fight the fire.

3. Fire equipment was not to use the walkways or sidewalks.

4. Disorderly members of a fire company had to be dismissed promptly.

5. Upon return from a fire, a company should move in an orderly fashion, moving to the right if it met another fire engine.

6. All fire hoses had to fit standard-size connections.

7. All firefighters had to wear their badges that displayed the name of the company and the fireman's individual number.

8. Minors were not allowed to be members of the company.

9–10. Dues were assessed.

11. Lists of members were submitted yearly.

12. No alcoholic beverages were to be consumed at a fire.

13. Committees policed the rules.

14. Firefighters who committed offenses were expelled; they could not return or join another fire company for 12 months.

15. Expelled firefighters' names were circulated to other companies; penalties were defined for expelled members and their companies.

16–20. These rules established grounds for expulsion, fines, and district boundaries.

21. Fire equipment was to use the streets only for a legitimate fire response.

22. A fireman wearing his badge was answerable for his behavior to the company.

23–24. These rules established more laws and fines.

25. Equipment left at the scene of a fire was to be returned to a central location for recovery.

26–28. Firefighters had to wear official badges.

29. Fire bells were to be used only for fire alarms.

30. "Rules of the road" defined how fire equipment was to be driven.[6]

Even with this organization, fire companies were frequently out of control. Scharf reported:

> Unfortunately, the rivalries and jealousies of the various companies had resulted at a comparatively early period in scenes of riot and bloodshed, and in spite of the formation of the United Fire Department, disorders and disturbances were of frequent occurrence between some of the organizations which composed it. "The alarm of fire," we are told, "sounded to the peaceful citizens as a war-whoop, and the scene of conflagration was the scene of riot, if not invariably of bloodshed. Gangs of disorderly blackguards, adopting the names of some of our fire companies, would marshal themselves under ringleaders, and, armed with bludgeons, knives, and even fire-arms, fight with each other like hordes of savages."[7]

Honest and law-abiding firemen were put at risk by this activity. In 1838 the city of Baltimore enacted ordinances to protect both the firemen and their equipment. Crime upon the equipment became a felony punishable by a prison term of two to five years; crimes upon the firemen likewise yielded both fines and prison terms.

In 1849 Baltimore was again divided into fire protection districts—this time, four. Baltimore was coming closer to a real unified fire department system. A paid fire department with 12 companies was proposed in 1849, but the city had insufficient funds for the salaries, station houses, and steam engines needed.

By 1851 there were 17 companies with 12 "spouting engines" and 27 "suction engines," 39 hose carriages, 21,250 feet of hose, and 2,400 volunteer firemen (Appendix, Table 4). In 1858, the city of Baltimore further organized its fire response teams to establish a paid staff, though volunteers remained at each of the companies' locations. However, rivalries among the companies persisted, and chaos often reigned at a fire scene. A fully paid fire department staff would not appear until 1865, and many attribute its formation to the impetus of George Kane, who had suggested the utility and efficiency of such an organization.

Kane belonged to the Baltimore United Fire Department as a member of the Independent Fire Company as early as 1837. He served as its Vice President from 1846 to 1848 and as President from 1851 to 1854. He was a member of the delegation of the Independent Fire Company to the Baltimore United Fire Department in 1837. Kane supervised the procurement of capes and hats as uniforms for the Company in early 1838, a year in which he was a member of both the electing committee and a committee to purchase a "new suction engine." He was active in the Company's social events and served on committees for balls and processions. Dues for this prestigious organization were $0.25 per quarter, far less expensive than membership in the Hibernian Society. In January 1839 he became one of three assistant engineers.

Kane, James B. Waters, and Samuel Kirk were the Independent representatives to the Baltimore United Fire Department in 1845. In January 1845 Kane was nominated to become Vice President of the organization; the results are not recorded, but he was elected Vice President in January 1846 and January 1847. At this time he was called "Captain Kane."[8] Kane continued as the Independents' representative to the Baltimore United Fire Department in 1848–1850.

Kane was a pioneer to suggest the concept of a paid fire department. In February 1853 the multiple fire departments in Baltimore began the painful and difficult decade-long process of consolidating into a system of paid employees, confusingly also called the Baltimore United Fire Department. Each individual company initially provided one representative for the negotiations for consolidation. Kane was the spokesperson for the Independent Fire Company.[9] He was chosen to be the Chairman of the Committee, and they established the following goals: "to render the Department more efficient" by "abolition of all the present companies; looking to a total reorganization; the paid system; a district system; the election of chief engineer, foreman and assistant foreman, &c., &c."[10] Unfortunately, the proposed paid Baltimore United Fire Department plan was rejected. In 1854, some businessmen again requested a reorganization of the fire department at the First Branch of the Baltimore City Council, but the proposal languished. It took considerable time for the concept of a unified fire department to take hold. In September 1854, "fire rioting" was still a problem. On this occasion, the New Market and the United Fire Companies both responded to a conflagration, and allegedly volunteers F. Baumonbough and Augustus Shelow ran the United fire engine into the New Market fire engine, "for the purpose of making a disturbance." The police intervened and avoided a full-scale riot. Officers arrested others involved in the melee, restoring calm.[11]

The concept of reorganization was again introduced in 1856. It also failed to pass. In 1857 the First Branch passed a resolution prohibiting the formation of any more volunteer fire companies. By 1858, action was beginning in committees of the city government, but there still were proponents of the volunteer system. The Baltimore United Fire Department passed a resolution "protesting against the violent dismemberment of the organization."[12] By this time there were 22 independent volunteer fire companies (three steam engine companies [Vigilant, First Baltimore, and Washington], 17 hand engine companies, and two hook-and-ladder companies), with over 1,000 active volunteers manning the equipment. Mayor Thomas Swann came on board supporting the concept of a paid firefighting force and a department based around steam fire engines. The organization was complete in 1859 when the city was divided into two major fire districts, with six steam fire engine companies and two hook-and-ladder companies. Kane was once again credited with much of the pressure to form this paid fire department.

Not all reports of firefighting in this era were negative, however. On March 25, 1858, Dr. John M. Johnston found his house ablaze, and Colonel Kane and the Independent Fire Company came to his rescue. Johnston was very thankful for the efforts of this Company:

> *To Col. Kane and the Gallant Independent* [Fire Company] my heart is overflowing with gratitude; for, like Hannibal leading the Legions of Carthage to thunder at the gates of Rome, with

the *brave Pioneer, the noble Friendship, the Washington, the Columbian, Western Hose* [all Baltimore fire companies]—and others which the excitement of the moment prevented me from observing, but to whom I shall ever feel grateful—boldly advancing to the charge, they continued with the most unwearied exertions, never deserting their post until the enemy was conquered.[13]

Transition of the fire departments to a paid force continued to proceed very slowly, in large part because of the resistance of each individual company to divest itself of the autonomy and prestige afforded by the old system. The early iterations of the Baltimore United Fire Department themselves had failed; therefore, centralization was inevitable. The advent of the steam-powered fire engine was upon the country, and the expense of such equipment was beyond the grasp of most independent volunteer units. The steam fire engine was far superior to hand-powered models, and it was not long before businessmen, politicians, and citizens were demanding this new technology.

The new Baltimore City Fire Department would introduce many innovative and practical forces for good:

    1. Firemen would be paid centrally, thus subjecting them to uniform rules and discipline;
    2. a chain of command was established with a powerful chief;
    3. steam fire engines improved the overall effectiveness of the firefighting effort; and
    4. a new system of fire alarms was introduced.

Fortunately for George Kane, who in 1860 was about to assume command of the Baltimore Police, the major contributors to the chaos and rioting in the city—the independent fire companies—were about to disappear just as he was charged with restoring order to the city.

7

Gangs of Baltimore and the Baltimore Elections

Baltimore was a center of immigration in the early 1800s. Thousands of immigrants poured into the Baltimore area, many of them German or Irish, "giving rise to problems that were in part religious, part economic, and part political."[1] Concentrations of immigrants in Baltimore neighborhoods caused ethnic tensions.[2] Baltimore of the 1840s–1860s had grown dramatically from this influx of immigrants—in 1860 it became the fourth largest city in the United States. The city had 212,418 residents in 1860, and one in four Baltimoreans was a recent immigrant.[3]

Locals resented the arrivals of large numbers of immigrants, and these resentments gave birth to multiple gangs in the city, euphemistically called "political clubs," most of them coalescing under the banner of the American Party. These gangs went by the names of the Blood Tubs, the Rip-Raps, the Plug Uglies, the Wampanoags, the Regulators, the Rough Skins, the Black Snakes, the Tigers, the Calithumpians, the York Roaders, and the Double Pumps. There was no shortage of clubs for young Baltimore toughs to join, and most of the names suggested an evil intent.[4]

Many clubs (such as the Blood Tubs) specifically targeted Catholic voters. The larger clubs had 50–150 members each; the 40 or so clubs in Baltimore had about 700–1,000 members total. Catholics responded by having social clubs of their own, named the Bloody Eights, the Bloats, and the Buttenders.[5] Each name may have had a peculiar significance, though the meaning of most has been lost to history. The "Plug Uglies," for example, could have been named for the "plug hats" (large round felt hats with a narrow brim—similar to bowlers or derbies). These hats had additional padding of paper, wool, and/or leather to function as helmets during fights. It could have referred to "plugging," another word for punching. It might have meant "stabbing," as the gang members often used shoemakers' awls to impale recalcitrant voters (awls were often attached to their legs or knees to make the attack more covert and surprising), and their shoes were said frequently to have spikes that could also be used to perforate an opponent. These Plug Ugly gang members were mostly affiliated with the Mount Vernon Hook-and-Ladder Fire Company.

The year 1855 was the first in which the *Baltimore Sun* used the term "plug ugly" or "plug uglies" for one of the gangs that intimidated voters. The newspapers documented many occasions of voters who were not allowed the right of suffrage:

7. Gangs of Baltimore and the Baltimore Elections

And some of the parties I heard crying out during the day rally, "plug uglies," after they had returned back to the polls.... I saw the same persons obstructing the gang way and preventing persons from voting....[6]

I was at the 19th ward on the 18th day of Oct., 1855, for the purpose of voting for a member of the city council. I made three different attempts to get up to the window. Was asked what ticket I voted. Said I was a Democrat. I did not succeed in getting to the window—was kicked by two different persons.[7]

I saw several German voters, who made an effort to vote, entirely driven from the polls and prevented from casting their votes....[8]

Many of these gangs were affiliated with the American Party, whose more popular name was the "Know-Nothing Party," attesting to the secrecy of many of the gangs and clubs. When asked about their affiliations with these gangs, members would reply, "I know nothing." As outlandish as it may seem, this party rose to power in Baltimore, largely on the strength of intimidation, terror, and violence. Police effectively assisted the formation and growth of these clubs by their open support, by their own membership in the clubs, and by their willingness to ignore the chaos that the gangs promoted. Many of the policemen had received their jobs as patronage favors given by the political bosses.[9] Tactics of the American Know-Nothings involved rioting and political scheming to influence votes. They participated in street fights that saw participants using rocks, bricks, paving stones, pistols, rifles, shotguns, and even cannons.

Each club or gang had its unique dominion within the city, often roughly corresponding to the fire districts. (Figure 18) By the mid–1850s the territories where each gang ruled in the city of Baltimore were loosely established. These groups were no more than ruthless men seeking domination over areas of the city, the political machines, and therefore the economy.

In 1858, one Baltimore Plug Ugly, Henry Clay Gambrill, murdered a police officer who had the audacity and bad judgment to arrest one of Gambrill's fellow Plug Uglies. Two policemen—Benjamin Benton and Robert Rigdon—had arrested this Plug Ugly for drunkenness and disorderly conduct. Gambrill came upon the scene and shot Benton in the head, killing him. Gambrill became famous, though he was convicted of the killing and subsequently executed. At his funeral the cortege were about "one hundred hacks and carriages," and an estimated 8,000–10,000 American Know-Nothings gathered to pay their ill-conceived respects to the hoodlum.[10]

Police were loath to intervene in the gang turf wars, and chaos often reigned, especially around election time. (Figure 19) Young toughs joined for adventure, for a sense of belonging to a group, or simply from boredom. The gangs provided a sense of camaraderie in a culture that often had bred isolation in the recently arrived immigrants. Some were decidedly Irish—they had anti–German sentiments. Some were German—they harbored anti–Irish feelings. Often the gangs were anti–Catholic.[11] In addition to their political activities, they often engaged in gambling, fighting, cockfighting, and prostitution. (Figure 20)

Gangs would notoriously kidnap potential voters (the homeless, the poor, immigrants, visitors to the city, transients or hoboes, and others), drug them or ply them

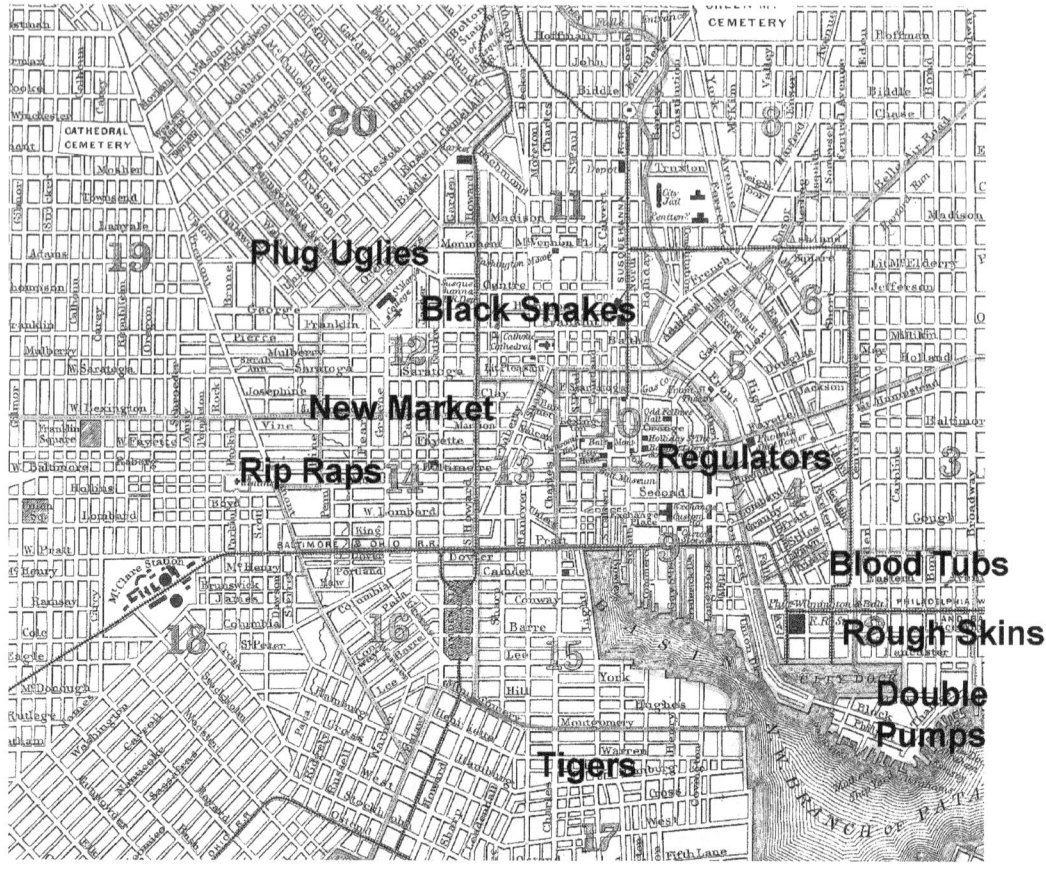

Figure 18. Approximate location of major gangs of Baltimore. From *Hanging Henry Gambrill* (Melton). Adapted from Samuel Augustus Mitchell, Jr.'s 1872 "Plan of Baltimore."

with alcohol to keep them until election day, and then carry them to polling places repeatedly to cast multiple votes, attempting to usher a favorite candidate to victory. Voter identification at the polls was haphazard at best, so bringing an "unregistered" voter to the polls was easy enough. This process was called "cooping" for the process of kidnapping and holding drugged potential voters in a coop—a small place of confinement or jail-like cell—until voting day. Some coops were reported to hold as many as 40–50 potential voters, and men cooped in this fashion would vote up to 10–20 times. Occasionally the illegitimate voters would be given a change of clothes as a disguise before their second or third passage through a polling station. In the November 2, 1859, election some estimates placed the number of cooped voters at 220, with a total of more than 1,000 illegitimate votes cast.[12] And that figure is just the fraudulent votes cast by cooped men; voter intimidation likely changed or eliminated far more votes. Other illegal votes by non-eligible voters further tainted the election process.

Some authors have claimed that Edgar Allan Poe may have died because of being cooped as he passed through Baltimore from Richmond, though the veracity of this story can't be confirmed. What is true and verifiable, though, is that he was

7. Gangs of Baltimore and the Baltimore Elections 47

Figure 19. "Plug Uglies Riot in Baltimore." From the Maryland State Archives.

found near the Fourth Ward Polling Station at 44 East Lombard Street on Election Day, October 3, 1849. He was clothed in garments that didn't belong to him, and he died in the Washington College Hospital (later known as Church Home and Hospital) on October 7, never having regained mental clarity, suggesting that he had been drugged. The Whigs were dominant during the Baltimore elections that year, but the Know-Nothings also used the cooping technique at about this time,[13] and they may have been responsible for Poe's death.

In addition, gangs would threaten legitimate voters. Formal voter registration was not initiated in Baltimore wards or precincts until 1865, so the identity of a legal voter at the polls was dependent upon the judgment of the voting official manning the ballot box. Baltimore was a huge city, and each election saw over 25,000 votes cast, a formidable number for the election judges to manage. Voting occurred at only one place in each of the 20 wards of Baltimore, often a tavern, a bar, a civic meeting hall, or even a private residence. These locations could be strategically chosen to be near a political party's offices, close to the home of a party boss, or in proximity to a dominant political club.[14] Polling places were often booths set up with a window through which ballots were presented to the polling judge.

Official voting requirements of the day included the following: male, white, over the age of 21, a U.S. citizen, and residing within the ward for 6–24 months (this requirement varied). Election judges at each of the 20 wards had the final say at each site, declaring who did and did not have the right to vote. If the judge recognized someone as a legal resident of that ward, he was supposed to allow that person to vote. Usually two clerks assisted the election judges, and voters were listed on rolls kept by individual parties. If a potential voter couldn't be found on the lists, the judge was given the discretion to qualify a voter if he had residency documents (such as naturalization papers), if he had the witness of a prominent citizen in that ward, or even if he just swore an oath. Each party had the right

Figure 20. "Plug Uglies, Political Argument on Railroad Train" (ca.1854–1856). From the Maryland State Archives.

to post a poll-watcher at the voting booth, someone who witnessed each voter and who could challenge the legitimacy of any vote. Police were supposed to be stationed nearby, though the police in the 1850s were often highly partisan themselves. Furthermore, each of the 20 Baltimore wards might have as many as 1,000–2,000 legitimate voters casting ballots, and the election judge would likely not be personally familiar with each man presenting himself to vote; however, ballots were distributed by the political parties themselves, and they were color-coded. If an official at the polls wanted to refuse to accept the ballot of someone because the paper was the "wrong" color (supporting the "wrong" party), it could be done. Therefore, straight party ticket votes were common, if not the rule. For this reason, it was common for one party to dominate the vote completely, with only a handful of dissenting votes, often the number equal to the number of voters assaulted after voting in that ward. Furthermore, if the voting official wasn't corrupt, gangs and thugs could intercept the voter before he ever arrived at the ballot box. Gangs could then force the voter to cast a ballot for the gangs' candidate by giving him the "correct" ballot.[15] The entire process was fraught with opportunity for corruption, and there were often multiple elections in the October–November time frame—one for municipal and local contests (often in September), one for state elections (October), and one for national races (November).

Gangs had many effective methods at their disposal for coercing a voter. Men with "awls" were commonly seen in the vicinity of the ballot boxes, "supervising" the elections. These awls were specially made pointed instruments, similar to a curved hook used to lift a bale of hay, or a straight shoemaker's awl that could be wielded by hand or tied to the gang members' legs to impale people with the audacity to vote contrary to the wishes of the local political boss. Amazingly, blacksmiths even conducted the business of making and selling awls close to the polling places. In the absence of awls, gangs could resort to the use of bricks, bats, guns, pikes, rocks, or the simple human fist as a means of torturing the prospective voter and convincing him to vote "properly."

When not using these more aggressive physical techniques to influence voters, gangs adopted their unique methods of intimidation. The Blood Tubs (or "Bloody Tubs"), for example, derived their name from the practice of bringing a tub filled with animal blood to the polling sites. Voters who had the wrong color ballots, signifying a vote for the party not favored by the gang, would have their ballots stolen and their heads plunged into the blood tub. Apparently the German immigrants feared this procedure the most and were effectively prevented from voting. Word of such tactics being used spread quickly, and voters intending to cast a ballot for the "wrong" party might be convinced to stay at home, rather than going to the polls and risking intimidation or physical harm. Riots often accompanied this voter intimidation. The Know-Nothings reaped the most votes from these illicit practices, especially in the latter half of the 1850s. It wasn't until the end of the 1850s that the Reform Party started to quell such tactics. "Ordinary acts of riot and intimidation" were the norm during this era.[16]

Baltimore's political parties also dominated the social and business scenes. The major parties of the presidential election of 1840 were the Democratic Party, the Liberty Party, and the Whig Party. Traditional Democratic–Whig rivalries were supplanted by the emergence of other parties as the Democrats experienced a split in loyalties. The Know-Nothing Party grew in part as a response to the anti–Catholic and anti-immigrant sentiment of the era. Political leanings were heavily dependent upon the area of Maryland being discussed. The Eastern Shore and many agricultural communities dependent on slavery voted Democratic; Whigs had lost dominance in Baltimore and were replaced by the Know-Nothings; western Maryland was mixed. The Know-Nothing Party had its own unique platform that emphasized anti-immigrant and anti–Catholic sentiments, Protestant preferences, nationalism, and "death to all foreign influences."[17] Those joining the Know-Nothing Party were required to answer questions about their beliefs and intentions. They were required to swear not to divulge the names of members of the party, that they were not Catholic, and that they were born in the United States. Further, they had to swear to vote only for native-born citizens and not to vote for Catholics or immigrants.[18] By the 1850s, the Know-Nothings had ascended to power.

As political involvement increased, gangs and fire departments effectively merged, further driving political agendas. Gangs accelerated their mayhem by purposefully setting fires or sounding alarms and then ambushing the rival fire department when it responded to the scene. On August 18, 1855,

It appears that the New Market fire company, in colleague with the United, had formed a plot whereby they designed giving the Mount Vernon Hook and Ladder company a severe thrashing.... [P]istols were fired and a skirmish of short duration ensued..., bricks thrown, and axes, picks and hooks used in the most desperate manner.... During the melee two men were mortally wounded, and a greater number severely.[19]

However, even more tumultuous times were approaching.

The election of 1856 was the pinnacle of intimidation and political riots in the city of Baltimore. The election for Mayor and the municipal offices was held on October 8. The mayoral candidates were Know-Nothing Thomas Swann (who would later become a Republican [1861–1866] and then a Democrat [1866–1879]) and Democrat Robert Clinton Wright in a very tight race. The Know-Nothing Party controlled the streets. Violence and disorder prevailed around the polling places for the 20 wards of Baltimore. Incumbent Mayor Samuel Hinks (1854–1856), himself elected Mayor as a representative of the Know-Nothing Party by a strongly contested margin of barely 1,000 votes, at first called the militia to quell anticipated disturbances, but he later rescinded that call. Violence was particularly extreme in the 2nd, 6th, and 8th wards, and many Baltimoreans (perhaps as many as 19) were killed, and scores of others were wounded.[20]

The scene was described as being "wild animation" and "riot and strife." "It was reckless and murderous in the extreme, conducted entirely in guerrilla fashion, and almost wholly with firearms." Most incriminated were the Rip-Raps and the Plug Uglies, along with the New Market Fire Company. Over 200 shots were fired from pistols, rifles, revolvers, "blunderbusses," muskets, shotguns, and "swivel guns." Rioters hurled bricks, rocks, and stones. Gang members again used their fists, brass knuckles, clubs, batons, "espantoons," awls, knives, razors, daggers, "dirks," blackjacks, slapjacks, "slungshots," "coshes," and "slug shots." It was revealing that newspapers reported: "[W]e heard of nothing more than usual fighting, except that voters were stopped and prevented from reaching the polls." The description of "usual fighting" exposed the undercurrents of unrest that reigned in the streets of Baltimore in 1856. Conflict and chaos were *expected*. After the gunfire ceased and the dust cleared, Swann had won, beating Wright by 1,567 votes, but partisans suspected massive voter fraud.[21]

The next election on November 4, 1856, for the presidency saw similar crowd dynamics. James Buchanan was the pick of the Democratic Party; John C. Fremont was the Republican (a new party that was a mix of Whigs and the Free Soil Party); and Millard Fillmore was a third party candidate representing the Know-Nothings. Riots were threatened once again, and the previous month's chaos instilled fear in most Baltimoreans. Mayor Samuel Hinks organized the police and the night watch, ordering all to be either on duty near polling stations or in readiness at the local police stations. Nearly 300 regular police were deployed to prevent or control rioting. Governor Thomas Watkins Ligon came to Baltimore to assess the situation and to see if additional troops were needed. Ligon's view was that the military should be activated, and he wanted to order them into position. Hinks, on the other hand, felt that the local police were sufficient and that a military presence might actually worsen the situation. By the end of their negotiations, balloting had already begun, and citizens from the 2nd, 4th, 8th, 16th, 19th, and 20th wards were arriving at the Mayor's office complaining that they were having difficulty voting. Nevertheless, the Governor deferred to the Mayor; however, by about 10:00 a.m. gunfire had erupted. Alcohol was contributing to the mood of the voters, even at this early hour.[22] Initial reports suggested at least 10 dead and 45 others with serious injuries; victims suffering less severe trauma were not even reported. Many children and teenagers were involved in the carnage. These riots were likely even worse than the ones seen in October 1856.

In Baltimore, Fillmore gathered 16,900 votes to Buchanan's 9,870; Fremont received only 270.[23] In Maryland, Fillmore received 47,452 votes; Buchanan had 39,123. Nationwide, it was Buchanan 1,835,140, Fremont 1,340,668, and Fillmore 872,703. Clearly, Baltimoreans were not drawn to the Republicans, and Marylanders, in general, likewise had no love for the Republican platform. The next presidential election would pit Republican Abraham Lincoln against three other candidates.

Contemporary Baltimore historian John Thomas Scharf recorded these scenes of the mayhem from the many elections of 1856 in great detail:

> On the 12th of September [1856] a bloody and disgraceful riot took place at the Seventeenth Ward House.... The house was attacked by the "Rip-Rap" and "Wampanoag" Clubs, and then commenced a bloody and desperate affray, which will long be remembered as one of the most bloodthirsty ruffianisms of the times.... During the melee one man was killed and some twenty badly wounded, some of them fatally.[24]

Further,

> The election of Oct. 8, 1856, was a frightful scene of disorder. The police were, to a great extent, affiliated to the Know-Nothing order, or intimidated by it, and shamefully failed in their duties. In various parts of the city pitched battles raged all day; muskets and pistols were freely used, and even cannon brought out into the streets....[25]

As the November elections approached, further rioting erupted:

> Our city, on the 4th of November [1856], was again made the theatre of the most prolonged and desperate rioting. Armed and organized associations, belonging to both political parties, resorted to firearms, with which they were liberally provided, and fought with ferocious and daring recklessness.... In both of these riots eight persons were killed and about 150 were wounded....[26]

The 1857 elections again prompted disagreements between Governor Thomas Watkins Ligon and the new Baltimore Mayor Thomas Swann. Ligon again wanted to use the militia; Swann didn't. Swann ultimately prevailed. Superficially polite words in their written communications hid their deep-seated disagreements.[27]

In an undated letter to Governor Ligon, apparently written on October 27, 1857, a group of lawyers, most of them from Baltimore, gave their opinion on the legality of the Governor intervening in the affairs of the city of Baltimore. They concluded that the Governor had the ultimate authority to call the militia, and that the determination of the necessity to bring this force to any city in the state was his alone. Specifically, these consultants addressed whether the potential for disruption of the elective process was a sufficient emergency to warrant the introduction of the state militia upon the city of Baltimore. They concluded that the answer was "Yes." It wasn't the

Figure 21. "At the Polls." From *Harper's Weekly*.

answer Mayor Swann wanted to hear. Swann was rather intransigent, and then he issued two proclamations that addressed the issues surrounding the maintenance of peace during an election. He implored citizens to cooperate with the police, and to report any police misbehavior. He defined the appropriate behavior of the election officials at the polls, and he declared that guns would be confiscated if they were being used to intimidate voters. He demanded the arrest of disorderly persons, and he declared that all "drinking houses" be closed on the day of elections. Thereafter, another group of lawyers, some of whom had advised the Governor about the legality of the his intervening in the affairs of Baltimore, wrote to the Governor, imploring him not to activate the militias. Governor Ligon relented, saying on November 1, "I now contemplate no use of the military force which I have ordered to be enrolled and organized." Ultimately, the militia didn't intervene in this 1857 Baltimore election.

During this era, no one even pretended that the elections in Baltimore were fair (Figure 21):

> As we remarked yesterday morning the nominal election on Wednesday last [October 14, 1857] was nothing better than a mockery—riotous and bloody—of the elective franchise. The scenes of that day, though not so frightfully distorted with massacre and wounds as were those of the election days last year, exhibit the political condition of our city at the very lowest ebb of demoralization.... The polls are notoriously places of danger to life and limb....
>
> This condition amounts to the positive fact that our political *status* is at this moment justly expressed by the term *anarchy*....[28]

Many Baltimoreans clearly wanted to see corruption removed from the political offices. Even before Reformers organized, some citizens had seen George Kane as a logical candidate for Mayor. One such citizen, who signed his letter "TAX PAYER," said,

> As all lovers of law and order seem desirous to select a candidate for the Mayoralty possessing the necessary qualifications for that office, one whose education and knowledge of the city will enable him to know her wants; one whose courage is beyond doubt; one whose activity, firmness, and manly bearing will command the respect of all; one who will lead his police army in person if it be necessary; one who will compel his officers to do their duty, and restore this city to its wonted peace and quiet.
>
> Such a one may be found in the person of Col. GEORGE P. KANE. I believe the times require such a man, and he is the man for the times. If he can be induced to serve he can be elected by a large vote, in defiance of the ruling rowdyism under which we are now suffering.[29]

Kane, soon to become Police Marshal, did not immediately respond.

Kane was willing to step into a fray if necessary to improve the city. His bravery had been documented many times over the years, and he again demonstrated his strength in October 1858. At this time gangs continued to dominate life on the streets. A group of local toughs from the "Rough Skins"—numbering about 10–15 young men—attacked an elderly man named Barney Bradey at the corner of Gay Street and Second Street. Kane was nearby, and he responded to the beating, rescuing Bradey and physically protecting him. It was this bravery and willingness to become involved even in mundane aspects of the public safety that endeared Kane to his fellow Baltimoreans.[30]

The average citizen began to rebel against the intimidation of the gangs beginning at about this same time in 1858. The founding of the City Reform Association that year under the guidance of George William Brown and Severn Teackle Wallis, both prominent Baltimore lawyers, was the beginning of the end of awls and blood tubs.[31] Often called simply the Reform Association, it organized Baltimoreans into poll watchers and ward committees that rallied in mass meetings in the streets and squares to fight the gangs. While the Reformers had pledged neutrality with respect to the other political parties, many if not most had Democratic—and Southern-leaning—tendencies.

The Reform Movement, begun by this City Reform Association, began to change the city's rowdy image. It was a cooperative venture between politicians and citizens to restore peace in Baltimore, especially during election cycles. Reform was the brainchild of many Baltimoreans; Samuel W. Smith would be its President, and George William Brown its Vice President. These men were all distressed at the chaos prevalent in Baltimore. The first meeting of this group was held on November 1, 1858. (Current Mayor Thomas Swann, Know-Nothing Party member, refused to participate in this group's reform efforts.) This conclave of 166 businessmen, politicians, lawyers, physicians, and other leaders counted many prominent citizens in its roster. They were determined to clean up city elections, the police force, and the judicial system:

> A number of the citizens of Baltimore, believing that a state of things exists in this community under which its members can no longer rest in safety or without disgrace, have united themselves under the name of the CITY REFORM ASSOCIATION, for the purpose of vindicating and preserving their political, personal and civil rights.... Outrages, by day and night,

upon unoffending citizens; robberies on the public highways; savage assaults upon voters while vainly attempting to exercise the right of suffrage; murders of men, at their own hearths and in the streets—have become the burden of the press.... The comparative infrequency of arrests; the facility with which the most notorious offenders find release upon insufficient security; the tardiness of trial, the uncertainty of conviction and the inadequacy of punishment, even when the crime is most heinous and glaring—all tend, if left alone, to the perpetuation of a misrule which is utterly subversive of the objects of civilized society....[32]

The City Reform Association pledged to restore the good name of Baltimore. However, the Reform Movement's activities and its results didn't come quickly. Even through the spring of 1859 they had little to show for their principles and efforts.

Making a push for results in the fall elections in 1859, the City Reform Association planned a rally on September 5, 1859, to "devise some means of rescuing our city from its present deplorable condition."[33] The call for this meeting was cosigned by over 2,000 of Baltimore's leading citizens. Bad weather forced the postponement of the gathering until September 8, when an estimated 10,000 or more assembled at Monument Square. The group formed an elaborate organizational structure that involved each of Baltimore's 20 wards, part of which was the "Reform Central Committee," charged with nominating candidates for public office without regard to political party affiliation. The major requirement was a dedication to the renovation of the political structure of the city along conservative lines that would restore peace and honesty to the city government. The Association was so well organized and favorably received that it was able to put forward candidates for the upcoming election the next month, October 1859, followed by the election on November 2. The Reform Party's platform included the revamping of the police force and fire department, placing the control of elections under the police, and overhauling the judicial system to ensure that gangs and American Know-Nothings were brought to justice.

The October 1859 election saw nearly the same riotous gang behavior as that seen in earlier years, but it was the first where politicians, news writers, and citizens could detect a difference in the *outcome* of the elections. Six Reform candidates were elected to the City Council out of 30 seats. The Know-Nothings watched the outcomes of this election, and they redoubled their efforts, holding their own rallies and augmenting the use of the awl.

The next election in November 1859 saw further violence. Severn Teackle Wallis reported, "There was not, at any part of the time while I was there, free access to the window for all voters; ... there was a wilful [sic] obstruction by a party of men not engaged in voting, who rallied under the cry of 'Regulators.'" Further, "the attack was so violent and so sustained; no interference made by the judges, and no policeman visible on the ground, that there was no alternative for the Reformers but to leave the ground or sacrifice their lives uselessly."[34] Mr. Charles D. Hinks also reported that the gangs "raved like madmen, swearing that they would kill the Reformers, and I heard McGonnigan, one of the Rip Raps, swear that no Reformer should vote; except over his dead body, this he said with horrid oaths and imprecations."[35]

The November 1859 election was also punctuated by fiery speeches and blatant voter intimidation. The *Sun* reported:

> [T]he clubs [gangs] assembled in Monument Square on Oct. 27, 1859, carrying banners and emblems of the most brutal and defiant character. Prominent among these were enormous models of *shoemakers' awls*, which they were in the habit of using to stab unfriendly voters as they advanced to the polls through lines of ruffians drawn up for the purpose. Clinched fists, with the motto, "With this we will do the work," bleeding heads labeled "Head of a Reformer," and other atrocious devices were displayed…. [T]hey struck terror into the hearts of all their opponents, and on this day they did their utmost.[36]

The entrenched, corrupt political structure had won, but the Reform Party persisted. Not dissuaded by their relative ineffectiveness in the fall 1859 elections, they reorganized at a convention held on November 17, 1859. Forming committees to address all of the major issues, including the presentation of evidence for the corruptness of the recent elections, they worked nonstop for the next six weeks. They wrote their "Reform Bills" that addressed the police, the elections, and the overwhelming evidence for judicial corruption.

The Know-Nothings had controlled the state legislature from 1855 to 1859; Thomas Hicks, Baltimore's Mayor from 1857 to 1861, was another Know-Nothing. But in January 1860 the Maryland Legislature (now Democratic by 12 to 10 in the Senate and 46 to 28 in the House) proposed three bills to deal with the mob violence in the city.[37] The first was to shift the control of the Baltimore Police Department to the State Board of Commissioners, the second was to make police responsible for the safety of voters and the integrity of the election process, and the third was allow militia to be used, if necessary, to keep the peace. The Know-Nothings fought these bills, but the most important—the shift of police control to the state—was passed on February 2, 1860. Included in the package was a nullification of some of the results of the fall 1859 elections. Legal challenges to this new law were unsuccessful. George P. Kane would soon be taking over the reins of this new post. He would later be described as a man with "remarkable self-confidence and a large ego."[38]

The control of the police in Baltimore was moved to the state-appointed board, effective February 1860. George Kane was its Marshal. His force would be responsible for bringing peace to the elective process. Reformers were encouraged. They re-assembled on August 18, 1860, and continued the process of nominating candidates for Baltimore offices. They chose George W. Brown, officially a member of the Constitutional Union Party, though he was instrumental in the formation and the activities of the Reform Party, as their mayoral pick. They were successful this time, and Brown was elected Mayor; he was swept into power along with the entire slate of Reform City Council candidates.[39]

"At the next election, on the 10th of October, 1860, not a shot was fired, not a knife drawn, not a brawl disturbed the quiet of the streets when a Reform mayor and city council were lifted into power by overwhelming and legitimate majorities."[40]

The presidential election of November 6, 1860, was a four-way race in Maryland. John C. Breckenridge ran as a Southern Democrat, Stephen Douglas as a Northern Democrat, John Bell as a Constitutional Union candidate (generally a combination of Whigs and Know-Nothings), and Abraham Lincoln as the Republican. Lincoln wasn't popular in either Maryland or Baltimore. This election was amazingly peaceful and quiet. The *Baltimore Sun* reported:

> Yesterday was the first general election under the new law, and the change in the moral aspect of the city was gratifying in the extreme. A visit to the polls of most of the precincts only presented scenes of quiet, and the police had little or nothing to do.[41]

Peace had prevailed.

Marshal Kane had successfully controlled the rioters, and Baltimore's nickname "Mobtown" seemed no longer relevant to the city. About the only incident of violence during election day or night was an accidental shooting of a policeman that occurred at the corner of Baltimore and South Streets, the Bell Headquarters. Following the shooting, Marshal Kane witnessed a spittoon being thrown from a window of the Bell Headquarters, striking another policeman. A few revelers were arrested, but soon released. This election stood in stark contrast to those of the previous four or five years.

8

Baltimore Police

Much of the story of George Kane's positive influence in Baltimore relates to his tenure as Marshal of the Baltimore Police. Initially a businessman, Kane would find himself surrendering a large yearly income for public service. This pattern was familiar to many public servants of the 1800s. Though the lure of political power often didn't translate to dollars, many politicians of the day surrendered wealth for a chance to either achieve political dominance or simply serve their fellow citizens. Attachment to the Baltimore police was a major step in Kane's service to his fellow Baltimoreans, those who favored the North as well as supporters of the South.

The Baltimore Police force in its early years was neither a leader in organization and techniques nor a bastion of honesty, integrity, or upright service. Baltimore began in 1659 as Baltimore *County*, much larger than the present-day Baltimore County. Baltimore *City* began in 1729 as surveyors outlined the streets of the city. Night watchmen and street lamps became the method of choice for preventing lawbreaking in 1773, "to preserve good order in our streets and to disperse all idle and tumultuous assemblies, at which blasphemy and vice usually preside." Civic-minded gadflies pled "for erecting lamps at proper distances in our streets and constituting a body of vigorous, trusty watchmen, for the public convenience and security."[1] These night watchmen—the first guardians of the streets of Baltimore—worked from 10:00 p.m. through daybreak, functioning also as town criers, announcing the time every 15 minutes. The organization of this "force" became more formalized with the Act of 1784 that empowered night watchmen (numbering 14 that year) to make arrests as they deemed necessary, similar to Baltimore constables, of which they needed only three. By the turn of the century, however, Baltimore had already begun its reputation as a rowdy metropolis. "Affairs became so unmanageable, that in 1801 a town meeting was held for the purpose of devising some plan for preventing the frequent thefts, robberies, disturbances and fires that had become so common."[2] The 31,514 citizens of Baltimore were well on their way to appending the name "Mobtown" to their city. By 1810 the city had 270 policemen.[3] In 1826 the Mayor was formally given command over the police force. In 1843 the police abandoned their practice of calling out the time as they went about their rounds, the correct assumption being that such announcements simply told the thieves and malefactors where the police were located, making hooligans' illegal activities easier to accomplish.

By the 1850s, the large number of immigrants had swelled the labor force, and unemployment rose. Murders and suicides increased. Beggars and the homeless contributed to the street crime. Violence abounded, and the average citizen felt generally unsafe.

The Baltimore police force was one of the last in the United States to become modernized. A Legislative Act in 1853 reorganized the force under a Marshal, and a hierarchy of rank was established. Rules were codified; officers were issued a badge and supplied with weapons. The Act required more precise record-keeping, and in theory it specified stricter discipline for the behavior of the policemen. After Samuel Hinks was elected Mayor in 1854, additional improvements in the police force were implemented: the night patrols were augmented, a Marshal was given command over the entire force, and the city was divided into four districts, improving logistics and administration.

Know-Nothing Party member Thomas Swann became Mayor in 1856, and improvements in the police force at the beginning of his tenure perhaps contributed to a lessening of crime, but they were not sufficient. Police regulations were again modified in 1857, specifying the chain of command that regulated the force, now at 405 officers, counting the Marshal, the Captains, Lieutenants, Sergeants, and the "turnkeys."[4] The "beat cops" numbered 350. Police were given expanded powers, and they were required to patrol the city round-the-clock. Their hours and duties were strictly defined (including meals and breaks), though all policemen were subject to being called to duty when needed, and police continued to wear their uniforms even when off duty to give the appearance of a stronger presence on the streets. (Police were required to purchase their own uniforms; only their badges with numbers and belts were supplied by the city.) The weapon provided was a "battoon," also called an "espantoon" (sometimes shortened to "spantoon"), today known as a "baton" or "billy club." The "battoon" in Baltimore remains even to this day a traditional part of the policeman's uniform. It was a wooden club, 22 inches long and 1.75 inches thick, worn on the belt or twirled at the end of a strip of leather attached to a swivel. Firearms were provided only as necessary.

In spite of this police presence, the security of the city deteriorated. The streets were essentially ruled by gangs and fire companies, which at times were one and the same. Police in Baltimore were not able—nor in many cases did they want—to quell the riots and disturbances. In fact, the police often identified with the gangs and looked the other way when violence was escalating—or worse, they sometimes participated. The police of that day—the mid- and late-1850s—were woefully undermanned, and the equipment they used didn't allow for rapid response times nor coordinated activity, even if the police were willing to intervene in such gangland disturbances, which they usually weren't. They patrolled the streets on foot and had only a "rattle" to warn bystanders or to summon additional aid. Even as the police force was augmented in 1857, the new officers hired were often members of the Know-Nothing Party, and their first allegiance was often to the political machine.[5] Thus, political patronage contributed most of the almost 300 new officers hired in 1857. The Reform Movement would not emerge for a few more years.

Marshal Benjamin W. Herring commanded the force in 1857. His reorganization of the police included establishing two shifts, one from 6:00 a.m. to 8:00 p.m., the other from 8:00 p.m. to 6:00 a.m. Since most mayhem occurred at night, one-third of the force worked the day shift, two-thirds the night. Meal breaks lasted one hour. Herring reported that he achieved 8,949 arrests during 1857, 25 for shooting at the police, most of these events occurring during the elections. By 1858 the arrests had increased to 10,877. Nevertheless, Herring's innovations could not match the corruption of the connections between the police and the Know-Nothing Party. Sadly, as de Francias Folsom, Baltimore police historian from the 1880s, reported, "the men sworn to enforce an observation of the law became the chief instruments in subverting it."[6] However, Herring would later contend that the real problem lay in the court system that refused to prosecute lawbreakers, and to some extent the fire departments that promoted violence: "We often arrested forty or fifty persons in one night, every one of whom were released the next morning by the magistrates.... The roughs defied the police, knowing how secure they were.... They were allowed to do as they pleased, until they thought any crime, even the murder of policemen, could be committed with immunity to themselves."[7]

The Reform Movement's members in 1859 suggested a number of major changes to Baltimore's police force in an attempt to release it from the grips of the gangs, the Know-Nothing Party, and the corrupt practices rampant in the election processes. One aspect of this reform was to move the control of the Baltimore Police from the city to the state, though the force was still headed by a Marshal. The state legislature passed this reorganization as law on February 2, 1860, and it formed a Board of Police Commissioners, a committee of four men plus the Mayor. The Commissioners had been nominated even before the Police Bill had been passed. They were Charles Howard (President), William H. Gatchell (Treasurer), Charles Dent Hinks, and John W. Davis. All were confirmed and sworn in on February 6. In an attempt to remove any Commissioner from the influence of outside interests, the law stipulated that the Commissioners could hold no other public office. Control of the police thus passed out of the sole hands of the Mayor to the Commission, even though the Mayor met with the Commissioners as a non-voting *ex officio* representative of the city government. Old laws that gave the Mayor supreme control over the police force were repealed. The new law specifically stated: "nothing in this section shall be construed to give to the said [Baltimore] Mayor and City Council, or any officer of said corporation, any control over said board or any officer or policeman appointed thereby."[8] Clearly, the Mayor and the City Council had been dealt out of the control of the police.

The transfer of supervision of the police from Baltimore city to the State of Maryland created a huge controversy. The powers of Baltimore City Hall vehemently opposed what they considered to be the usurpation of their authority.

The Baltimore Mayor initially refused to meet with the Commissioners because the Baltimore City Council was challenging the constitutionality of the law transferring the control of Baltimore City's police to the state. Many Baltimoreans believed that only Baltimore residents could judge what was best for the city and that losing control of the police to the state was simply unacceptable. Skeptics said that wanting to keep control of the police within the city was really just a desire to continue the corrupt politics of the past. Nevertheless, the *Baltimore Sun* stated, "We have thoroughly examined both these bills, and cordially accept them as the best combination of power, not simply for the occasion, but for the general maintenance of law and order, and the protection of our citizens."[9] The editors argued that in fact state control of the Baltimore police would actually restore rights and privileges of Baltimoreans. They railed against politicians who had used their connections with the Baltimore police to their own ends, who had "shed blood remorselessly," and who dared to "oppose all measures which strike at their unhallowed career." They put their trust in "A board of commissioners … of honest men, without regard to their politics, inasmuch as they will be indebted to no party for their appointment."

The legislation was immediately challenged in court by the city and then-Mayor Thomas Swann. They argued that the move of control of the police to the state violated the Maryland State Constitution. However, the Superior Court of Baltimore City held it to be constitutional on March 13, 1860, and the Court of Appeals[10] confirmed this decision on April 17, 1860.[11]

By the end of March 1860, even though the force had not been officially constituted and had not begun its work, simply "the prospect of such a police as the law creating it contemplated has had a marked effect on the moral condition of the city."[12] Anticipation of police reform in itself had created a salutary effect.

Mayor George William Brown soon joined the first Police Commissioners as an ex officio member of the Commission. Charles Howard, another member, was an aristocratic member of the elite rich, a member of a prominent Baltimore family, and a Democrat who supported the South and pro-slavery principles. In later life, however, he was a spokesperson for the common man and a philanthropist. Charles Hinks was a merchant like Kane, in the flour and grain business, and Hinks and Kane were actually business partners. John Davis was Democratic, and he had worked for the Port of Baltimore as a customs official, as had Kane. William Gatchell was also a Democratic slaveholder who was a co-owner of the *Baltimore Exchange*, which was a pro–Southern newspaper. Mayor Brown was described as a rather small, aristocratic-appearing man with a moustache and having an air of sophistication. All of the Commissioners were rather well-to-do, with close connections to the power structure and legal and business centers of Baltimore.[13]

The Board of Commissioners quickly appointed George Proctor Kane as the Marshal on February 21, 1860. Their choice of Kane was not exactly random. By this time Kane was a Democrat, having previously been a Whig. He owned slaves, rather firmly establishing him as a supporter of the South. Furthermore, some historians believe that Kane harbored a strong dislike for the Know-Nothings because he believed that they had been responsible for his unsuccessful bid to become an elected City Council member in 1856.[14] Kane's job was to rid the city of gangs, to bring order to elections, and to clean up the corruption in the police department. Baltimore by this time was one of the three or four largest cities in the United States at about 212,000 inhabitants, so the task was huge.

Kane was chosen based upon his history of community service, his prior employment positions, and his experience with the militias. Newspapers immediately reported that Kane had "no intention to hold the position permanently."[15] Another Baltimore newspaper said,

> The appointment of Col. George P. Kane to be Marshal of Police, under the new law, has given universal satisfaction. Col. Kane is every way qualified for the post, and his appointment, which was entirely unsolicited on his part, is regarded as an earnest of the intention of the Commissioners to make a thorough re-organization of the force.[16]

Thomas Gifford was soon appointed as deputy marshal, and the new police force officially began its duties on May 1, 1860. Applications for police positions came pouring into the office, with an estimated 1,050 men seeking jobs in the first two days. Men previously employed on the force applied, but it was noted that "there are many applying whose habits render them improper persons in whose hands to trust the peace of the city and the establishment of general good order." Baltimore wanted a new wave of honesty in the police force, not a return to political allegiances that in the past had destroyed their ability to patrol the streets.[17] Hiring and organization of the force were rapid. By early May all police positions were filled. The police force was initially fixed at 350 "beat cops," though the number could be increased to 450, if necessary. Pay was set at $10.00 per week for ordinary policemen; sergeants made $10.50, lieutenants $11.50, and captains $13.00; the Marshal himself received $1,500.00 per year, or about $28.85 per week.[18]

Police were still required to wear their uniforms at all times, whether on duty or not. In fact, "they are to be considered as always on duty, and liable to be called on at any moment. They are therefore required invariably to wear their uniform dress when they appear in public, unless they are under suspension."[19] Regulations were tight, even including "proper regard paid the bathing of the person."[20] And "[p]olice officers and men are strictly forbidden to enter any public bar-room, or drinking room, except in the discharge of their duty; nor can they be allowed to smoke on the public streets." Police were forbidden from taking any extra pay, tips, gifts, or compensation from the public, unless approved by the Board of Commissioners; if approved, such gratuities were to be deposited in an aid fund for injured policemen and for rewards for gallantry, as decided by the board. Policemen could not even leave the city without permission, since they were considered always to be on duty. Importantly, all police officers were likewise prohibited from holding other jobs. To avoid political entanglements, police additionally

> are all required to refrain from attending any primary or other political meeting for the purpose of making nominations or promoting the election of any public officers, or of electing delegates to any political convention; neither can they be permitted to be delegates to any such convention, or members of, or connected with any club or other association, whose objects or other purposes may have reference to the nomination or election of any candidate for office.[21]

Police were also to refrain from engaging in "political discussion," and "[n]o member of the police force will be allowed to make or to solicit from others, contributions for political purposes."[22] To add to their duties, police were also involved in the response to fires and to public health emergencies, such as epidemics. Finally, lest the police be accused of shirking their duty, they could not, "under any circumstances, unless in the discharge of their duties, stop at the corners of the streets, or linger on their routes, or enter any house, but are expected constantly to patrol their beats."[23]

A major aspect of the 1860 law was the handing of the duties of election supervision to the police. In addition, it voided the results of recent Baltimore elections because of suspected fraud. City politicians, bosses, political operatives and gangs all had vehemently opposed the transfer of police supervision to the state because they all realized that their influence would be dramatically reduced. And it was. Immediately after the ruling of the appeals Court, on April 21, the Mayor turned over all police control, equipment, station houses, and arms to the new Board of Police.

Officers initially hired took their oath of office on Saturday, May 5, in preparation for their new duties. The new police force took charge of Baltimore's streets on Monday, May 7, 1860. By then, most officers had at least their caps and belts, and the transformation of Baltimore began, moving from its historic "Mobtown" image to a respectable city.[24] "With the neat French military cap, blue coat and gray pants, together with white gloves, the men looked as if under proper management and discipline they will fully answer the expectations of all in the preservation of good order and the detection of those who violate the laws."[25] On May 7 the new board revoked the appointments and commissions of previous police. The old force under Marshal B. W. Herring retired and received its final pay, Mayor Thomas Swann offering them his thanks and good wishes.

By October 3, the hiring, the turnover of the force, and the training had all been completed. Not long thereafter, a new mayoral election was held. On October 10, 1860, George William Brown became the new Mayor and the ex officio member of the Board of Police Commissioners.[26]

The discipline Kane imposed and the honesty he brought to the task would be evident in the results he produced. He had gangs to disperse, political machines to dismantle, volunteer fire departments to control, and rowdy election ward structures to subdue. He would succeed.

The new police initially functioned under the old system of patrolling the streets, though Kane began by augmenting the number of men on duty during the night shift, when most crimes were committed. Kane immediately demanded that all laws be enforced impartially and completely.

One of Kane's primary targets was to enforce the "vagrancy laws" on the books. Laws in Maryland as early as 1804 allowed warrants to be issued "against any person or persons, on information founded upon the oath of any competent witness, that such person or persons in the said affidavit named is a vagrant, vagabond, disorderly person or common prostitute." Such persons had to post security for good behavior for 12 months. If the vagrant could not immediately post bail, the judge could sentence him (or her) to residence in Baltimore's almshouse. The statute defined "vagrants, vagabonds and disorderly persons" as persons

> who have no visible means of maintenance from property or personal labour, and lives idle, without employment, and every person who wanders about and begs in the streets from door to door, and any person who wanders about and lodges in out-houses, market places, or in the open air, and cannot give a good account of the means by which he, she or they, procure a livelihood, and every woman who is generally reputed a common prostitute, and every juggler or fortune-teller, or common-gambler, shall be adjudged a vagrant, vagabond , prostitute or disorderly person, within the meaning of this act.

Such persons could be sentenced "to hard labor in the alms-house for a space of time not less than one week, nor more than two months."[27] The almshouse itself was located about two miles to the west of Baltimore on Calverton Road.[28] Later laws allowed such persons to be sent out of town, to be put in the House of Refuge, or to be remanded to the almshouse for two to six months. The number of vagrants so confined in 1853 had been 230 whites and 37 blacks; 269 whites and 39 blacks in 1854; more than 400 whites and fewer than 50 blacks in 1857; and more than 500 whites and fewer than 50 blacks in 1858. In 1858, another alternative for confinement of vagrants was the Baltimore jail.[29] These were the years before Kane took office as Marshal; the numbers rose dramatically thereafter.[30]

Kane crusaded to keep the street corners free of loiterers, especially young men and boys, and particularly on Sunday. Local newspapers took notice and informed their readers about the new strict enforcement.[31]

Furthermore, laws existed that forbade driving through the Centre Market during business hours. Enforcement of these relatively innocuous rules told the inhabitants of Baltimore (residents and visitors alike) that no violations of *any law* were going to be tolerated.[32] Strict enforcement pertained to the citizenry, but also to the police officers themselves. Marshal Kane quickly handled any infractions committed by the police. Sleeping on the job, wearing the uniform improperly, fraternizing with people on his beat, or any other violations of police rules met quick retribution from city officials.

Marshal Kane used all manner of techniques to identify and arrest lawbreakers. In May 1860, as he took control of the police force, petty burglaries and thefts had been on the increase. Kane ordered his men to report the names of men in their districts who were either visitors or residents who seemed to have no identifiable source of income. These men would fit into the category of vagrants, as defined by the Code of Maryland. Kane dispatched one "careful and intelligent officer" from each police station "whose time shall be exclusively devoted to this particular business." Kane also instructed these officers to furnish the names of men who kept "low groggeries," cheap drinking houses, also called "cribs" (not to be confused with "coops") and the names of the men who frequented them. The intent was "to drive the thieves from the city, or arrest and put them in prison." These same intelligence officers would often station themselves at the railroad depots and observe men coming into town who might be thieves or known criminals.[33] All of these activities yielded results, some arrests, but likely the word spread that Kane was not going to tolerate criminal activity, regardless of how small it might be. Newspapers reported these activities in a positive light: "The instructions carried out will make Baltimore a delightful place for residents and honest strangers."[34] Visitors to the city commonly found themselves hauled before the local judges and questioned about their means of livelihood. The unemployed—the "vagrants"—were sentenced to 30–60 days in jail. It was only a few days before Kane saw results from his crackdown. Newspapers reported that Kane's action "has thrown consternation into the ranks of that class of individuals who have no visible means of support, and many of them have left the city."[35]

Arresting vagrants was not without its own inherent dangers. On one occasion early in his tenure, Kane arrested James Jeffers, the son of one Madison Jeffers, on the charge of vagrancy. The elder Jeffers took exception to the arrest of his son, and he pressed charges against Kane and two of his officers for "illegal arrest and detention." Jeffers was actually challenging the propriety of the police to arrest vagrants. The day after Jeffers filed these charges, Kane and the elder Jeffers encountered each other on the street, apparently by chance. Words were exchanged and a scuffle ensued, and Kane arrested Jeffers for "disorderly conduct and resisting George P. Kane in the discharge of his duty." Jeffers then filed a counter lawsuit against Kane for "assault and false imprisonment." Kane had to post $500 bail, pending trial. Kane's good friend and personal attorney George W. Dobbin represented him. A magistrate initially ruled against Kane and his fellow police officers for the arrest of James Jeffers, and they were fined $100 each for this act. An appeal was filed in the Court of Common Pleas. A grand jury then cited Kane for assault and illegal arrest of Madison Jeffers. The entire sequence of lawsuits seemed to disappear when the court discovered that James Jeffers had deserted his military post in Carlisle, Pennsylvania, and he was sent back to his base for punishment. A few weeks later, the case of Madison Jeffers assaulting Kane came before the court, and Jeffers pleaded *nolo contendere*, meaning that Jeffers did not admit guilt but that he accepted the consequences as if a guilty plea had been entered, with Jeffers being fined $1 and court costs.[36] Kane would frequently suffer such legal entanglements resulting from the discharge of his duties.[37]

Next on Kane's hit list, after the vagrants and the cribs, came gaming houses. He ordered the police to find and report such houses and give a list of the names of the proprietors, as well as those who frequented these gambling dens. All were reported to the grand jury, and Kane assigned officers to be stationed at the doors of these establishments. He believed that these locations were the sites where thieves gathered, and the presence of a policeman near the door was a strong deterrent to such men gathering for illicit purposes.

Pickpockets were another of Marshal Kane's targets. Pickpocketing was a common low-level crime, and Kane was determined to eliminate it from the city. The *Sun* reported,

> It is the intention of the marshal to cause the arrest of all known thieves, and in the absence of proof on which to convict them on a specific charge, to have all such taken to the several police stations so that all the police can have the opportunity to see them. As fast as arrested, they will be warned to leave the city within twenty-four hours, and in default will be re-arrested and confined in jail as vagrants.[38]

The Police Board was serious about enforcing all laws, without exception, including Sunday restrictions. On May 28 Charles Howard, the President of the Board of Police Commissioners, issued an order to Marshal Kane:

> Section 172. No person whatsoever shall work or do any bodily labor, or wittingly or willingly suffer his or her children, servants or slaves, to do any bodily labor on Sunday (work of necessity and charity always excepted), nor shall suffer or permit any children, servants or slaves to profane the Lord's Day by gaming, fishing, fowling, hunting or unlawful pastime or recreation, under a penalty of five dollars.
>
> Section 173. No housekeeper shall sell any strong liquors on Sunday (except in case of absolute necessity), or suffer any drunkenness, gaming, or unlawful sports or recreation in his house, on pain of forfeiting twenty-five dollars.

Section 174. No person shall sell, dispose of or barter any spirituous or fermented liquors, or cordials of any kind, in any quantity whatsoever, on Sunday, under a penalty of not less than twenty nor more than one hundred dollars for the first offence, and if convicted a second time for a like offence, the license of the person so offending shall be declared null and void.

The Police Board was serious about reestablishing order within the confines of Baltimore city.[39] From sales of cigars on Sunday to the future protection of the President-Elect, Kane discharged his duty to enforce all laws indiscriminately.

Though communication in 1860 was rather primitive, it was not uncommon for authorities in one city to warn the police of another city about traveling bands of thieves or disruptive persons about to arrive, usually by train, to wreak havoc on the destination's populace. Police chiefs in New York, Philadelphia, Baltimore, and Washington, D.C. commonly cooperated and issued warnings of such activity. Recipient cities organized police to meet the criminals at the train stations. Such was the case for Kane and his colleagues.[40] Similar cooperation between police forces helped to curb the frequent games of confidence men who often traveled from city to city.

Kane slowly introduced new methods of policing the city. First he concentrated on changing the ratio of nighttime to daytime police officers. Then he devised a system to rotate the coverage, having police serve only for a few hours before being relieved by a replacement. He wanted always to have "fresh men" on duty, enabling them to keep moving on the beat without becoming fatigued.[41] His innovations actually drove the lawbreakers to the suburbs, where the policing was not as intense. Kane then petitioned the Board of Commissioners to increase the strength of the force in the outlying areas of town as well.[42]

One of the major problems at the outset of Kane's tenure as Marshal was the frequency of false alarms for both police and fire activity. Kane established a program whereby the only men to have access to the alarm boxes were the men actually on duty at the time. Other off-duty police and the public were prohibited from being able to activate the alarm boxes. This way the responsibility for any given alarm could be established unequivocally, and the number of false alarms thus decreased dramatically.[43]

Soon after Marshal Kane took office, the Democratic National Convention gathered in Baltimore. The majority of the delegates arrived on Saturday, June 16, 1860. This event taxed the capability of the newly reformed police to keep the peace. Kane took a first step of prohibiting any military display during or after the Convention. He forbade the firing of cannons within the city during this gathering.[44] Kane soon received information by telegraph warning him of the arrival of "well known New York thieves." He arrested them as they disembarked from the train in Baltimore, and he kept them in jail until the Democratic Convention had concluded. Such "preventive arrests" would not be tolerated today, but they were both allowed and effective in 1860 in Baltimore.[45]

As the presidential race progressed, Kane found it necessary to control gatherings and demonstrations in the city. One such rally was a meeting to promote Southern Democrats John C. Breckinridge and Joseph Lane, held at Monument Square on July 6. The *Baltimore Sun* estimated that the attendance was between 8,000 and

10,000, but Kane and his force controlled the crowd "to perfection, no disturbance of any kind occurring to destroy the harmony of the meeting."[46]

Marshal Kane also found it necessary to enforce limitations on the use of fireworks in 1860. Most of the Baltimore structures were wooden, and fireworks had been responsible for at least 30–40 house and business fires in the previous year. The law read, "it shall not be lawful for any person or persons to sell or offer for sale, within the limits of the city, any crackers, squibs, rockets, or other combustible fireworks…; every offender against any of the provisions of this section shall pay for each and every offense two dollars." Also, "no person shall cast, throw or fire any squib, rocket, cracker, torpedo, grenade or other combustible fireworks or explosive preparation, within the city; and every person, for every such offense, shall forfeit and pay a sum not exceeding five dollars."[47] Kane enforced these laws strictly,[48] and his efforts were successful. Newspapers reported that he had "prevented the recurrence of the scenes of last year, when the demons of fire and rowdyism stalked forth unchecked."[49]

Part of Marshal Kane's effectiveness stemmed from his enforcement of discipline within the police force. He was unafraid to punish policemen who misbehaved, knowing that having a team of men who both obeyed the law and enforced it was essential to the good function of Baltimore's police. Early in his tenure his men discovered that sloppy behavior could result in their suspension or expulsion from the force.[50] Even vague "infractions" such as fraternization with the public caught Kane's attention.[51]

One of Kane's most visible duties was to ensure the integrity and peacefulness of the election process. Even after Kane became Marshal, cooping was still practiced, though on a smaller scale. This technique was again practiced in October 1860, the first election cycle to occur after Kane took office. In the previous year cooping was common, some sites imprisoning up to 60 voters, with some men voting 8–10 times each.[52] Kane pursued these criminals with vigor. Judges finally cooperated with the police, and some men arrested were held on $2,000 bail, equivalent to about $40,000 today.[53] Coinciding with the transfer of the police control and oversight to the State of Maryland and Kane's appointment, new laws were written controlling the conduct of elections and the relationship of the judges of elections. They were broadly divided into six categories:

- Citizens might be required to assist in the conduct of elections. Failure to comply would result in a fine of $150. Election judges were considered to be peace officers, and as such could send offenders to jail for disturbing the peace, creating a riot or disorder, or interfering with voters.
- A police officer failing to uphold the law would be fined $500. Any police officer or other Baltimore official who interfered in the jailing of an offender would be fined $1,000 and could receive a jail term himself of 60 days.
- Drinking establishments were to be closed on Election Day. Violations would result in the forfeiture of the bar's liquor license, a fine of $500, and such persons could not obtain another liquor license for five years.
- Any person interfering with another person's attempt to vote, or forcing another person to vote against his will or under compulsion, would be charged with a

- felony and would be imprisoned for not less than two years, and not more than six years.
- Gatherings of two or more persons for the purpose of keeping voters away from the polls (including obstructing, beating, intimidating, injuring, etc.) or who did the same to a voter who had already voted would be guilty of a felony, punishable by not less than three and not more than six years in the penitentiary. The same penalties were applied to men inflicting violence upon election officials.
- Any officer or employee of the Mayor and City Council who forcibly resisted or obstructed the execution of the law would be subject to a fine of $1,000 and would forfeit the right to employment or the holding of any office under the jurisdiction of the Mayor and City Council of the City of Baltimore.[54]

These rules were strict; minimum sentences were harsh, and their enforcement went a great distance toward creating peaceful elections. Further, Kane continued to receive information from law enforcement in other cities that warned of gangs coming to Baltimore to influence elections. Police arrested these men upon arrival and kept them confined until the election was completed.[55]

The Board of Police supported Kane's tight discipline of the police force. Charles Howard, the President of the Board of Police, often issued statements to the press outlining protocols and principles so the public would be aware of the guidelines under which the patrolmen operated. Especially around the time of elections, police were charged with keeping unruly mobs and disorderly persons under control.[56] Howard made it clear that he held the commanding officers responsible for the behavior of their subordinates.

These policies were effective. On October 11, 1860, the *Baltimore Sun* reported, "The charter election yesterday was so quiet that a stranger could not have known that an important occasion to the great interest of the people of Baltimore was going on." The scene was so calm that police "had little or nothing to do"; and "[i]t is a remarkable fact that during the whole day there was no person arrested for discharging firearms, nor was there a pistol discharged, so far as could be ascertained. The contrast with the elections for six years past was so great as to excite almost general surprise, notwithstanding the ample police arrangements which had been made." George William Brown, the Mayor-Elect, said in summary, "The long reign of terror is over."[57]

It became obvious that changing the control of the police had made a huge difference in the conduct of elections, as well as in the general calm and safety of the city. Newspapers described Kane positively:

> A man of resolute purpose, tireless energy and unflinching nerve, he has suffered no personal considerations, no halting policy to conflict with the stern performance of his duty. He has been abused and slandered, the usual tribute to public worthiness from those who hate and dare not emulate it. The evil-doers have been sought out in their obscurity—in their fancied security—and placed within the power of the law.[58]

But the city was about to experience a shock.

On October 13 Kane announced his intention to resign from his position of Chief Marshal, effective immediately after the November elections. Kane had intended to hold his office for only as long as seemed necessary to revamp the police force, and after only a few months in command he felt that the job had been accomplished. He had taken the position at considerable personal and financial loss, and he believed that his job was completed.[59] The presidential election was upcoming, and Kane would oversee the police for that tumultuous event, but he intended to resign thereafter.

The November 6 election came and went with little to no upheaval in Baltimore. Political demonstrations were peaceful, and the four-way race among Lincoln, Bell, Douglas, and Breckinridge was generally quiet. One accidental shooting occurred at the Bell headquarters near South and Baltimore Streets, where 3,000–4,000 people had gathered, but the old Baltimore-style riots were nonexistent.[60]

Law-abiding Baltimoreans objected to Kane's planned departure from his Marshal's position. The *Baltimore Daily Exchange* said that his resignation

> will cause sincere regret in all quarters, and if the grateful acknowledgements of the whole community to this gallant officer, for the energetic, intelligent and unwearied discharge of his most responsible and difficult duties, and its unanimous wish that he should remain at his post, could avail to alter his determination, we are sure they would be freely tendered.[61]

The sentiment was uniform: "On the inauguration of the new police system, with Col. Kane at its head, there was neither law nor order respected, and now, after a period of only seven months, there is no city in the Union where law is more respected, and where better order prevails."[62] In response, Kane bowed to public pressure and rescinded his resignation on November 16. He would remain as Marshal. Only his arrest in June 1861 for his Southern proclivities would be successful in removing him from office.

After deciding to remain in control of the police, Kane continued his strict discipline of the force. He insisted upon literal and punctilious observance of all rules, regulations, and enforcement of all laws on the books. Kane specified that "those who do not feel disposed to submit to a strict observance will be required to give way for those who will."[63]

Overall, Kane's policies were positive, and the police force improved dramatically, but in June 1861 Kane and all of the Police Commissioners would find themselves arrested by Union military troops and behind bars at Fort McHenry (what the *New York Times* called the "Hospital for Sick Patriotism").[64] Soon thereafter, the Mayor himself was arrested, and he too became a resident in military stockades.

But before that, after Kane had been Marshal for scarcely four months, he became so popular that his friends floated his name as a possible candidate for Mayor. Kane responded with a notice in the newspaper: "The undersigned having been presented in your columns as a Candidate for the Mayoralty, deems it proper to state that the announcement was without his knowledge or approval, and that *under no circumstances* would he consent to be a candidate. GEORGE P. KANE."[65] Kane's future looked good, but the "collision" that would become the Civil War was about to descend upon him.

9

Slavery in Maryland and Baltimore

Maryland at the start of the Civil War was often described as having a Southern personality, but a Northern economy. Baltimore in 1860 was a Southern city in its character. In fact, some described Baltimore as "Southern soil."[1] While Maryland didn't become a secessionist state, many slaves existed in Maryland nevertheless. The Mason-Dixon line formed the northern border of the Maryland, but Baltimore and Maryland were more than just geographically Southern. Though Maryland as a state was divided, most Baltimore citizens in 1860–1861 were rabidly Southern in mindset and were pro-slavery. The election of November 1860 testified to Southern sentiments. Lincoln received so few votes that he was not even a major candidate in the city or state.

As a border state, Maryland could have easily been two states. Southern Maryland (Anne Arundel, Calvert, Charles, Prince George's, Montgomery, and St. Mary's Counties), depending upon slavery for tobacco and wheat farming and other agricultural products, was strongly Southern-leaning. However, other regions of the state—northern and western Maryland (Allegany, Baltimore, Carroll, Frederick, Harford, and Washington Counties)—ultimately sided with the Union, not needing slave labor for their other agricultural pursuits, manufacturing, and industrial-based employment. Baltimore City was somewhat different from Baltimore County. The city at the end of the 1850s leaned strongly toward the South. Even more split was the Eastern Shore (Caroline, Cecil, Dorchester, Kent, Queen Anne's, Somerset, Talbot, and Worcester Counties). The Eastern Shore was not as Southern as Southern Maryland nor as Northern as Northern Maryland.[2] The areas of Southern sentiment heavily supported the Democratic Party, including Baltimore's traditionally Democratic base. The American Party (the "Know-Nothings") was decidedly anti-immigrant and anti–Catholic, as well as nativist and opposed to political parties in general. The immigrant population in Baltimore had swelled, with mostly German and Irish Catholics coming to the area. Between 1840 and 1860, over 177,000 immigrants had arrived in Baltimore, with many of them staying there. By 1860, 25 percent of Baltimoreans had been born in another country. This same year, John C. Breckinridge, a Southern Democrat, gathered the plurality of the votes for President. Baltimore in 1860, with its population of 212,418, was the fourth largest city in the United States, behind only New York, Brooklyn (which was then considered to be a separate city), and Philadelphia. Baltimore had about 52,000 foreign-born inhabitants, and about 25,000 free blacks, in addition to 2,218 slaves. Maryland had the largest population of free blacks in the country—83,942, or 49.1 percent of the entire population of blacks in the state. One in every six families in Maryland owned slaves, though compared to other states the number of slaves per Maryland family unit was smaller than the national average. The total number of slaves in Maryland in 1860 was 87,189.³

Kane, as a Southerner at heart, owned slaves. The 1860 Baltimore census for Ward 11 reported that Colonel Kane, age 41 and Marshal of Police, owned two male black slaves, ages 50 and 30; his father-in-law John Griffith also owned five slaves that year, one male (age 30) and four female (ages 30, 30, 22, and 7). Griffith had previously reported four male and six female slaves in the 1858 Baltimore tax records (Appendix, Table 5). In that 1860 census Kane lived with his wife Ann C. Kane, age 30, and her father John Griffith, age 70.⁴ Black servants were in Kane's home until at least 1870, as the 1870 census listed black females named Charlotte Tubman (55 years old), Charlotte Chester (29 years old), and Sarrah Chester (12 years old) as "domestic servants."⁵ The 1870 census had as other members of the household Ann C. Kane, age 43 (George's wife), and Mary Griffith, age 45, likely Ann's older sister. In spite of being pro–Southern and owning slaves, George Kane was said to oppose secession and war.

Free blacks in Maryland, as well as elsewhere, were often kidnapped and sold as slaves, even though they had previously been emancipated. Most commonly these newly enslaved people were shipped to the South, though some remained in Maryland. Marshal Kane found himself involved in searching for these kidnapped souls in other states, and he lobbied the Governor of Maryland to deal with the governments of Southern states for the return of these men and women.⁶ Baltimore was the site of a lucrative slave trade, with many of the men, women, and children sold to places further south, mostly New Orleans. Notorious slave houses near Baltimore's Inner Harbor kept blacks captive until they were sold.

Thomas H. Hicks, the Maryland Governor in early 1861, wrestled with the divisive issues that plagued the entire country. Hicks was born in Dorchester County, Maryland, on the Eastern Shore, where enslavement was part of the agricultural system. He was ultimately pro–Union, though he himself was an enslaver. He has been called indecisive in his political pronouncements and actions, but the choices available to him were all bad. One description applied to Hicks's behavior was "masterly inactivity." Many Marylanders were calling for a special session of the Legislature to declare where Maryland stood in the secession frenzy. Hicks issued a broadside on January 3, 1861, addressing the questions that would determine what Maryland's course might be in the coming months. He declared to his fellow Marylanders:

> The exciting character of the events now transpiring in our country, naturally agitates and fills with care the minds of the citizens of this state....
>
> I firmly believe that the division of this Government [of the United States] would inevitably produce civil war. The secession leaders in South Carolina, and fanatical demagogues of the North, have alike proclaimed that such would be the result, and no man of sense, in my opinion, can question it.
>
> Is it not then the bounden duty of all of us, and especially of those placed in authority, to endeavor to prevent the occurrence of such a catastrophe, by opposing any thing even tending to produce it?
>
> I fervently hope, and firmly believe, that the Union may be preserved....
>
> It is unnecessary for me to make extravagant professions of devotion to the South.... I am

a Marylander by birth, and descent, and by a residence of more than sixty years. Every dollar of property I own is invested in this state. I am a slaveholder, not by accident, but by purchase, out of the hard earnings of a long life of toil. I have not a conviction or prejudice which is not in favor of my native State. I have never lived and should be sorry to be obliged to live, in a State where slavery does not exist, and I never will do so if I can avoid it. Whatever would impair the rights of slaveholders in Maryland, would equally injure me, and the instinct of self-interest, if no higher motive, would impel me to stand by the South while life shall last.[7]

Hicks felt pressured to "allow Maryland to slide into the ranks of the seceding States," but he also believed that such a choice would bring "ruin upon my country." He therefore chose to attempt to await the course of events as calmly as humanly possible. He fully recognized the position of border states:

Believing that the interests of Maryland were bound up with those of the border slaveholding States, I have been engaged, for months past, in a full interchange of views with the Governors of Virginia, Kentucky, Tenessee [sic] and Missouri, with a view to concerted action on our part. These consultations, which are still in progress, I feel justified in saying, have resulted in good; so that when the proper time for action arrives, these sister States, bound up in a common destiny, will, I trust, be prepared to act together.

Hicks believed that a special session of the Legislature to address secession was not in the best interests of the State of Maryland. Those most fervent for disunion and secession were the ones Hicks believed were pushing for such a session, so he believed that convening the Legislature would be tantamount to promoting the withdrawal of Maryland from the Union, an action he opposed.

Furthermore, Hicks believed that the nation already appreciated that Maryland stood firmly on the side of the South: "That Maryland is a conservative Southern State all know who know any thing of her people or her history." Hicks was aware that secessionists wanted to seize the federal capital and the crucial buildings of the government, and he knew that Maryland needed to be a part of that plan for it to have any chance of success. In addition, "The plan contemplates forcible opposition to Mr. Lincoln's inauguration, and consequently civil war, upon Maryland soil, and a transfer of its horrors from the States which are to provoke it." Clearly, talk was circulating in Maryland, and in Baltimore in particular, about the "Baltimore Plot" to assassinate Lincoln on his journey through the state and Baltimore on his way to Washington for his inauguration.

As the Civil War progressed, Marylanders shifted their sentiments toward the North. More men joined the army of the North, by a margin of 60,000 to 25,000, from the overall population of 687,000. Maryland residents appreciated that the local economy was heading toward agriculture and industry that depended less upon enslavement than it had in the past. Furthermore, they could see early that the North was likely to win the war. The Emancipation Proclamation, effective in January 1863, freed the slaves of the South, though Maryland was exempted from this declaration because of its location as a border state and its ultimate allegiance to the North. In the end, Maryland's new constitution in 1864 abolished slavery. However, the vote passed by only a narrow margin, 30,174 to 29,799, reflecting the ambivalence of Maryland's citizens that persisted from 1860 through to the end of the Civil War.

10

The Baltimore Plot

The first attempt on Abraham Lincoln's life occurred on the route of the inaugural train from Springfield, Illinois, to Washington, D.C. Lincoln's entourage took an indirect route through the upper portion of the United States, making many stops along the way (Figures 22–23). It was his celebratory excursion through the North. The route of the train began in Springfield on February 11, 1861, and ended in Washington, D.C., in the early morning hours of Friday, February 23.

Lincoln's trip from Springfield, Illinois, to Washington, D.C., was anything but leisurely and restful. As Lincoln departed Springfield, his short speech included some brief references to what some believe to be the beginning of his premonition of a premature death:

Figure 22. Lincoln's inaugural train route. His entourage traveled a circuitous route from Springfield to Washington: Springfield, State Line, Lafayette, Indianapolis, Cincinnati, Columbus, Steubenville, Pittsburgh, Alliance, Cleveland, Westfield, Buffalo, Rochester, Syracuse, Utica, Albany, Troy, Poughkeepsie, New York, Trenton, and then to Philadelphia. From there, the proposed route was from Philadelphia to Harrisburg to Baltimore to Washington. The actual route was from Philadelphia to Harrisburg, back to Philadelphia, and then on to Baltimore and finally Washington. Adapted from "A Map of the Baltimore & Ohio Railroad and its Principal Connecting Lines Uniting All Parts of the East & West," Library of Congress.

10. The Baltimore Plot

Figure 23A. Early proposed route from Philadelphia to Washington, D.C. The first proposed route had Lincoln traveling from Philadelphia to Baltimore to Washington. Adapted from "A Map of the Baltimore & Ohio Railroad and its Principal Connecting Lines Uniting All Parts of the East & West," Library of Congress.

> I now leave, not knowing when or whether ever I may return, with a task before me greater than that which rested upon Washington. Without the assistance of that Divine Being who ever attended him, I cannot succeed. With that assistance, I cannot fail. Trusting in Him who can go with me, and remain with you, and be everywhere for good, let us confidently hope that all will yet be well. To His care commending you, as I hope in your prayers you will commend me, I bid you an affectionate farewell.[1]

The train left Springfield and soon encountered an unsuccessful attempt to kill Lincoln by way of a bomb planted in one of the cars. It then was scheduled to go to Cleveland and then to Buffalo, New York, via Erie, Pennsylvania, on February 16. Lincoln would have a day to attend church in Buffalo on the 17th, then he would travel to Albany via Rochester, New York, on the 18th, then to New York City via Troy and East Albany on the 19th, and finally he was to give speeches and attend receptions in New York City on the 20th.

Surprising to the reader of today, the President-Elect (and even later the President) did not have an organized security detail. To us, the Secret Service seems to have always been there, but it did not exist in the mid–1800s. Nor was there a consistent military presence around Lincoln during his inaugural train trip. Furthermore, everyone knew Lincoln's schedule and itinerary, which were published in all of the newspapers.

John Wilkes Booth just happened to be in Albany on the 18th and 19th when

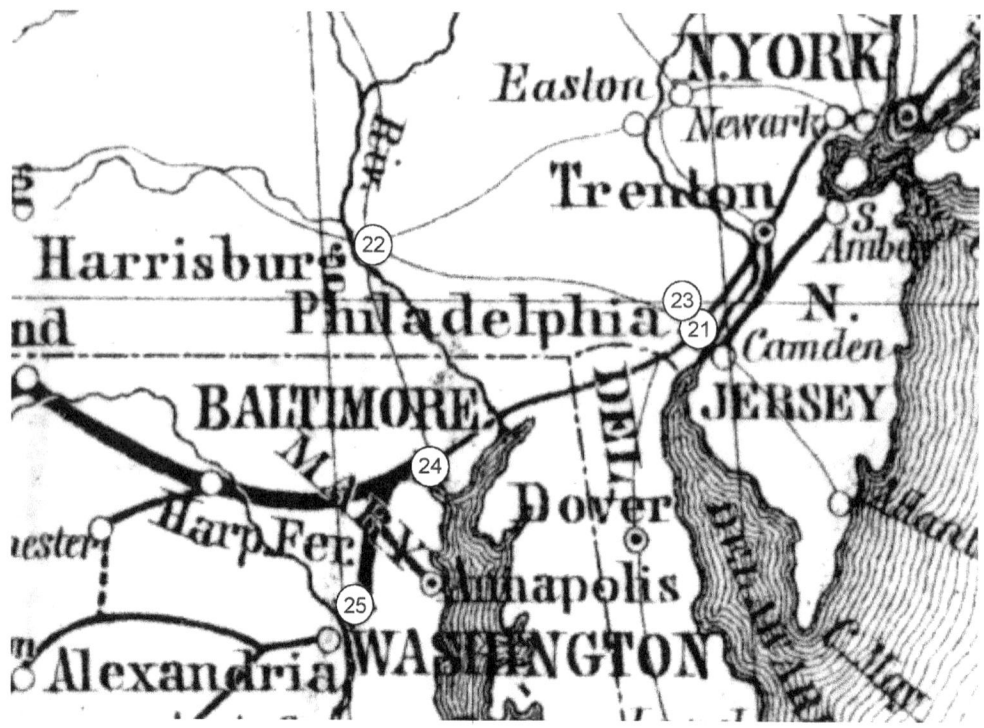

Figure 23B. Actual route from Philadelphia to Washington, D.C. Lincoln actually traveled from Philadelphia to Harrisburg, then back to Philadelphia, and onward to Baltimore and then Washington. Adapted from "A Map of the Baltimore & Ohio Railroad and its Principal Connecting Lines Uniting All Parts of the East & West," Library of Congress.

Lincoln passed through that city. Booth was acting in a production there at the New Gayety Theater on Green Street.[2] It could have been an opportunity for Booth to strike the assassin's blow, but his passion against Lincoln at that time likely hadn't risen to the level required for murder. Booth had performed as Duke Pescara in *The Apostate* on the 12th and had injured himself falling on a knife. This wound kept him from performing again while Lincoln was in town.[3] His absence from the stage would have given Booth ample time to study Lincoln's itinerary, but Booth didn't strike in Albany. Lincoln's entourage continued on toward Washington, D.C.

William S. Wood, a railroad employee, was chosen to arrange Lincoln's many moves, not because he was an expert in security, but because he knew the railroads, their routes, and their schedules. Lincoln allowed a few select men to serve as his unofficial protectors. These included Major David Hunter, Colonel Elmer Ephraim Ellsworth, Colonel Edwin V. Sumner, Captain John Pope, and Captain George Washington Whitfield Hazzard. Ward Hill Lamon also served in a security capacity, in part because he was both a longtime friend and legal associate of Lincoln and was always near the President-Elect, but also because he had an imposing physical strength and was not afraid to carry weapons.[4]

Hazzard was one of the first to warn Lincoln about his trip through Baltimore, a short journey from one railroad station to another, but completely exposed to any potential assassin. Hazzard was familiar with Baltimore because he had lived there and knew the sentiments of the population. He also knew the routes likely to be taken from the Northern Central Railroad Station on Calvert Street to the Baltimore and Ohio (B&O) Railroad Station on Camden Street.

Hazzard wrote a note to Lincoln (undated, likely penned in late January or early February 1861), outlining his concerns and proposing alternative strategies to provide for Lincoln's safety:

> [T]he greatest risk your excellency will have to encounter on your way to the national capitol will be in the city of Baltimore and on the road from that point to Washington. I have for many years known Col. George P. Kane, the chief of the Baltimore police.... I am constrained to state that I have but little confidence in Col. Kane's abilities and less in the integrity of his character. Independent of this there are men in that city who, I candidly believe, would glory in being hanged for having stabbed a "black republican president...."
>
> Before arriving at Baltimore you can decide on any one of three courses of conduct each of which can be executed in a variety of ways and I beg to submit my thoughts on the advantages or disadvantages of each separately.
>
> 1st You may travel openly and boldly through in the manner you have passed through others; or 2dly You may avoid the city—and 3d. You may pass through incognito and without the knowledge of any one, except such as you choose to confide in.
>
> 1st. <u>Going publicly through the city</u>. I have heard it suggested that <u>regular troops</u> should be employed as an escort.
>
> To this I would reply that it would take an army of 50,000 men and a weeks preparation to make a perfectly safe passage through a hostile city as large as Baltimore. Thousands of marksmen could fire from windows and housetops without the slightest danger to themselves....
>
> From the foregoing I think it is incontestable that if your excellency visits the city <u>publicly</u> you must yield yourself unreservedly to the protection of the local civil and militia authorities.
>
> 2d. <u>Avoiding the city of Baltimore</u>....
>
> 3d. <u>Passing through Baltimore incognito</u>
>
> This could be accomplished
>
> 1st By leaving Philadelphia privately and unannounced with a very few friends (not more than five) at 10 o'clock 50 minutes at night and taking the sleeping car all the way through to Washington, by which means you would avoid the exposure at the crossing of the Susquehanna and the transhipment at Baltimore. You would arrive in Washington at 5 o'clock 48 minutes in the morning. A false mustache, an old slouched hat and a long cloak or overcoat for concealment could be provided, by a friend, while in N.Y. City....
>
> 2d. By leaving Harrisburg secretly at 3 o'clock any morning except Sunday, disguised and accompanied as above; getting off the cars at the outer (Bolton) depot at Baltimore and then making your way <u>on foot</u> through obscure streets....
>
> Respectfully yours,
Capt Hazzard
No answer is expected[5]

Hazzard's suggestions were almost prophetic for the manner in which Lincoln would ultimately pass through Baltimore incognito (third option, first route). But as his route was later changed, Lincoln was scheduled to pass from Harrisburg to Baltimore on the Northern Central Railroad (Figure 24).

Samuel Morse Felton was the President of the Philadelphia, Wilmington, and Baltimore (PW&B) Railway. One Saturday in January 1861, Dorothea Dix approached Felton privately. She had earned the respect and admiration of proponents of both sides of the slavery/secession questions. And Dix had other credentials that caught Felton's attention. She was a socialite, educator, philanthropist, political advocate, social worker, and champion of prisoners and of the mentally ill. She hated

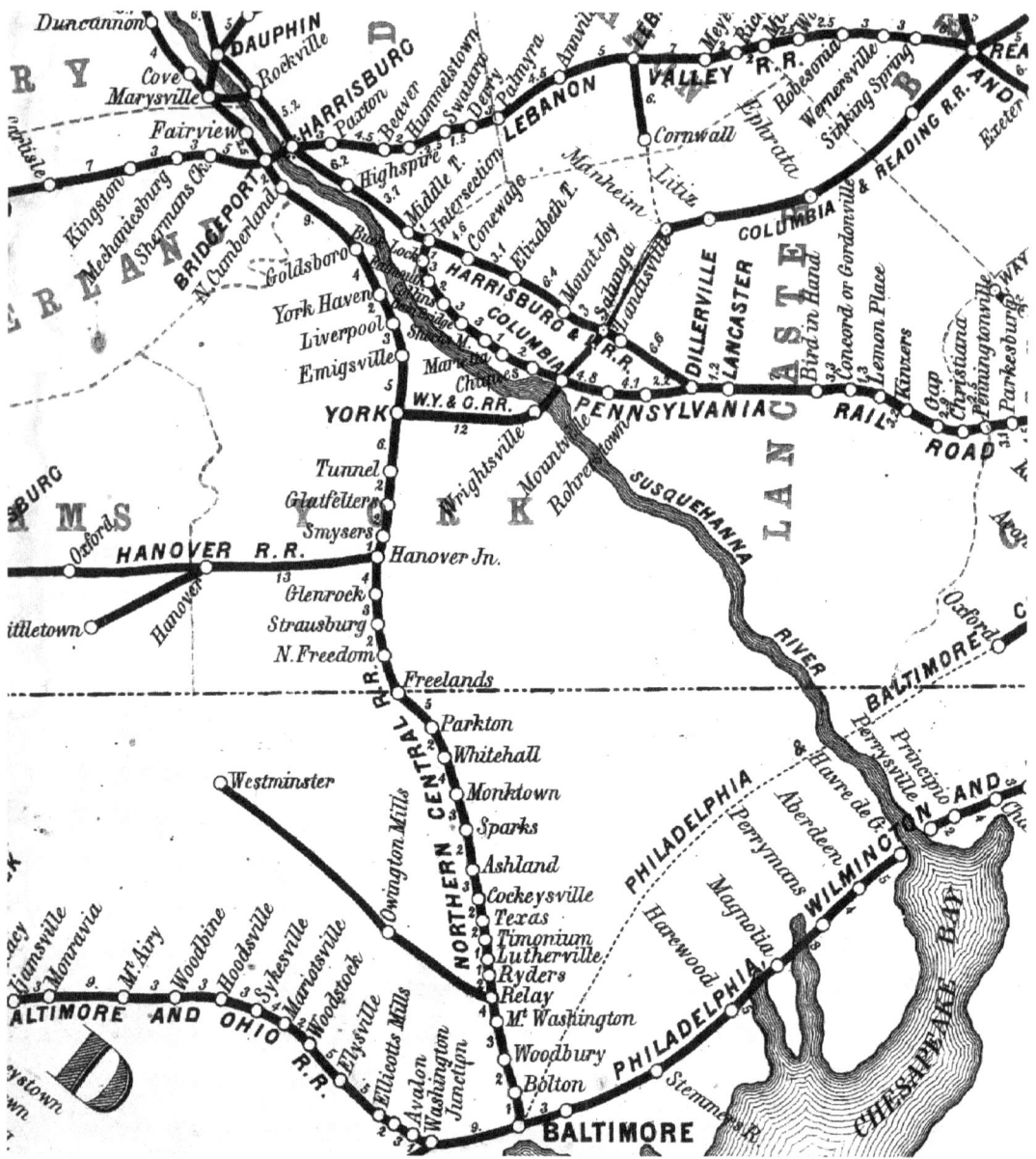

Figure 24. Northern Central Railroad Line from York, Pennsylvania, to Baltimore. This was the proposed route. Adapted from W. Barrington, *New Railway Guide Containing all the Rail Roads in Pennsylvania & N. Jersey with Portions of New York, Ohio, Maryland & Virginia*. 1863, Library of Congress.

publicity, so her testimony was believable: she had no reason to lie. She had an exciting and troubling tale to relay to Felton, and he was willing to listen to her story.[6]

During her recent travels through the South, Dix had caught wind of many plots to thwart Lincoln's plans, and some to assassinate him. Hundreds, if not thousands, of Southerners were agitating against Lincoln's inauguration on March 4. Sentiment was heated, and men were raging against the prospect of the abolition of slavery. She had also heard rumors of specific plots against the President-Elect. The agitators were planning to take over Washington, D.C., and replace Lincoln's government

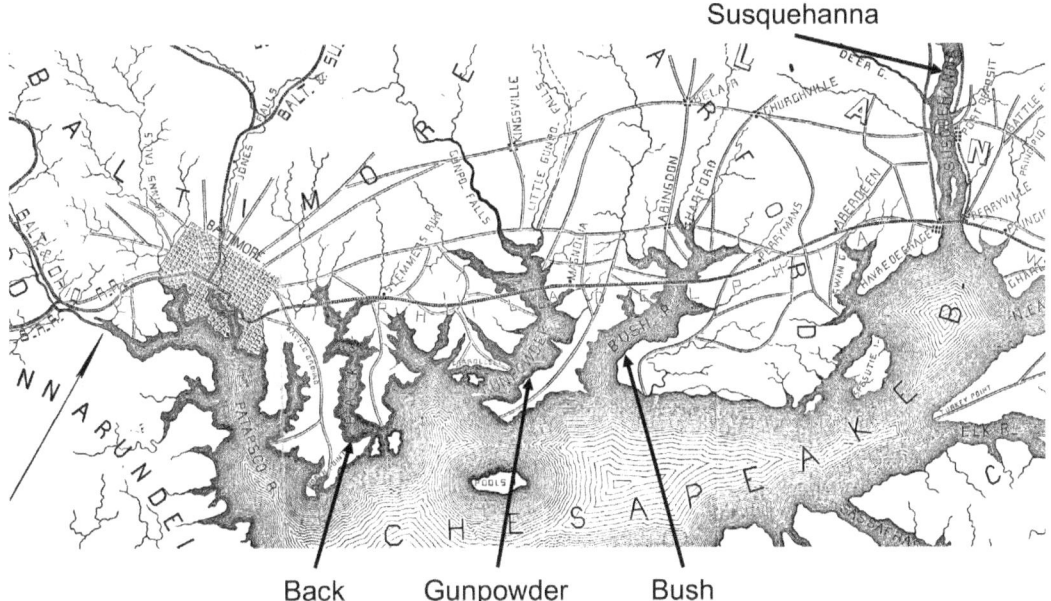

Figure 25. Philadelphia, Wilmington, and Baltimore Railroad Lines. Havre de Grace and Perryville are on opposite sides of the Susquehanna River. Ferries were used to cross the Susquehanna before a bridge was built. Note the locations of the Bush, Gunpowder and Back Rivers and their bridges, from right to left. These four crucial locations could be sites for interrupting Lincoln's passage to Washington, D.C. Adapted from "Map of the Philadelphia, Wilmington, & Baltimore Railroad shewing [sic] its connections," Library of Congress.

with one of a Southern Confederacy. The plans were many-pronged, even prioritized in a sense; if one didn't work, the next would be tried. First was the plot to interrupt rail service to the Capitol; this one would affect Felton and his railroad most directly. It would isolate the North and make any Union military shipments to the South impossible. Felton's railroad had three major bridges to the north of Baltimore—one each over the Bush, the Gunpowder, and the Back Rivers. The bridges over the Bush and Gunpowder Rivers were about one mile long each (Figure 25).

Conspirators would try to burn railroad bridges, disrupt the rails, and sink ferries. One such ferry was the *Maryland*, a ship capable of carrying an entire train across the Susquehanna River from Perryville on the northeast to Havre de Grace on the southwest shore. The conspirators were planning to sink it to disrupt travel to and from Baltimore and ultimately to Washington, D.C. They would also cut communication wires for the telegraph. They were determined to keep Lincoln from being inaugurated.

After Dix's report, Felton communicated with Nicholas Philip Trist, Felton's assistant and paymaster for the railroad, and told him to go to Washington, D.C., immediately to tell General Winfield Scott of these plots. Trist advised Scott to amass troops in Washington to prevent any trouble, and even suggested that Lincoln be inaugurated in Philadelphia, where conditions were safer and could be better controlled.

A few days later an independent source advised Felton that a group in Baltimore was indeed planning to destroy railroad bridges and tracks along the various routes from the North, but specifically the routes expected for President-Elect Lincoln as he traveled to his inauguration in Washington, D.C. Intelligence at this point was a bit sketchy, with the prime source of the information being an unidentified man from Baltimore who repeatedly visited the Back River Bridge railway office, about five miles north and east of Baltimore, informing the attendant there that plans were afoot to burn the bridges. On February 7, 1861, George Stearns, a Baltimore resident, wrote to Governor Thomas H. Hicks, telling him of the plot to burn the bridge and assassinate Lincoln.[7] The white perpetrators were to disguise themselves as black people, and they had already organized and had acquired combustible materials to accomplish their foul deed. It was unclear if all of this intelligence was even the slightest bit reliable, but Felton decided that he had to act. As President of the railroad, Felton had a lot to lose if his rail lines and/or bridges were disrupted. It was a dilemma: should he trust an unknown informant and expend resources on defense of the railroad? But Dix had told a similar story, so Felton acted. The reports further contended that if the burned bridges didn't stop Lincoln, the conspirators would cause the train to derail—perhaps down an embankment—stop the procession with grenades, or board his train and kill him. If none of these tactics were successful, they would attack Lincoln in Baltimore.[8] Even Governor Hicks himself believed in the plot, and he wrote to Lieutenant General Winfield Scott on February 9, 1861, telling of his concerns.[9]

Felton himself went to D.C. and met with someone who knew George Proctor Kane, the 40-year-old Marshal of Police in Baltimore. Kane had been described to Felton as honest and reliable (in contrast to Captain George W. W. Hazzard's description), so Felton told his friend the plot he had heard and asked that it be relayed to Kane, which it was. Kane reportedly investigated the matter, but he concluded that the story was preposterous and didn't require that he do anything to prevent it, declaring that there "was not the slightest foundation for such rumors."[10] Felton was not convinced of the thoroughness of Kane's investigation, and he was by now convinced that he couldn't trust Kane. William Henry Herndon, Lincoln's law partner and biographer, later said, "At that time the Baltimore police were entirely in the hands of the Secessionists; their Chief being George P. Kane, a rabid Rebel, who was subsequently a long time imprisoned in Ft. McHenry…. He is a man with some feelings, but thoroughly Southern, and in that respect unscrupulous."[11] Thereafter, Felton ignored Kane and decided to proceed on his own.

Felton had first hired Allan Pinkerton, head of the Pinkerton National Detective Agency, on February 3, 1861, to investigate whether the reported plots were true or simply unfounded rumors that had no chance of coming to pass.[12] Pinkerton's detective agency had been founded in 1850, and by 1860 it had developed a sound reputation for both honesty and successful investigations.[13] Pinkerton and his assistants immediately took up the evaluation of the threats of sabotage and assassination. They insinuated themselves into the secessionist groups in Baltimore, joined them in their meetings, and convinced them that Pinkerton's agents could be trusted. Pinkerton himself posed as a stockbroker and set up an office about four blocks from Barnum's City Hotel in downtown Baltimore (at 44 South Street, near

Lombard Street),[14] calling himself John H. Hutchinson (spelled "Hutcheson" in some accounts). The other agents claimed to be from New Orleans or Charleston. Felton would base his decisions on the information gleaned from these informants.

On one hand, Kane could be characterized as a dissolute Southerner, frequenting rebel haunts such as Barnum's City Hotel and consorting with disreputable men such as Cipriano Ferrandini (incorrectly identified repeatedly by Detective Allan Pinkerton as "Fernandina").[15] On the other hand, Kane had a history of bravery in fulfilling his duty to keep the law and the peace.[16] He could be brave when necessary. But could he be trusted to protect President-Elect Lincoln?

Pinkerton himself claimed to have met with some of the conspirators in Baltimore, specifically mentioning Barnum's City Hotel as the epicenter of Southern secession sentiments. He reported that "in the evenings the corridors and parlors would be thronged by the tall, lank forms of the long-haired gentlemen who represented the aristocracy of the slaveholding interests. Their conversations were loud and unrestrained, and anyone bold enough or sufficiently indiscreet to venture an opinion contrary to the righteousness of their cause, would soon find himself in an unenviable position and frequently the subject of violence."[17] Kane seemed to be the leader of many of these Southern supporters, and Pinkerton stated as well that "The entire police force of the city—officers and men—were in full sympathy with the rebellion, and it became apparent to him [the Pinkerton spy] that a strict watch was kept over every man who expressed Northern opinions, or who was not identified with the cause which they had espoused."[18] Kane and his police force were described as being "almost entirely composed of men with disunion proclivities. Their leader [Kane] was pronouncedly in favor of secession, and by his orders the broadest license was given to disorderly persons and to the dissemination of insurrectionary information."[19] Later, Pinkerton said that the Baltimore police force was "in active sympathy with the [Southern] movement."[20] Pinkerton claimed that he met with Kane and others, including Cipriano Ferrandini, at a meeting of a secret society at Barnum's Hotel. Some believe that Kane and Ferrandini were members of the Knights of the Golden Circle, the Palmetto Guards, or similar organizations, though no firm evidence exists for such connections. While Pinkerton was known to embellish his accounts, these descriptions had a ring of truth to them.

The Harbor Basin formed the heart of downtown Baltimore (now called the Inner Harbor). Less than a mile square, the extent of the conspirators' haunts was roughly the downtown area. The majority of the Southern activity revolved around the hotels, bars, and restaurants within a radius of about 1000 feet from Barnum's City Hotel. The central focus of the activity was Monument Square, the site of the memorial to the Battle of Baltimore in the War of 1812, not to be confused with the Washington Monument on Monument Street, only about eight blocks to the north and slightly east. The central location, Barnum's City Hotel (Figures 26–27), at the southwest corner of Fayette and Calvert, was where secessionists liked to meet. Barnum's was sometimes called the "Democratic headquarters." Guy's Monument House was diagonally opposite Barnum's at Fayette and Calvert. Pinkerton lived at the Howard House at 5 North Howard.[21] So all of the activity that Pinkerton and his operatives monitored was located within a small district of downtown Baltimore.

Figure 26. Barnum's City Hotel, ca. 1870. From the New York Public Library.

Baltimore had its share of rowdies during the 1860s. In addition to the political/military organizations like the National Volunteers and the Knights of the Golden Circle, street gangs still ruled certain areas of the city. Baltimore was not known for its restraint, and men in Baltimore said that they "would just as leave shoot Lincoln as they would a rat."[22]

Barnum's City Hotel was an elegant seven-story building on the southwest corner of Calvert and Fayette Streets, only about five blocks from the Calvert Street Railroad Station where the Lincoln entourage would ultimately arrive on February 23. Barnum's was a fashionable meeting place for the rich and influential, as well as the disaffected and secessionist conspirators. Pinkerton called it "the Head Quarters [sic] of Secessionists from all parts of the country."[23] A nearby hotel, Guy's Monument House, on the corner opposite Barnum's Hotel, was also frequented by the upper class of society, often Southerners. These were the haunts of men watched by both Kane and Pinkerton.

Pinkerton immediately began to organize "covert operations" within the city of Baltimore. He deployed seven of his best detectives, plus himself. His primary assistant was Kate Warne, slender, blue-eyed, brown-haired, a widow, and the first female detective in the United States. She was a constant companion to Pinkerton, much to the dismay of his wife. Warne was described as graceful, self-possessed, and captivating, and she was hired not only for these qualities but also as a woman

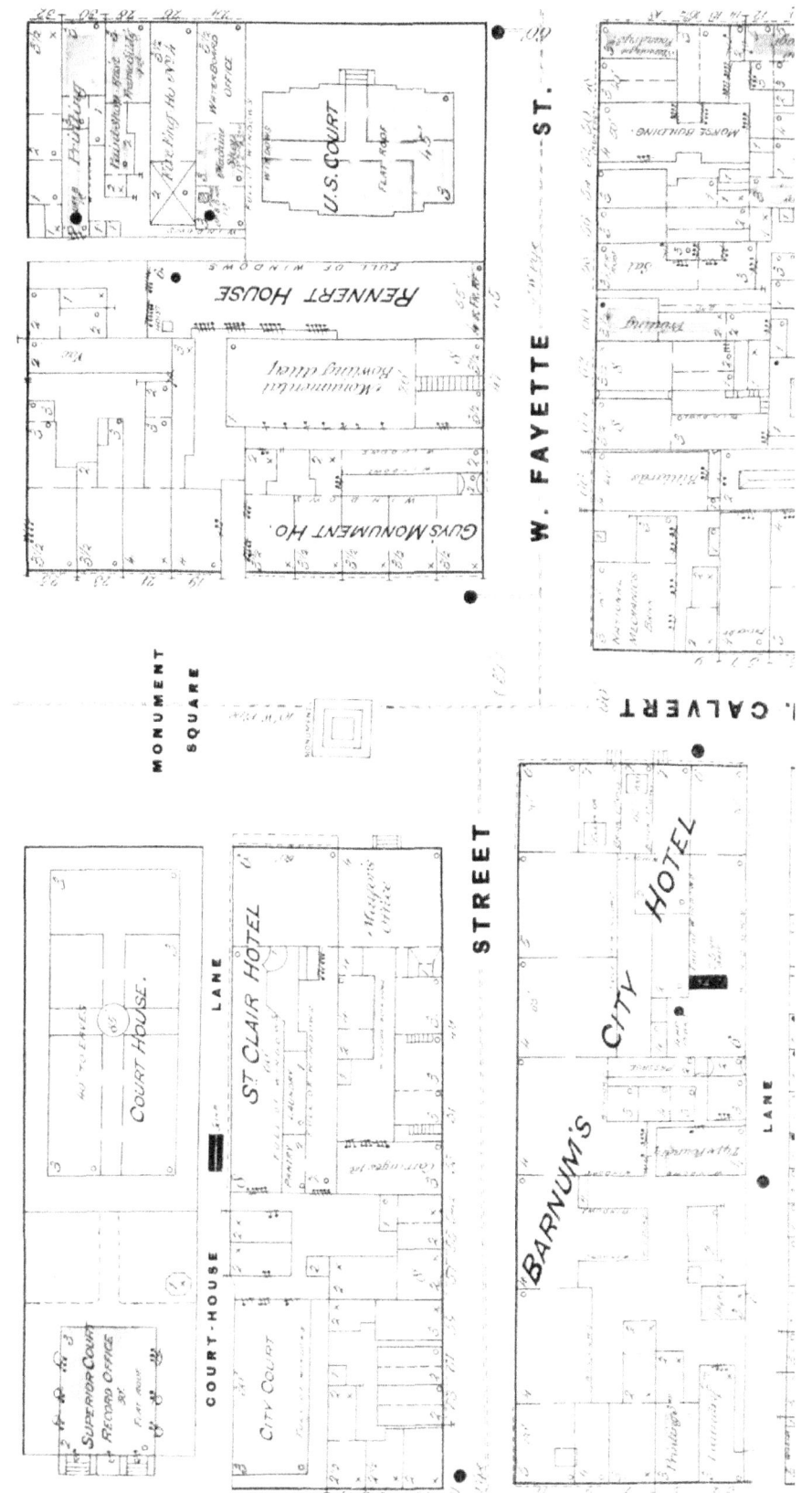

Figure 27. Downtown Baltimore where much of the Southern conspiratorial activity took place. Barnum's City Hotel and Guy's Monument Hotel (or "Guy's Monument House") were on opposite corners of the intersection of Calvert and Fayette Streets. From Papenfuse: Atlases and Maps of Baltimore City and County, 1876–1915.

who could go places a man couldn't go. Furthermore, she could seek intelligence by feminine means. Warne never left Pinkerton's side, even in death—she is buried next to him in the Pinkerton family plot in Graceland Cemetery in Chicago. Pinkerton used the alias John H. Hutcheson (or Hutchinson), or E. J. Allen (or E. I. Allen); Warne went by any number of aliases—Mrs. M. Barley, Mrs. Cherry, Kay Warne, Kay Waren, Kate Waren, Kittie Warren, or any number of variants of her real name.[24] Other Pinkerton agents used aliases, too. Deployed in and around the city, they insinuated themselves in the local community, in which there was no deficiency of secessionists, enemies of Lincoln, and Southern sympathizers. Pinkerton himself was disguised as a stockbroker; Warne embedded herself in local Baltimore high society, where she pretended to be a rich Southern belle from Montgomery, Alabama, with a strong Southern accent. Others in the spy group pretended to be Southern patriots to win the favor of local organizations.[25]

The Pinkerton team's first assessment didn't bode well for Lincoln. The mood was "increasingly tense, the attitude of the press decidedly hostile, and the warnings more and more ominous. At length it became quite evident that the hospitality of the city was not to be extended to Lincoln's presidential party. The omission of an official welcome, with the usual speeches, receptions, fanfare, and parade was highly significant."[26]

After some of the conspirators developed trust in Pinkerton, they introduced him to that fanatical supporter of the South, Cipriano Ferrandini. He was a Corsican (Pinkerton identified him as an Italian) who had immigrated to the United States, and he connected himself with the Southern cause. He had traveled to Mexico in 1860 to train for the secessionist militia. Upon returning to Baltimore, he attached the title "Captain" to his name. He was described as a 38-year-old barber or "hairdresser," who was a "fine looking, intelligent appearing person … whose eyes fairly glared and glistened."[27] Some believe, however, that his title "Captain" referred to his position in the Knights of the Golden Circle, an organization devoted to the expansion of Southern influence in the Caribbean and Central America. Knights swore "to bear hatred, that nothing but blood shall satisfy, against all men of the North who are not friendly to our cause." Furthermore, "we swear death and destruction to Northern Abolitionists." The penalty if a Knight of the Golden Circle broke this pledge was death.[28] The Knights' General President was George Bickley.[29] Since this organization was well known, widely reported upon, and even advertised in Baltimore newspapers, Kane would certainly have been aware of their activities.[30] Nevertheless, Kane's public stance was that Lincoln's passage through Baltimore on the way to his inauguration was safe. It was rumored that Kane would send only a small contingent of police to the train station where Lincoln might arrive, and that no police were scheduled to accompany the Lincoln entourage as it passed through the city.[31] It seemed—if correct—to be almost an invitation for Lincoln's enemies to attempt assassination.

The Knights of the Golden Circle comprised a small band of men who were plotting to overthrow the Northern government, with Lincoln targeted in particular. It was one of the so-called Southern Rights Clubs.[32] John Wilkes Booth was said to be a member of the Knights of the Golden Circle.[33] The Knights advocated for the maintenance of slavery and the slave trade and the promotion of farming of cotton, tobacco, sugar, rice, coffee, indigo and mining, all of which required intense heavy manual labor, i.e. slaves. General George William Lamb Bickley founded the Civil War–era Knights organization on July 4, 1854. The original group likely went back at least to 1834–1835.[34] Capitalizing on men's fascination with secret organizations, Bickley imbued the Knights with multiple levels of organization, initiation rites, passwords, rituals, oaths, handshakes, codes, signs, and rules known only to members. The Knights wanted to create a "Golden Circle" of North American, Central American, and Caribbean possessions that depended upon, and supported, slavery. It included areas in Mexico, Central America, and the island nations of the West Indies. The center of the Circle, which was 2,400 miles in diameter, was Havana, Cuba.[35]

Local conclaves of the Knights of the Golden Circle were called "castles."[36] Each local Castle was very hierarchical and militaristic. While the plan was to extend the influence of slave-owning regions, the activity to destabilize the Union government and to kidnap or kill Lincoln was based primarily around Baltimore. The Knights were dedicated to the "destruction of the Union and the annihilation of the Constitution."[37]

Further, they plotted to

"assaminato [sic] him [Lincoln], and capture Washington, inasmuch as such a thrilling movement would strike terror to the hearts of the "Abolitionists," afford an opportunity to rob the National Treasury, and thus secure the entire field in advance.[38]

This plan was bold:

About one thousand men, armed with bowie knives and pistols, were to meet secretly at Baltimore, where they were to secure the services of the Plug Uglies. Thence they were to proceed to Washington, on the day previous to the inauguration, and stop at the hotels as private citizens, aftor [sic] which their leader was to reconnoiter and select the most effective mode of operations on the succeeding day. This schemo [sic] was not encouraged by Jeff Davis, as he was not yet quite crazy onough [sic] to think that a few dozen of the "chivalry" could terrify the whole world by one demonstration.[39]

Finally,

But one thing above all others, some one of them is to distinguish himself for, *if he can,* and that is, the assassination of the "Abolition" President.[40]

Some experts in the history of the Knights of the Golden Circle believe that members of the Baltimore Castle included John Wilkes Booth, John Surratt, Patrick Charles Martin, George Sanders, Michael O'Laughlen, John C. Breckinridge, George P. Kane, George W. Brown, and even Jesse James. They also believe that Jefferson Davis was a member of the Knights, though in a different Castle.[41] The *Baltimore Sun* reported in 1859, "The headquarters of this recent military organization appear to be in the city of Baltimore."[42] One publication claimed that the Baltimore Castle was headquartered at the Maltby Hotel, located in downtown Baltimore.[43] Yet another source reported that at least one meeting place for the Knights was a building on the corner of Hanover and Lombard Streets.[44]

Through a series of meetings, the Baltimore Castle conspired with another group called the National Volunteers. The membership of the Volunteers was smaller and more tightly controlled, but mostly came from the Knights of the Golden Circle itself.[45] The Volunteers was founded by William Byrne, a businessman in Baltimore who was also a liquor dealer, ran a gambling house, and was an ardent secessionist, possibly even the leader of the assassins in Baltimore who targeted Lincoln on his passage through town.[46] Its governing body had 54 members.[47] Its original function had been to promote John C. Breckinridge as President of the United States (it was even referred to as the "Breckinridge and Lane Club" in its early existence). They had been modestly successful in this goal, with Breckinridge receiving the most votes of any candidate in Maryland—42,482 of 92,502, with Lincoln receiving only 2,294.[48] (Appendix, Table 6)

There were multiple National Volunteer Companies within Baltimore.[49] All members had to take an oath to be willing to kill Lincoln as a requirement of membership,[50] so there were thousands of men in Baltimore sworn to kill him as he passed through the city. Later events would even suggest that Byrne was more centrally involved in the plot. At a trial in Richmond in 1862, charged with running a gambling house and being disloyal to the rebel cause, a witness testified that Byrne was the leader of the plot to take Lincoln's life.[51]

Members of the Baltimore National Volunteers also included Otis K. Hillard and Cipriano Ferrandini.[52] Ferrandini had been "commissioned" by George Bickley on August 8, 1859. Hilliard was also likely a member of the Knights, but no firm proof is extant.[53] The leader of the estimated 5,000 National Volunteers in Washington, D.C., was Dr. Cornelius Boyle, a physician.

Pinkerton was a supremely gifted detective. He had made friends with James H. Luckett, a man who shared Pinkerton's office suite on the same floor at 44 South Street (at times Pinkerton referred to him as "Luckitt").[54] When Luckett had introduced Pinkerton to Cipriano Ferrandini, William H. H. Turner, clerk of the Baltimore Circuit Court, was also present at the meeting. There, even Pinkerton was mesmerized by Ferrandini's personality, and Pinkerton commented that Ferrandini seemed to exude some "strange power."[55] Ward Lamon had a different opinion of Ferrandini, and he would later say, "He drank and talked, and made swelling speeches; but he never took, nor seriously thought of taking, the first step toward the frightful tragedy he is said to have contemplated."[56]

Ferrandini's Corsican background made Pinkerton think that violence and murder were certainly within the realm of options that Ferrandini might be considering. Ferrandini had said, "Murder of any kind is justifiable and right to save the rights of the Southern people."[57] Pinkerton read him as a fanatic, an extremist devoted to preventing Lincoln from taking office. Pinkerton quoted Ferrandini as saying, "Lincoln shall never, never be President. My life is of no consequence. I am willing to give it for his. I will sell my life for that of that abolitionist. As Orsini gave his life for Italy, I am ready to die for the rights of the South…. [D]ie he must and shall…. [W]e will, if necessary, all die together…. [I]f I alone must do it, I shall not hesitate!" Ferrandini compared himself to Felice Orsini, the Italian extremist who was executed for trying to assassinate Napoleon III. Ferrandini also apparently used the nickname or alias "Ruscelli," a name of uncertain significance.[58] One of Ferrandini's conspirators said the next day, "one week from to-day the North shall want a new President, for Lincoln will be dead." Others quoted Ferrandini as saying, "The first shot fired and the head traitor, Lincoln, dead, all Maryland will be with us and the South will be free. If I alone must do the deed, I swear that Abraham Lincoln will die in this city."[59]

At least the conspirators believed that Kane was in their camp and that he would only go through the motions of appearing to protect the President-Elect. One conspirator said, "I have seen Colonel Kane, Chief of Police, and he is all right."[60] Some stories reported Kane as promising only 20 police in the President-Elect's protective detail, claiming that all stories of danger to Lincoln were fabricated, or at least extremely exaggerated. Northerners believed that Kane was purposefully denying protection so that the assassins could do their work.

In fact, Republicans had indeed petitioned the Marshal's office for a protective detail for Lincoln's party as it passed though Baltimore. Many considered Baltimore to be the most dangerous of all of the cities traversed by the inauguration train. Certainly Baltimore was one of the southernmost points on the route, and there were more than a few rabid secessionists with which to contend. Kane refused the petition for heightened protection, saying that calling attention to the President-Elect's caravan would only increase the likelihood of violence. Whether that was his real belief or whether he truly wanted Lincoln to be assassinated will never be known.

The accuracy of Pinkerton's accounts has always been suspect, but they must be considered, nevertheless. He reported on February 21, 1861:

> I also argued that it was impossible for Marshall [sic] Kane not to know that there would be a necessity for an Escort for Mr. Lincoln on his arrival in Baltimore, and, that if with this knowledge Marshall [sic] Kane failed to give a Police Escort, then I should from this time out doubt the loyalty of the Baltimore Police.[61]

Unknown to the conspirators, Pinkerton's men had so infiltrated this band of assassins that two of the Pinkerton operatives—Timothy Webster and Harry W. Davies (alias "AFC," alias "Joseph Howard")—actually drew ballots with the rest of the group.

> [T]he Police were not to interfere only sufficient to make it appear that they were endeavoring to do their duty.... [E]ven if they had interfered what could they have done? We had four thousand of the [National] Volunteers at and about the Depot besides what were at Monument Square, and if you did not see Marshall [sic] Kane around, He knows his business.[62]

Another conspirator said about Lincoln's passage through Baltimore, "It is determined that that G-d d-d Lincoln shall never pass through here alive! The d-d abolitionist shall never set foot on Southern soil but to find a grave."[63]

Felton also enlisted spies to join three alleged Union troop detachments that were conducting military drills close to the railways. The spies pretended to have some Southern sympathies, so they might more easily detect plots to damage the cause of the North. After drilling with the detachments, and becoming familiar with all aspects of the operation, the spies determined that at least two of the three detachments were disloyal to the Northern cause. They were planning to disrupt the rails and march to Washington to overthrow the government. Indeed, they were a part of the coup d'etat. Felton became more trustful of Pinkerton than of Kane.

Upon hearing the news about threats to the railroad bridges, Felton also immediately dispatched 200 men—his own armed forces—to guard and protect the bridges to the north between Baltimore and the Susquehanna River, where the rumors had claimed that the mayhem was to occur. Felton's men needed a covering, a subterfuge to hide the real purpose of their activities. Not wanting the conspirators/arsonists to know that he had received advance warning of the attacks, Felton devised a ruse that would both keep the armed protectors in place and actually fortify the bridges. He deployed his men to whitewash the bridges with a compound that was a mixture of alum and salt, a combination that retarded fire and made the bridges more fireproof. They applied as many as six or seven coats of this whitewash to local bridges. Felton called it his "nine days' wonder." Locals were perplexed at the sudden activity that—on the surface—seemed to be simply a large beautification project. Citizens were unaware that the "paint" actually had fire-retardant properties. Furthermore, since the projects were time-consuming, completion of the job at multiple bridge sites guaranteed that Felton's guards could remain in the area for a number of weeks to observe any suspicious activity around the bridges.

As it later became known that Lincoln was changing his travel itinerary, the conspirators abandoned their plans to burn bridges on the PW&B line. Lincoln had added a stop in Harrisburg, Pennsylvania, where he would address the Pennsylvania legislators, and he would therefore be traveling from Harrisburg to Baltimore on the Northern Central Railway, a different route to the west of the previously planned trip on the PW&B Railway. As the attention of the conspirators switched to the Harrisburg-Baltimore route, Pinkerton's team kept pace with the plans.

By February 9, more specific threats had emerged. Otis K. Hilliard had said, "Give me an article of agreement that you will give my mother Five Hundred Dollars, and I will kill Lincoln between here and Havre-de-Grace."[64]

On February 12, Pinkerton sent a telegram through George H. Bangs to Norman B. Judd, alluding to a "message of importance."[65] Judd was Lincoln's close friend traveling with him on the inaugural train. Judd replied how Pinkerton could connect with Lincoln by telling him what he already knew—the schedule of the trip which included stops at Columbus on the 13th and Pittsburgh on the 14th. William H. Scott, a Pinkerton detective and special messenger, delivered a note to Judd early on the morning of February 13, but Judd decided not to inform Lincoln about Pinkerton's intelligence. The note itself has not survived, so it's unclear exactly what details Pinkerton had sent to Lincoln, but apparently Judd felt that the information was too sketchy to bother Lincoln at precisely that time. Judd took it upon himself to keep the communication secret, telling no one about whatever was known regarding the unfolding plot at that time.[66]

Meanwhile, Pinkerton assigned his agent Harry W. Davies to shadow Hillard, and he did his job admirably, following Hillard everywhere throughout Baltimore, from hotels to bars and even to Madame Annette Travis's brothel at 70 Davis Street, where Hillard spent a good deal of time with Anna Hughes, "his woman."[67]

When the Electoral College succeeded in confirming Lincoln as President on February 13, 1861, the conspirators lost one of their options. They had to proceed to the alternate methods that were more violent.

Rumors of these many plots were circulating throughout the country. On January 26, the House of Representatives (at the instruction of President James Buchanan) had convened a Select Committee (later called the "Select Committee of Five," referring to the five members who questioned the alleged conspirators) to investigate the reported threats, in addition to investigating other important matters. Testimony began on January 29 and continued through February 13. A total of 27 men were questioned, both suspected conspirators and their accusers, including James G. Berrett (Mayor of Washington), General Winfield Scott (Army Commander), Colonel Charles P. Stone (Inspector General of the Washington, D.C., Militia), Dr. Cornelius Boyle (Head of the National Volunteers in Washington, D.C.), Jacob Thompson (Secretary of the Interior), and Enoch Lowe (former Governor of Maryland). Thomas H. Hicks (Governor of Maryland) was scheduled to testify, but he refused to appear. Governor Hicks was a very coy and reluctant witness, and two of the Committee actually had to go to Annapolis to question him, along with a clerk to record the proceedings. Upon their arrival in Annapolis, the two Committee representatives were inexplicably told that Hicks was unavailable to testify.[68] This behavior was common for Hicks, who often played one side of a controversy against the other. In this case, his evasiveness covered his Southern-leaning tendencies without committing himself to support for either side. Hicks ultimately met with the Select Committee on Wednesday, February 13, the last day of the Committee's deliberations, and was again evasive in his testimony; though he said that he had heard rumors of plots, he refused to name names. He reported his own assessment of the veracity of the widely reported schemes, testifying that they were not believable. While he admitted that he had heard rumors, he opined that the conspirators weren't talented enough to carry out their plans. So, by implication, if he could assess the skills of the alleged assassins, he must have known who they were. But the members of the Select Committee didn't ask the tough questions.[69] Furthermore, Marshal George Kane, as Chief of Police of Baltimore, would have been a prime candidate to have useful information about conspirators, plots, and schemes afoot in Baltimore, but the Committee did not call Kane.

Those two members of the National Volunteers, Cipriano Ferrandini and Otis K. Hillard, had also been questioned by the Committee earlier. Ferrandini and Hilliard admitted that they were committed to prevent Northern troops from passing through Baltimore, but Hilliard denied any knowledge of a conspiracy. And both refused to name anyone who might try to impede the passage of Northern troops or Lincoln through Baltimore. They had both lied to the Committee. Ferrandini wanted to become a hero and to make a name for himself, and he wanted Maryland to join the Southern bloc, liberating it from what he perceived as the tyranny and unconstitutional behavior of the abolitionists.[70] The Committee of Five finally declared in summary that it was "unanimously of the opinion that the evidence produced before them does not prove the existence of a secret organization here or elsewhere hostile to the government, that has for its object, upon its own responsibility, an attack upon the Capitol, or any of the public property here, or an interruption of any of the functions of the government."[71]

The "rules of engagement" for the Civil War were different from other conflicts. Previous wars and conflicts had declared the commanders out-of-bounds for attack. But as early as Lincoln's election in November 1860, plots against Lincoln's life emerged. He was not protected. Likewise, early in the war Jefferson Davis also became a target for murder and kidnapping. Edward Steers describes this change in strategy in *Blood on the Moon*. It was called "Black Flag Warfare." It simply meant that no leader nor warfare technique was ruled out-of-bounds. Even germ warfare was on the table.[72] Nothing was held back; nothing was too immoral; nothing was sacred. Arson of cities was tried; poisoning of water supplies was considered. For the first time, the Presidents of each side were targeted.

Another group plotting to assassinate Lincoln was the Palmetto Guard. Formed as a volunteer military unit on June 28, 1851, the majority of its members lived in the South Carolina area. It was a part of the South Carolina Infantry Regiment, Fourth Brigade. This unit participated in the attack on Fort Sumter. In fact, Edmund Ruffin, a secessionist and member of the Palmetto Guard, allegedly took the first shot on the fort.[73] One of Pinkerton's investigators had discovered that portions of the Palmetto Guard were in Baltimore plotting to murder the President-Elect. Pinkerton Detective Agent Joseph Howard (referred to as "Howard of New Orleans") had trained as a Jesuit priest and was well-educated in college, fluent in many languages, and widely traveled; he spoke well and presented himself as a refined gentleman. He fit into Baltimore high society. During his first days in Baltimore, he broadcast his bogus but ardent secessionist beliefs, and he knew enough about Southern sentiments and manners to convince anyone of his credentials. He reported that he had made the acquaintance of a man known only by the name of Mr. Hill. They became friends when Howard pretended to be rabidly anti–Union, and the two frequented bars and went to entertainment in the city together. After Hill became convinced that Howard was a legitimate Southern sympathizer, he opened up one night and said, "What a pity that this glorious Union must be destroyed all on account of that monster Lincoln."[74] Hill went on to say, "I am destined to die shrouded with glory. If a man had the nerve he could immortalize himself by plunging a knife into Lincoln's heart. Let us have another Brutus. I swear I will kill Lincoln before he reaches the Washington depot, not that I love Lincoln less, but my country more. I am ready to do the deed…. When our company draws lots, if the red ballot falls to me, I will do it willingly…. I will go out there and kill him if it is so ordered."[75]

Pinkerton was again informed of this plot to occur in Baltimore, and he sent another letter to Judd, who had now arrived in Buffalo. In addition, Pinkerton sent Kate Warne to meet the Lincoln entourage in New York on February 18. The parties agreed to meet in Philadelphia to discuss strategy to avoid any threats to Lincoln as he passed through Baltimore.[76]

Baltimore was central to the operation of the railroads along the east coast of the United States. Situated between Philadelphia and Washington, D.C., it comprised a major part of the rail connection from North to South. In addition, Baltimore had a good port to and from which goods could be shipped. Each railroad built and operated its own depots and terminals. Within a large city such as Baltimore, an individual railroad might even have multiple depots. A traveler who needed to transfer from one railway to another had to coordinate and arrange transportation from one terminal to another, often on different sides of town. It was this system that Marshal George Kane needed to protect as Lincoln passed through the city.

Baltimore city during Lincoln's time had at least eight passenger train depots with which a traveler had to contend (not counting over 40 commercial freight

Figure 28. Major passenger train depots in Baltimore in the early 1860s. Adapted from Samuel Augustus Mitchell, Jr.'s 1872 "Plan of Baltimore."

depots, most terminating at various locations on the waterfront). Rails connected many of the independent terminals, but Baltimore city ordinances prohibited steam engines from traveling these routes.[77] Therefore, no connections *by locomotive* existed among any of the many railroad terminal buildings in Baltimore.

For the purposes of understanding the assassination attempt on Lincoln, only three stations are important.[78] Lincoln's first scheduled arrival was from Philadelphia at the President Street Station, followed by a crosstown journey to Camden Street Station. The second planned arrival was from Harrisburg at the Calvert Street Station, where he would then likewise transfer across downtown Baltimore to the Camden Street Station. In fact, his actual arrival point would finally be moved back to the President Street Station for his nighttime incognito passage through "Mobtown."

Bridges were crucial to the integrity of the rail systems, though some rivers and waterways had no bridges and were served by ferries. Difficult as it is to imagine, for example, when a train from Philadelphia to Baltimore on the PW&B Railway came to the Susquehanna River, it was necessary to put the cars on a ferry (the *Maryland*, a full 238 feet long) to traverse the river, reconnecting to rails on the other side at Havre de Grace (Harford County, Maryland). Disruption of this line, therefore, could be accomplished simply by sinking or otherwise disabling the ferry. It was not until 1866 that a single-rail wooden bridge was constructed over the Susquehanna that rendered ferries obsolete.

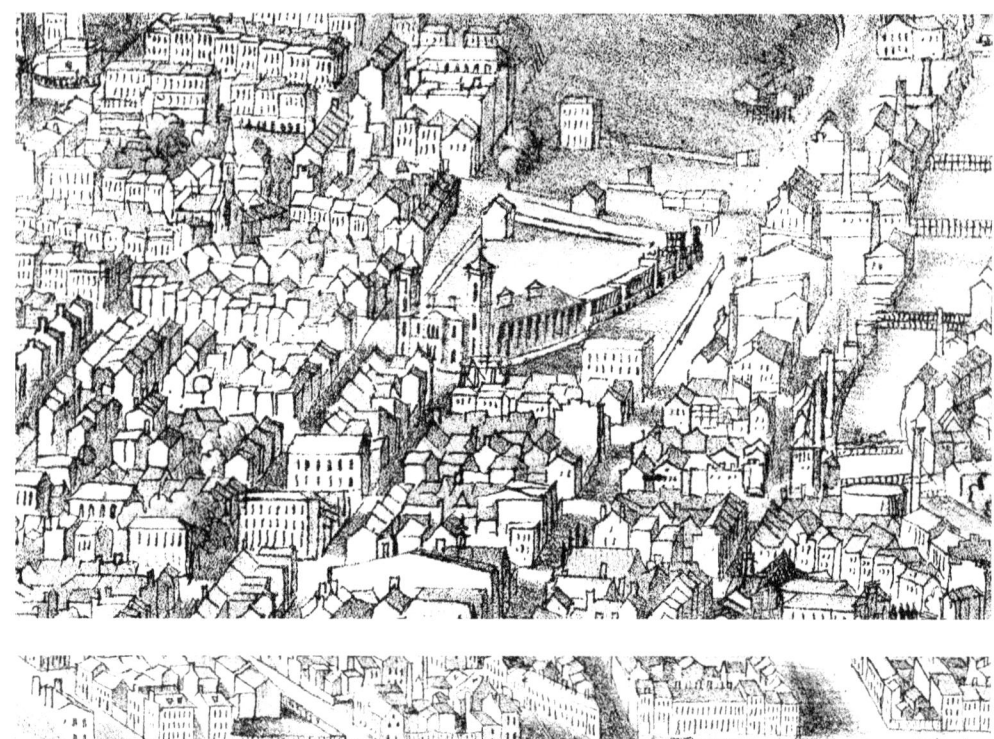

Above and opposite top: **Figure 29. Major train stations in Baltimore in 1858. Calvert Street Station.** *Bottom:* **President Street Station**

The three largest railroad companies were the B&O, the Northern Central, and the PW&B Railroads (Figures 28–33). The first railroad terminal built in Baltimore was the President Street Station, which in 1861 was the depot for the PW&B. The line ended there, one block north of the major Baltimore city dock. Travelers who needed to connect with the B&O passenger terminal had to traverse the downtown Baltimore area along President Street for four blocks, then join Pratt Street for 12–14 blocks to the Camden Street Station (also called the Washington Station) between Eutaw and Howard Streets. This trip of slightly more than a mile could be

10. The Baltimore Plot

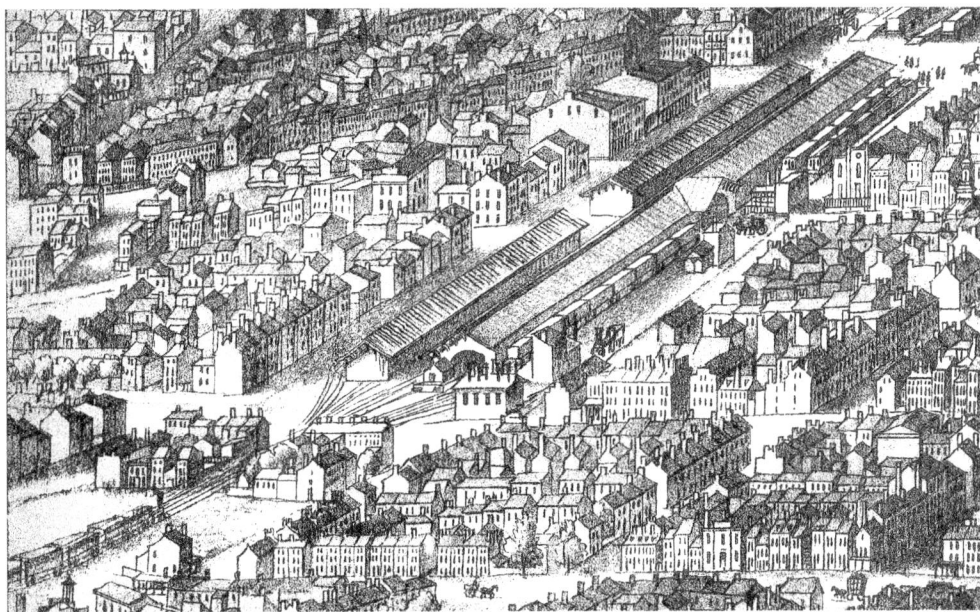

PASSENGER AND FREIGHT STATIONS, PRESIDENT STREET, BALTIMORE.

Top: Camden Street Station From "E. Sachse & Co's Bird's Eye View of the City of Baltimore"; The Sheridan Libraries, Johns Hopkins University, Baltimore, Maryland. *Bottom:* Figure 30. President Street Station. Baltimore home of the Philadelphia, Wilmington, and Baltimore Railroad. From the Library of Congress.

accomplished on foot or by horse or carriage, or at times the railroad cars would be hitched to horses that pulled the cars from one station to another on crosstown rails (again, steam locomotives were prohibited), but it also took a route through downtown Baltimore, past waterfront, wharf, and dock areas where the toughs and gangs hung out. It was not necessarily guaranteed to be a safe passage. Originally Lincoln

Figure 31. Camden Station, Camden Street, between Howard and Eutaw Streets. From the Maryland Center for History and Culture.

was scheduled to arrive at the President Street Station, but the plans were changed at the last minute for Lincoln to come to Baltimore from Harrisburg, Pennsylvania, on the Northern Central line, using the Calvert Street Station.

The Calvert Street Station—the second planned site for Lincoln's arrival—was the terminus of the Northern Central Railroad, occupying the area between North and Calvert Streets and Franklin and Centre Streets. The plot against Lincoln apparently was to be executed in a narrow vestibule passageway exiting the building. An architectural gem in the 1860s,[79] the building is no longer standing, demolished in 1948 and replaced by the Baltimore Sunpapers Building.

Travel between the Calvert Street Station and the Camden Street B&O Station (which occupied the area between Eutaw and Howard Streets) likewise required a trip of about eight blocks southeast across downtown. This trip, while not a great distance, was exposed, just like the trip from the President Street Station would have been, and it offered any determined assassin plenty of room to maneuver and wreak havoc on the President-Elect's party.

Republican presence was nearly nonexistent in Baltimore in 1861. Much of the state harbored Southern sympathies. Even Governor Thomas H. Hicks had written on November 9, 1860, referring to distribution of some arms to men in the area, "Will they be good men to send out to kill Lincoln and his men?" Anti-Lincoln sentiment therefore pervaded the state from lowly barbers to the Governor.[80] Only 2,294 of 92,502 votes in 1860 were cast for Lincoln in the entire state of Maryland; Lincoln received only 1,083 votes in Baltimore, out of 30,146 total votes cast.[81] Four years earlier, the "Plug Uglies" had threatened and assaulted President-Elect Buchanan,

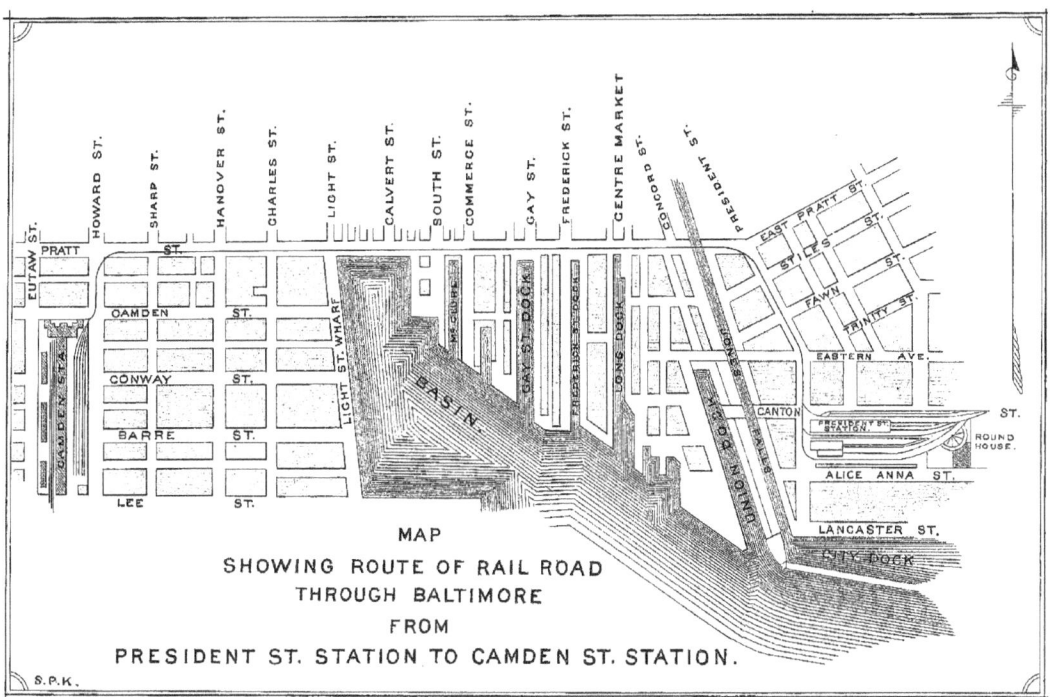

Figure 32. Map of the route Lincoln was initially scheduled to take in Baltimore on his journey from Philadelphia to Washington, D.C. (also the route used by the Massachusetts 6th Regiment on April 19, 1861). From *Baltimore and the Nineteenth of April 1861*.

so violence was a traditional part of the Baltimore political scene.[82] The Republicans had planned no large reception, gathering, or speech for Lincoln as he passed through this great metropolis. William S. Wood was in charge of activities in Baltimore for the President-Elect's arrival.[83] Wood was given the title "Superintendent of Arrangements,"[84] but Lincoln didn't even know him, and there were no "arrangements" contemplated until just before Lincoln was to pass through the city. The Baltimore Republican Committee considered hosting a reception for Lincoln, but it had to be discreet, so no *public* invitation was ever forthcoming.[85] Mayor George William Brown was an ardent secessionist (he would later be jailed for these sympathies), so he planned no reception nor meeting while Lincoln traveled through Baltimore. Nor did the Legislature, the City Council, nor the Governor. Baltimore Republican attorney and staunch Unionist Worthington Garrettson Snethen wrote to Lincoln on February 15,

> On consultation with some of our leading Republican friends, it has been deemed inadvisable, in the present state of things, to attempt any organized public display on our part, as Republicans, on the occasion of your approach to and passage through Baltimore.[86]

Snethen detected that the flavor of any reception given Lincoln in Baltimore might make a negative rather than a positive impression.[87]

George Kane believed that Lincoln could pass through Baltimore without being harmed, as long as the trip wasn't punctuated by any elaborate receptions or demonstrations. A quiet passage was the best option, he thought. Newspapers concurred in this assessment[88]:

> A set of unscrupulous political knaves in Baltimore, who had determined to turn Mr. Lincoln's visit there to their own account, arranged for a procession from the depot to the hotel. Protection was asked by these rowdies of Marshal Kane, who protested against such a proceeding.[89]

A party or parade given by Republicans ("unscrupulous political knaves," "rowdies") would likely incite a riot.

Kane's belief that extensive police protection for Lincoln was not necessary led him to write to James Gabriel Berret, the Mayor of Washington, D.C., on January 16, 1861. Kane said,

> I would state to you my opinion with reference to the truth of the rumors ... that associations of armed men are being formed here for the purpose of making unlawful demonstrations at the seat of government on the 4th of March.... [Lincoln's Inauguration Day]. I beg to say ... that they are wholly without foundation. No such organization now exists, none has existed, nor will the citizens of Baltimore tolerate any such....
>
> That the citizens of Maryland have a strong sympathy with their Southern brethren, and that upon every lawful occasion for the expression of that sympathy, it will doubtless be emphatically heard, cannot be denied; but that they will tolerate or connive at the unlawful doings of a mob, or permit violence or indignity to any public functionary passing through the State, I believe to be entirely devoid of truth....
>
> The President elect will need no armed escort in passing through or sojourning within the limits of this city or State, and, in my view, the provision of any such at this time, would be ill-judged.[90]

This is not to say that the members of the police force themselves weren't opposed to Lincoln. The police were simply a sampling of the general population of Baltimore, perhaps with even a more prominent Southern bias than the average Baltimorean, most of whom opposed Lincoln's election. Most police, likewise, harbored ill feelings toward the President-Elect. "The entire police force of the city—officers and men—were in full sympathy with the rebellion."[91]

On January 24, Robert B. Coleman invited Lincoln to a gathering at the Eutaw House when he passed through Baltimore, though the invitation was proffered through a third party, Simeon Draper.[92] Coleman was the manager of the Eutaw House Hotel at the corner of Baltimore and Eutaw Streets from 1859 to 1874.[93] At the last minute, a different luncheon was scheduled for a portion of the President-Elect's

CALVERT STATION. NORTHERN CENTRAL RAIL WAY, N. E. COR. FRANKLIN & CALVERT STREETS.

party at the home of General John S. Gittings, a local businessman who was the President and owner of the Northern Central Railway, which was scheduled to bring Lincoln from Harrisburg to Baltimore. In fact, Police Chief Kane was instrumental in arranging this luncheon, and he also convinced Gittings to go to Harrisburg with James C. Clark, the Northern Central Superintendent, to meet Lincoln and accompany him to Baltimore, along with the small Republican committee that already had planned to escort Lincoln to Baltimore. Kane, of course, knew that Lincoln was scheduled to be using Gittings's railroad for his travel to Baltimore, and having the railroad owner and boss on the trip might cause the Northern Central employees to exert more caution on the journey. Furthermore, Gittings was a Democrat, and having a prominent and popular Democrat accompany the Republican President-Elect might cause rowdies to think twice about disrupting the procession. Little did they know that the President-Elect would at that very time be considering an alternative plan to pass through Baltimore.

The men traveling with the President-Elect mistrusted Marshal Kane. Newspapers called Lincoln's route through Baltimore "the first Southern soil" to be traversed by the President-Elect. Many feared that the Southern sentiment and dominance in the city itself at that time would lead to rioting, or at least an unpleasant reception for Lincoln and his entourage.[94] Pinkerton especially worried that Kane might be turning a blind eye in hopes that someone would be successful in assassinating Lincoln.

Opposite and above: **Figure 33. Calvert Street Station, ca. 1925. The Calvert Street Station was to be the stopping point in Baltimore for Lincoln on his inaugural trip from Harrisburg to Washington, D.C. From the Library of Congress.**

The tumult in Baltimore might not include any plans for assassination, but it certainly could turn ugly and give the city a bad name. Having Gittings in the group (he was also a slaveholder, as well as a Democrat) might lessen the risk to the entourage. Gittings at worst was a neutral influence and at best could be a calming force. Finally, Gittings owned a large mansion suitable for receiving Lincoln; it was close to the rail line from Harrisburg, and it also had reasonable access to the B&O line to Washington. Gittings listened to these arguments and agreed to host the President-Elect.

However, Baltimore radicals were still discussing plans for an assassination. Lincoln and his group would arrive at the Calvert Street (Northern Central Railroad) Station at about noon, would then pass by carriage to the Gittings Mansion on Eutaw Street near Mount Vernon Square, and after dining there would proceed to the Camden Street (B&O) Station. The conspirators allegedly planned to make a demonstration or disturbance at the Calvert Street Station, using crowd tactics, rotten eggs, and brickbats where the police force under the command of Colonel Kane would be distracted. Lincoln's exposure there would be the greatest. While the ruckus was underway, any of 20 or so assassins would complete the deed before the party was able to mount carriages for the trip to the Gittings Mansion. Others in the party were not targeted, but there could indeed be some "collateral damage." That was the nature of the messy business of assassination.

Perhaps Kane's protestations about Republican unpopularity and the need to avoid any procession in Baltimore were just a cover-up for him to justify planning for only a small force of police for the protection of Lincoln as he passed through the city. Either Kane knew of the plot to kill Lincoln and was complicit in the scheme, or he was oblivious to the real threat against the President-Elect. Clearly Kane was a Southerner at heart, but his duty was to protect the Northerner passing through his city.

The conspirators apparently had no shortage of willing assassins. About 20 gathered on February 18 to draw lots (colored ballots) from a hat in a dark room to see who would be the real assassin. If you secretly drew a white ballot, you were relieved of your duty to kill; if you secretly drew a red ballot, you were the assassin. But to ensure success, there were eight red ballots in the bag. Unbeknownst to the lottery "winners," any holder of a red ballot would have seven other killers vying for the "honor" of assassinating the President-Elect. The assassin could choose his own method—shooting or knifing. With eight assassins, one would doubtless succeed. Unknown to the conspirators, Pinkerton's men had so infiltrated this band of assassins that two of the Pinkerton operatives—Timothy Webster (alias "A.F.C.") and Harry W. Davies (alias Joseph Howard)—actually drew ballots with the rest of the group. Legend has it that both drew red ballots, meaning that only six true assassins were chosen. But even having "only six" was probably firepower enough to eliminate Lincoln.[95]

Armed with all of this information, Pinkerton sent word to Norman B. Judd about the planned assassination. Judd decided to wait until he could meet face-to-face with Pinkerton in Philadelphia before informing Lincoln of the plot. It was too unclear what might happen, too preposterous to worry the President-Elect until they could give him more details.

10. The Baltimore Plot

As the President-Elect arrived in Philadelphia's Kensington Street Station on February 21, those aware of the plots were finally able to meet. Samuel Felton, Allan Pinkerton, and Norman Judd gathered at the St. Louis Hotel. Judd thought that Lincoln should travel immediately to Baltimore, and subsequently to Washington secretly under the cover of night. At 10:25 p.m., Lincoln came to Judd's room in the hotel, and Judd introduced Pinkerton to Lincoln. The President-Elect listened to Judd and Pinkerton's recounting of how the plot would be executed as they passed through Baltimore.[96] Felton's first recommendation had been that the President-Elect travel directly to Baltimore from Philadelphia on that very night, even before Lincoln's planned speech and flag-raising over Independence Hall on Thursday, February 21. Felton had offered the service of his railway company and said that he would arrange the details. The President-Elect wouldn't hear of such a plan; he rejected it outright. Lincoln is reported to have said, "Both these appointments I will keep *if it costs me my life*."[97] He felt obligated to appear at the event at Independence Hall, and he was also adamant that he meet with the Pennsylvania legislators in Harrisburg on Friday, February 22. Furthermore, he wasn't absolutely sure that he even believed the reports of his impending assassination, though he did say in his speech at Independence Hall in Philadelphia on the morning of February 22, "I will preserve the Union even if the assassin's knife is at my heart."[98] He also said, "But if this country cannot be saved without giving up that principle [of the Declaration of Independence]—I was about to say I would rather be assassinated on this spot than to surrender it." And "I have said nothing but what I am willing to live by, and, in the pleasure of Almighty God, die by."[99] Lincoln did agree, however, to reconsider advice that might be proffered after the meeting in Harrisburg on Friday the 22nd.

After returning to his own room, Lincoln found another urgent meeting awaiting him. Frederick Seward, son of Senator William H. Seward, had come from Washington, D.C., and he had information gleaned from John A. Kennedy, the chief ("General Superintendent") of police of New York City, who himself had been investigating rumors of an assassination. Kennedy had sent three detectives—David S. Bookstaver, Thomas Sampson, and Eli DeVoe—to Baltimore on February 1. They reported their findings to Colonel Charles P. Stone, an assistant to General Winfield Scott (the Commander of the United States Army in Washington) in Washington.[100] Bookstaver had relayed a summary of his findings to Stone, and the information was then transmitted to both the elder Seward and Scott. Senator Seward actually had additional information gathered from other sources. They then sent Frederick Seward to Lincoln with this information.[101] The details of all the informants were remarkably similar to Pinkerton's description. Evidence was mounting. Dix had a story. Pinkerton's version was the same. Kennedy's story was consistent. And Seward's tale was almost identical. Like a good lawyer, Lincoln sought to determine if all stories had the same origin, or if they were in fact independent. He became convinced that each of the reports was original, so the story became more sinister; it might be the truth. Nevertheless, Lincoln was not ready to change his plans; he was still intransigent. He would raise the flag in Philadelphia, address the legislators in Harrisburg, and then go to a dinner and reception with Pennsylvania Governor

Andrew Gregg Curtin. Then, and only then, would he reconsider fleeing to Washington in secret. He needed the night to think about the plot. Tomorrow he would reconsider changing his travel.

Even though it was still unclear whether Lincoln would agree to a secret journey to Washington, Pinkerton and Felton made arrangements for the trip. Pinkerton negotiated with George Charles Franciscus, the Pennsylvania Railroad Division Superintendent, to secure a secret train to transport Lincoln from Harrisburg back to Philadelphia on Friday night, the 22nd. Felton would make arrangements for the 11:50 p.m. PW&B train from Philadelphia to Baltimore to be ready for the President-Elect. Then in Baltimore Lincoln would transfer to the B&O line for the Baltimore-to-Washington run.

Lincoln kept to his schedule on Friday, February 22, raising the flag over Independence Hall and there giving a short speech. In it, he alluded to the plans afoot to harm him as he passed through Baltimore.[102] Felton and Pinkerton confirmed their secret plans, and elsewhere Lamon told Seward that Lincoln had decided to return to Philadelphia and then on through Baltimore and to Washington that night. Lincoln then went to the West Philadelphia train terminal that was owned by the Pennsylvania Railroad and boarded the train for Harrisburg at 9:30 a.m., making an uneventful trip in the three-car special train to Harrisburg.[103]

Lincoln remained jovial throughout the trip, even knowing that he might be in danger. He joked at one stop to well-wishers that he "had merely come out to see them and let them see him." He then added that he thought that he "had the best of the bargain." When Mary Lincoln came to the train platform at one stop, Lincoln commented that now you have seen "the long and the short of it" (Lincoln was six feet four inches tall, and she was five feet three inches). Later in the trip, like many politicians who detect a good response from the crowd and milk the line for all it's worth, Lincoln said, "I come before you to see and be seen, and, as regards the ladies, I have the best of the bargain; but, as to the gentlemen, I cannot say as much."[104]

Lincoln arrived in Harrisburg at 1:30 p.m. He was taken to the Jones House Hotel at the southeast corner of Market and Second Streets. After receiving guests at the hotel, Lincoln traveled the three blocks to the Pennsylvania State Capitol Building where he met with Pennsylvania legislators and addressed the General Assembly at 2:30 p.m. Lincoln then returned to the hotel at about 4:00 p.m. There he attended a dinner given by Governor Curtin. At the dinner, the guests present were informed of the potential assassination and the danger to Lincoln of traveling through Baltimore. His "handlers" reminded him that he had two options: proceed as planned with a strong military or police escort, or pass through in secret. At one point, Lincoln had said that if a Republican Committee came from Baltimore to Harrisburg to welcome him and escort him to and through Baltimore, his decision would be not to make the secretive journey to Baltimore at night. Thus far, Lincoln had heard no word of such a Committee coming to Harrisburg. Unbeknownst to him, there was indeed one traveling to Harrisburg that very night. It would include Worthington G. Snethen, Judge William L. Marshall, Leopold Blumenberg, James E. Bishop, William E. Gleeson, William E. Beale, Judge Joseph M. Palmer, and Francis S. Corkran, some of them no doubt seeking to lobby for their own appointments in Lincoln's cabinet, or at least high positions in the government. Though allegedly pursuing the same goal of welcoming and honoring the President-Elect, "the utmost harmony did not exist among the committee, the usual rivalries and jealousies which mark the success of party being very perceptibly manifested."[105] The chairmanship of the Committee was in dispute: both Snethen and Marshall claimed to be in charge of the delegation. In addition, John Sterrett Gittings, the President of the Northern Central Railroad, and James C. Clark, its Superintendent, had traveled to Harrisburg to accompany Lincoln to the Gittings Mansion in Baltimore for lunch. All would be chagrined and distressed if Lincoln went to Baltimore by another route or at another time without them. But Lincoln knew nothing of this committee and their plans at the time he needed to make his final decision. It was too late to muster a military escort. Lincoln was quiet during the final discussion of his options, but when it came time to make the final decision, he acquiesced to the subterfuge. He would secretly go to Washington, D.C., this night.

Ward Lamon accompanied Lincoln to the train station. Governor Curtin asked Lamon if he was armed, and Lamon showed Curtin a virtual arsenal under his coat—two revolvers, brass knuckles, a slug shot (a heavy weight on a rope that could be brandished as a weapon), and a large knife.

For this trip, Lincoln wore a rather large overcoat (variably described as a trench coat, a "bobtail overcoat" resembling a "sailor's pea jacket,"[106] or a "very long military cloak"). He also wore a small soft brown felt hat. By contrast, Lincoln usually wore a top hat, or stovepipe hat, made of felted beaver fur, silk, or even wool. Later reports that Lincoln wore a Scottish plaid hat or "Tam o' Shanter woolen cap" were apparently inventions of the press. Nevertheless, Lincoln's clothing was different than his usual attire, and he was at least slightly more difficult to recognize. Some reports had Lincoln carrying or wearing a shawl as though he were an invalid. Newspapers would describe Lincoln skulking around in a plaid Scottish cap, with drawings of him exiting a freight car (Figure 34). These were caricatures, published to embarrass him, emphasizing his "cowardly" trip to the Capitol. Lincoln described himself as not being recognized because he wasn't the same man.[107]

Lincoln himself in 1864, apparently because the escapade still haunted him, gave his version of the choice of headwear:

> In New York some friend had given me a new beaver hat in a box, and in it had placed a soft wool hat. I had never worn one of the latter in my life. I had this box in my room.... Having informed a very few friends of the secret of my new movements [to Baltimore], and the cause, I put on an old overcoat that I had with me, and putting the soft hat in my pocket, I walked out of the house at the backdoor, bareheaded, without exciting any special curiosity. Then I put on the soft hat and joined my friends without being recognized by strangers, for I was not the same man.[108]

Lincoln needed to travel only a couple of miles to arrive at that special train prepared for him by the Pennsylvania Railroad line, consisting of the engine, a baggage car, a single passenger car for guests, and the special car for Lincoln.[109] The arrangements for the railroad transport required the help of officers of the Pennsylvania Railroad. Pinkerton enlisted the services of George Charles Franciscus, the Pennsylvania Railroad Division Superintendent, and Enoch Lewis, the General Superintendent.

Edward S. Sanford, the President of the American Telegraph Company, handled the telegraph details, and he deployed John Pitcairn, Jr., to travel on the train and send any emergency messages necessary by telegraph. Franciscus, Lewis, Pitcairn, and Ward Lamon accompanied Lincoln on the train. The only other person riding this train to Philadelphia was T. E. Garrett, the general baggage agent.[110] All other trains that were supposed to be on this line that night were sidetracked. All telegraph lines out of Harrisburg were cut, meaning that Kane received no news of this travel. The lights were extinguished in Lincoln's car to avoid anyone seeing the President-Elect through the windows, which themselves were covered by thick red curtains. Pinkerton tested the success of their telegraph sabotage after returning to Harrisburg by asking for a message to be sent to Baltimore from Harrisburg. The telegram could not be transmitted. They had effectively isolated Harrisburg from communications with the outside world.[111]

Figure 34. "Passage through Baltimore." Lincoln is depicted as sneaking through Baltimore in a railroad freight car. From the Metropolitan Museum of New York.

Lincoln's train arrived at the West Philadelphia Terminal at Thirty-second and Market Streets at 10:30 p.m., where Felton and Pinkerton met Lincoln, Lamon, Franciscus, and Lewis. The train from Harrisburg was actually too early to make an immediate transfer to the Baltimore-bound sleeping car that had been reserved by Kate Warne and another Pinkerton detective, George R. Dunn. Pinkerton therefore stalled by driving Lincoln, Lamon, and Henry F. Kenney (another Superintendent of the PW&B Railroad) around in a carriage in Philadelphia for about 30 minutes until it was time for the departure of his next train—the PW&B line from the Broad and Prime Street Station. Still, Baltimore Police Chief Kane knew of none of these plans.

Because Felton was afraid that Lincoln might actually arrive late for this train in Philadelphia, he had instructed John Litzenburg, the conductor of the Baltimore-bound train, to wait for departure until he had received a package of important documents to be delivered to Washington. Felton had wrapped a bundle of worthless papers in a package, labeling them as crucial government records. He did the same for the Baltimore-Washington train. Only a man as important as Felton—and his passenger Lincoln—could have delayed these two trains simply on a man's order.

Lincoln and his companions were to be situated in the back four sleeping compartments of the last car of the train. Pinkerton operative George Dunn had been able to obtain the keys to the back door of the sleeping car from the conductor. There they boarded the train from the rear to minimize the likelihood that anyone would see Lincoln. The excuse was that one of the passengers for the sleeping car was disabled and ill, and he couldn't walk further forward. Lincoln was still disguised, and this time he walked bent over to appear to be disabled. Warne pretended to be the "old man's" sister. Pinkerton, Lamon, and Warne were armed. Lincoln was offered a revolver and a Bowie knife, but he refused.[112]

Lincoln boarded the train in his "disguise," accompanied by Lamon, Pinkerton, and Warne, slightly before 11:00 p.m. on Friday. Lincoln was described to railroad employees as "the sleeper [who] should not be disturbed."[113] Henry F. Kenney, Superintendent of the PW&B, handed the "important papers" to John Litzenburg the conductor, and the train was off, departing at about 10:55 p.m.[114]

The trip to Baltimore went without a hitch. As they arrived at the President Street Station at 3:30 a.m., Saturday, February 23, Pinkerton briefly exited the car to assess the situation. Warne left the group to go to her hotel in Baltimore, where she would stay the night. She was planning to investigate the prevailing sentiment and activity in Baltimore, since Pinkerton was to return to Baltimore immediately after delivering Lincoln to Washington, D.C. The rest of the Lincoln entourage would be arriving from Harrisburg midday Saturday, as well. The sleeping car was disconnected from the PW&B train and towed by a team of horses along the rails on the cobblestone Pratt Street across the center of Baltimore about 14 blocks to the B&O terminal at Camden Street. The wait at the B&O Station itself was about 30 minutes.[115] The car was finally attached to the Washington-bound B&O train. Felton's package of "important papers" was delivered to the conductor, as it had been at the West Philadelphia station, and the journey continued. All of these events transpired without Marshal Kane's knowledge.

From Baltimore, Lincoln left for Washington at 4:15 a.m. The trip again proceeded without interruption, arriving in D.C. at 6:00 a.m. Saturday, February 23. Lincoln, Lamon, and Pinkerton then departed for the Willard Hotel. Along the route, Lincoln encountered an old friend, Congressman Elihu B. Washburne, and his secret trip was thus revealed.[116] Telegraph lines were reconnected at 8:00 a.m., and the word was sent back to Felton that the President-Elect had safely arrived at the Willard Hotel. The message, in code, read, "Plums delivered nuts safely." ("Plums" was the code word for Pinkerton; "nuts" was Lincoln). And that package of "important papers" was also delivered to the Willard Hotel, along with the President-Elect.

Mrs. Lincoln and the rest of the inaugural train departed for Baltimore on Saturday, February 23, as scheduled. Colonel John S. Gittings, the owner of the Northern Central Railroad, and James C. Clarke, the Superintendent of the Northern Central, boarded the train in Harrisburg to accompany the Lincoln entourage safely to Gittings's mansion. To prove that he had supreme confidence in the safe passage of the train, Clarke had his only son, aged five, with him. Northern Central employees were stationed every half mile to watch the tracks and protect against sabotage. Guards were stationed at every bridge. At least the segment of the trip from Harrisburg to the outskirts of Baltimore was likely to be safe.

Mrs. Lincoln left Harrisburg at 9:00 a.m. and arrived in Baltimore at 1:00 p.m. In the first car were the journalists, some political friends, and the Lincolns' son Robert. In the second car were the visitors from Baltimore, including that Republican Committee. In the third car were Mrs. Lincoln and their two youngest boys, William (Willie) and Thomas (Tad), the family physician Dr. W. S. Wallace, Norman B. Judd, John G. Nicolay, Colonel E. V. Sumner, John S. Gittings, and some other dignitaries.[117]

Since about 11:00 a.m., thousands of people had been gathering in the general area surrounding both Northern Central depots, the Bolton Street Terminal and the Calvert Street Station. By this time the entire police force of about 400 men had been mustered for the job of protecting the President-Elect, Kane's previous statements notwithstanding.[118] Mrs. Lincoln and her party passed nearly to the Calvert Street Station without any problems.[119]

The train stopped several blocks short of the Calvert Street Station, much to the chagrin of the crowd that had gathered at the station itself. Only about 200 people were present at this location between the Bolton and Calvert Street Stations, while crowd estimates at the Calvert Street Station itself were 10,000–20,000. Mrs. Lincoln and her party were escorted to the carriages awaiting her from Colonel Gittings. Gittings, Sumner, and Judge David Davis accompanied her to the Gittings Mansion near Mount Vernon Place. From the Calvert Street Station Robert B. Coleman escorted the rest of the party to the Eutaw House at the northwest corner of Baltimore and Eutaw Streets for a reception. Originally, the entire Lincoln party had been scheduled to go to the Eutaw House Hotel for a small, inconspicuous reception, but Gittings's invitation to Mr. and Mrs. Lincoln had split the party.[120]

The expressed reason for Mrs. Lincoln's early departure from the train just prior to the arrival at the Calvert Street Station was to avoid the crush of the crowd there and annoyance, noise, and confusion, rather than for fear of any violence (Figure 35). In addition, by departing the train early, Mrs. Lincoln could have the best views of Baltimore, including the Washington Monument.[121] This plan would have obviated the concern over Mrs. Lincoln's passage through the narrow vestibule in the Calvert Street Station where the assassins were to do their dirty work on President-Elect Lincoln. The *Baltimore Sun* said, "Every thing possible had been done to guarantee his [Lincoln's] safe arrival in Baltimore, and the mayor of the city had determined to give him a courteous reception, while the *entire police of the city* [emphasis added] was brought into requisition to preserve the peace, and to prevent the crowd from pressing too closely on the presidential party." The same *Sun* article also said,

10. The Baltimore Plot

Police arrangements for the reception were the amplest ever provided for any public occasion in Baltimore. Over two hundred and seventy men were detailed from the four districts for special duty, under the command of their respective captains and sergeants.[122]

In fact, the entire area proved to be relatively free of violence. Perhaps the group seeking to kill the President-Elect had heard about Lincoln's earlier secretive passage through town, and they saw no reason to harm other members of the party. Certainly the assassins had no beef to pick with Mrs. Lincoln. This was still an era when the President's family would not be considered to be an appropriate target for harm. She was not the object of their ire, so she was allowed to pass unharmed. Though she and part of her entourage went to the Gittings Mansion, the entire party was registered as attending the gathering at Coleman's Eutaw House Hotel on February 23.[123]

Newspapers reported that the sketchy news of Lincoln's previous passage "did not prevent such an assemblage of people at the Calvert Station as was probably never before witnessed in our city. At one o'clock it was actually impossible to approach within a square of the depot from any direction, and the ascent of Franklin street was crowded with people up to Courtland street."[124] The police presence was notable.[125] As Mrs. Lincoln arrived, Marshal Kane received word that President-Elect Lincoln had passed through Baltimore the previous night. He immediately dismissed many of the gathered force, knowing that the object of his protection wasn't on that train from Harrisburg.[126] Despite the large crowd, little serious mayhem occurred.[127]

Figure 35. "The Crowd at Baltimore Waiting for Mr. Lincoln, President-Elect of the United States." From the New York Public Library.

Mrs. Lincoln and her party, including her sons William ("Willie") and Thomas ("Tad") and the Baltimore Republican Reception Committee, completed their transport in carriages to the home of Colonel John S. Gittings as planned, absent her husband. The Baltimore Republican Reception Committee had been both hastily formed and confusingly organized. They expressed dismay at the President-Elect's absence.[128] One Baltimore newspaper said, "The Baltimore delegation were [sic] in particular very much mortified at the want of confidence displayed in thus avoiding a public reception in Baltimore."[129]

At the Gittings Mansion, Mrs. Lincoln was upset at the entire series of events over the last 24 hours. She saw no need for her husband's secretive passage to Washington, and she was distressed at the advice that Lincoln's friends had given him. Perhaps the great ultimate success of everyone's safe travel had hidden the danger from her eyes. Nevertheless, she was displeased.[130] The rest of the party on the train, including the Lincolns' son Robert, had gone to the Eutaw House for their luncheon.[131] All luggage went directly to the B&O Camden Street Station.

At about 3:00 p.m., both Lincoln parties were escorted to the Camden Street Station, where several thousand spectators had amassed to watch them depart for the trip from Baltimore to Washington, D.C. The contingents from both the Gittings Mansion and the Eutaw House made the trip across Baltimore without incident. There at the B&O Railroad Station Mrs. Lincoln and the other dignitaries boarded the train that took them to Washington. It left at 3:10 p.m., and a telegram at 5:00 p.m. announced that the party had arrived safely in D.C.

Lincoln's method of travel to Washington ultimately proved to be a great embarrassment. He was vilified by not only his enemies, but by some of his friends and supporters as well. The *Baltimore American and Commercial Advertiser* called the entry "not exactly capable of being praised as dignified or courageous." Newspapers said that "he should not have run on his first approach to slave territory."[132]

Lincoln himself later regretted the subterfuge, forgetting the real danger of assassination that had been present on the trip through Baltimore. He later told Lamon, "You know that the way we skulked into this city [Washington] has been a source of shame and regret for me, for it did look so cowardly."[133] A triumphant President-Elect became a comical coward to many observers, and his political reputation never entirely recovered from this secret entry to the Capitol. First impressions can be lasting. One newspaper said,

> Had we any respect for Mr. Lincoln, official or personal, as a man, or as President of the United States … the final escapade by which he reached the Capitol would have utterly demolished it, and overwhelmed us with mortification.… We do not believe the Presidency can ever be more degraded by any of his successors than it has by him, even before his inauguration.[134]

The Gettysburg *Compiler* of March 4, 1861, read, "The whole nation is humiliated, degraded by this wretched and cowardly conduct of the President elect."[135] Even Lincoln's friend Horace Greeley said, "Mr. Lincoln ought to have come through [Baltimore] by daylight, if one-hundred guns had been pointed at him."[136] The press was not happy with Lincoln.

After Lincoln's passage through Baltimore, Pinkerton returned to Baltimore on the night of February 23. There he conferred again with James H. Luckett, one of the real conspirators, to try to determine if the assassins had other plans to kill Lincoln. Pinkerton's memoirs recorded Luckett as saying that "they would yet make an attempt to assassinate Lincoln." Furthermore, Luckett repeatedly confirmed the plans he had set in place for Lincoln's passage through Baltimore: "if it had not been for d----d spies somewhere, Lincoln could never have passed through Baltimore; that the men were all ready to have done the job, and were in their places, and would have murdered the d----d Abolitionist had it not been that they were cheated."[137]

In the days after Lincoln's passage through Baltimore, Kane would recount his version of events. Kane had feared that the crowds would demonstrate against the Baltimore Republicans themselves in the gathering, though not Lincoln specifically. The *Baltimore American* later said that Lincoln had altered his travel plans "to avoid the attention of his political friends here whose unpopularity with the great mass of the people is so notorious."[138] The *Baltimore Clipper* concluded that Lincoln "*decamped to* avoid the *Baltimore Committee*, of whose approach he was secretly advised."[139] The *Baltimore American* said on February 26,

> It appears that a few hundred men, particularly obnoxious to the people and public sentiment of Baltimore, had determined to avail themselves of the opportunity to use Mr. Lincoln, and to accompany him in procession from the depot to his hotel.
>
> They applied to Marshal Kane for protection by the police. He advised against the proceeding, assuring the parties that while Mr. Lincoln, in his passage through Baltimore, would be treated with the respect due to him personally and to his high official position, there was no guaranty that the proposed procession would be similarly respected....
>
> It appears, however, that the parties insisted upon their programme, when Mr. Lincoln was advised of the facts, and urged [him] to pass immediately through to Washington....
>
> [T]he change of route and incognito entrance to Washington was caused by a desire to escape from his pretended friends here, and thus prevent a breach of the peace that would have been disgraceful to the city and derogatory to American character. We do not believe there was any intention to assault or even insult the president elect on the part of any portion of our community, but it is a notorious fact that the Baltimore republican committee, who proceeded to Harrisburg and declared their determination to escort Mr. Lincoln to his quarters, would have been pelted with eggs, if not otherwise maltreated.[140]

Kane, in a published letter dated February 27, 1861, said, "when I spoke of the rumors which had reached me of an intended republican display, by certain parties here, which, in my opinion, would be deemed offensive to the masses of our people..., [I feared that it] would invite decided marks of disapproval."[141]

The Board of Police of Baltimore also published a report on February 28:

> The Board of Police deem it proper to state, for the information of their fellow-citizens, that the accounts which have appeared in some newspapers of other cities that "the police authorities of Baltimore had determined to employ a force of only twenty men for the special duty of attending to the route of the President's cortège through Baltimore" on Saturday last, that, "yielding to the pressure of public opinion, they determined to have out the whole force, though they still believed that twenty men would be all-sufficient," or that they were influenced in the slightest degree in making or changing any of their arrangements by representations alleged to have been made to them by Mr. Kennedy, superintendent of the New York police, or by any other person or persons from New York or Washington, are all and each of them utterly untrue.[142]

Whether this plot would ever have been carried to completion if Lincoln had passed through Baltimore during daylight hours will never be known. One person traveling with Lincoln felt that the threat was real enough that he himself "made his will, sealed up the papers, and prepared for sudden death in case Mr. Lincoln should insist upon going this morning."[143] Charles P. Stone wrote to Lincoln on February 21 about a report from a New York detective: "there is serious danger of violence to and the assassination of Mr. Lincoln in his passage through that city."[144] Charles Gould wrote to his friend Henry Bowen on February 5: "Will you tell Mr. Lincoln that these facts are real, that they are unexaggerated—and that my statements can be relied on?"[145] Others thought that the plot was "manufactured by the New York sensation reporters."[146] The Baltimore Mayor at the time was George William Brown, and he wrote a retrospective in 1887 trying to clear the good name of Baltimore, saying, "much that is exaggerated and sensational has been circulated."[147] He surmised that some people were consumed "by the temptation of getting up a sensation of the first class," that Lincoln's flight was a "signal deliverance from an imaginary peril," and that his action exhibited a "want of confidence and respect manifested towards the city of Baltimore."[148]

Ferrandini and his co-conspirators had been suspected of planning foul play, but no charges were ever brought against him or his friends. Apparently no one had enough evidence then, and certainly now it's difficult to find concrete proof that he would have killed Lincoln if given the chance.

Even New York Superintendent of Police John Kennedy soon recanted his warnings about an assassination attempt. Perhaps his letter was politically motivated since Marshal George Kane had objected to the published versions of Kennedy's findings and advice to Lincoln, but Kennedy wrote to Kane on February 28:

> On the evening of Tuesday, 26th, several friends came into my office to learn the facts, whether any attempt was to have been made to assassinate Mr. Lincoln. I assured them there was no foundation in the story.... But no officer of mine has reported to me the actual existence of any band "organized for the purpose of assassinating the President elect." ...[T]hey have not reported to me that even these bodies [the Southern Volunteers] have resolved on assassination.... [O]n the 22nd, I sent a telegraph to Mr. Wood of Mr. Lincoln's party, advising him to go down on the Susquehannah [sic] road as perfectly safe.[149]

Kennedy appears to have told two versions of the story.

As Lincoln went to his inauguration on March 4, the plotters continued to scheme. While they planned further attempts at assassination, they were less organized and less likely to succeed. Indeed, they were unsuccessful. Lincoln was sworn in as President without any shots being fired, but hundreds of thousands of shots were about to commence as the Civil War began.

Ward Lamon wrote his memoirs about 11 years after the event, and in them he gave two conflicting views of the events. One claimed that the plot against Lincoln was real, the other that no plot existed. He said:

"For ten years the author [Lamon] implicitly believed in the reality of the atrocious plot.... It is perfectly manifest that there was no conspiracy,—no conspiracy of a hundred, of fifty, of twenty, of three; no definite purpose in the heart of even one man to murder Mr. Lincoln in Baltimore."

But later he said:

"It is now an acknowledged fact that there never was a moment from the day he [Lincoln] crossed the Maryland line, up to the time of his assassination, that he was not in danger by violence, that his life was spared until the night of the 14th of April, 1865, only through the ceaseless and watchful care of the guards thrown around him."[150]

Perhaps the passage of time had sharpened Lamon's deductive skills; perhaps hindsight had revealed the truth to him. Perspective changes as time passes. But certainly the man who saw it necessary to carry two guns, brass knuckles, a knife, and a "slug shot," and who offered Lincoln a gun to carry through Philadelphia and Baltimore, must have thought that a real danger existed. So his later protestations to the contrary seem disingenuous, or at least generated under a different set of assumptions and fears. Lending further skepticism to any version of Lamon's account is the fact that Pinkerton thought that Lamon was a buffoon, a "brainless egotistical fool."[151]

Most reports denying the reality of the plot came years after Lincoln traveled through Baltimore. Pinkerton's letters were written daily, in real time, concurrent with his investigation. They contained specific places, names, and dates. In this respect, they are the most compelling evidence extant. Furthermore, three independent and separate lines of evidence—from Dix, Seward (through Kennedy via letters from Scott and Seward senior), and Pinkerton—all yielded the same conclusions. So the plot was likely real, and Lincoln escaped assassination.

Even later, Kane again felt a need to present his side of the story of Lincoln's passage through Baltimore in a lengthy rebuttal to those who claimed that he had been in danger.[152] Stories continued to show Kane in a bad light, and perhaps he was considering running for office, so he told his perspective on Lincoln's trip, finishing with:

> I feel quite certain that no intelligent and honest mind will continue to credit the oft-reported slanders upon Baltimoreans of having contemplated a deed of such savage atrocity as that alleged to have been threatened by these detective policemen. That Mrs. Lincoln was not imposed upon by the invention of such people was abundantly shown in the fact that before starting from Baltimore for Washington she sent a request that I would call and afford her an opportunity of making her acknowledgments for the interest I had shown in the arrangements which had been made; but sudden and severe indisposition prevented me from doing so. As effectually as her husband may for the time have been duped by these people, and led to a course which was subsequently a matter of deep regret to himself and his friends, I had the very best reason to know that he was very soon undeceived, and that I could have enjoyed the most substantial evidence of his confidence and favor after he became the President, had I felt inclined to embrace it.
>
> Yours, very respectfully,
> Geo. P. Kane, Danville, Va.[153]

At this juncture, Kane was trying to convince his readers that no real threat to Lincoln had ever really existed in Baltimore. He had dispatched—to his mind—an appropriate police force to the Baltimore arrival of the Lincoln party.

11

The Baltimore Riot

The Baltimore riot of April 19, 1861, would become the second major defining moment of George Proctor Kane's career.

Threats and fears of Civil War abounded, and on April 15 President Lincoln issued a proclamation, requesting 75,000 militia troops "to cause the laws to be duly executed." He appealed "to all loyal citizens to favor, facilitate and aid this effort to maintain the honor, the integrity and existence of our National Union, and the perpetuity of popular government, and to redress wrongs already long enough endured." Many Southerners interpreted his plea for 75,000 soldiers as a de facto declaration of war. At the very least, it greatly increased the tension and excitement of the people of Baltimore. The quota of volunteers for Maryland was four regiments; Maryland's exact allocation was 3,123 soldiers, and these men were to serve for only 90 days.[1]

Northern state governments would respond quickly to Lincoln's request for 75,000 soldiers to protect Washington, D.C., a city vulnerable to the South's military. With Maryland to the north and Virginia to the south, Washington was in a perilous location. It could be isolated quickly, and such isolation might spell failure in any conflict about to arise. As Union troops gathered in the North and moved toward the Capitol, they encountered cheering crowds and warm welcomes. They would soon be disillusioned. The reception became more hostile as they moved closer to the South. Food lavished on the men by laudatory supporters in Massachusetts, New York, and Pennsylvania would be replaced by bricks and stones hurled by angry crowds in Maryland. Most Baltimoreans at that time thought that the troops were being recruited for war upon the South, though Lincoln would later argue that the request for Northern troops passing through Baltimore had been only to protect the Capitol itself from the Southern forces amassing across the Potomac River in Virginia.

Thomas H. Hicks, Governor of Maryland, was—as always—hesitant and ambivalent, vacillating and indecisive. He knew that Union troops were about to cross Maryland on their march to Washington. Hicks wrote to Lincoln on April 17, 1861, asking for confirmation that any soldiers recruited from Maryland would be used only for "defense of the United States Government, the maintenance of Federal authority, and the protection of the Federal capital. I [Hicks] also understand it was the intention of the United States Government not to require their services outside of Maryland except in defense of the District of Columbia." Secretary of War

Simon Cameron replied, assuring Hicks that soldiers from Maryland would be used exactly as Hicks understood.[2] Initially, Hicks had successfully avoided addressing the secession issue by refusing to call the Maryland Legislature to a special session to debate whether Maryland would remain in the Union or secede. For the entirety of the winter of 1860–1861 he had continued to withstand pressures to call this special session, but by April 1861 he had to make his choice. Lincoln was calling for troops. Hicks thought that defending Maryland itself, the federal capital, and the District of Columbia was acceptable for deployment of Maryland troops, and he issued a proclamation on April 18, reassuring the citizens of Baltimore and Maryland that the Maryland troops' deployment would be limited. But only three days after calling for troops to serve for 90 days, the length of estimated service was extended to three years.[3] Hicks requested not only that guns be possessed only by men loyal to the federal government, but also that he be given sufficient weapons to arm the troops requested by Lincoln from the State of Maryland.[4] John Nicolay and John Hay, in their history of Lincoln, said, "the Governor of Maryland was a friend of the Union, though hardly of that unflinching fearlessness needed in revolutionary emergencies. Whatever of hesitancy or vacillation he sometimes gave way to, resulted from a constitutional timidity rather than from a want of patriotism."[5]

Hicks made a proclamation on April 19, 1861, that said in part, "The unfortunate state of affairs now existing in the country has greatly excited the people of Maryland. In consequence of our peculiar position, it is not to be expected that the people of the State can unanimously agree upon the best mode of preserving the honor and integrity of the State, and of maintaining within her limits that peace so earnestly desired by all good citizens."[6] Mayor George William Brown concurred and said, "I cannot withhold my expression of satisfaction at his resolution that no troops shall be sent from Maryland to the soil of any other state."[7] Emotions ran high, and Marshal Kane was called upon to intervene at many confrontations. Kane supported the rights of citizens to display symbols—Confederate or Union—as long as the Baltimoreans remained orderly and did not "break the peace."[8]

As the Civil War was about to explode, Union troops were moving south, traveling to protect Washington. The first soldiers, estimated to be between 460 and 530 men, were to come from Pennsylvania in two trains of 21 railroad cars at about 8:00 a.m. on April 18, 1861.[9] On April 16, Governor Andrew Gregg Curtin of Pennsylvania had ordered men and artillery to go to Harrisburg for their trip to Washington.[10] On April 18, Governor Hicks arrived in Baltimore. Marshal Kane had tried to learn details of these troop movements earlier, writing on April 16 to Mr. William Crawford, an agent for the PW&B Railroad, asking, "Is it true as stated that an attempt will be made to pass the volunteers from New York intended to war upon the South over your road to-day? It is important that we have an explicit understanding on the subject."[11]

As Baltimoreans considered the implications of Northern troops passing through the city, a local chapter of the National Volunteers met on the morning of April 18. Gathering at the Taylor Building on Fayette Street, T. Parkin Scott talked of the anticipated movement of Union troops through the streets of Baltimore. Though Scott's speech strongly favored the South, Scott urged calm and tolerance because he felt that the soldiers "could do no harm" in their passage through the city. Dr. James A. Stewart made a motion at the meeting to urge the presidents of the local railroads (the Northern Central, the B&O, and the PW&B lines) to refuse to transport Northern troops on their trains. The motion passed.[12]

The first wave of soldiers from Pennsylvania arrived at the outer depot of the Northern Central Railroad (the Bolton Street Station) at the projected time of 1:00 p.m. on April 18. Kane was there with Mayor Brown upon their arrival, but Brown was called away to confer with Governor Hicks just as the troops arrived. These 600 Pennsylvania troops marched to the Camden Station, but they discovered that the train to Washington had already departed, and they were forced to march slightly further west to the Mount Clare Station. These troops were ill-outfitted—many had no guns, most had no uniforms, and they appeared hungry.

Several thousand people awaited the arrival of these men from the North, and the Baltimoreans entertained themselves by singing "Dixie's Land." One estimate set the number of police at nearly 300, another at 120 (the entire contingent of Baltimore police at that time was 398 officers). Even before the troops reached the Mount Clare Depot, they "were subjected to numerous indignities, such as being spit upon, having their coat tails pulled, and references made to their beggarly appearance; cries of 'let the police go, and we'll lick you,' 'wait till you see Jeff Davis,' 'we'll see you before long,' 'you'll never go back to Pennsylvania,' and many similar expressions. But for the efficient police arrangements there would undoubtedly have been a collision between the populace and the military."[13] The passage of these first troops through Baltimore city was otherwise reasonably uneventful.[14] Baltimoreans hadn't welcomed this first wave of Northern troops from Pennsylvania; however, their troops' march was safely conducted without death or injury because of the police protection afforded them:

> Marshal Kane was present in person with about 120 policemen, who guarded as well as they could the persons of the troops from actual assault, and prevented a breach of the peace. They could not stop the mouths of the people, however, and the scene that ensued and continued along the march was ludicrous, and the expressions not at all complimentary to the military excursionists. Hisses, groans, cheers, and imprecations were mingled by the crowd....
> ... More northern troops will arrive to-day, and henceforth the sight of marching soldiers and beating drums will be no novelty in this city.[15]

Other reports from more Southern-leaning newspapers told the story with a bit more flavor. *The Daily Exchange and Gazette*, whose editor, Thomas W. Hall, Jr., would soon be arrested for having treasonous thoughts that supported the South, claimed that most Northern troops joined the military simply to be fed and to acquire a new set of clothes.[16]

Kane then awaited the next trainload of soldiers, expected later that afternoon at the President Street Station. In fact, they did not arrive as expected, and Kane dismissed his police force to await their arrival at some unknown future hour. About 800 pro-secession men mingled in the streets of Baltimore on that night of April 18, wearing small Confederate flags on their lapels. Secession badges were visible everywhere. Around this time they were holding that Southern Rights Convention at the Taylor Building, and they frequently clashed with the few Union supporters—some of them belonging to a group called "Minute Men"—in the city. The *Baltimore Sun* reported, "Secession badges and flags of the Southern Confederacy have grown with the last 48 hours into universal demand, and their sale brings money to the pockets of scores of boys who cry them vociferously through the streets from morning till night and away into the night…. A great number of Confederate flags have been flung out."[17] Confrontations numbered in the hundreds of participants, sometimes in the thousands. Marshal Kane frequently needed to intervene in these disputes.[18] Kane was not content simply to issue orders to the police. He joined his men in the streets to quell disturbances, often putting his own life at risk. Fortunately the opposing sides chose to gather at separate locations, about 1.5 miles apart. The Southerners amassed near the Bolton Street Station, while the Northerners gathered on the two-block segment of Baltimore Street between Holliday Street and Calvert Street.

Southern Rights men raised a Confederate flag at the corner of Greenmount and Charles Streets. They also succeeded in firing a one-hundred-gun salute to the South, and they managed to keep the flag flying for all to see.[19] However, only a few arrests were necessary during the entire day.[20] Another contingent of Northern troops would soon arrive and march through the center of Baltimore.

Simon Cameron, Secretary of War, wrote to Governor Hicks on April 18 after hearing that future Northern troops might have some difficulty passing through Baltimore:

> The President is informed that threats are made, and measures taken, by unlawful combinations of misguided citizens of Maryland to prevent by force the transit of United States troops across Maryland, on their way, pursuant to orders, to the defense of this capital….
> Such an attempt could have only the most deplorable consequences; and it would be as agreeable to the President as it would be to yourself that it should be prevented or overcome by the loyal authorities and citizens of Maryland, rather than averted by any other means.
>
> I am, very respectfully, yours, &c.,
> Simon Cameron, Secretary of War[21]

Both Hicks and Brown acknowledged the emergency and urged calm.

Lincoln's call for soldiers to defend Washington, D.C., had been answered quickly by the Sixth Regiment of Massachusetts Volunteers. It was composed of many diverse companies, all with different uniforms, training, and backgrounds, most men with weapons, though a few were unarmed. Soldiers in the Regiment came from four Massachusetts counties—Middlesex, Essex, Suffolk, and Worcester—and from over 30 towns. Their strength was estimated to be about 700 soldiers. Emotions were high. Marshal Kane still had been given no details about the troops' arrival. He began assembling his police force again, not knowing exactly what was happening. He had been ready the day before, on April 18, but the troops had not arrived.[22] In addition to these Massachusetts troops, ten companies of Pennsylvania soldiers, numbering about 1,800, being parts of two regiments of the Washington Brigade of Philadelphia with General William F. Small as commander, joined forces and traveled in the same train to Baltimore. The vast majority of these latter troops likewise had no uniforms or weapons, and the Pennsylvania men were essentially untrained.

The train left Philadelphia at 3:00 a.m. on April 19. It passed to Perryville on the eastern shore of the Susquehanna River, where the troops were ferried across on the steamboat *Maryland* to Havre de Grace. From there the train journey continued to the President Street Station in Baltimore.

During the trip, Quartermaster James Munroe had issued six rounds of ammunition to each soldier in the Massachusetts Regiment.[23] Colonel Edward F. Jones gave them their orders for the "rules of engagement":

> After leaving Philadelphia I received intimation that our passage through the city of Baltimore would be resisted. I caused ammunition to be distributed and arms loaded, and went personally through the cars, and issued the following order, viz: "The regiment will march through Baltimore in column of sections, arms at will. You will undoubtedly be insulted, abused, and, perhaps, assaulted, to which you must pay no attention whatever, but march with your faces to the front, and pay no attention to the mob, even if they throw stones, bricks, or other missiles; but, if you are fired upon and any one of you is hit, your officers will order you to fire. Do not fire into any promiscuous crowds, but select any man whom you may see aiming at you, and be sure you drop him."[24]

At 11:00 a.m. on April 19, this train of 35 cars arrived at the President Street Station. On board the train were the soldiers of those 11 companies of the Sixth Regiment of Massachusetts, the First and Fourth Regiments of Pennsylvania, and Philadelphia's Washington Brigade. In command were Colonel Edward F. Jones for the Massachusetts troops from Lowell, Boston, and Acton; General William F. Small commanded the soldiers from Philadelphia. Little did they know it, but within their ranks would be the first fatalities of the Civil War.

Kane first received word about the Massachusetts troops in a message on Friday, April 19, at 8:20 a.m., stating that the soldiers would be at the Camden Station in about 30 minutes, meaning that they had already arrived at the President Street Station and were en route across town. Kane and 50 men of his police force hurried to the Camden Station, at which time Kane received a contradictory word that the trainload had just left the Susquehanna River, meaning that they were still 40–50 miles away from President Street Station. Unsure exactly what was happening, Kane sent most of the police to a nearby police station to await further word about the troops' movements. Kane called for Mayor Brown, Police Commissioner Davis, and the rest of the Police Commissioners (except for Hinks, who was out of town) to come to the Camden Station to await the arrival of the troops, where they would board the next train to Washington. Why Kane positioned himself and the police command officials at the terminus of the Massachusetts troops' journey and not at the beginning of their trip across town is perplexing, though reports from the time said that "the police were requested by the agent of the [rail]road to be in attendance at the latter [Camden] station."[25] Presumably, both Kane and Brown suspected that if any trouble occurred, it would be at the B&O's Camden Station. They knew, though, that the route of the soldiers would take them about one mile through the heart of downtown Baltimore, most of the march being along Pratt Street. Their passage through town would be extremely exposed to the citizenry that had proved on the previous day to contain many Southern agitators, many of whom were easily aroused to confrontation and perhaps to violence. While troops were beginning their trek across town, Marshal Kane next heard that a riot was in progress along the route from the President Street Station to the Camden Station. The Police Commissioners ordered Kane to use the entirety of his police force, if necessary, to protect the Massachusetts troops and to keep order in the city. Kane replied that "if he and his whole force lost their lives the troops should be protected."[26] Kane then hurried with his force of about 50 men to Pratt Street and ran eastward toward the President Street Station. The *Daily Exchange* reported that the city expressed "sheer indignation by groans for Hicks, Lincoln and the Federal Government, and cheers for Jefferson Davis and the Southern Confederacy."[27] The *South* said that the gathered crowd "vociferously cheered for Jeff. Davis and the Southern Confederacy."[28]

The first of the Massachusetts soldiers traveled across town in nine horse-drawn cars that left the President Street Station at about 11:30 a.m. While horses pulled the cars within the city of Baltimore, the cars traveled on train tracks, obeying regulations that steam engines not be used within the city. Relative peace prevailed at the start of this transfer. Soldiers were frightened as they rode the cars through the city, and they closed the windows to avoid being seen and perhaps being the targets of rocks or bullets. These first nine cars passed essentially unhindered, except for verbal taunts and abuse. They peacefully loaded into the cars at the B&O Camden Station to take them to Washington, about 31 miles away, but at about this time word came that rioters were attempting to tear up the train tracks between Baltimore and Washington. Marshal Kane thus dispatched some of the police to go as far as Relay House, a station about nine miles southwest of Baltimore, to protect the rails.

The next car, the tenth, inexplicably stopped opposite Commerce Street, only halfway to its destination at the Camden Station.[29] Here the crowd started throwing rocks and bricks, and the driver of the car quickly attached the horse team to the opposite end of the car, pulling it back nearly to the President Street Station. By now, the Baltimore crowds were working to block and destroy the crosstown train tracks. This tenth car carrying the troops then made another attempt to reach the Camden Station but was derailed by the obstructions already placed on the tracks. A passing work crew briefly placed the car back on the tracks. It wasn't long before the crowd—now estimated at between 800 and 1,000 persons—was throwing rocks, bricks, and stones at the troops in the car. The Pratt Street Bridge itself was being repaired, and rocks and bricks were readily available to be used as missiles. Rocks shattered the windows, and some of the soldiers were struck. True to their orders, the soldiers at first refrained from responding to the attack.

As the car neared Gay Street, bystanders further obstructed the tracks using more rocks, paving stones, cobblestones, and sand being used to repair Pratt Street. In other places, rioters destroyed the tracks themselves. In addition, they piled ships' anchors pulled from the Gay Street dock onto the rubble, one estimate reporting eight massive anchors obstructing the passage of the horse-drawn cars. It was clear that no more soldiers would be traveling to the Camden Station by railroad car. All further travel would be by foot.

This tenth car had to stop once again and return to the President Street Station. There the men disembarked and prepared to march through the city with the remainder of the men on the train, taking about 15 minutes to achieve their military marching formations. Four companies now remained to march the gauntlet on foot.³⁰ As they awaited the organization of the men into rows and columns—about 220 soldiers in total—the crowds were increasing, both in size and in anger. There were now as many as 2,000 Baltimoreans watching the troops, hooting and hissing and cheering the Confederacy. As the soldiers left the horse-drawn cars, they gathered initially in single file, then in double file, then in columns of four, while the crowds pressed toward them.³¹

At about this same time, additional crowds were gathering around the President Street Station. One group, allegedly directed by a local tough and political leader of the American Party named George Konig, bore a secession flag (a circle of eight white stars on solid blue). They positioned themselves in the front of the Union troops as the soldiers began to march toward the Camden Station. It was an unusual sight, and one that would remain etched in the memories of many Baltimoreans—Northern soldiers following the Southern symbol, some reports having Konig as the man carrying the flag. All of the Union troops remained calm, except for one. This soldier tried to grab the flag, but the rioters restrained him. Southern sympathizers rescued and protected the Confederate flag, and they continued to march in front of the Massachusetts and Pennsylvania soldiers.

Only about 100 yards from the railroad depot, civilians supporting the Union again tried to grab that Confederate flag leading the procession, and the Confederate sympathizers attacked them. The Unionists fled to be closer to the troops, upon which movement the crowd began to throw more rocks and stones. As the troops reached Fawn Street, the rocks found their mark, and William Patch from Massachusetts was struck. He fell to the gutter and was beaten by the crowd before the police could intervene. Immediately thereafter a second soldier was struck and seriously injured. With this indignity, the troops began to march "double time," running at a faster pace as the shower of missiles increased, and two other soldiers were hit by rocks near the corner of President and Stiles Streets. Here a few police worked diligently to prevent additional injury, and they aided the fallen soldiers.

Once the report of a riot in progress reached Mayor Brown, he himself departed for Pratt Street. Marshal Kane dispatched the officers who had been waiting at the B&O Camden Station to the scene, and Kane likewise went as quickly as he could. Both Kane and Brown were running toward the collision between the soldiers and the Baltimore rioters.

Here the police intervened to try to restore calm. The Baltimore crowd stood firmly in front of the soldiers, who turned as if trying to retreat back to the railroad station. To the cries of "Head them off," others in the crowd moved to the rear of the marching troops, completely blocking their ability to move either forward or backward. Then the police escort formed protective groups both in the front and at the rear of the troops, and they resumed their march across town toward the B&O depot. The police were described here as "untiring in their efforts to preserve the peace."³² Kane had not yet personally arrived at this particular scene.

Mayor Brown had left the Camden Station with Police Commissioners Gatchell, Howard and Davis slightly earlier than Kane, and Brown reached the scene first, somewhere near the Maltby House at the northwest corner of Light and Pratt Streets, only about five blocks from the Camden Station. He identified himself to the troops, saying, "I'm the Mayor of Baltimore," and they accepted him at his word. Brown convinced them not to march or run so rapidly, as he thought that their rapid pace was agitating the crowd. Brown continued to Smith's Wharf, where he ordered men to remove impediments on the tracks. Pandemonium in the crowd was fierce. Guns were already being discharged, and men had already been killed and wounded. Captain Albert S. Follansbee of Company C said, "We have been attacked without provocation." By this time, Mayor Brown was standing with the Union soldiers, and he told them, "You must defend yourselves."[33]

Kane and some additional 40–50 policemen encountered the Union troops at Light Street, not far from the Camden Station. Whether Kane did everything he could do to quell the riot will never be known. Men in the crowd actually cheered Kane, saying, "Hurra[h] for Marshal Kane—drive the damned sons of bitches back," so at least the local perception was that Kane was firmly committed to the Southern side of the evolving riot. He ordered the police to open their ranks to allow the troops to pass through them; then the police closed ranks again to re-form a barrier at the rear against the crowd of the mob. Kane thereafter positioned himself between the troops and the Baltimore citizens at the tail of the marching soldiers. By now many in the crowd were exchanging gunfire with the soldiers, and many on both sides were being killed or injured. Kane shouted at the crowd between Light and Charles Streets, "Keep back, men, or I'll shoot!"[34] Surprisingly, this calmed the situation, and the soldiers continued toward the train to take them to Washington.

The crowd continued its march to the Camden Station. People began to rush the train at this B&O station where the Massachusetts troops were preparing to leave for Washington. As Kane arrived back at Camden Station, bricks and stones continued to fly, and the occasional shot was fired. Soon a slight calm returned as the last of the troops arrived. The soldiers initially quickly boarded the train cars that were bound for Washington, and they aimed their muskets out the windows of the cars, but Police Commissioner Davis convinced Commander Jones to order them to withdraw their guns.[35] The Southern men in the crowd next shouted commands to their cohorts to destroy the track between Baltimore and Washington, but again the police intervened.

Calm finally descended on the scene, and Kane subsequently dismissed the police force, thinking that the conflict had ended. He was headed back toward his office when he heard that there were some stranded soldiers still remaining at the President Street Station. He next hurried there to find that the Massachusetts regimental marching band had been attacked near the President Street Station, and many of them had fled the scene. Some Pennsylvania troops also remained near the President Street Station.[36] The police again had to rescue the soldiers, helping them to board the train cars to take them back toward the Susquehanna River and then to Philadelphia. However, some of these stragglers had already disappeared into local Baltimore neighborhoods where sympathetic citizens gave them refuge. Kane felt vindicated in his actions: "The earnest expressions of gratitude which I received from the persons thus rescued, left on my mind the conviction that I had done my duty."[37] Some of the soldiers sought safety at the police stations; from there they were soon transported back to Philadelphia or at least as far as Havre de Grace by rail.[38]

The size of this riot has been hotly debated for over 150 years. Some estimates put the number of the Baltimore rioters at 8,000–10,000. One newspaper estimated the crowd at the Camden Station alone to be 6,000–7,000.[39] Others estimate as few as 250 "active participants." Likely many of the attendees were simply onlookers and not belligerents themselves. The fact that Marshal Kane was able to quell the fighting—or at least to protect the Massachusetts troops—suggests that the smaller number of actual rioters was more accurate.[40]

It's unclear who fired the first shot of the melee, though it is generally accepted that it was near the intersection of President Street and Pratt Street, while the heaviest fighting occurred near Pratt Street at South Street. All reports suggested that initiation of the gunfire was not the result of any official military order to shoot at the Baltimore citizens, though some reports blame Follansbee for such an order. Mayor Brown had shouted at both the soldiers and the crowd, "For God's sake don't shoot!" However, his entreaties went unheeded. It seemed to Brown that the innocent bystanders were suffering more from the gunfire than the citizens actually shooting at the soldiers[41] (Figure 36).

Likely the most accurate representation of the beginning of gunfire came from George W. Booth, a 16-year-old member of the Baltimore militia, the Independent Greys. He claimed that a rock or stone struck a Union soldier in the ranks of the marching troops at approximately Pratt and Commerce Streets. That soldier dropped his musket, and a citizen immediately picked it up and fired it into the columns of marching soldiers. Then apparently the rest of the soldiers began to fire back at the crowd, starting a wild exchange of bullets from all manner of weapons.

Union reports said that the gunfire started earlier, when the last of the railroad cars was being towed across the city to Camden Station.[42] Soldiers were being wounded by the fusillade of paving stones being thrown by the rioters, but the soldiers did not shoot into the crowd of citizens lining the street. One of the Massachusetts soldiers then had a thumb blown off by a shot from the Baltimore mob, and he pleaded with his Commander to be allowed to return fire. The Commander, Major Benjamin F. Watson, told the soldiers to lie on the floor of the railroad car and to load their guns, then rise and shoot out the windows "at will." The order to the troops from Captain Albert S. Follansbee apparently came later as they marched through Baltimore on Pratt Street, after they themselves had also taken gunfire from the mob.[43]

Colonel Edward Jones, the Commander of the soldiers, claimed that the citizens discharged their weapons first: "pistol-shots were numerously fired into the ranks."[44] Some later reports even named the actual first shooter as E. W. Beatty.[45] Baltimore citizens disagreed, averring that the soldiers loosed the first volley. Feeling themselves without other options, someone—likely one of the commanding officers—gave the soldiers the order to fire their weapons; whether that was before or after citizens had opened fire will never be known conclusively. Even in court, responsibility for beginning the shooting during the riot was never completely settled. Charges were filed, however, against some men *participating* in the riot, though not charging them with *starting* the riot. On July 11, 1861, a grand jury of the United States District Court rendered a wordy indictment against one Baltimorean named Samuel Mactier, saying that he

11. The Baltimore Riot

Figure 36. "First Blood: The Sixth Massachusetts Regiment Fighting Their Way Through Baltimore, April 19, 1861." From *Harper's Weekly*.

with force of arms, maliciously and traitorously did conspire, consent and agree with divers other false traitors, whose names are to the jurors aforesaid unknown, to aid and assist the aforesaid evil-disposed bodies of men so as aforesaid levying and carrying on an open and public insurrection, rebellion and war, to subvert and overthrow the government established in the United States of America.[46]

Mactier's bail was set at $40,000, and the trial was scheduled for November 1861. Five other men were also indicted with same charges.[47] The case dragged through the courts, with Mactier pleading for clemency to Secretary of War Edwin M. Stanton on March 28, 1864 (his plea was denied). The case was not dismissed until November 4, 1868.[48] Furthermore, the United States Circuit Court of Justices Roger B. Taney and William F. Giles indicted a total of 61 men for treason in 1861, including George P. Kane. Each man indicted had the $40,000 bail applied uniformly. While Kane was listed in the indictment,[49] he was never prosecuted for this particular charge.[50]

The first Baltimorean to be struck by a bullet apparently was Francis X. Ward, a young lawyer and a member of the City Guard Battalion, who was wounded in the left groin.[51] Ward returned the gunfire after being shot, striking the soldier who shot him.[52] Police protected this soldier from being beaten to death by the crowd, and citizens carried him to safety in a nearby store. However, his wound would prove fatal.

The last chance for the Baltimore citizens to express their disgust for the passage of federal troops through the city would be as the train left the Camden Station on its way to Washington. Marshal Kane's presence at the depot had calmed the tensions somewhat. The Union troops, however, believed that many of the police force didn't want to protect them: "*the police having—and many of them caring to have—no power to stay the tumult.*"⁵³ Union observers had their own opinion about the lack of police protection they were afforded during their march across Baltimore, though they appreciated the refuge provided by some Baltimore citizens. One soldier said,

> On our way [marching across Baltimore] we saw squads of police, who took no notice of us, evidently regarding the whole thing as a good joke…. After running in this way for a half mile, as near as we could judge, we were encountered by a party of women, partly Irish, partly German, and some American, who took us into their houses, removed the stripes from our pants, and we were furnished with old clothes of every description for disguise. We were treated here as well as we could have been in our own homes. Everything we wished was furnished, and nothing would be taken therefor [sic]; but we were told that it would be an insult to offer it.⁵⁴

Citizens continued to throw rocks as the 13 cars pulled away from the Camden Station platform at 12:45 p.m. Kane "ascended the steps of the building of the Railroad Company, amid deafening cheers for 'Marshal Kane,' and the assurances of those present that they would do whatever he directed."⁵⁵ Kane pleaded with them to obey the laws. He urged them to disperse, which they did.

The initial portion of the trip from Camden Station to Washington was difficult, as well. The crowd followed the train, attempting to halt its progress at many points.

At the same time, many of the Pennsylvania militia (estimated to be about a thousand) and the Regimental Marching Band of the Sixth Massachusetts Infantry Regiment and portions of Companies C, D, I, and L (about 130 men), who had been left stranded at or near the President Street Station, began their return to the North. Most returned to Philadelphia by the same train route at about 2:00 p.m., arriving at the Broad Street Philadelphia Station at about 11:00 p.m.⁵⁶

By the end of this April 19 riot, four soldiers lay dead, as well as 12 Baltimore civilians.⁵⁷ Approximately another 35–36 of the troops were injured, as well as countless civilian rioters and bystanders. The first soldier mortally wounded—Corporal Sumner Henry Needham of Company I, the Sixth Massachusetts Infantry from Lawrence, Massachusetts—is often cited as the first fatality of the Civil War, the victim of a skull fracture, dying on April 27.⁵⁸ While Needham was the first struck with a mortal wound, the other three Massachusetts soldiers actually died before Needham.

Newspapers reported, somewhat incorrectly, "The city is in great excitement. Martial law has been proclaimed [it hadn't]. The military are rushing to their armories. Civil war has commenced. The railroad track is said to be torn up outside of the city. Parties threaten to destroy the Pratt street bridge."⁵⁹ Of the thousands of civilians involved in the April 19 riot, only seven men were recorded as having been immediately arrested, though newspapers cited "great numbers" of arrests.⁶⁰ This event would come to be called "The Riot of April 19," "The Pratt Street Riot," or "The April 19 Riot."

In the excitement of the activity along Pratt Street, Kane was also called upon to protect a cache of ammunition and gunpowder from the rioting mobs in an ammunition magazine in Canton, east of the city center and across the water, northeast of

Fort McHenry. Kane took charge of the gunpowder and provided police protection for it. He also arranged the use of a tugboat to defend Fort McHenry from the water side, near the gunpowder storage facility. By the end of the riot and its aftermath, both the gunpowder and Fort McHenry remained safe.[61] Kane had discharged his duty to protect the city, in spite of his Southern leanings.

A little-known fact is that John Wilkes Booth was in Baltimore during this riot, as well as during Lincoln's passage through Baltimore on the way to his inauguration earlier in February. One "J. W. Booth" from Boston registered at Coleman's Eutaw House on Saturday, April 20, and he was given room #76 (Figure 37).

The April 19 riot was one of the cardinal tests of Kane's duty to enforce Northern laws. Here was a police chief bound to keep the peace in Baltimore, but his innate sentiments lay in the camps of the South. Kane had been accused of deploying only a small force to protect President-Elect Lincoln on his passage through Baltimore a few weeks earlier. While his initial response to guard Lincoln may have been rather anemic, he ultimately provided a sufficient protective force for the Lincoln entourage, which of course didn't include Lincoln himself, as the course of events evolved. Kane was now confronted by angry Baltimoreans wanting to harm the Northern troops, and he was willing to risk his own life to keep the peace, even though his heart identified with the sentiments of the South and the rioters. He positioned himself between the Massachusetts troops and the mob, a maneuver that could have cost him his life.

Many sources reported that Kane distinguished himself perhaps better on April 19 than at any other time during his public service. By some accounts, his courage shone through his own partisan leanings, and he discharged his duty in a manner that gained him national recognition. Mayor Brown would say of Kane, "It is doing bare justice to say that the board of police, the marshal of police, and the men under his command, exerted themselves bravely, efficiently, skillfully, and in good faith to preserve the peace and protect life.... [But] for the timely arrival of Marshal Kane with his force, as I have described, the bloodshed would have been great."[62] Even years later, Massachusetts soldiers who had been protected lauded Kane's bravery and calm command of the situation in the mean streets of Baltimore. Kane was commonly painted as the hero who waded into a riot, standing between angry Baltimoreans and the Massachusetts troops, with his famous shout, "Keep back, men, or I'll shoot."[63]

Some witnesses even described Kane as a hero. Richard Norris, Jr., wrote a letter to the Board of Police about what he saw on the streets of Baltimore on April 19:

> Marshal Kane made every possible effort to protect the troops; caught hold of many of the assailants, drove them back and prevented them from continuing their attacks; addressed others declaring they were bringing disgrace on the city by assailing unarmed men. His whole conduct was perfectly fearless.[64]

The Massachusetts soldiers believed that Mayor Brown had also acted honorably during their passage through Baltimore. Their testimonials spoke of Brown's bravery and of his pivotal role in protecting them:

> I have my doubts whether we should have gotten through [the streets of Baltimore] at all without his [Brown's] aid. (Charles Babbidge, Chaplain, Sixth Regiment, Massachusetts Volunteer Militia)

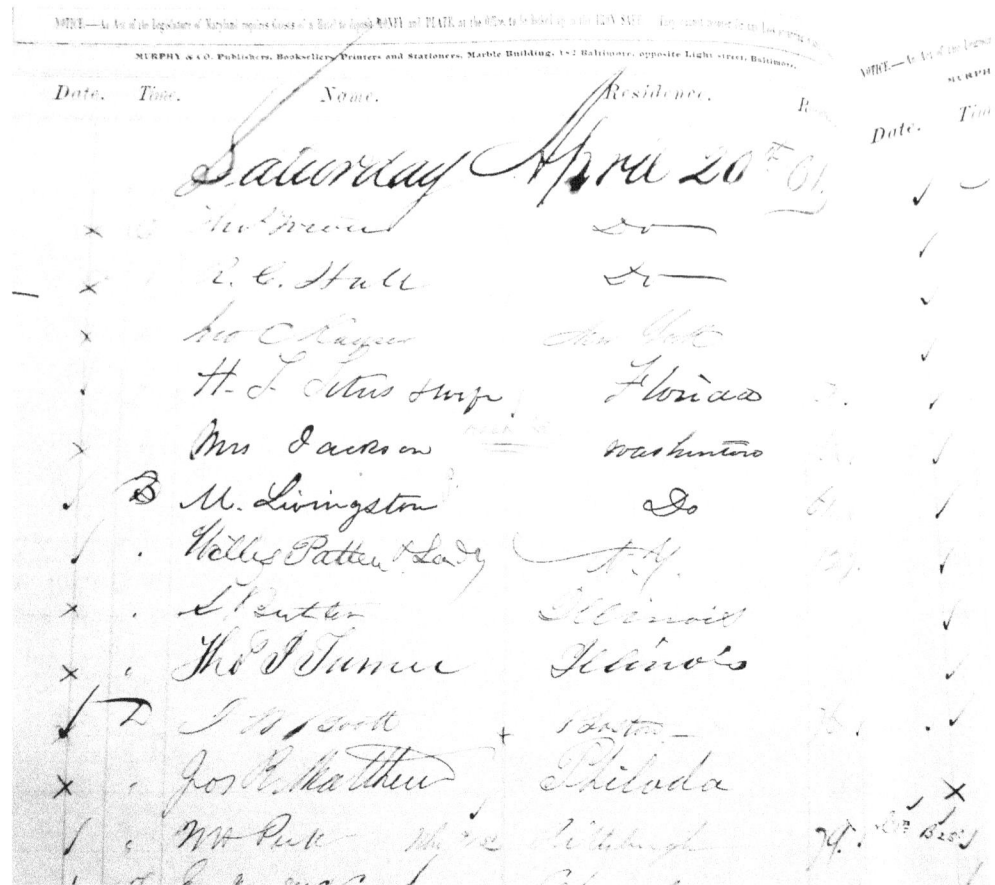

Figure 37. Page from the Eutaw House Hotel register dated April 20, 1861, showing that one "J. W. Booth" from Boston (10th entry from the top) was given room #76 in the hotel. From the Maryland Center for History and Culture.

> I can bear witness to his [Brown's] patriotic and heroic conduct on that occasion. (A. S. Follansbee, Captain, Company C, Sixth Regiment, Massachusetts Volunteer Militia)[65]

Colonel Edward F. Jones of the Sixth Regiment, Massachusetts Volunteer Militia, wrote to Marshal Kane on April 28, 1861: "I am, with my command, much indebted to you. Many, many thanks for the Christian conduct of the authorities of Baltimore in this truly unfortunate affair."[66] Furthermore, Mayor Brown himself lauded Kane's behavior on that fateful day: "the wrath of the mob [of Baltimore citizens against the Massachusetts troops] was directed against the militia, and an attack would certainly have been made but for the vigilance and determination of the police, under the command of Marshal Kane."[67]

However, opinions of Kane's behavior were deeply polarized. Witnesses near the President Street Station claimed that police officers nearby refused to arrest the men who were protesting the passage of the Union troops. They contended that the tone of the Baltimore police force, trickling down from its chief,[68] reflected their Southern allegiance. Some accounts even painted Kane in far darker colors. The witnesses at the federal grand jury convened between September 4 and October 12, 1861, to investigate the riot were far less laudatory. Most said that Kane allowed the crowd to escape from his control at a time when a riot could have been prevented. Representative testimonies reported:

> William P. Smith, Baltimore resident, reported that the police "did not offer to protect the [Massachusetts] troops, even 'pushing them [the Massachusetts troops] about in a hostile manner.... I told them [the police] ten men if resolute could put down the riot.'"[69]
>
> Edward Airey, Baltimore carter: "The police could have stopped the riot but did not try. Stones came from right among the police."[70]
>
> John Ehrman, Baltimore carpenter: "The police acted in such a way that I told some of them they were heading the mob."[71]
>
> William J. Stowell, Depot Master of the President Street Railroad Station: "My impression was the officers did not want to make any arrests—when urged to do so would laugh. There were officers enough there to stop the riot; but evidently did not want to do so."[72]

Of these testimonies at the grand jury referencing the police in general[73] or Kane in particular, virtually all spoke negatively about the conduct of the Baltimore Police force under Marshal Kane. It appeared that Kane initially allowed rioting and mayhem because it fit his sentiments about the Northern troops passing through the city. It seemed as though Kane had a change of heart after the riot's intensity exploded. His initial acceptance, sanctioning, or endorsement of the mob's abuse of the Massachusetts troops changed to a recognition of the duty he had to protect the soldiers on their passage through Baltimore. Kane thus became famous as Maryland's "most loyal rebel."[74]

One of the issues for which Kane received serious condemnation was his note to a friend—Bradley T. Johnson, a lawyer, militia organizer, State's Attorney for Frederick County, Maryland, and newspaper editor in Frederick, Maryland. Many newspapers also decried Johnson as a "notorious traitor." Kane wrote to Johnson, asking for help to defend the city: "Bring your men by the first train, and we will arrange with the railroad afterwards. Streets red with Maryland blood. Send expresses [express trains] over the mountains of Maryland and Virginia for the riflemen to come without delay. Fresh hordes will be down upon us to-morrow (the 20th). We will fight them, and whip them, or die."[75] Kane's note was circulated around Frederick, Maryland, the next day, along with Johnson's words affixed: "All men who will go with me will report themselves as soon as possible, providing themselves with such arms and accoutrements as they can. Double-barreled shot-guns and buckshot are efficient. They will assemble, after reporting themselves, at 10 1/2 o'clock, so as to go down in the 11 1/2 train."[76] These communications aroused excitement and accounted for the recruitment of about 70 men who came to Baltimore to fight against the Northern troops. Northern sympathizers viewed this communication as inflaming the already riotous citizens of Baltimore. General Banks "charged that Marshal Kane, instead of seeking to win back the mad populace to their proper allegiance, had, by his dispatch to Bradley T. Johnson, … stirred up to their very depth their evil passions." Southern sympathizers, on the other hand, claimed that Kane "had time and again risked his life on that day to protect the Massachusetts soldiers" and that Kane was "as faithful and honest an officer as the country could produce."[77] History would later conclude, however, based on his deeds during 1862–1865, that Kane was indeed a rabid Southern sympathizer.[78] Two of Lincoln's biographers and confidants—John Nicolay and John Hay—would say, "It is impossible to resist the conviction that Mayor Brown and Marshal Kane were secessionists at heart, and while they were too sagacious to have prompted or encouraged the mob of April 19, they were quite ready to join in any sweeping popular movement to precipitate Maryland into rebellion, even if they were not actually then in a secret conspiracy to that end."[79] In all of these emotional events, everyone—Kane's supporters and detractors alike—agreed that at least at some points during the riot the Marshal had acted honorably and, in spite of what may have been his own political beliefs, protected the Northern troops at the risk of his own life. Most importantly, many of the Massachusetts troops themselves lauded Kane and his bravery in protecting them.

Once the Massachusetts Regiment had departed the Camden Street Station on the afternoon of April 19, spontaneous gatherings began in the downtown area. By 4:00 p.m. Friday, large crowds gathered in Monument Square to hear their representatives address the crisis. At about the same time, Governor Hicks and Mayor Brown called out the militias to respond to perceived threats looming on the horizon. They also advised the owners of the railroads to refuse to bring further troops to the city and to return those still present to the Maryland-Pennsylvania border.[80] Samuel Felton of the PW&B Railroad agreed with the plan and said he would transport no more troops over his railroad line at present. The Baltimore Directors of the Northern Central Railroad (though not constituting the entire Board of Directors) sent a letter of protest against the transport of any more federal troops from the North over their railroad.

The mass meeting at Monument Square was a spirited gathering; some reports stated that 10,000 people were present.[81] Speakers were passionate and eloquent, and the sentiment leaned toward the South. Striking was the absence of the flag of the United States; it had been replaced with the flag of Maryland.[82] Dr. Alexander C. Robinson, a prominent Baltimore secessionist whose arrest would later be ordered (though he fled to Virginia and avoided the arrest),[83] said, "We now stand as a unit. Not another Northern soldier shall pass over our soil to defend the Northern Government or the so-called Capital of the United States."[84] Mayor Brown was more conciliatory in his speech, asking that the good name of Baltimore not be "sullied." He pointed out that he had risked his own life to try to protect the Massachusetts soldiers, as well as the citizens of Baltimore. He called for calm and expressed a desire for peace, while the crowd expressed some displeasure at the tone of his words. Brown declared that he was not a supporter of the President's call for troops to go to Washington, and the crowd seemed more pleased at this statement, cheering him enthusiastically. He confirmed that he and Governor Hicks had negotiated with the railroad companies to bring no more Northern troops through Baltimore, and that those still remaining in the city needed to be returned to their home in the North. Again the crowd cheered when Mayor Brown said that "it is folly and madness for one portion of this great nation to attempt to subjugate another portion. It can never be done. If the North cannot live with the South, let us part in peace, and each section work out its destiny under the overruling providence of God."[85]

William P. Preston, a Baltimore lawyer who supported states' rights, talked next, saying, "The blood which had this day been shed on the soil of Maryland had united her sons, and they were now of one mind in regard to the aggressions of the North."[86] He said, "Let no more troops pass through Baltimore!" to which the crowd roared, "We won't, indeed. Never."[87] S. Teackle Wallis, another respected Baltimorean who was also a strong Southern supporter, then spoke. Wallis began by saying, "if the blood of your fellow citizens, this day shed in your own streets, does not cry aloud to you, all other voices had as well be silent." Wallis initially spoke for peace and order, but he also pleaded for "the honor of the city of Baltimore and the sanctity of the soil of Maryland."[88] The newspapers reported, "the immense concourse of people, animated by a single impulse, responded to the sentiment expressed by the speaker with the waving of hats and caps and the most vociferous cheering." Other speeches continued with a decidedly Southern inclination. Governor Hicks addressed the crowd toward the end of the gathering and admitted that the Union had apparently been broken, but he expressed hope that "its reconstruction may yet be brought about," to which the crowd shouted vehemently "Never, never." At this point he issued his now-famous statement: "But, if otherwise, I bow in submission to the mandate of the people. If separate we must, in God's name let us separate in peace; for I would rather this right arm should be separated from my body, than raise it against a brother."[89] Hicks seemed to respond to the feelings of the crowd, starting his speech with a calm plea for peace and order, and ending with a flourish toward the South.

At about this time, the city and the Board of Police began to try to acquire all possible arms and ammunition wherever they might be found—whether owned by the city, the county, the state, the federal government, or privately. Most arms were simply confiscated, though some were purchased. Kane, later in his letter defending his actions, concluded by justifying these confiscations and purchases. Specifically, he denied that he had taken weapons to be ultimately delivered to forces of the South.[90]

Late on the evening of Friday, April 19, Mayor Brown and Marshal Kane gathered with Brown's brother, John Cumming Brown, and ex-governor Enoch Louis Lowe. They discussed the rumors that more troops were headed to Baltimore on their journey toward Washington. Baltimore was leaning strongly toward the South at this time, and the City Council had even passed a regulation banning the display of the American flag within the city limits.[91]

Governor Hicks was staying as a guest at the home of Mayor Brown that night. Hicks had been warned that danger existed in the hotel where he had been staying, and Mayor Brown offered his home as a refuge. In addition, Hicks was ill, and the Mayor's home provided more comfort for the Governor. They all desperately wanted to avoid any more bloodshed, and it seemed that the best plan was to try to avoid having any more Northern troops pass through the city. None of the options to achieve this goal were ideal. They needed, at least temporarily, to halt the march of Northern troops through the city. Whether one favored the North or the South, all agreed that more Northern troops passing through would mean more rioting, fighting, injuries, and death.

At about 11:00 p.m. on April 19, Mayor Brown and Governor Hicks sent a telegram to President Lincoln:

> Sir: A collision between the citizens and Northern troops has taken place in Baltimore, and the excitement is fearful. Send no more troops here. We will endeavor to prevent all bloodshed.
>
> A public meeting of citizens has been called, and the troops of the State and the city have been called out to preserve the peace. They will be enough.
>
> Respectfully,
> Thomas W. Hicks
> Geo. Wm. Brown, Mayor[92]

To ensure that he received the message in a timely manner, Brown and Hicks had William Prescott Smith immediately carry the message personally to President Lincoln by special train car to Washington. Smith sent an additional message by telegraph from Camden Station: "The Governor of Maryland + Mayor of Baltimore have sent you a highly important despatch for fear [sic, meaning '…despatch. For fear…'] you may not receive it promptly, we have sent a special express engine + messenger to deliver it to you. W. P. Smith, Master of Transportation, B + O R R."[93] To guarantee that there was no question about the perilous state of emotions in the city of Baltimore, Hicks and Brown also sent three trusted Baltimoreans that same Friday night—Hugh Lennox Bond, a Judge of the Baltimore Criminal Court; John C. Brune, President of the Baltimore City Board of Trade and member of the Maryland House of Delegates; and George W. Dobbin, Baltimore judge—to Washington with another letter and asking for a personal audience with Lincoln. Brown's letter was dated April 18 (likely incorrectly—it was actually the 19th), but would be presented to Lincoln on the 20th:

> The people are exasperated to the highest degree by the passage of troops, and the citizens are universally decided in the opinion that no more should be ordered to come. The authorities of the city did their best to-day to protect both strangers and citizens, and to prevent a collision, but in vain, and but for their great efforts a fearful slaughter would have occurred. Under these circumstances, it is my solemn duty to inform you that it is not possible for more soldiers to pass through Baltimore unless they fight their way at every step. I therefore hope and trust, and most earnestly request, that no more troops be permitted or ordered by the Government to pass through the city. If they should attempt it, the responsibility for the bloodshed will not rest upon me.
>
> With great respect, your ob'dt serv't,
> Geo. Wm. Brown, Mayor[94]

Governor Hicks appended a letter stating that he concurred with the sentiments of Mayor Brown: "I have been in Baltimore city since Tuesday evening last, and co-operated with Mayor G. W. Brown, in his untiring efforts to allay and prevent the excitement and suppress the fearful outbreak as indicated above, and I fully concur in all that is said by him in the above communication."[95]

Indeed, President Lincoln and General Scott initially had different interpretations of Brown and Hicks's short telegram. Lincoln thought that it meant only that the Maryland officials were able to handle the confrontation themselves and that the federal government didn't need to respond with more troops. Scott, however, read it correctly, understanding the real message that they wanted no more federal troops to march through Baltimore, as the citizen riots could recur.

Eliminating easy access to Baltimore seemed to be an obvious method to keep troops away and to prevent further bloodshed on the city streets. Even before the government officials made a decision to stop the passage of Northern troops through Baltimore by burning the railroad bridges, citizens of Baltimore had the same ideas. Some citizens were plotting violence as a means of taking charge of the situation. They threatened to burn the B&O's office at Camden Station if that rail line transported any more federal troops, and they damaged the track between Relay House and Washington. Furthermore, they threatened John Work Garrett, President of the B&O line:

> One Hundred of us, Firm, Respectable, Resolute men—have determined & Sworn to each other, to destroy "every" Bridge & tear up your Track on both lines of your Road–(the Main & the Branch) between this City & their head points—If you carry another Soldier over either line of your Road after Saturday April 20th. We trust Dear Sir that you will harken unto the request of your Southern Fellow Citizens & save us this labour which we will very much regret to undertake. This organization of ours extends from here to Grafton & Washington & your trains will be watched. Spare us Dear Sir this to us unpleasant duty. Many of our Committee know you personally, some intimately, but the nature of our Oaths prevent us from seeing you in person. I am requested Sir to thus notify you. We have a large force ready to answer our calls.[96]

Soon after dark on Friday, bands of citizens went to destroy the bridges of the Northern Central and the PW&B Railroads. By the time government officials were willing to attempt the same deeds, some destruction had already occurred. Nevertheless, even at this late time Northern sympathizers were asking for privilege of passage of Northern troops through the city. Mr. J. Edgar Thompson, President of the Pennsylvania Central Railroad from Philadelphia, said, "Arm your Union men, and put down the populace." This report was relayed to Marshal Kane, the Baltimore Police Commissioners, Mayor Brown, and Governor Hicks, but it seemed to have the effect of steeling their resolve to burn the bridges.

Throughout the evening and night of April 19–20, Friday and Saturday, unrest prevailed in all quarters of the city. Volunteer soldiers in the various militias, as well as armed citizens, patrolled the streets.

By 11:00 p.m. Baltimoreans were fearful that other assaults on their city were imminent. Wanting weapons with which to protect themselves, they broke into multiple stores where guns were available. The Baltimore City Council would eventually appropriate $500,000 for the defense of the city. At this time, at least, all forces within Baltimore were amassing to resist any Union presence. Mayor Brown issued a proclamation: "All citizens having arms suitable for the defense of the city, and which they are willing to contribute for that purpose, are requested to deposit them at the office of the Marshal of Police."[97] Not many responded to this request, however, because everyone wanted to have his own weapon to use as needed. Some establishments donated substantial numbers of weapons to the city. Police confiscated arms from wherever they could locate them, while citizens also staged a run on the stores of Baltimore to purchase any weapons remaining. The entire city seemed to be preparing for war.

At 1:00 a.m. on Saturday, April 20, the signal was displayed to rally all of the local militias for the defense of the city. A red lantern was hung from the armory of the Maryland Guard at the corner of Calvert and Baltimore Streets. This notice was a pre-arranged signal for the militias of the city to congregate to protect Baltimore against attack. The Calvert Street Station was designated as the meeting point for these many organizations of troops and volunteers. Medical personnel also organized as a military board of surgeons to prepare for expected casualties of the next passage of troops through the city.

Men who had been attending the rallies, as well as those who had armed themselves by taking guns from local stores and warehouses, congregated at their predetermined meeting places, expecting to repel the New York Seventh Regiment that had been rumored to be on its way, soon to pass through Baltimore as the Massachusetts Regiment had done.

Major General George H. Steuart was the Commander in charge of all the diverse militia organizations. Contrasted to those somewhat organized preexisting militias under Steuart, Baltimore was now seeing volunteers who were mostly untrained, not uniformed, and unarmed. Recruitment of these civilians was very successful; over 30 companies of civilians (2,265 men) quickly came into existence,[98] exclusive of the previously existing militias commanded by Steuart. They were to be organized under the direction of Colonel Isaac R. Trimble,[99] who ordered Francis J. Thomas, Adjutant-General of the Volunteer Forces, to procure weapons—guns and cannons—from Virginia for the defense of the city. Money for the purchase of the guns and transportation of the ordnance had been drawn on an account of Marshal Kane.[100]

In late April 1861 Union forces could be found only at Fort McHenry, commanded by Captain John C. Robinson.[101] The fort was rather defenseless at this juncture, with many of the weapons being non-functional (some were even faked—tree trunks painted to look like guns), and with few soldiers available on site.

At Mayor Brown's home on the night of April 19, Kane discussed plans to prevent troop movements through Baltimore, future riots, and loss of life. Initially with Mayor Brown, John Cumming Brown, and Enoch Lewis Lowe, Kane was told "that it was impossible to prevent these troops from going through Baltimore; the Union men must be aroused to resist the mob."[102] Kane disagreed. Burning the railroad bridges so trains carrying troops could not reach Baltimore seemed to be the best option. Brown, Kane, Brown, and Lowe then went to consult with Hicks in his bedchamber. Hicks had already retired for the night, in part because he was ill. Brown presented the idea of burning the bridges on the train routes to Baltimore, knowing that this idea was unprecedented—destruction of private property at the order of governmental officials in an attempt to prevent bloodshed. Hicks was indecisive at first, but the men finally agreed that burning the railroad bridges on the approaches to the city would make it impossible for Union troops to access the city, and thus would prevent riots and death. Any movement of troops from the North would then need to utilize rail lines and ships that did not pass directly through the city itself.

Kane would later insist that the decision to burn the bridges was unanimous—all were in agreement:

> The Governor then sent for me, and in company with the Mayor I went to his chamber, and the condition of the city, the dangers of a sanguinary conflict in the event of troops coming to it whilst the public mind was highly inflamed, being fully discussed, the Governor deemed

it proper, and agreed with Mayor Brown and myself that the bridges on the roads by which troops would likely come, should be destroyed, as the only means of impeding them and avoiding the threatened conflict, and the Mayor and Board of Police then issued the order to that effect.

Kane would always remain convinced that his actions had been justified: "What the condition of Baltimore city would be at this time had I failed to execute the order to destroy the bridges referred to, by which the troops were arrested at Cockeysville on the morning of Sunday, the 21st of April, instead of coming to the city, is too horrible to contemplate, and can better be imagined than described."[103]

The exact content of the conversations held by Hicks, Brown, Brown, Lowe, and Kane would be hotly disputed in the ensuing years. George W. Brown and Kane distinctly remembered that Hicks had supported the burning of the bridges, though Hicks later asserted that he hadn't approved of the plan. However, nobody at Mayor Brown's house transcribed their conversations at the time. Furthermore, documents used to direct the teams to burn the railroad bridges, if any were produced, were not preserved. All of the men were walking uncharted ground. Never before had governmental officials considered destroying private property, let alone railroad transportation routes owned by their friends and supporters, to prevent troop movements ordered by the President of the United States. These acts were indeed unique. Kane had no jurisdiction to order destruction of property. Mayor Brown, even if he had jurisdiction, was limited in his authority to the borders of the city of Baltimore. The bridges were outside the city limits, so they needed Hicks's assent. Hicks apparently agreed that preventing troop movement—if it could be accomplished—would be a solution to the problem, and he wanted to avoid any more bloodshed like they had seen earlier that day. Hicks later would dispute their statements, contending that he had said "that the Mayor could do as he pleased—that I had no power to interfere in his design; if this be consent to the destruction of the bridges, then I consented." Hicks would later also say, "I do not deny that the proposed act, unlawful though it was, seemed to be the very means of averting bloodshed. But it would have little become me as Governor of the State to consent to an infraction of the laws which I had sworn to enforce."[104] Hicks would further contend that since the burning of the bridges began one hour after his alleged consent, it really wasn't his consent that led to their destruction.

Those gathered in Mayor Brown's home did not know who exactly might have the jurisdiction to issue such an order. Apparently Mayor Brown gave the order at about 2:30 a.m. to destroy the bridges on both the Northern Central and the PW&B Railroads on their approaches to Baltimore. Any documents written to Kane authorizing the use of the Baltimore police, or to Colonel Isaac Ridgeway Trimble, the head of the militias being organized in the city for defense, have disappeared. Nevertheless, two groups of men then deployed themselves to attempt to destroy the railroad bridges, one for the Northern Central Railway and one for the PW&B Railway. They armed themselves with turpentine and camphene to start the fires, and with picks, axes, shovels, and crowbars for manual disassembly of the bridges.

One team comprised policemen under Marshal Kane, civilian volunteers, and a company of the Baltimore City Guard Militia under the command of Captain John G.

Johannes. It headed to the Northern Central line toward Harrisburg. They went to the Melville bridge (near the current-day Cold Spring Lane), a structure that had originally cost about $6,000 to build, about five miles from Baltimore, where they told the watchman their plans. He surrendered the bridge to them. First the crew dismantled part of the bridge; then they demolished the watch house and threw pieces of it under and on the bridge itself, setting the bridge rubble on fire. After doing their work, some men remained on site until daylight. Thereafter, the crew went to the bridge at Relay House (located directly to the north of Baltimore near current-day Lake Roland). There they dismantled that iron structure and threw it into the river. Next they went to Cockeysville and destroyed the bridge between it and Ashland, about 11 miles from Baltimore. As the group disbanded they cut telegraph wires and destroyed telegraph poles along the route of the railroads. Others of their colleagues even removed the buoys in the Baltimore harbor to make navigation more difficult for any Union ships.

The other team comprised the Maryland Guard Battalion Companies—a militia that had been formed in 1859—who went to their armory where they spent the first part of the night. Early in the morning of the next day, Saturday, April 20, a squad was formed by taking four men from each company, and they combined forces with 40 Baltimore policemen. Trimble directed this group under the command of Captain Boyd and Lieutenant Fisher. They attacked the lines of the PW&B. Riding on the 3:00 a.m. train to the Bush River—the most distant—they destroyed the bridge. Trimble's team found a private party of about five citizens at that bridge who had independently gone by horseback to accomplish the same task. Some of the team, including the local volunteers, destroyed the Canton Bridge over Harris Creek and then went on to the Gunpowder River bridge, which they burned. This team then went to the Back River Bridge—the closest to Baltimore—which they also burned. Trimble's team had originally intended to capture or disable the ferry *Maryland* over the Susquehanna River, but two different reports caused them to scuttle this plan. One report suggested that there were other ferries that could transport Union troops across that river, and another communication reported that 2,000 Pennsylvania soldiers would already have reached the crossing by the time Trimble and his men could arrive there, so they abandoned that scheme. Trimble returned to Baltimore by about 1:00 p.m. Saturday, while Kane had returned somewhat earlier.

All of these maneuvers were successful, causing Union troops to skirt around Baltimore in their passage to Washington, D.C., most often going by boat to Annapolis and then by train to Washington.

A few days later the Baltimore County Horse Guard—which included Lieutenant John Merryman—traveled a bit further north and destroyed more bridges of the Northern Central Railroad and cut telegraph wires. For these deeds, Merryman was arrested on May 25 and imprisoned at Fort McHenry, and he was later denied habeas corpus. His court case became famous as *Ex parte Merryman*, with a ruling from Supreme Court Justice Roger Brooke Taney, then functioning as a federal circuit court judge, declaring that only Congress, not the President, had the authority to suspend the writ of habeas corpus.[105] Merryman was released on $20,000 bail, pending trial. The trial was never held, in part because Judge Taney believed that Merryman could not receive a fair trial during the Civil War.[106]

The effect of burning the bridges was short-lived. The damage to the Northern Central line was estimated to be $117,000. Repairs began on April 22, a mere two days after they were destroyed. Pennsylvania troops protected 150 repairmen, also from Pennsylvania, who completed their job on May 9. The repairs on the PW&B line began on May 10, and took only three days. The B&O's damages between Baltimore and Washington had already been repaired by April 26.[107]

The disagreement about what happened in Mayor Brown's home the night of April 19 regarding the burning of the bridges continued for years. Brown asserted that Hicks consented to torching the structures. Hicks would later deny Brown's report. Mayor Brown said, "I seriously regret that so grave a misunderstanding exists between the governor and myself on so important a subject."[108] Brown explained the midnight meeting with Hicks in Brown's home:

> The point was pressed that if troops were suddenly to come to Baltimore with a determination to pass through, a terrible collision and bloodshed would take place, and the consequences to Baltimore would be fearful, and that the only way to avert the calamity was to destroy the bridges. To this the governor replied, "It seems to be necessary," or words to that effect. He [Governor Hicks] was then asked by me whether he gave his consent to the destruction of the bridges, and he distinctly, although apparently with great reluctance, replied in the affirmative. I do not assert that I have given the precise language used by Governor Hicks, but I am very clear that I have stated it with substantial correctness, and that his assent was unequivocal, and in answer to a question by me which elicited a distinct affirmative reply.[109]

Mayor Brown asked the others who attended the meeting with Governor Hicks to record their impressions of the conduct of the discussions after the fact, and Governor Hicks himself responded to them in a lengthy explanation given about two months after the event.

Marshal Kane had earlier reported:

> The conversation resulted in the governor's distinctly and unequivocally consenting, in response to the direct question put to him by the mayor, that the bridges on the roads by which the troops were expected to come should be destroyed as the only means of averting the consequences referred to of their coming at that time.[110]

The Mayor's brother, John Cumming Brown, reported the event:

> The destruction of the bridges on the Northern Central and the Philadelphia, Wilmington and Baltimore Railroads was, in the opinion of my brother, the best and most effective method to obstruct their progress. In this opinion Governor Hicks fully concurred.... [Hicks said] "I see nothing else to be done." "But sir," said my brother, "I cannot act without your consent; do you give it?" The governor's reply was distinctly given in the affirmative.[111]

Finally, E. Louis Lowe said of the conversation:

> Governor Hicks replied that it was a serious affair to undertake to destroy the bridges, and he expressed some doubt as to his authority to give such an order.... Governor Hicks fully and most distinctly assented to all this, and said, "Well, I suppose it must be done," or words of precisely that import, to which the mayor replied, substantially, "Governor, I have no authority to act beyond the city limits, and can do nothing in this matter except by your direction; shall the bridges be destroyed?" Governor Hicks emphatically and distinctly replied in the affirmative. It is absolutely impossible for any misapprehension to exist on this point.... The mayor then issued written orders for the destruction of the bridges.[112]

Members of the Maryland Senate later asked Governor Hicks himself if he consented to or authorized the burning of the bridges on the Northern Central and the Baltimore, Wilmington and Philadelphia Railroads. He replied, "I have to say: That I neither authorised or consented to the destruction of said bridges; but left the whole matter in the hands of the Mayor of the city of Baltimore;—with the declaration that I had no authority in the premises—that I was a lover of law and order, and could not participate in such proceedings."[113]

Hicks first objected to the notion that his agreement to the burning of the bridges would have been given only verbally. He claimed that the act was so important, and so controversial, that any agreement with the plot would have to be in writing. Hicks then quoted his accusers in stating that their recollection of his words was not verbatim. Next he claimed that he had no power to consent to the burning of the bridges, and that furthermore he had no power to prevent these "evil men" (Brown, Brown, Lowe, and Kane) from doing what they were determined to do, anyway. He contended that because earlier in the day he had rejected the idea of sinking or pirating the steamship *Maryland* at Perryville as a similar means of preventing the transport of troops and the avoidance of violence, he—to remain consistent—would have also had to reject the burning of the bridges. Hicks' aide-de-camp, Colonel R. S. Mercer, agreed that Hicks had rejected the idea of removing or destroying the *Maryland*. Mercer argued that Hicks remained true to the principle that he "insisted upon the right of the government to pass troops through Maryland to the capital."[114] Finally, Hicks argued that even though the men addressing him about the burning of the bridges seemed to be seeking his approval, indeed they had already begun their actions to burn the bridges. Hicks's assent was neither needed nor wanted; Hicks thought all of the discussion was a subterfuge to try to involve him in an unlawful act, one designed to "precipitate Maryland into rebellion." He said, in summary, "I unhesitatingly assert that I refused my consent, and gave as my reason therefor [sic] that I had no authority in the premises—that the bridges were private property—that the proposed act was unlawful—that I was a lover of law and order—that the Mayor could act as he pleased—and that I had no power to interfere with his designs."[115]

The bulk of the testimony had Governor Hicks assenting to the plan to burn the bridges, though it is noteworthy that apparently Mayor Brown was the one who actually gave the order for the torching, destroying, and rendering the railroads inoperable. Regardless of the debate about who agreed to the actions, the closure of the routes to Baltimore probably saved countless lives. Nevertheless, the other participants in the discussion at Mayor Brown's house fared poorly. Kane and Mayor Brown were later arrested; Lowe escaped to the South.

On Saturday morning, April 20, the Baltimore militias had gathered, and news bulletins reported Union troops coming from the North, from Harrisburg and Philadelphia, on both the Northern Central and the PW&B lines. All able-bodied men wanted to participate in the defense of Baltimore, the assumption being that any further Union troops passing through the city *should* meet severe resistance. Citizens and members of the militia were arming themselves.

The delegation of Bond, Brune, and Dobbin, sent to Washington, had reported to Mayor Brown early on Saturday the 20th, saying, "We have seen the President and

General Scott. We bear from the former a letter to the Mayor and Governor, declaring that no troops should be brought through Baltimore, if, in a military point of view, and without opposition, they can be marched around Baltimore."[116]

At about the same time on April 20, Mayor Brown sent a telegram to President Lincoln: "Every effort will be made to prevent parties from leaving the city to molest troops marching to Wash'n. Baltimore seeks only to protect herself. Gov. Hicks has gone to Annapolis but I have teleghd ['telegraphed'] to him."[117]

Also on Saturday the 20th, Governor Hicks wrote to Simon Cameron, the Secretary of War, explaining the situation:

> Since I saw you in Washington last I have been in Baltimore City laboring, in conjunction with the mayor of that city, to preserve peace and order, but I regret to say with little success. Up to yesterday there appeared promise, but the outbreak came; the turbulent passions of the riotous element prevailed; fear for safety became reality; … the rebellious element had the control of things…. I therefore think it prudent to decline (for the present) responding affirmatively to the requisition made by President Lincoln for four regiments of infantry.[118]

Hicks returned to Annapolis that same day, citing illness as the reason for his apparently untimely departure, and now expressing confidence in Mayor Brown's ability to manage the crisis. Hicks would not withdraw from his participation in the negotiations, however, and he wrote to President Lincoln on April 22:

> I feel it my duty most respectfully to advise you that no more troops be ordered or allowed to pass through Maryland, and that the troops now off Annapolis be sent elsewhere, and I most respectfully urge that a truce be offered by you, so that the effusion of blood may be prevented. I respectfully suggest that Lord Lyons be requested to act as mediator between the contending parties of our country.[119]

Secretary of State William H. Seward would reply immediately on April 22 that troops to defend Washington should be welcome in Maryland and that suggesting that a foreign dignitary, especially the representative of a European monarchy, be appointed to be a mediator between opposing forces was inappropriate.[120]

During that morning of Saturday, April 20, both the First Branch and the Second Branch of the Baltimore City Council met in emergency session and voted to allocate $500,000 for the defense of the city. Immediately thereafter, local banks supported this vote by making the funds available for the purchase of arms and ammunition, and for whatever else might be necessary to repel Union troops.

The response in Baltimore to President Lincoln's letter, stating that "no troops should be brought through Baltimore,"[121] was less than enthusiastic. The *Daily Exchange* reported:

> THE FEELING IN REGARD TO THE PRESIDENT'S ANSWER. There was considerable dissatisfaction expressed on the streets at the unsatisfactory tone of the President's reply, many being of the opinion that these foreign troops should not be allowed to pollute the soil of the State of Maryland by their march to the rendezvous, where preparations are making for the slaughter of Southern citizens, who only ask to be let alone and allowed to govern themselves.[122]

Lincoln's response contained no apology, and their quotation about his statement declaring that no more troops should pass through Baltimore seemed to be couched in equivocal terms.

Lincoln's next letter to Hicks and Brown, also written on Saturday, April 20, after his meeting with Dobbin, Brune, and Bond, revealed that the misinterpretation of the previous telegram had been clarified, and that Lincoln's words weren't quite as obscure as the emissaries had reported:

> Gov. Hicks, & Mayor Brown
>
> Gentlemen: Your letter by Messrs. Bond, Dobbin & Brune, is received. I tender you both my sincere thanks for your efforts to keep the peace in the trying situation in which you are placed. For the future, troops *must* be brought here, but I make no point of bringing them *through* Baltimore. Without any military knowledge myself, of course I must leave details to Gen. Scott. He hastily said, this morning, in the presence of these gentlemen, "March them *around* Baltimore, and not through it." I sincerely hope the General, on fuller reflection, will consider this practical and proper, and that you will not object to it. By this, a collision of the people of Baltimore with the troops will be avoided, unless they go out of their way to seek it. I hope you will exert your influence to prevent this.
>
> Now, and ever, I shall do all in my power for peace, consistently with the maintainance [*sic*] of government.
>
> Your Obt. Servt.
> A. Lincoln[123]

At the same time, Maryland Senator Anthony Kennedy and former Maryland Third District Representative J. Morrison Harris, who had taken a special train to Washington on Saturday morning, had been talking with President Lincoln in Washington, and with the Secretaries of War, State, Navy, and Treasury, as well as with General Winfield Scott. They reported that the result of their meetings was "the transmission of orders that will stop the passage of troops through or around the city."[124] The new planned route for the troops through Maryland was to go by train to Perryville, north of Baltimore on the Susquehanna River, by boat from there to Annapolis, and then again by the Annapolis and Elk Ridge Railroad to Washington. An alternative plan was to transport the soldiers from Pennsylvania on the Northern Central Railroad as far as Relay House, about seven miles north of Baltimore, march to the B&O Railroad Relay House, about seven miles southwest of Baltimore, and then continue by train to Washington. Kennedy and Harris sent a telegram to Mayor Brown stating that troops would pass <u>around</u> Baltimore, rather than <u>through</u> it. Though the wording of their telegram was more definitive than prior communications, unease persisted on the streets of Baltimore.

As darkness approached on Saturday night, April 20, Mayor Brown could see the potential for mob violence, and he ordered the closure of all taverns and restaurants for the night. Militias continued to assemble, and men not already belonging to any militia affiliated themselves with one or another as quickly as they could. On Saturday alone, over 2,000 new recruits were added to these militias' rolls. Many of these men were given guns, but without any training.

Bradley Johnson with his 70 recruits from the Frederick, Maryland, area had responded quickly to Kane's plea and arrived in Catonsville near Baltimore via the B&O Relay House. They then marched into the city and encamped at 34 Holliday Street, opposite the Marshal's office. Johnson would remain with his troops in Baltimore until April 26, when he returned to Frederick, but with the promise to return if needed.[125]

Very early on Sunday, April 21, at 3:00 a.m., Mayor Brown and Governor Hicks received a telegram from President Lincoln (written on Saturday night, April 20), asking them to come to Washington to discuss the crisis: "Gov. Hicks, I desire to consult with you and the Mayor of Baltimore relative to preserving the peace of Maryland. Please come immediately by special train, which you can take at Baltimore, or if necessary one can be sent from hence. Answer forthwith. LINCOLN."[126] Brown telegraphed to Lincoln early Sunday, "I am coming immediately. Hope to see you at once."[127] Clearly everyone understood the gravity of the situation.

Hicks had already returned to Annapolis, and Dobbin, Brune, and Bond had returned to Baltimore following their Saturday meeting with Lincoln. So Brown went to Washington without Hicks, accompanied this time by advisors S. Teackle Wallis, Dobbin, and Brune (Bond did not accompany this second delegation). They left Baltimore at 7:30 a.m. Sunday and arrived in Washington at about 10:00 a.m. There they met with Lincoln, General Scott, and some unnamed members of Lincoln's Cabinet. Brown assured Lincoln that the burning of railroad bridges was not an act of aggression against the Union, but one designed to prevent more riots and death in the streets of Baltimore. Lincoln, on the other hand, passionately told Brown that his call for 75,000 Northern troops was not an act of aggression against Maryland, but one designed to protect Washington, D.C., from Southern military forces. Lincoln emphasized his point by saying, "Mr. Brown, I am not a learned man! I am not a learned man!," meaning that his intentions were honorable but had been misinterpreted.[128] Lincoln and General Scott deliberated upon how to accomplish defense without again endangering the citizens of Baltimore, and they agreed that movement of troops *around, rather than through* Baltimore was an acceptable alternative. They asked Mayor Brown if he would agree to such a plan and if the police and militias could facilitate such a circuitous route. Brown responded that he would do everything in his power to support such a scheme, but that he only had jurisdiction within the city of Baltimore, and that he couldn't necessarily control Baltimoreans if they tried to confront the federal troops outside of the city limits. Lincoln and Scott acknowledged that Brown was correct, but they accepted Brown's promise to try to "use all lawful means to prevent their citizens from leaving Baltimore to attack the troops in passing at a distance." Then, "The interview terminated with the distinct assurance on the part of the President that no more troops would be sent through Baltimore unless obstructed in their transit in other directions, and with the understanding that the city authorities should do their best to restrain their own people."[129] At the end of the meeting, Brown felt that he understood Lincoln to have pledged to try to limit any more troop movements through Maryland, and avoid them completely through Baltimore, as long as sufficient numbers of soldiers could be transported around the city to Washington.

Mayor Brown and his traveling companions then returned to the railroad cars to begin their trip back to Baltimore, seemingly assured that all possible had been done to prevent the passage of more soldiers through Baltimore. However, no sooner had they arrived at the rail depot at about 2:00 p.m. but they were given a telegram from John Garrett stating that federal troops at Cockeysville were about to march down to Baltimore, through the city, and on to Washington. Garrett said, "Three thousand Northern troops are reported to be at Cockeysville. Intense excitement prevails. Churches have been dismissed, and the people are arming in mass. To prevent terrific bloodshed, the results of your interview and arrangements [with President Lincoln] are awaited."[130]

Indeed, more Union troops had headed toward Baltimore on Sunday, April 21. These soldiers had originally amassed at Camp Curtin near Harrisburg, Pennsylvania, and consisted of the 1st, 2nd, and 3rd Regiments of the Pennsylvania Volunteers. That Sunday, between midnight and 1:00 a.m., they took the Northern Central Railroad as far as they could travel, considering that many railroad bridges had been burned the previous Friday night and Saturday morning. Their progress was halted at Ashland Station, near Cockeysville, Maryland, only about 16 miles from Baltimore, as a result of the burned bridge there.[131] They camped at 8:00 a.m., just a few miles north of Baltimore, between the railroad and the "turnpike"[132] in a wheat field on the property of Peter Cockey, a Union supporter. It was sometimes called "Cockey's Fields," about one mile north of Cockeysville itself. The new troop encampment was called "Camp Carroll." The majority of residents of this portion of Baltimore County indeed supported the Union, even though Baltimore City itself was a hotbed of Southern sentiments. Some of these Union supporters provided the troops with needed supplies for their brief stay in Maryland. Estimates of the size of this force varied wildly, some as high as 10,000 men, but the real number was more likely about 2,400–2,500. As the troops were hastily gathered, most had arms but were generally without ammunition, only about one-quarter had uniforms, and food was scarce. Most men had not eaten for over 24 hours as they arrived at Cockeysville, their last food having been on Saturday morning as they left Harrisburg.[133] Local Marylanders swarmed to the area on Sunday afternoon to get a glimpse of the camp. At this time it was unclear if the soldiers would attempt passage through Baltimore, skirt around the city, or return to Pennsylvania. At about this time, all telegraph lines north of Baltimore had been cut, and lines to the south were under the control of Marshal Kane.

Brigadier General George G. Wynkoop instructed the Pennsylvania troops to respect local landowners and property rights as much as possible, considering that they were encamped on private property.[134] Rumors were rampant that a battle was about to begin. Full preparations were made in Baltimore for an armed conflict. Guns were distributed to the Baltimore militias, and additional cannons were placed in the streets, expected to be used for the march of the Northern troops through the city.

Marshal Kane positioned himself in front of City Hall and spoke to the unruly crowds, telling them that he would not tolerate unorganized and untrained men having guns, even if the expressed purpose were to defend the city. These men he considered to be a mob, and he knew that mobs were a detriment to the safety of the citizens of Baltimore. He instructed them to volunteer for military companies if they wanted to help, and many of them organized themselves into groups that subsequently went to affiliate with a militia.

Independently, on Sunday, April 21, Kane sent William H. Quincey, his representative from Baltimore, to talk with the leaders of the Northern troops at Cockeysville. Quincey discussed the situation with General Wynkoop, who was himself a Marylander. Quincey said, "I hope you have no intention to march through Baltimore, for the people are in arms and there will be a terrible slaughter." Wynkoop replied, "I have no intention of going to Baltimore, and have been endeavoring to get a map of the county, so as to pick out some other route to Washington. I am a Marylander, born in Montgomery county, and nothing would give me more pain than to be compelled to shed the blood of Maryland citizens."[135] Baltimoreans nevertheless remained fearful of the intentions of these Pennsylvania troops. Though rumors confirmed that Lincoln and General Scott had agreed not to bring any more troops through the city of Baltimore, many observers were skeptical. All feared that the troops might suddenly launch a movement toward the center of the city, but for the time the troops progressed no further to the south.

Meanwhile, in Washington, Mayor Brown telegraphed back to John W. Garrett, President of the Baltimore and Ohio Railroad, at 1:25 p.m.: "Be calm, and do nothing till you hear from me again. I return to see the President at once, and will telegraph again. Wallis, Brune and Dobbin are with me."[136]

Immediately Brown and his delegation returned to the White House and demanded another meeting with Lincoln. It seemed that the assurances that they had been given were false. Troops in Cockeysville might be on the move. However, Lincoln's response to this report seemed to be genuine surprise, and Lincoln requested Scott to order the troops back to Harrisburg or York, Pennsylvania. They gave an order to Major James Belger, Assistant Quartermaster of the U.S. Army, to carry personally to the Cockeysville troops, ordering them to return to Harrisburg, then to proceed to Philadelphia, followed by travel to Perryville on the Susquehanna River, where they would board steamships to Annapolis and thence travel to Washington by rail (Figure 38).

At 3:15 p.m., Brown again telegraphed Garrett: "We have again seen the President, Gen. Scott, Secretary of War, and other members of the cabinet, and the troops are ordered to return forthwith to Harrisburg. A messenger goes with us from Gen. Scott. We return immediately."[137]

News finally arrived in Baltimore from Mayor Brown at about 4:00 p.m., saying that President Lincoln and General Scott had ordered the Cockeysville troops back to Pennsylvania, but the report was again greeted with skepticism. Only later, at about 8:00 p.m., did Trimble report that the earlier communication had been correct: Union troops were being ordered to return to Pennsylvania. Calm enveloped Baltimore once more.

Isaac Trimble had been named Commander of the militias in Baltimore city, including the Maryland Guards, the Baltimore City Guards, the Independent Greys, and the Law Greys. Dozens of others needed to coalesce into a manageable fighting force. Trimble quickly organized the diverse militias and issued orders providing for the coordination of the forces, one of which said, "Should there be a demand for active service tonight, the fire bells of the city will be rung in a continuous peal, when the troops will all assemble at the Calvert station as soon as possible."[138]

Mayor Brown arrived back in Baltimore at about 6:00 p.m. Sunday, with rest of his delegation and the messenger Lincoln and Scott had sent to communicate with

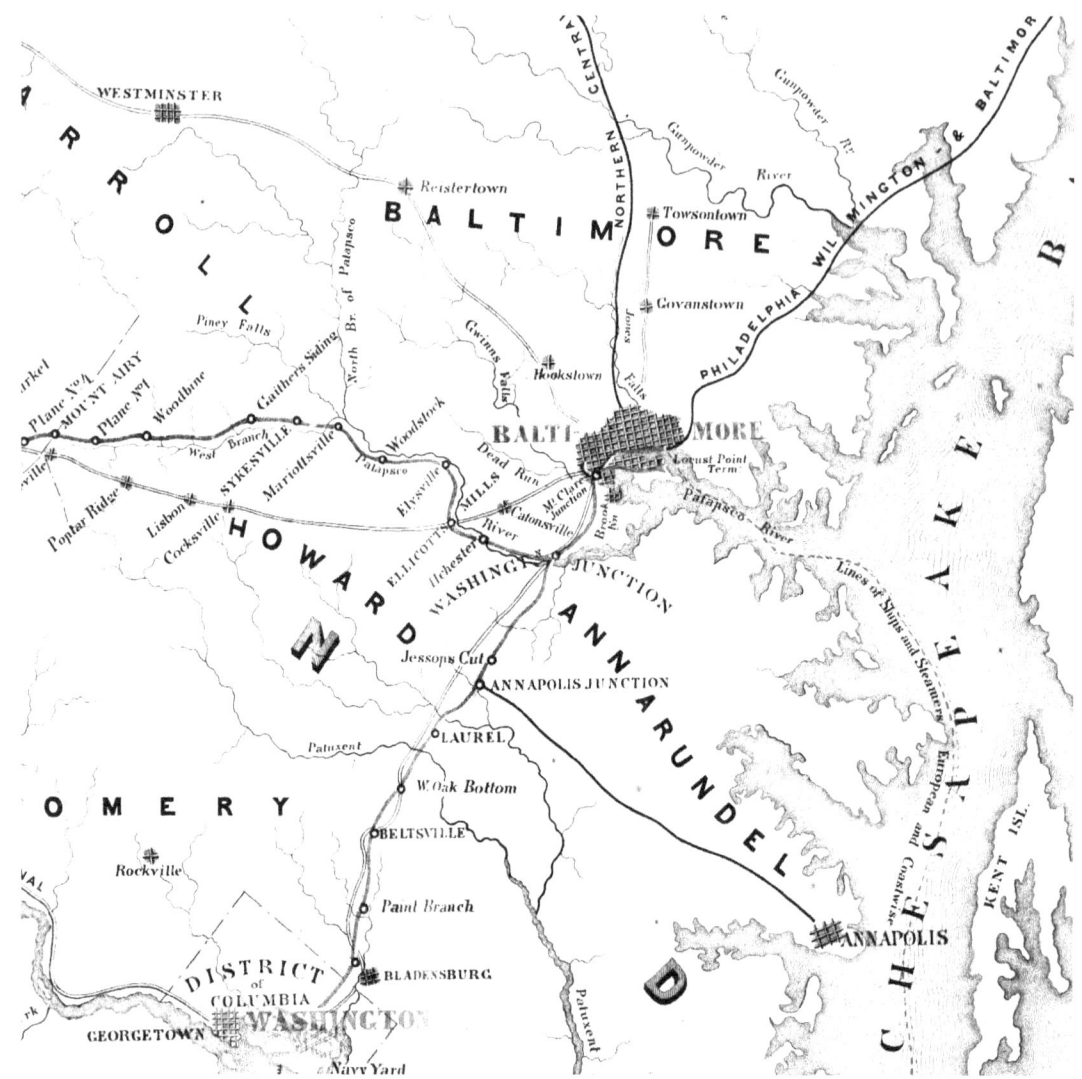

Figure 38. Rail lines around Baltimore and Washington. From the Library of Congress.

the Pennsylvania troops now stationed in Cockeysville. Kane himself accompanied U.S. Army Major James Belger from Baltimore to Cockeysville on Sunday evening to meet with General Wynkoop. As Marshal Kane met with General Wynkoop, tensions seemed to diminish. Kane also saw the immediate plight of these troops who had been hastily mustered. Even local Northern-leaning newspapers recognized Kane's merciful heart, saying, "By order of Marshal Kane, several wagon loads of bread and meat were sent to the camp of the Pennsylvania troops, it being understood that a number were sick and suffering for proper food and nourishment. The act was a humane one, and deserves to be recorded."[139] However, not only did Kane provide food for the *Union* troops at Cockeysville, but the citizens of Baltimore also provided their own militias with supplies, as well. In the midst of this overwhelming crisis, Baltimoreans rallied to support their local protectors.[140]

11. The Baltimore Riot

No conflict emerged through Sunday night, and the troops on both sides slept peacefully. The next morning—Monday, April 22—the entire Union military contingent returned to York, Pennsylvania, defusing what could have been a volatile situation.[141] The crisis seemed to have been averted. Nevertheless, the Baltimore militias placed sentries every half mile along the road between Cockeysville and Baltimore to warn of any troop movements, but by Tuesday, April 23, all of the Pennsylvania troops had withdrawn back to Harrisburg.[142]

Reaction to the April 19 riot and the subsequent burning of the railroad bridges was both swift and partisan. Kane himself later issued a lengthy defense of his actions, submitted to the Board of Police Commissioners and to the press on May 3:

> An Official Narrative of the Facts in Relation to the Occurrences which took place in this City on Friday, April 19, 1861.
> POLICE DEPARTMENT, OFFICE OF THE MARSHAL,
>
> Baltimore, May 3, 1861.
> Chas. Howard, Esq.,
> President of the Board of Police:
>
> SIR:—The columns of the *Baltimore American* of this date contain an assault upon my official conduct as commanding officer of the police force of this city, in connection with the occurrences of the 19th of April last, which seems to require some notice, in order that the facts of the case may be duly registered on the journals of your office....
>
> [Kane then detailed his version of the events of April 19.]
>
> ... I fought hard for their [the Massachusetts troops'] protection; at first almost alone, but soon had the assistance of a part of my force, who hurried from the neighboring beats, and had the gratification of seeing all but those who took shelter in neighboring houses, put on another train, and under escort of police, accompanied by myself, sent safely out of the city on their return to Philadelphia. The earnest expressions of gratitude which I received from the persons thus rescued, left on my mind the conviction that I had done my duty....
>
> The Governor then sent for me, and in company with the Mayor I went to his chamber.... [T]he Governor deemed it proper, and agreed with Mayor Brown and myself that the bridges on the roads by which troops would likely come, should be destroyed, as the only means of impeding them and avoiding the threatened conflict, and the Mayor and Board of Police then issued the order to that effect....
>
> What the condition of Baltimore city would be at this time had I failed to execute the order to destroy the bridges referred to, by which the troops were arrested at Cockeysville on the morning of Sunday, the 21st of April, instead of coming to the city, is too horrible to contemplate, and can better be imagined than described....
>
> I have the conviction that I have faithfully discharged the duties of the office of Marshal of Police during the extraordinary excitement which has pervaded this community, probably beyond anything of the kind in its previous history, and that the force under my command has been successful in protecting the persons and property of people of the most intensely obnoxious character to another portion of our community from the slightest violence or injury. I feel that I can well afford to endure assaults, coming from such sources.
>
> It may be proper in this connection to refer to the insinuation so broadly conveyed of complicity on the part of the police in appropriating property of the Federal Government [guns and ammunition] to improper uses. The charge is untrue. It was taken into the custody of the police solely for the purpose of preserving it—of which proper notice was given to the authorities of the United States Government, in Washington and in this city.
>
> Yours, very respectfully,
> GEO. P. KANE, Marshal[143]

The New York *Tribune*, chronically an opponent of Kane and his actions, denounced the explanation given by him of the passage of the Massachusetts troops:

The substance of his declaration [justifying his actions] is that by a series of unfortunate accidents he was repeatedly during the day prevented from getting correct information as to what was going on, and did not in general know that his services were wanted until it was just too late to render them efficiently.... He alleges that he then hurried to the rescue [of the troops], and succeeded by great exertions in rescuing them, for which they were duly grateful, and their gratitude, he says, left on his mind the conviction that he had done his duty.

... Marshal Kane's ... heart was not in the business of putting down the mob, and protecting the troops who were passing, all of them peaceably, and most of them unarmed, through the streets of Baltimore. It will not do for him to allege that he had no information of what was happening....

The truth is that Marshal Kane is a Secessionist in feeling, and would be a traitor in act if he dared. His conduct on the occasion of the expected public passage of President Lincoln through Baltimore was not free from suspicion of sinister design on his part.... A fact like this indicates either great inefficiency, stupidity or culpable indifference on the part of the Head of the Police.[144]

During this excitement, Kane ordered all persons marching or parading in the streets to disperse unless they were part of organized militias practicing under the orders of their commanders.[145] On April 22, Police Commissioner Charles Howard ordered that everyone was to refrain from using "martial music," especially drums, as it might incite agitation, rumors, or even riots.[146] He also issued an order imploring parents to keep their minor children at home and under control, and imposed a curfew on the city. Anyone caught on the streets after 6:00 p.m. would be arrested and confined at the police station houses. "Places of amusement" were to be closed. Kane also ordered that bands were prohibited from playing music in the streets or near crowds of people.[147] Steamers leaving the Baltimore harbor would need a special permit, though travel was not categorically prohibited. However, shipment of any weapons, ammunition, other "munitions of war," blankets, saltpeter, sulphur, flour, pork/beef/bacon, and coal was specifically restricted (by any conveyance). "Droves of horses" likewise could not leave the city.[148] Supplies (2,000 guns) arriving from Virginia for the defense of Baltimore from Union troops were allowed to come into the city, but food intended for the Union troops coming from New York and Philadelphia was confiscated. Any gunpowder or guns located in the city were also confiscated for use of the militia or the police. All of the shot in the Baltimore Merchants' Shot Tower was taken and delivered to Marshal Kane's office. Citizens rallied behind Kane by organizing three different auxiliary police forces to augment the services that the Baltimore police regulars could provide. Vigilante groups formed to protect local neighborhoods were often given a more socially acceptable title, such as the "Home Guard." Many members of the militias were deputized to assist the police forces in their various locations.[149] These militias were often composed of men too infirm or too old to join the regular troops. Hotels, restaurants, and businesses, as well as everyday citizens, continued to provide food for the Baltimore militias.

Militias throughout the state had already begun mobilizing and drilling. They elected officers, inducted new recruits, established protocols, arranged medical and surgical backup, and in general got ready to fight.

Kane found himself having to enforce rules that were more even-handed than he might have wanted. On April 26 word spread that display of Union flags was about to incite riots in the city. The Board of Police instructed Kane to issue and enforce an order to ban the display of all flags. Kane's order read, "I do hereby, by their [the Board's] instructions, order that *no flag, of any description*, shall be raised in any place or carried through the streets."[150] Most citizens complied, though Union flags were briefly raised in Fells Point and on Federal Hill. Police promptly dealt with both.

By Monday, April 22, Mayor Brown would again order all bars and liquor establishments to close, even though the populace was calmer than it had been on Friday, Saturday, or Sunday.

Governor Hicks could see the potential for unrest to accelerate again, and he called for an emergency session of the Maryland General Assembly to be held on Friday, April 26, in Annapolis. He knew that the question of secession needed to be addressed. At this time, President Lincoln thought it prudent to allow the Maryland Legislature to meet (later this judgment would change). Lincoln wrote that he believed they had a right to assemble and deliberate the issue, and—practically—he felt that it would be impossible to prevent their gathering. He said, "I therefore conclude that it is only left to the commanding general to watch and wait their action, which, if it shall be to arm their people against the United States, he is to adopt the most prompt and efficient means to counteract, even, if necessary, to the bombardment of their cities, and in the extremest necessity, the suspension of the writ of habeas corpus."[151] Mayor Brown quickly called for a special election of ten delegates from Baltimore to attend this meeting in Annapolis.

Lincoln, in many of his pronouncements about the suspension of the writ of habeas corpus, delegated the decision for this action to his generals. For example, in an order to General Scott, he wrote:

> You are engaged in suppressing an insurrection against the laws of the United States. If at any point on or in the vicinity of any military line which is now or which shall be used between the city of Philadelphia and the city of Washington you find resistance which renders it necessary to suspend the writ of habeas corpus for the public safety, you personally, or through the officer in command at the point at which resistance occurs, are authorized to suspend that writ. Abraham Lincoln, Washington, April 27, 1861.

He did the same on July 2, 1861, with similar wording for the region between New York and Washington.[152] While much has been said about Lincoln's suspension of habeas corpus, his actions in this regard were clearly attempts to save the Union. Difficult though it may be to understand his actions in the mid–1800s through the lens of the 21st century, no one can impugn his motives.

Lincoln argued that the suspension of habeas corpus

> is allowed by the Constitution on purpose that men may be arrested and held, who cannot be proved to be guilty of defined crime, "when, in cases of Rebellion or Invasion, the public safety may require it." This is precisely our present case, a case of Rebellion, wherein the public safety does require the suspension. Indeed, arrests by process of courts, and arrests in cases of rebellion, do not proceed altogether upon the same basis. The former is directed at the small percentage of ordinary and continuous perpetration of crime; while the latter is directed at sudden and extensive uprisings against the government, which, at most, will succeed or fail, in no great length of time. In the latter case, arrests are made, not so much for what has been done, as for what probably would be done. The latter is more for the preventive, and less for the vindictive, than the former.[153]

Lincoln went so far as to predict, "I think the time not unlikely to come when I shall be blamed for having made too few arrests rather than too many." He argued that arrests could be made both in areas of active insurrection and in areas where insurrection was only *likely* to occur. Lincoln would later ask the question, "Must I shoot a simple-minded soldier boy who deserts, while I must not touch a hair of a wiley agitator who induces him to desert?"

Even though the response of the citizens in Baltimore prevented the immediate repeat of federal troops marching through the city, it wasn't long before they became aware of Union soldiers traveling to Washington, bypassing the center of the city itself. Citizens responded less violently to the use of this more circuitous route, though Marshal Kane and his police were needed to control the crowds. Most onlookers viewed the troop movements from the wharves on the city side of the harbor, though a few ventured to the Locust Point wharf of the B&O. However, violence was averted.[154]

Unbeknownst to Baltimore officials, including Marshal Kane, General Benjamin Butler had arrived on April 20 in Perryville, Maryland, about 40 miles to the north of the center of the city, with approximately 1,000 soldiers: men from the Boston Light Artillery, the Massachusetts Sixth Infantry, and 500 men from the Eighth New York. By Sunday, April 21, Butler had advanced to Annapolis. From there, he moved on May 5 to Relay House on the B&O, southwest of Baltimore City. Soon Butler would occupy the city of Baltimore in a preemptive strike against the secessionists, including Kane, and he would begin arrests of Southern sympathizers for such ill-defined crimes as "treasonable language."[155] Butler had heard of Southern sympathies within Baltimore, as well as stories of caches of guns and ammunition to be used for rebellion. General Winfield Scott gave Butler permission to confiscate the munitions, but Butler took it upon himself to take 950 men (500 from the Sixth Massachusetts and 450 from the Eighth New York Regiments) and enter Baltimore on May 13. Under the cover of a heavy thunderstorm, Butler went to Federal Hill and Fort McHenry, establishing his presence even before most of the citizens, police, and militias were aware of his movements. Baltimoreans awoke the next morning to find nearly one thousand Union troops occupying Federal Hill, overlooking the central business district of the city. Butler encountered no opposition to his invasion of Baltimore and confiscation of the city's arms caches. Butler would later report in his memoirs, "it was comparatively as easy to capture Baltimore as it was to capture my supper."[156] Mayor Brown was infuriated both at the invasion and at the rather loquacious proclamation Butler issued on May 14 that said, in part:

> A detachment of the forces of the Federal Government under my command have occupied the city of Baltimore for the purpose, among other things, of enforcing respect and obedience to the laws, as well of the State—if requested thereto by the civil authorities—as of the United States laws, which are being violated within its limits by some malignant and traitorous men.... I thereby, ... do now command and make known that no loyal and well-disposed citizen will be disturbed in his lawful occupation or business; that private property will not be interfered with by the men under my command, or allowed to be interfered with by others, except in so far as it may be used to afford aid and comfort to those in rebellion against the Government.... [M]unitions of war, and that fitted to aid and support the rebellion, will be seized and held subject to confiscation.... No transportation from the city to the rebels of articles fitted to aid and support troops in the field will be permitted....

All assemblages, except the ordinary police, of armed bodies of men, other than those regularly organized and commissioned by the State of Maryland, and acting under the orders of the governor thereof, for drill and other purposes, are forbidden within the department....

No flag, banner, ensign, or device of the so-called Confederate States, or any of them, will be permitted to be raised or shown in this department, and the exhibition of either of them by evil-disposed persons will be deemed and taken to be evidence of a design to afford aid and comfort to the enemies of the country.[157]

General Scott replied,

Your hazardous occupation of Baltimore was made without my knowledge, and of course without my approbation. It is a God-send that it was without conflict of arms. It is also reported that you have sent a detachment to Frederick, but this is impossible. Not a word have I received from you as to either movement. Let me hear from you.[158]

On May 15, Scott's tone was more irritated as he wrote again to Butler:

Issue no more proclamations.
   Why assume the authority to call for re-enforcements from General Patterson?
   Answer my letter of last evening.
   Did you leave any men at Relay House? Look to their safety.
   Not a word received from you in several days.[159]

That same day, May 14, 1861, General Orders #2 from the Headquarters, Maryland Militia, in Frederick, Maryland, read: "Brigadier General John R. Kenly of the Third Brigade M.M. [Maryland Militia] is assigned to the command of the four Regiments M.M. called out in pursuance of the Proclamation of the President of the United States dated at Washington the 15th day of April 1861." Governor Thomas H. Hicks confirmed this appointment.[160]

Butler replied quickly to Scott on May 15, stating that he had been given verbal orders from the War Department to advance upon Baltimore. He then proceeded to describe how he took possession of Federal Hill "amid the plaudits of many of the people." He continued to detail the finding of arms under the custody of the Board of Police. He justified issuing a proclamation "in order to set right the thousand conflicting stories and rumors of the intentions of the Government as to Baltimore, which were taken advantage of by the mob to incite insubordination and encourage a spirit of insurrection, and which showed itself upon our taking possession of the Government arms, but was instantly suppressed upon a show of force."[161] Scott was both surprised and angered that Butler had apparently acted on his own recognizance. The command of federal troops in Baltimore (officially called the Department of Annapolis) passed through many hands in 1861 and 1862. Benjamin Butler's tenure as Commander in Baltimore was brought short almost as soon as it had begun. General Winfield Scott swiftly rebuked Butler for overstepping his orders, removing him and replacing him with Brevet Major General George Cadwalader on May 15. Cadwalader's headquarters was Fort McHenry in Baltimore.

Cadwalader was given two primary jobs to accomplish, one being to keep order and enforce laws, the other to suppress any Southern supporters that might tend to push Maryland toward secession. Lincoln believed that the loss of Maryland would cause the fall of Washington and likely the entire Union. Cadwalader continued Butler's prohibition of Southern symbols, including the display of blatantly

Confederate images such as flags and banners, as well as simple or more subtle items such as juxtapositioned red and white colors, and the singing of Southern songs. Cadwalader was actually thought by many to be too lenient on the secessionists and Southern sympathizers in Baltimore, and he also was quickly relieved of his command. General Nathaniel P. Banks replaced Cadwalader on June 11, 1861. Baltimore citizens subsequently made Banks their scapegoat, accusing him of using deceptive tactics and secret informants to trick them into situations that resulted in the arrest of many pro–Southern citizens. General Banks also continued the suppression of displays of Southern solidarity. General John Adams Dix replaced Banks only a few weeks later, on July 23, 1861. Dix was a more formidable commander and a strict disciplinarian. Under his command, the Department of Annapolis was renamed the Department of Maryland, though the headquarters was still at Fort McHenry. Dix felt that Baltimore was both crucial for the maintenance of the Union and fabled as

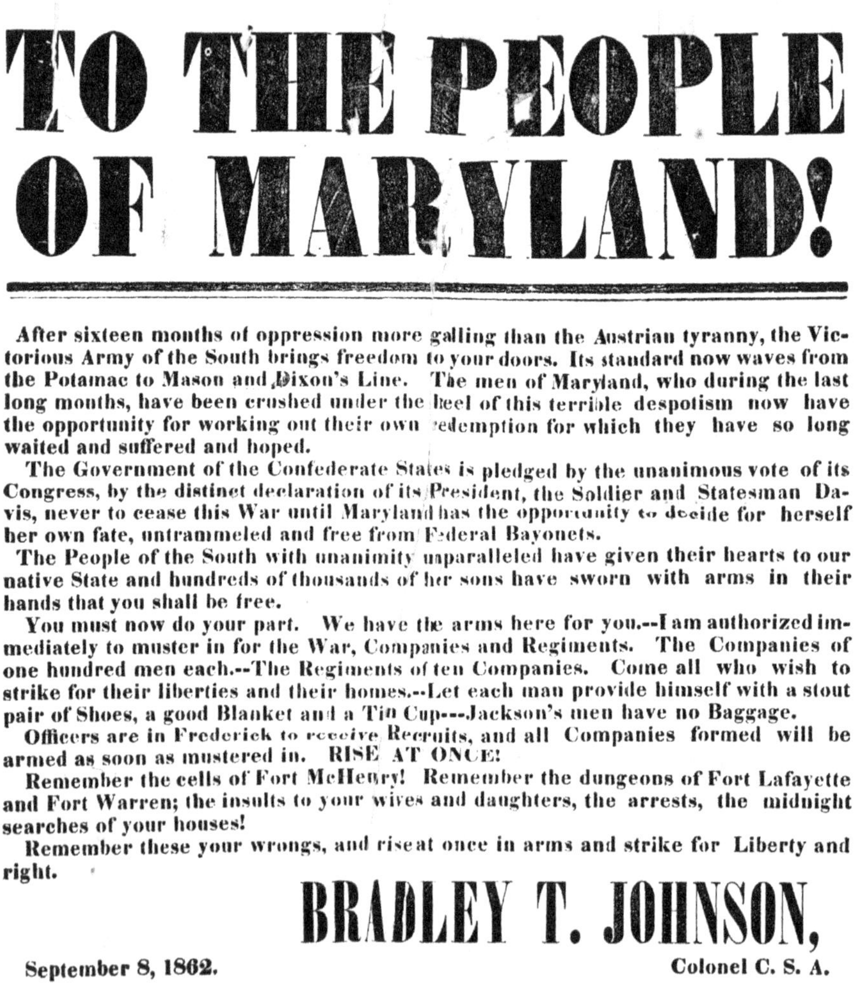

TO THE PEOPLE OF MARYLAND!

After sixteen months of oppression more galling than the Austrian tyranny, the Victorious Army of the South brings freedom to your doors. Its standard now waves from the Potomac to Mason and Dixon's Line. The men of Maryland, who during the last long months, have been crushed under the heel of this terrible despotism now have the opportunity for working out their own redemption for which they have so long waited and suffered and hoped.

The Government of the Confederate States is pledged by the unanimous vote of its Congress, by the distinct declaration of its President, the Soldier and Statesman Davis, never to cease this War until Maryland has the opportunity to decide for herself her own fate, untrammeled and free from Federal Bayonets.

The People of the South with unanimity unparalleled have given their hearts to our native State and hundreds of thousands of her sons have sworn with arms in their hands that you shall be free.

You must now do your part. We have the arms here for you.--I am authorized immediately to muster in for the War, Companies and Regiments. The Companies of one hundred men each.--The Regiments of ten Companies. Come all who wish to strike for their liberties and their homes.--Let each man provide himself with a stout pair of Shoes, a good Blanket and a Tin Cup---Jackson's men have no Baggage.

Officers are in Frederick to receive Recruits, and all Companies formed will be armed as soon as mustered in. RISE AT ONCE!

Remember the cells of Fort McHenry! Remember the dungeons of Fort Lafayette and Fort Warren; the insults to your wives and daughters, the arrests, the midnight searches of your houses!

Remember these your wrongs, and rise at once in arms and strike for Liberty and right.

BRADLEY T. JOHNSON,

September 8, 1862.   Colonel C. S. A.

Figure 39. Broadside from Colonel Bradley Johnson, September 8, 1862, seeking troops for the Confederate cause. From the Maryland Center for History and Culture.

a center of rowdies and riotous activity.¹⁶² He thought that he needed to control the city with an iron hand, and for this reason he was even less popular than previous commanders.

Sarcastic comments abounded among the citizenry about Dix's suppression of Southern symbols, particularly the combinations of red and white colors, including a published broadside that read:

> It is said that all mint candy and barber poles of that color were forbidden, and that: All white persons having red hair and moustaches, or whiskers, are hereby warned to have the one or the other dyed blue. No sunrises or sunsets which exhibit such combinations will be permitted on pain of suppression. Persons are forbidden to drink red and white wine alternately. His Majesty (Abraham 1st) is however graciously pleased to make an exception in favor of red noses, these last being greatly in vogue among Federal officers....
> Done at the Baltimore Bastille [Ft. McHenry], this 4th day of September the 1st year of Abraham's glorious and peaceful reign.
>
> Signed: JOHN L. [*sic*] DIX, Maj. Gen.¹⁶³

General John E. Wool replaced Dix on June 1, 1862. If possible, Wool was yet even more unpopular. He was strict and expressed disdain for any secessionist thought. He began a new series of arrests for any perceived Southern sympathies. Subsequently, General Robert C. Schenck took over for General Wool on December 23, 1862. After Wool, almost any commander would have seemed acceptable to Baltimoreans, but the honeymoon was quickly dashed as Schenck and his subordinates—especially his Provost Marshal, William S. Fish—made even more arrests for disloyalty. Schenck also instituted martial law on June 30, 1863. Each new Union commander seemed more odious than the previous one.

Weapons continued to be a major factor in the activity of the federal troops in Baltimore. Mr. Washington Bonifant, the United States' Marshal for the District of Maryland, butted heads with Marshal Kane over the possession of some guns stored in the McKim House on Greenmount Avenue in the city. General Cadwalader later sent

Figure 40. George Kane, tintype photograph, ca. July 1861; prototype for the drawing in *Harper's Weekly*, Figure 41, below: From the Maryland Center for History and Culture.

100 soldiers to that location to take control of the large cache of weapons stored there. Kane, under the Board's direction, objected in principle to the seizure of the guns, but he and his officers ultimately allowed the federal government to take control of the weapons. A total of 480 muskets and 1,500 pikes were transported by 18–20 wagons to the Locust Point area and stored at Fort McHenry.[164] Furthermore, in early June 1861, Union Colonel Edward Petherbridge approached Marshal Kane and told him that Governor Hicks had ordered Kane to relinquish all of the arms belonging to the State of Maryland. Once again, Kane objected to this action, but because he was presented with an order from the Board of Police directing him to comply, he did.[165]

Wholesale arrests of anyone who had any hint of Southern sympathies were common, and they continued throughout the war. Newspapers were censored, newspaper editors and writers were arrested, documents were randomly seized, and ordinary citizens were arrested if a person merely suggested that his neighbor harbored Southern sentiments. No proof was needed; suspicion was sufficient. The arrested and confined men did not sit idle. They bombarded the government with letters demanding their release, complaining about being arrested without due process and about their living conditions, seeking a speedy trial, and refusing to sign the oath of allegiance because it would be a passive admission of some sort of guilt.[166]

Meanwhile, Kane's friend and secessionist supporter Bradley T. Johnson was busy in western Maryland recruiting troops for the Confederate Army (Figure 39).

Activities of women of the time are often overlooked, but some of Marshal Kane's relatives would also be cited for

Figure 41A. George Proctor Kane. From *Harper's Weekly.*

treasonable activities. In October 1863 Elizabeth Kane, Kane's sister, and Clara Kane, his niece, were sent to the South from Baltimore for writing "treasonable letters" to their relatives in the Confederate Army.[167]

Maryland did not have the luxury of choosing her own allegiance; Lincoln and the Union chose Maryland's destiny for her. Arbitrary arrests, suspension of habeas corpus, suppression of the state legislature, control of elections, martial law, occupation by federal troops, and the control of the press were all deemed necessary for the preservation of the Union. Arrests were originally ordered solely by the Department of State, then jointly by the Department of State and the Department of War, then by the Department of War alone. William Seward was considered to be the villain by many Marylanders arrested early in the Civil War, including Kane (Figures 40–41) and his co-prisoners. For a lot of them, Seward was worse than Lincoln. On September 26, 1862, Lincoln established Provost-Marshals in each state, and these men soon dominated the law enforcement processes. The Provost-Marshals employed other law enforcement agencies and military forces, as well as citizens, to enforce restrictions on secessionist activities. Those arrested for "treasonable activities" were to be tried by military courts. The appropriateness and legality of Lincoln's and the federal government's actions during the Civil War have now been debated for over 150 years.[168] The debate likely will never end.

Figure 41B. From the New York Public Library.

12

Kane's Arrest

Kane had conducted himself reasonably well during the April 19 riot, but most people knew his Southern sympathies. After General Benjamin Butler occupied Baltimore on May 13, Butler began to pursue the stories that Kane and the Baltimore police harbored large quantities of weapons and ammunition, supposedly to be sent to the South. When soldiers from Butler's command confronted Kane and tried to inspect a local warehouse, Kane objected. He refused admission of the federal troops to the building and challenged their authority to search premises that contained what Kane interpreted to be a legitimate storage of weaponry for the city of Baltimore. When Kane refused to give Butler's men the key to the warehouse, he asked by what authority they came. Allegedly the Commander responded, "By the authority of my sword!"[1]

George P. Kane was quietly arrested at his home at 163 St. Paul Street at 3:00 a.m., June 27, 1861 (Appendix, Table 7). Major General Nathaniel P. Banks sent a cadre of federal soldiers from the Maryland Volunteers from Camp Carroll and the Pennsylvania Regiment from Federal Hill. They apparently expected a fight because Major General Banks had sent 500[2]–1,800[3] men. Banks made the arrest in secrecy. Kane appeared at his door only partially dressed, wearing a head cap, and offered no resistance. When Kane asked what the soldiers wanted, the Commander said that Kane himself was the object of their attention. Kane replied, in a joking manner, "I'll supply that demand."[4] Kane seemed astonished at the large number of troops mustered for his arrest. He allegedly said, "Good God! Why did you not bring five or six more regiments, and some artillery? If you had sent me a note and a carriage, I would have come without all this fuss"[5] (Figure 42). Union troops guarded every street near his home and detained any nearby Baltimore police in case they might fight the arrest. However, everything proceeded so quietly that few of Kane's neighbors even knew what was happening. The federal troops transported Kane to Fort McHenry where he was jailed, and the detained Baltimore police were then released. *Frank Leslie's Illustrated Newspaper*, reporting the event, touted Kane as "the most active rebel in Maryland."[6] He would soon be joined in Fort McHenry by many of his friends.

Word of Kane's arrest soon spread to the residents of Baltimore, and polarization of their North-South sentiments became more evident. Allegedly the cause of Kane's arrest was his "plot in this city to oppose the military orders of the administration by force."[7] Union sympathizers lauded the arrest, while Southern-leaning persons denounced it as unconstitutional. Kane's detention and imprisonment sparked small demonstrations throughout the city.

Figure 42. "Arrest of Marshal Kane, at his house in Baltimore, at three o'clock a.m., on Thursday, June 27, by order of Major-General Banks on a charge of treason." From *Frank Leslie's Illustrated Newspaper*.

General Banks himself created a stir that same day with a proclamation that declared his arrest of Marshal Kane and the reasons behind the action:

> I have arrested, and do now detain in custody, Mr. George P. Kane, Chief of Police of the City of Baltimore....
>
> [U]nlawful combinations of men, organized for resistance to such laws, that provide hidden deposits of arms and ammunition, encourage contraband traffic with men at war with the Government ... are not among the recognized or legal rights of any class of men, and cannot be permitted under any form of government whatever.... Under such circumstances the Government cannot regard him [Kane] otherwise than as the head of an armed force, hostile to its authority and acting in concert with its avowed enemies.[8]

However, Banks tried to reassure the populace that it was not his intention to interpose himself in the business of the city. The same day, June 27, Major General Banks sent Colonel John Reese Kenly and Kenly's Secretary Lieutenant Frederick Tarr to the office of the Police Commissioners to relieve them of their duties. Banks later issued another proclamation to the city:

> The police headquarters, under charge of the board, when abandoned by their officers, resembled in some respects a concealed arsenal. After public recognition and protest against the

"suspension of their functions," they [the Police Commissioners] continue in daily secret sessions. Upon a forced and unwarrantable construction of my proclamation of the 27th ultimo, they declared the police law itself suspended, and the officers and men off duty for the present, intending to leave the city without any police protection whatsoever.[9]

After a brief consultation among themselves, the Police Commissioners immediately protested the takeover of the police force by federal agents. Thomas Gifford, the Deputy Marshal under Kane, wrote to his men, "The police force will continue in the discharge of their duty as theretofore. No military force is intended to take the place of the present force, without necessity calls [sic] for it."[10]

Colonel Kenly was not unknown to Kane and the Commissioners. Kenly was a Baltimore native, born in 1822,[11] and was educated there, including his study of law. He passed the bar in 1845 and was active in the Baltimore military scene, first as a member of the Eagle Artillery, the same militia where Kane was an officer. Kenly became a lieutenant in this group before joining William H. Watson's militia called "Baltimore's Own," formed to respond to the Mexican War. Kenly served in the Mexican War initially as a captain, and he fought in the battle of Monterey, where he distinguished himself as an outstanding soldier. Upon returning to Baltimore in June 1847, he resumed his practice of law until June 11, 1861, when Lincoln appointed him as a colonel in the Union Army. So Kenly was well qualified to take over as chief of police. Kenly and Kane had worked side by side on many projects in the Eagle Artillery. Kenly was both well known and loved by most Baltimoreans. His appointment as Provost Marshal after Kane's arrest placed him in the unenviable position of dealing with the fallout of the arrest of his friend and another beloved Baltimorean and enforcing federal rule on a city that had not yet decided where its loyalties should fall.

General Winfield Scott had given orders to Major General Banks on June 24: "[Y]ou should take measures quietly to seize at once and securely hold the four members of the Baltimore police board, viz: Charles Howard, Wm. H. Gatchell, J. W. Davis, and C. D. Hinks, esqrs., together with the chief of police, G. P. Kane."[12] Banks had first ordered Kane's arrest; then he instructed Colonel Edward Jones, Commander of the Sixth Massachusetts Regiment, the very Regiment that had been attacked as it passed through Baltimore on April 19: "[Y]ou will proceed with a detachment of nine companies of your regiment immediately upon receipt of this order to the residence of Mr. Charles Howard, late a member of the board of police commissioners, or wherever else he may be found and him the said Howard arrest and securely hold and bring him to Fort McHenry in this department without fail."[13] There was a brief delay, but on July 1 federal troops arrested the entire rest of the Board of Police Commissioners—Davis, Hinks, and Gatchell, in that order— between 2:00 and 3:00 a.m., all of whom were sent to Fort McHenry. It was rather amazing the amount of manpower and firepower used to arrest these men: Kane ~1,000 men; Howard ~900 men, Gatchell ~400 men, Davis and Hinks ~700 men each.[14] Hinks was in ill health and was quickly released upon the receipt of a letter on July 3 certifying his illness ("consumption," another term for tuberculosis) and stating that his incarceration might prove to be fatal.[15]

Kenly served the Police Commissioners and the police force with a resolution:

"I [Colonel Kenly] assume and take command of the police force of the City of Baltimore, to superintend and, with the aid of the subordinate officers of the Police Department, to execute and cause to be executed the Police law provided by the Legislature of Maryland 'for the government of the City of Baltimore.'"[16] Kenly then proceeded to the Central Police Station to inform Deputy Police Marshal Thomas Gifford of the administrative changes and to assume charge of the police force. Banks had also provided Kenly with a declaration that confirmed Kenly's appointment.[17]

Reaction to these arrests immediately caused Simon Cameron, Secretary of War, to write to Brigadier General J. K. F. Mansfield, warning him to be careful how he chose to arrest the secessionists and subversives: "Complaints are received at this department of arrests and searches in Maryland by troops from this District. You will please give directions to prevent such proceedings except for good cause and by your order and to have your own necessary orders for such arrests and searches executed by discreet officers from the native camps."[18]

In an explanatory document written slightly later on July 29, 1861, from their confinement at Fort McHenry, the Police Commissioners (Howard, Gatchell and Davis—Hinks had at this point already been released because of his poor health) explained that Major General Banks and Provost Marshal John Kenly had on June 27 "suspended the active operation of the Police law, and put for the time off duty, all the officers and men, who could not without directly violating both the letter and spirit of the law, recognize the authority or be subject to the control of any other head than the Board of Police."

The Police Commissioners continued to object strenuously to their arrest. On July 29, Howard, Gatchell, and Davis wrote from Fort McHenry to the U.S. Senate and House of Representatives: "[we] received no information as to the cause of [our] arrest…, nor have [we] since been informed of any charges whatever."[19] They called Banks's actions an "unwarrantable and unlawful violation of [our] personal liberty."[20] They contended that the "arsenal" found in the police offices "were the lawful property of the city; that they were insignificant in quantity, constituting but little more than the customary armament of the force for its public duties, and were lawfully concealed to prevent unlawful seizure."[21] They argued that only the Board of Police Commissioners had the power to hire and fire policemen and that such action by Major General Banks was illegal. Mayor Brown likewise wrote to the U.S. Senate and the House of Representatives confirming the assertions of the Commissioners, and saying that "Arms belonging to the City of Baltimore and rightfully in the custody of its authorities have been taken."[22] The House of Representatives responded on July 24 by writing a resolution to President Lincoln, asking for an explanation of the government's actions. Lincoln refused.[23]

Memoranda from the State Department regarding the arrests of Kane, the Mayor, and the Police Commissioners stated vague charges by federal government officials, but did not identify specific acts of treason that these men had committed. The most common word used in the charges was "precaution":

> **KANE:** "Kane was notoriously in deep sympathy with the rebels and his arrest was a measure of military precaution. No testimony has been furnished to the State Department by the military department at Baltimore of any specific acts of disloyalty by Kane."

GEORGE W. BROWN [who was arrested in September, later than the others]: "There are no papers in the State Department showing the precise character of the charges against Brown."

CHARLES HOWARD: "So far as the Department of State is advised the arrest and detention of Charles Howard seem to have been military precautionary measures founded upon his well-known sympathies with treason."

WILLIAM H. GATCHELL: "This arrest was made as a measure of military precaution to guard against the abuse of authority in furtherance of the interests of the insurrection to which the police commissioners were contributing all their exertions."

JOHN W. DAVIS: "The arrest and detention of John W. Davis were purely military precautionary measures founded upon his known sympathies with treason, so far as the State Department is advised."[24]

Such arbitrary arrests were exceedingly common during the Civil War. One estimate places the number at 14,401 arrested by the North during the entire War, meaning that about 1 in 1,500 Northerners would be arrested during the course of the conflict.[25] Another estimate placed 2,094 "political" arrests during the Civil War in the state of Maryland alone—politicians, legislators, government officers, businessmen, newspaper editors and owners, doctors, bankers, lawyers, and others.[26] Political prisoners were distinguished from combatants in the prisons, and they were often treated differently. Political prisoners often were paroled quite rapidly, most commonly simply upon taking an oath of allegiance to the United States. William H. Seward in the Department of State was notoriously quick to have someone arrested on suspicion of disloyalty. Seward once wrote to Lord Richard B. P. Lyons (British Minister to the United States, 1858–1865), bragging about his powers of arrest: "My Lord, I can touch a bell on my right hand, and order the arrest of a citizen of Ohio; I can touch a bell again, and order the imprisonment of a citizen of New York; and no power on earth, except that of the President, can release them. Can the Queen of England do so much?"[27] Edwin M. Stanton in the War Department was more adept at administration than was his predecessor Simon Cameron, and Seward apparently relinquished his internal security duties without objection. However, Stanton correspondingly gave Joseph Holt, the Judge Advocate General, many of the duties of protecting security, which included making arrests of suspected traitors or at least those who might have traitorous tendencies.[28]

Prisons were filled with these two major classes of prisoners—combatants and political prisoners. Because most political prisoners were held without charges and without the benefit of habeas corpus, they frequently petitioned authorities for release, or at least to have charges brought against them and to be brought to trial. Major John A. Dix received many of these entreaties, and he ruled that some were too dangerous for release or parole: George P. Kane, Charles Howard, Frank Key Howard, T. Parkin Scott, S. Teackle Wallis, H. M. Warfield, Richard Thomas (Zarvona—"the French Lady"), and some members of the Maryland Legislature. Contrary to practices today, however, many of the political prisoners were allowed to be briefly released for urgent personal needs—deaths or illnesses of close family members, pressing business obligations, etc., only to return to prison on their own recognizance and honor.

Suppression of voting in some areas was another goal of the federal government. Commander John A. Dix wrote from Baltimore on November 1, 1861, stating that he had been asked if an election official could demand an oath of allegiance from any voter who appeared "of doubtful loyalty." Dix replied that he would like to answer in the affirmative, but that he could not interfere in the voting process of Marylanders. Then he added, "But it is in the power of the judges of the election under the authority given them to satisfy themselves as to the qualifications of the voters—*to put to those who offer to poll such searching questions in regard to residence and citizenship as to detect traitors* and without any violation of the constitution or laws of Maryland to *prevent the pollution of the ballot boxes by their votes*."[29] He wrote another letter the same day saying that his officers were to arrest voters who were attempting to "convert the elective franchise into an engine for the subversion of the government." He was seeking to "prevent the ballot boxes from being polluted by treasonable votes."[30] In other words, let them vote, as long as they support the Union's candidates and principles.

In many areas the criteria for declaration of secessionist tendencies were extremely loose. Major General John A. Dix wrote about some Baltimoreans that they "had committed no particular acts of hostility to the Government subsequently to the 19th of April last but were offensive in their conduct and conversation as secessionists." Many displays that were interpreted as Confederate sympathies were outlawed—the colors red and white, certain flags (especially any resembling Confederate designs and including some state flags), certain decorations, "secession slippers," "secession caps," emblems, "cockades," and envelopes.[31] Even the singing of certain songs was forbidden. Musical bands, marching, and parades were prohibited, and on certain days when the risk of rioting seemed the worst, the bars and taverns were also closed.[32]

Baltimore was said to be under martial law during this time, but in fact it wasn't. Generally accepted definitions of martial law require the takeover of civil functions by the military. Often curfews are imposed; the right of habeas corpus is often abrogated; civil rights can be limited; military rules and laws are enforced. While the application of the term "martial law" to the circumstances in Baltimore might be questioned, at no time did military courts replace civil judicial authority. Civil courts were open. Though the (replaced) city police force was functioning under the authority of federal officials, the civil powers were still operating otherwise. The Mayor still performed his duties; the laws in effect were the ones previously set in place by the municipal and state governments. Curfews were imposed, and certain activities were limited or prohibited.[33] However, martial law was indeed proclaimed officially on June 30, 1863, by Major General Robert E. Schenck, and it was not rescinded until after the November 1863 elections.[34]

In their own defense, Police Commissioners Howard, Gatchell and Davis filed a "Memorial" sent to the U.S. Senate and House of Representatives, explaining their view of the circumstances. They complained that they had been arrested without being told of the cause of their arrest and that no formal charges had been filed against them. They cited the only document that they could access—a proclamation—which stated that their arrest was made "in pursuance of orders issued from headquarters of the army at Washington, for the preservation of the public peace" and that the Police Commissioners were refusing to acknowledge the legality of the federal government's assumption of the control of the Baltimore Police. The Police Commissioners continued to meet daily, even after they were imprisoned at Fort McHenry. Federal officials claimed that the Commissioners had "suspended Police Law" and had declared the Baltimore police force to be "off duty, 'intending to leave the city without any police protection whatsoever.'" The Commissioners denied any such intentions. They were accused of refusing to acknowledge the authority of Provost Marshal Kenly (under General Banks), and they were said to be harboring a "concealed arsenal" at the headquarters of the Force. The Commissioners contended under "the explicit terms of the law, that no police force can lawfully exist in Baltimore, unless appointed and governed by the Police Board." They claimed that "None of them [the Police Commissioners] are subject to removal, except by the Legislature of Maryland, from which they derive their authority and functions." Finally, the Board objected to the use of a Provost Marshal to control the police because martial law had not been officially declared in Baltimore; state and federal courts were open and functioning.[35]

The Police Commissioners declared that the removal of the Board also constituted the suspension of the rank-and-file officers:

> *Resolved*, That this Board do solemnly protest against the orders and proceedings above referred to of Major General Banks, as an arbitrary exercise of military power, not warranted by any provision of the Constitution or Laws of the United States, or of the State of Maryland, but in derogation of all of them.
> *Resolved*, That whilst the Board ... cannot, consistently with their views of official duty, and of the obligations of their oaths of office, recognize the right of any of the officers and men of the Police force, as such, to receive orders or directions from any other authority than from this Board.
> *Resolved*, That, in the opinion of the Board, the forcible suspension of their functions, suspends at the same time the active operation of the Police law, and puts the officers and men off duty for the present.[36]

This resolution was signed by all of the Police Commissioners—Charles Howard (President), William H. Gatchell, Charles D. Hinks, and John W. Davis—as well as Mayor George William Brown, an ex officio Member of the Board.

Banks countered on July 1, summarizing his points of previous communications: he had discovered an "arsenal" of weapons; the board suspended the police, and the board did not recognize the police appointed by Banks.[37]

Banks also stated that the entire police force remained intact, save for the Commissioners and the Chief of Police, under orders from the new federal Provost Marshal Colonel Kenly,[38] who was charged with the authority to replace any police officer who refused to comply with the change in command of the force. Nevertheless, the now-defunct Board of Police Commissioners directed the entire police force to disband, calling upon them to return to their respective station houses. The Board objected to any entity, even the federal government, usurping the powers conferred upon the Board by the State of Maryland. The Board directed the police officers to remove their "stars and numbers," signifying that they were off duty. Most of the 400-plus policemen were opposed to the recent actions of the federal government, as was Kane. The Board told them that they would continue to be paid, even though they were "off duty." Kenly immediately issued a directive: "No act or resolution of the late Board of Commissioners of Police can operate as a suspension of any officer now in service. Every man [on the force] will be continued until he voluntarily retires from the discharge of his duties." Kenly then implored the citizens of Baltimore to assist in the maintenance of law and order: "I call upon all good citizens to aid me in preserving the peace of this city, and respectfully suggest that no more effectual way to do this can be devised than to exhort you all to avoid congregating at the corners of streets or any given point, and heads of families to keep their household in doors [sic] after nightfall."[39] Also, perhaps expecting widespread disorder, he proclaimed, "Ordered that all bar-rooms and places for the sale of intoxicating liquors be immediately closed."

The police in general tended to comply with the former Board of Commissioners, rather than Colonel Kenly. Fully 360 of the nearly 400 members of the police force initially disbanded.[40] In so doing, they removed their uniforms, badges, caps, and batons. Most police returned to their station houses, where they proceeded to take many of the items from the station needed for effective police function: "official records and dockets, blank warrants, revolvers, muskets, rattles, sticks and other appurtenances of the force, and the houses appeared quite desolate."[41] Any new police would find it more difficult to function with the station houses stripped of equipment and supplies.

Nevertheless, Colonel Kenly rapidly organized a new police force, naming four new captains, each of which was authorized to hire one hundred men for the new force. The new federal control of the police had to seek and hire nearly 400 officers to man the duties required to keep the peace. Major General John A. Dix, Commander of the Baltimore Regiment, would write to Major General G. B. McClellan on September 4, 1861:

> The old police when disbanded consisted of 416 persons. Twenty-seven are in our service. Several have been discharged. There are now about 350 left. The great part of them are obscure and inoffensive persons. Some of them are Union men. There are I am confident not over forty or fifty who would not take the oath of allegiance. There are some very mischievous, worthless fellows, but they are quiet. We only want a pretext for arresting them. They have up to this time been paid by the city. Yesterday I addressed a letter to the mayor ordering the payment to be discontinued. I think he will obey it. If he does not I shall arrest him and make a like order on the city comptroller who will obey.[42]

Most of the new recruits were actually police from the old force who were "reenlisting" to keep their jobs and income, though the overall composition of the new police force was more Union in sentiment. Southern sympathies within the police force rapidly reverted to Union support, mostly triggered by a desire to maintain a job and income. Initially lacking uniforms, these new recruits were identified in public by the wearing of a special scarlet ribbon on their clothing.

John R. Kenly's command of the police force under his title of Provost Marshal was then rapidly accepted. Banks dispatched his troops to the major streets of Baltimore to restore order, and Kenly searched Kane's office and nearby quarters in the building for contraband arms thought to be stored for the use of the secessionists. Symbolically, a cannon was found at the entrance to Kane's office. In addition, more stores of munitions were found "in an old back building of the City Hall."[43] The old City Hall Building had been used by Kane as his office, and an old building in the back, "formerly occupied as the City Collector's office,"[44] concealed guns and ammunition that were hidden in floors, ceilings, under rafters, beneath mounds of coal, and in walls of the building, indicating "no lack of evidence of the traitorous sentiments of Marshal Kane and his coadjutors."[45] Furthermore, at least one report alleged that Kane had constructed a storage building on Gallows Hill (near where the Maryland Penitentiary sits now) to hide munitions to be used for secessionist activity.[46]

On July 10 Banks appointed Baltimore citizen George R. Dodge to be the new Marshal of Police, assuming duty and replacing Provost Marshal Kenly the next day on July 11. Kenly would leave Baltimore on July 16 to rejoin his regiment, the First Maryland Infantry, where his rank was Colonel.

The exact timing and mechanism of the removal of the original police force from the streets of Baltimore was in itself an issue. Commissioners would argue that even though the police withdrew from active duty, they were still employees of the city entitled to pay, even though they were "on leave." The Board, furthermore, stated that it would refuse to pay *both* the "old" Baltimore force and the "new" federal force, though most men were the same for both. The Board refused to acknowledge Colonel Kenly's recent hires. This issue of payment of police salaries would plague negotiations over the new police force for months.

For all of the arrests made by Union officials of pro–Southern adherents during 1861–1865, very few cases were brought to trial. In fact, Kane and the Mayor and

Figure 43. "Interior of the outbuilding attached to Marshal Kane's police headquarters, Holliday Street, Baltimore—discovery of cannon, muskets, ball and ammunition intended for the service of the secessionists." From *Frank Leslie's Illustrated Newspaper*.

Police Commissioners were never tried, though some preliminary proceedings were instituted against Kane. The only case for these men that made it completely through the court system was this obscure issue dealing with the use of the funds allocated to the Police Department early in the Civil War. The Board of Police Commissioners contended that the original Baltimore police were "on duty" but "on leave" during the summer of 1861 when Colonel Kenly supposedly disbanded the Baltimore force and installed his own men. Furthermore, the actual disbursement of funds itself from the police account became an issue. On February 6, 1862, William Gatchell, the Treasurer of the Commissioners, wrote a check to Charles Hinks for $1,000, supposedly paying him his salary from August 6, 1861, through February 6, 1862. Gatchell actually wrote this check to Hinks (who himself was not imprisoned) from his prison cell at Fort Warren in Boston. The new Mayor and the City Council of Baltimore notified the Farmers and Planters Bank of Baltimore that it should not cash the check, and it didn't. This action started a lawsuit challenging the right of the former Commissioners to dispense money from the police fund. Courts eventually ruled that the Commissioners did indeed have the right to disburse the money, even from their Boston prison cells. This ruling led to the Revocation Act and the Establishment Act.[47] The Maryland State Legislature passed the Revocation Act on February 12, 1862, removing the power of the four Commissioners (Howard, Gatchell, Hinks, and Davis) to access money in the police funds (but it did not grant this power to the Mayor or the City Council of Baltimore). Furthermore, it authorized the payment of the police appointed by the military after the takeover of the police force by Colonel Kenly. The same body passed the Establishment Act on February 18, 1862, creating a new Police Board of Commissioners, removing Howard, Gatchell, Hinks and Davis, installing Samuel Hinds and Nicholas L. Woods, and authorizing the new police force and the payment of their salaries (about $10 per week).[48] So by early 1862 the control of the Baltimore police seemed secure.

After Kane was arrested and the Police Commissioners were removed from duty, Banks reported to Lieutenant General Scott: "The city has remained in perfect order and quiet since the organization of the new police. The headquarters of the police, when vacated by the officers appointed by the board, resembled a concealed arsenal. Large quantities of arms and ammunition were found secreted in such places and with such skill as to forbid the thought of their being held for just or lawful purposes."[49] The "concealed arsenal" was tabulated as "six 6-pounder iron cannon; two 4-pounder iron cannon; 332 muskets, rifles and pistols, and a large quantity of ammunition, &c."[50] (Figure 43). Federal authorities believed that Kane and the Police Commissioners were trafficking these weapons for the South. Indeed, Governor Hicks even issued an order demanding that all weapons officially the property of the State be given to the federal officers.

Other newspapers itemized what Kane had amassed in this "arsenal" in the building he occupied. The tallies all varied greatly, with multiple sites of storage, but one report stated:

> 1 six pound iron gun, with limber only [limber is a 2-wheeled carriage]
> 1 six-pound iron gun, without limber

2 four-pound iron guns without limber
1.5 tons assorted shot
1.5 kegs shot for steam gun
120 flint muskets
2 Hall's carbines
8 rifles
3 double barreled shot guns
8 single barreled shot guns
9 horse pistols
65 small pistols
132 bullet molds
3 cartridge boxes
8 dirk knives
5 swords
8 kettle drums
1 lot of worm and screw drivers
1 box musket cartridges
33 gum coats
35 rifles
3 8–12 dozen copper powder flasks
1 8–12 dozen small powder flasks
6 muskets
117 cannisters
1 lot of flannel bags
12 old muskets
25 Minié muskets
46 Hall's carbines
1 set of slow matches
48 millions hat caps
2 kegs ball cartridges
100 rifle ball cartridges
735 Hall's rifle cartridges
3,162 rounds ball cartridges
6,520 long ball Minié cartridges
7 cannisters of shot
1 12-pound cannon ball

The entire number of muskets was 600–700, with 40,000 rounds of ammunition.[51]

Additional items were found in a detective's room (20–30 revolvers), outhouses (a "small number" of revolvers), and the Middle District Police Station (2 six-pounder cannons, 2 four-pounder cannons, 6 shotguns, 15 lock and 9 flint muskets, "a lot of bayonets," and a "moderate sized basket containing flints").[52]

Union sympathizers deduced that this cache of weaponry was sufficient evidence for Kane's disloyalty and support of the Confederacy. Worthington G. Snethen, a Baltimore lawyer, Unionist, and staunch Republican, said,

> Last night, a further depot of 800 stand of arms was discovered at Jackson Hall in the 8th [Baltimore] Ward.... [T]he late Police Board and its Marshal, and the Mayor too, have

demonstrated that they are traitors, rebels, conspirators murderers and liars, by their acts and deeds. I repeat, that justice and the future peace of the city demand the arrest of the four Police Commissioners.

Their attempt to inaugurate anarchy, night before last, by disbanding the Police force, or rather ordering them off duty, and continuing them under pay, was most atrocious.[53]

Many other warehouses were reported to contain weapons intended for the Confederate cause. One cache of arms required 35 wagons to transport everything to Fort McHenry—110 boxes contained 2,200 muskets; another 67 boxes had spikes and spears, numbering over 4,000. Sixty thousand pounds of gunpowder was seized from a warehouse in Canton, and the Merrill & Thomas manufactory of breech-loading rifles was seized. The contents of these storehouses were used as some of the reasons given for Kane's arrest.

Some newspapers even reported (incorrectly) that the arresting officers found a commission in Kane's pocket that made him a Brigadier General in the rebel army.[54] Kane's title of "Colonel" had been with him for years already, long before the Civil War started, though he never appeared in any accounting of troops or officers of the Confederacy, as Brigadier General or Colonel or otherwise.

Kane argued that the arms discovered in his offices and storehouses were legitimate weapons of Baltimore and the State of Maryland, as militias were entitled and even required to provide their own weaponry. However, he was unable to explain satisfactorily why many of the weapons were stored concealed in floors, walls, and ceilings. It seemed obvious to many Northern newspapers that such hiding was *prima facie* evidence that the guns and ammunition were to be used for illegal purposes. Weaponry rightfully used by lawful militias shouldn't have needed such clandestine storage. Kane simply said that the guns were hidden to prevent theft.

There were cries to release the Police Commissioners, but military officials objected. General Nathaniel Banks wrote to William H. Seward on July 9:

> Mr: [sic] Howard without being, perhaps, a bad man at heart is one of the worst influences here. He was emphatically the most mischievous man, connected with the Police. He has three sons in the Confederate army and a fourth is editor of the "Exchange" published here that does not hesitate to reccommend [sic] assassination as a remedy for the obstacles the secessionists encounter in their work.—"It is difficult to determine," his paper said the other day, "whether the country most needs a Brutus or a Washington." To release the head of such a family would alarm all the friends of the governmt [sic] here for their safety.[55]

Mayor George Brown would soon submit a letter to the Baltimore City Council (July 11, 1861), defending Marshal Kane's actions and explaining the arms found in Kane's offices and storehouses:

> The board of police considered it proper that there should be a sufficient number of efficient weapons to arm the entire police force in case of an emergency.... That some of the arms and ammunition were concealed about the building is sufficiently explained by the fact that the officers in charge desired to secure them from seizure, but such concealment was made without my knowledge.[56]

Kane immediately retained his Baltimore lawyer and close friend, George W. Dobbin, for his defense. He also immediately wrote to the Honorable Henry May, a Congressional Representative of the Fourth Maryland District (and a supporter of the Southern cause, who would find himself arrested in mid–September, as well) to plead his case:

> I take the liberty of informing you that I am not advised of the causes of my arrest and challenge my accusers if any there be to bring me into a court of justice or to substantiate any charge against me affecting my character as an officer or gentleman.

He claimed that he was also the target of "a constant, systematic and willful abuse … in the Northern press ever since."[57]

Though George Kane claimed that he was arrested and held in prison without charges, newspapers reported that he had been indicted for treason by a Grand Jury of the United States District Court of Baltimore[58] (Figure 44). Kane quickly declared that he was unaware of the reason(s) for his arrest, though he stated that he was initially well treated, considering the circumstances.

The June 1861 session of the grand jury of the District Court of the United States in Maryland charged that Kane did

> commit treason against the said United States by levying war against the United States and by adhering to and giving aid and comfort to the said evil disposed persons by force and arms by obstruction the means of communication between the government of the United States and the troops of the said United States by ordering the destruction of bridges and telegraphs on the line of the Northern Central Rail Road while the aforesaid troops were on their way by orders of the government of the United States to defend the capitol of the government of the United States and by other means being in communication and connection with the aforesaid evil disposed persons by sending telegrams to them.

This "presentment" was filed July 16, 1861, after Kane was arrested. The document stated, rather repetitively, that Kane had committed treason.[59] In support of the charges, the government attached the handbill published in Frederick, Maryland, quoting Kane as saying to Bradley T. Johnson, "Bring your men by the first train, and we will arrange with the railroad afterwards. *Streets red with Maryland blood!* Send expresses over the mountains and valleys of Maryland and Virginia for the riflemen to come without delay. Fresh hordes will be down upon us tomorrow (the 20th). We will fight them, and whip them or die." Johnson was a secessionist, and the message certainly fueled the claim that Kane had acted in a treasonous manner to burn the bridges and cut the telegraph wires. This message from Kane to Johnson was considered to be a major indiscretion in Kane's behavior during this tumultuous time. The indictment claimed that Kane intended "to raise and levy war, insurrection and rebellion against the United States of America." It stated that over 500 persons were involved in the insurrection, which was primarily the riot that occurred as the Massachusetts troops passed from the President Street Station to the Camden Station on April 19. The latter portion of the indictment named the burning of six bridges serving the Northern Central Railroad and the cutting of telegraph wires traveling alongside it as some of Kane's major misdeeds, his "acts of treason." These charges were officially filed on July 19, 1861. Kane's initial hearing was to be on the first Monday of November 1861. According to Kane, court authorities never presented him with a warrant nor this indictment. Troops had arrested Kane, though his tentative November court date in Baltimore would never materialize. Kane would be incarcerated in the military prison at Fort Warren in Boston at that time (Figure 45).

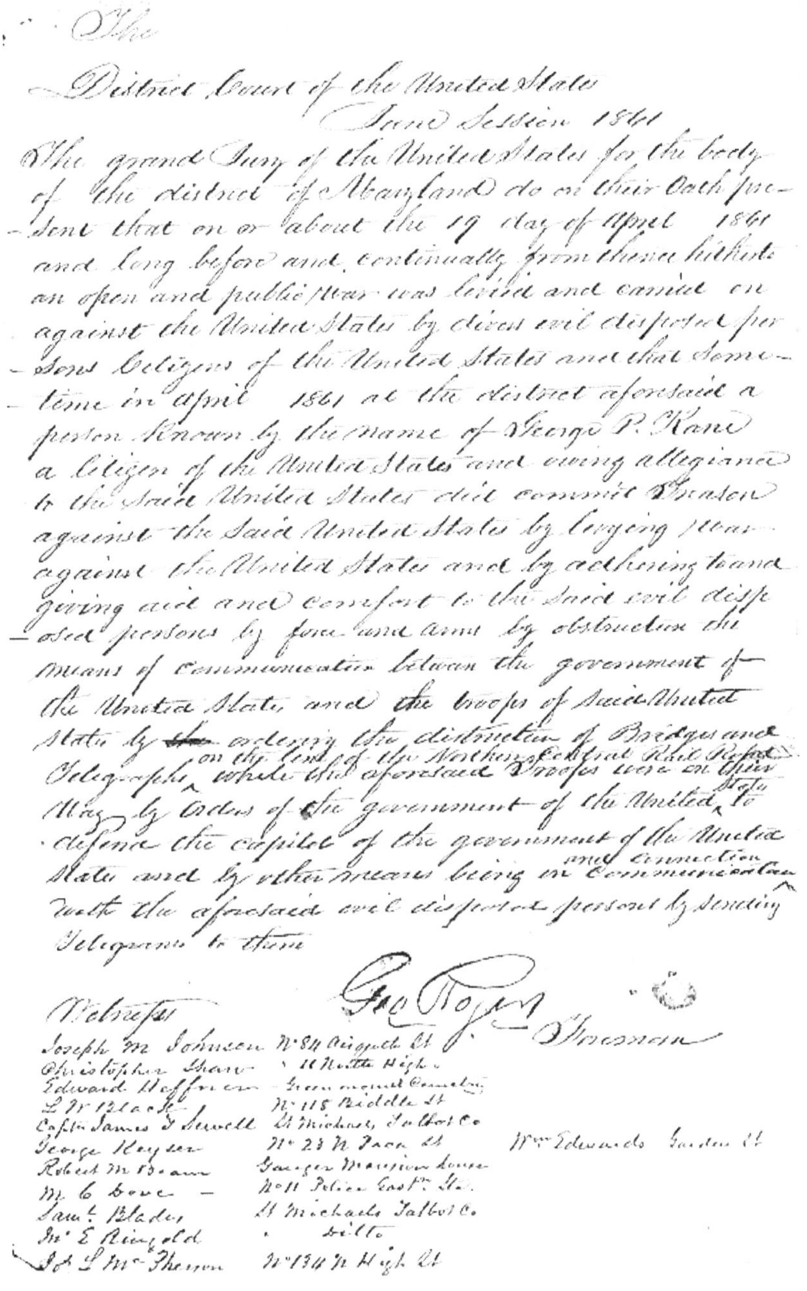

Figure 44. Portion of the grand jury action against George P. Kane for treasonous activity related to the April 19 Baltimore Riot. From the National Archives and Records Administration.

In November 1861 the U.S. Circuit Court met in Baltimore before Chief Justice Roger B. Taney and Judge William F. Giles, attending to the matter of the treason cases before this jurisdiction. Marshal Kane was described as "beyond the reach of the court" (meaning that he was jailed at Fort Warren), and his lawyer explained that Kane was indeed interested in having a speedy trial. Nevertheless, some of the witnesses were also jailed at Fort Warren, so the trial was "continued" (postponed) until the April term.⁶⁰ It was unclear if the military authorities would be willing to release Kane to the civil courts for trial.

In spite of these charges, Kane seems to have been well-respected by his fellow Baltimoreans for his behavior during the Riot of April 19. Even his detractors and enemies admitted that he had behaved bravely and honorably. U.S. Senator Anthony Kennedy, an American Party member, gave a speech in the Senate lauding Kane:

> No body of men were ever more zealous to perform their duty, and did it more daringly and openly, than the mayor, city authorities, and police of Baltimore, on that day.... I would appeal to the Massachusetts regiment itself to say whether this very man, Marshal Kane, did not interpose his fire between them and the mob, fighting gallantly to conduct the troops through the city? ... But, sir, notwithstanding he and I have ever been politically opposed, I will do him the justice to say, that no police force in this country ever exerted itself more nobly and more daringly than did the police force of Baltimore on the 19th of April, to maintain and enforce the dignity of the laws.

Kennedy also spoke in defense of Kane's possession of the "arsenal" of weapons, saying that it was grossly overstated, and that all weapons were simply kept for safekeeping to keep them out of "improper hands."[61]

Members of the Massachusetts Regiment would later write laudatory letters about Marshal Kane's behavior during this event, and Kane kept these letters and proudly displayed them to visitors to his office in subsequent years.[62]

Both the House of Representatives and the Senate initially supported Kane. The House resolved that President Lincoln needed to explain his actions. Lincoln said that it was "incompatible with the public interest at this time to furnish the information called for by the resolution." The Senate resolved on July 29 that Kane and the Police Board should either be turned over to the civil courts for trial or released, and that the Board should resume control of the police.

The House then offered another resolution, after being rebuffed by President Lincoln:

> Resolution offered in the House of Representatives July 31, 1861.
> Resolved, That the arrest and imprisonment of Charles Howard, William H. Gatchell and John W. Davis and others without warrant and process of law is flagrantly unconstitutional and illegal; and they should without delay be released, or their case remitted to the proper judicial tribunals to be lawfully heard and determined.

All of these entreaties were rejected.[63]

The Maryland Legislature usually met only every two years, but after the agitation evident over the possible secession of Southern states in early 1861, after President-Elect Lincoln's passage through Baltimore in February, and after the Baltimore riot of April 19, Governor Thomas Holliday Hicks called a special session (both the House and the Senate) for April 26 in Frederick, Maryland. He chose that city to discuss the crisis because the federal troops under General Benjamin F. Butler had occupied Annapolis on April 22, and Hicks feared that anti–Union feelings could spark conflict if the Legislature met there. Frederick, as a whole, leaned more toward pro–Union sentiments, anyway. President Lincoln, knowing that it was possible for the Legislature to address the question of secession, considered arresting the entire body of elected officials, but he decided against such a course of action. The Legislature met to discuss secession, but believed that it didn't have the statuary authority to vote for such a radical move. Legislators thought that for Maryland to withdraw from the Union there would need to be a special convention called with representatives elected specifically for the purpose of discussing and voting on such an action. On April 27 the Maryland Senate voted unanimously to declare that it had no authority to secede; the House of Delegates voted about 4:1, declaring the same sentiment. They agreed that the General Assembly needed to call for any such convention to deliberate secession, and it didn't happen. Neutrality remained important to most lawmakers, though they successfully passed a resolution objecting to any Union occupation of Maryland.[64]

Coincidentally, it was also on April 27 that President Lincoln authorized the suspension of habeas corpus in Maryland "in the extremest necessity." Lincoln wrote to General Winfield Scott, "You are engaged in repressing an insurrection against the laws of the United States. If at any point on or in the vicinity of the military line…, you find resistance which renders it necessary to suspend the writ of Habeas Corpus for the public safety, you, personally or through the officer in command at the point where the resistance occurs, are authorized to suspend that writ."[65]

Later in May 1861 the General Assembly clarified its stance, reporting that it believed that the war was unconstitutional and unjust, and that it wanted Maryland to have no part in the conflict. Further, it suggested that the Southern states be recognized as their own country, and that it objected to any military occupation of Maryland. One of the resolutions passed during August called for the "immediate recognition of the independence of the Confederate States."

The Maryland General Assembly again met in the summer in Frederick and adjourned on August 7, planning to reconvene on September 17. By now Governor Hicks had become more pro–Union.

By September, President Lincoln had determined that the Maryland Legislature needed to be arrested. While he had considered such arrests to be an unconstitutional abuse of power in April 1861, he now felt that it was necessary to preserve the Union and to assure the protection of the Capitol in Washington, D.C. He could not allow secession of the State of Maryland because such an action would isolate the seat of the federal government geographically from the rest of the Union and might cause the fall of the country.

On September 12, 1861, Major General George B. McClellan, after conferring with President Lincoln, Assistant Secretary of State Frederick W. Seward, and Secretary of War Simon Cameron, ordered General Banks (who commanded the Union forces in western Maryland) and General Dix (who commanded them in eastern Maryland) to arrange the arrest of the "disloyal" members of the Maryland Legislature in Frederick. Lincoln, Seward, Cameron, McClellan, Banks, and Dix suspected that the Maryland Legislature was about to pass a resolution of secession since about two-thirds of both branches of the Maryland Legislature were thought to be secessionists. Cameron had written to Banks on September 11, "The passage of any act of secession by the legislature of Maryland must be prevented. If necessary, all or any part of the members must be arrested. Exercise your own judgment as to the time and manner, but do the work effectively."[66] Further, McClellan told Banks, who passed the order on to Major General John Adams Dix, on September 12, "When they meet on the 17th, you will please have everything prepared to arrest the whole party and be sure that none escape…. If successfully carried out, it will go far towards breaking the backbone of the rebellion…. I have but one thing to impress upon you, the absolute necessity of secrecy and success."[67] Then Cameron wrote to Dix, also on September 11:

> You are directed to arrest forthwith the following-named persons, viz: T. Parkin Scott, S. Teackle Wallis, Henry M. Warfield, F. Key Howard, Thomas W. Hall, Jr., and Henry May, and to keep them in close custody, suffering no one to communicate with them, and to convey them at once to Fortress Monroe there to remain in close custody until they shall be forwarded to their ultimate destination. You will also seize their papers and cause them to be carefully examined.[68]

Howard was the editor of the *Baltimore Exchange*, and Hall was the editor of the Baltimore *South*, both Southern-leaning newspapers. Banks and Dix had their orders. They were to monitor the movements of the Maryland legislators, allowing the loyal Unionists clear passage to the assembly, but they were to interfere with the disloyal members by either impeding their travel or arresting them. In reality, military officials were generally cognizant of which legislators were loyal and which were secessionists. Most had already proclaimed their allegiances. In fact, Lincoln himself had said that there would be no difficulty "separating the sheep from the goats."[69] Nevertheless, Banks and Dix had discovered a "litmus test" for Union loyalty. It was a resolution proposed by S. Teackle Wallis that would clearly identify the sentiments of those legislators whose Southern ties were unclear.

The Legislature reconvened on September 17; it began in the afternoon with a roll call of the members and subsequent adjournment. S. Teackle Wallis was the Chairman of a Committee on Federal Relations, and he submitted his report to the Maryland State Assembly after a majority of that Committee had taken a stand against the Union and had spoken out against the concept of the military necessity for revoking certain civil liberties.[70] Wallis's report concluded:

> The Committee respectfully recommend [*sic*] the adoption of the following resolutions:
> WHEREAS, The military authorities of the Government of the United States in Baltimore have assumed to remove from office the Marshal of Police of that city, an officer of the State of Maryland, … and have further assumed to dismiss from office the Board of Police of Baltimore…; and
> WHEREAS, The Congress of the United States, instead of rebuking the wrong and usurpation aforesaid, has justified and approved the same, under color of a "military necessity…"; and
> WHEREAS, Charles Howard, William H. Gatchell and John W. Davis, Police Commissioners aforesaid, having been arrested by order of the General commanding the army of the United States, and imprisoned in Fort McHenry, under frivolous and arbitrary pretexts, without oath, warrant, presentment of a Grand Jury, or lawful cause…, in utter defiance of law and constitution, and in criminal violation of the plainest and dearest rights to which American citizens are born; now, therefore, it is
> Resolved by the General Assembly of Maryland, That we solemnly protest … against the proceedings aforesaid, … pronouncing the same … a gross and unconstitutional abuse of power….

Figure 45. Civil War prisons where Confederates such as George P. Kane were kept. Adapted from Richard Swainson Fisher, *Dinsmore's Complete Map of the Railroads and Canals in the United States & Canada Carefully Compiled from Authentic Sources* (1856). Library of Congress.

Union Prisons Where Kane Was Held.

1. Fort McHenry, Baltimore
2. Fort Columbus, Fort Lafayette, and Fort Hamilton, New York
3. Fort Warren, Boston

Resolved, That we appeal … to the whole people of the country…[to] come to the rescue of the free institutions of the Republic.⁷¹

The sentiments expressed in this document were considered to be treasonous. Members of the Legislature who voted to approve Wallis's report were to be arrested, since their assent thus constituted treason in itself. Furthermore, federal authorities found in the possession of F. Key Howard, a Baltimore newspaper editor, a list of citizens supporting secession. These men, too, were targeted for arrest.⁷² Federal agents had no difficulty in identifying their subjects.

Reports of the numbers of arrests varied, but the Third Wisconsin Regiment, stationed in Frederick, beginning on September 13, 1861, took into custody between 19 and 31 persons, mostly in the dead of night, mostly Maryland state legislators, in addition to employees of the Maryland Assembly (both House and Senate), prominent Southern-leaning newspaper editors, and even local hotel keepers.⁷³

Major General Nathaniel P. Banks reported on September 20, 1861: "all the members of the Maryland Legislature assembled at Frederick City on the 17th instant known or suspected to be disloyal in their relations Government have been arrested."⁷⁴ Not surprisingly, Governor Hicks, now leaning strongly toward the Union, wrote on September 20 to General Banks, "We see the good fruit already

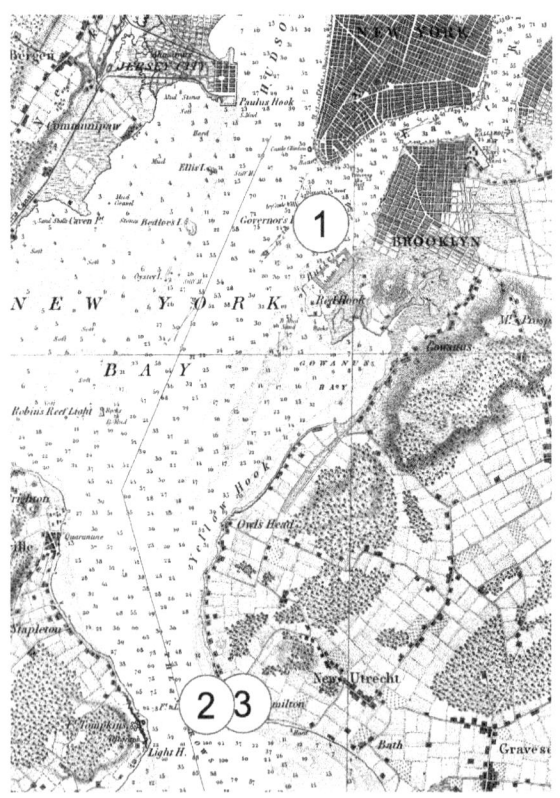

Union Prisons
Near New York City
for Confederate Soldiers
and Political Prisoners:

1. Fort Columbus
(formerly Fort Jay)
2. Fort Lafayette
3. Fort Hamilton

Figure 46. Prisons in the New York area where George P. Kane was held. Adapted from Ferdinand Rudolph Hassler and Alexander Dallas Bache, *Map of New-York Bay and Harbor and the Environs* **(1845). Library of Congress.**

produced by the arrests. We can no longer mince matters with these desperate people. I concur in all you have done."[75]

Ironically, Allan Pinkerton, the detective involved in the investigation of the Lincoln assassination plot, which was to have occurred in Baltimore earlier in the year, was employed in the arrest of the Marylanders. Pinkerton actually carried the arrest order for Scott, Wallis, Howard, Hall, May, and Warfield from Secretary Cameron and Major General McClellan to Major General Dix.[76] Before the Civil War ended, 2,094 Marylanders would be summarily arrested, most without any charges being proffered.[77] Most of the arrestees would ultimately be transferred to Fort Warren.

Federal officials also targeted the newspapers of the region. Baltimore had many newspapers, some of them catering to only a small segment of the population. The *Baltimore Sun* is the only Civil War newspaper that survives today (General John Dix, the federal Commander in Baltimore in August 1861, said that the *Sun* was "in sympathy [with the South] but less diabolical").[78] Frank Key Howard, William Wilkins Glenn, and William H. Carpenter edited the *Daily Exchange*. Howard and Glenn were both arrested for suspicion of traitorous leanings, and the paper was also banned from distribution through the mails on September 10, 1861. The *South* was also closed on September 15, 1861, and its editor, Thomas W. Hall, Jr., was arrested.[79] The Lincoln administration thus severely restricted the freedom of the press.

Lincoln wrote a public notice on September 15, 1861, in reply to a question about why Mayor George W. Brown of Baltimore had been arrested:

> The public safety renders it necessary that the grounds of these arrests should at present be withheld, but at the proper time they will be made public. Of one thing the people of Maryland may rest assured: that no arrest has been made, or will be made, not based on substantial and unmistakable complicity with those in armed rebellion against the Government of the United States. In no case has an arrest been made on mere suspicion, or through personal or partisan animosities, but in all cases the Government is in possession of tangible and unmistakable evidence, which will, when made public, be satisfactory to every loyal citizen.[80]

Marshal Kane would find himself progressively transferred from Fort McHenry in Baltimore to Fort Lafayette (passing briefly through Fort Hamilton) in New York on September 13, 1861; to Fort Columbus (originally called Fort Jay, renamed in 1806) in New York on October 11, 1861; (again passing briefly through Fort Hamilton in New York) and then to Fort Warren in Boston on November 1, 1861 (Figure 46; see also Appendix, Table 8).[81]

13

Fort McHenry

Fort McHenry is, of course, most commonly remembered as the birthplace of Francis Scott Key's "The Star-Spangled Banner." It was here during the War of 1812 that the fort survived the attack by the British on September 13–14, 1814, and successfully defended the Baltimore harbor. The fort occupies about 43 acres at the entrance to what is now Baltimore's Inner Harbor. Here in 1861 Union troops used the fort as a prison for men suspected of being Confederate sympathizers, beginning with the arrest of Marshal Kane on June 27, 1861. Prisoners usually were not kept here for long, but were transferred to other Union facilities that were better able to house political or "state" prisoners. In addition, Fort McHenry was small, and its capacity was limited. Kane would be transferred to Fort Lafayette on September 11, 1861.[1]

Kane and his colleagues were political prisoners at Fort McHenry, and they were granted many amenities supplied by friends, relatives, and purchased from the prisoners' own funds. William Wilkins Glenn, an editor of the *Daily Exchange*, a Southern-leaning newspaper in Baltimore, who was imprisoned for disloyalty to the Union, described the conditions at Fort McHenry:

> By the first of this month [October 1861] I was, strange to say, tolerably comfortable in my prison quarters. I had received from home bedding and books, I was allowed provisions of liquors and my wife came to see me frequently. A few other friends were allowed to come from time to time. Other prisoners were detained at Fort McHenry only for a short time. They were allowed no comforts and as soon as a sufficient number had accumulated to warrant the expense, a steamboat was ordered down and they were shipped to some larger Fort.

Glenn had strong attitudes about the officers at Fort McHenry, Colonel William W. Morris in particular, saying that Morris

> displayed unpardonable ignorance. At times he was a perfect brute; then again he would be kind and good natured. He often manifested a strong friendship & was willing to serve you, while at the same time his love of trickery so predominated that it was a real pleasure for him to catch a friend in a trap. He would call up prisoners and use every argument to induce them to forsake their opinions and take the oath of Allegiance and the moment it was done he would turn from them in contempt and speak of them most disparagingly.[2]

The conditions at Fort McHenry were not ideal by any means. On September 5, 1861, Major General John A. Dix, then the commanding officer of the fort, wrote to Major General G. B. McClellan about the conditions there:

Fort McHenry which has not sufficient space for the convenient accommodation of the number of men necessary to man its guns is crowded with prisoners. Beside our own criminals awaiting trial or under sentence we have eleven State [political] prisoners. To this number six more will be added tomorrow. I do not think this a suitable place for them if we had ample room. It is too near the seat of war which may possibly be extended to us. It is also too near a great town in which there are multitudes who sympathize with them who are constantly applying for interviews and who must be admitted with the hazard of becoming the media of improper communications, or who go away with the feeling that they have been harshly treated because they have been denied access to their friends.... I certainly do not think them perfectly safe here considering the population by which they are surrounded and the opportunities for evading the vigilance of the guards.[3]

Virtually all of the political prisoners from Maryland were first jailed at Fort McHenry before being transferred elsewhere. Kane and the Baltimore Police Commissioners followed this pattern. Soon after Kane was incarcerated at Fort McHenry, he became ill with presumed malaria. Though he recovered rather quickly, he would later claim that he suffered aftereffects of malaria (though other reports would call this disease "typhoid fever"), which indeed are common. The *Baltimore Sun* reported on July 29, 1861, that Kane "has almost entirely recovered from his late illness."

Kane petitioned to have his restrictions lifted somewhat while he was at Fort McHenry. On August 12, 1861, he wrote, "The undersigned requests that for the benefit of his health, the limits of his confinement may be extended to include the public grounds at this post, and on condition that his request be granted, hereby pledges himself on honor that he will make no attempt to escape. Geo. P. Kane." The commander of the post issued General Orders #52, which stated, "Pursuant to instructions from Major General Dix ... the limits of confinement of Col. Geo. P. Kane are extended to include the public grounds at this fort, he having pledged himself on honor that he will make no attempts to escape if his limits are so extended."[4]

Fort McHenry was chronically overpopulated. Much of the hardship experienced there was not the result of hatred or hostility on the part of the Union soldiers, but of trying to house too many prisoners in a small space. One inmate described his stay at Fort McHenry by telling how he and his roommates lived above the horses in the stable and where the "hot, steamy air from below had full access to us, and during the oppressive days and sultry nights of July and August ... our situation was anything but comfortable." Further, "The bunks were never supplied with straw. There were no chairs or stools. No basins or towels." Food was "so-called coffee," bean soup, pickled beef, "mess pork, usually ancient and rancid," hard tack that "was always stale, often moulded, not infrequently wormy and putrescent." Fortunately, some kind citizens in Baltimore frequently supplemented their diet, as well as donating clothing and room fixtures.[5]

Frank Key Howard, the editor of the *Baltimore Exchange*, also began his imprisonment. He was arrested at his home between 12:30 and 1:00 a.m. in the morning of September 13, 1861, and was transported to Fort McHenry. The soldiers arresting Howard were unable to produce a warrant, saying only that they were arresting him at the orders of Secretary of State William Seward. The troops treated

Howard roughly, but he recognized the futility of resistance, so he complied with their instructions as they ransacked his home and personal belongings. Upon arrival at Fort McHenry, he discovered many of his friends likewise imprisoned there—Kane, Mayor Brown, and members of the Maryland Legislature, about 15 in total, all arrested for their political beliefs. Howard remained imprisoned in Baltimore only until 5:00 p.m. the afternoon of September 13 when he was sent to Fortress Monroe on the steamer *Adelaide*, then subsequently to Fort Lafayette and then to Fort Warren. While Howard was at Fort McHenry, the guards refused to allow his friends and family to visit him; a few gained access to the fort, but they were kept distant from Howard, speaking only a few words with the guards present, with the visitors on the ground level and Howard on the second floor balcony. Howard described the setting:

> Two small rooms were assigned us during our stay. In the smaller one of these I was placed, with three companions. The furniture consisted of three or four chairs and an old rickety bedstead, upon which was the filthiest apology for a bed I ever saw. There was also a tolerably clean-looking mattress lying in one corner. Upon this mattress, and upon the chairs and bedstead, we vainly tried to get a few hours' sleep. The rooms were in the second story of the building, and opened upon a narrow balcony, which we were allowed to use, sentinels, however, being stationed on it. When I looked out in the morning, I could not help being struck by an odd and not pleasant coincidence. On that day, forty-seven years before, my grandfather, Mr. F. S. Key, then a prisoner on a British ship, had witnessed the bombardment of Fort McHenry. When, on the following morning, the hostile fleet drew off, defeated, he wrote the song so long popular throughout the country, the "Star-spangled Banner." As I stood upon the very scene of that conflict, I could not but contrast my position with his, forty-seven years before. The flag which he had then so proudly hailed, I saw waving, at the same place, over the victims of as vulgar and brutal a despotism as modern times have witnessed.[6]

Lawrence Sangston was another Maryland legislator to be imprisoned, having been arrested on September 12.[7] Sangston was a member of the House of Delegates representing Baltimore County. He was known to be sympathetic to the rebel cause. Union military officials suspected him of supporting secession and believed that he was conspiring to have the Maryland Legislature push for withdrawal from the Union. Police awakened Sangston at about midnight on September 12, saying that they had orders to arrest him and take him to Fort McHenry. Sangston requested to see a written order or warrant for his arrest, but they had none, only a telegram from Washington and a verbal order from the Deputy Provost Marshal. At Fort McHenry Sangston discovered that others had been arrested at the same time so as to prevent the Legislature from meeting and to suppress dissent, including Ross Winans, T. Parkin Scott, S. Teackle Wallis, William G. Harrison, Henry M. Warfield, Thomas W. Hall, F. Key Howard, and Henry May.[8] Fort McHenry was not prepared to receive these prisoners, as it had not even enough chairs for the arriving "guests." Sangston's wife had to bring him clothing and bedding, though he claimed that it was confiscated before reaching him. Soldiers allowed him to buy a few personal articles, including cigars and tobacco. Within a day he also was transferred to Fortress Monroe on the steamship *Adelaide*, arriving at 8:00 a.m. on September 14.

The number of inmates at Fort McHenry quickly exceeded the capacity of the jail cells. General Dix, when he was the commander of the fort, wrote to General

McClellan about the prisoners on September 8, 1861: "I have all these persons in custody; what shall be done with them? I must again call your attention to the crowded state of Fort McHenry. Every room is full and we had about fifty prisoners last night in tents on the parade ground with hardly room left for the guard to parade."[9]

Kane was transferred following orders received on September 11, 1861. Kane immediately sought the advice of his lawyer, George W. Dobbin, but he was taken to Fort Lafayette in the New York harbor on that same day.[10]

14

Forts Hamilton, Lafayette and Columbus

Fort Hamilton was only a few hundred yards from Fort Lafayette. Lafayette was on a small island; Hamilton was located on land now called Brooklyn. Because of their proximity, both often had similar military command. While political prisoners often were screened at Fort Hamilton, most were actually imprisoned at Fort Lafayette.

Handling of prisoners between Fort Hamilton and Fort Lafayette was quite routine. Most were first taken to Fort Hamilton, where they were screened and recorded by members of Colonel Martin Burke's command. The vast majority were then conveyed by a very short boat trip to Fort Lafayette, under the command of Lieutenant Charles O. Wood. At Fort Lafayette, prisoners were again searched, and their weapons, money, and other valuables confiscated. Each prisoner was allowed to keep a financial account with which to purchase additional food and sundries, as well as more elaborate items such as tables and chairs. This pattern was common at most Northern prisons where political prisoners were kept, though the majority were too poor to take advantage of this system.

Fort Lafayette registered its first prisoner of the Civil War on July 22, 1861. Fort Lafayette, built on a small island between Staten Island and Long Island, was located near New York City, just a few thousand feet offshore from Fort Hamilton. (Fort Lafayette was demolished in 1960 and replaced by the northeastern pillar of the Verrazano-Narrows Bridge spanning to Brooklyn.) Forts Hamilton, Lafayette, and Richmond were in a line guarding the New York harbor, with Lafayette being the smallest of the three. Fort Lafayette was never intended to be a prison, rather a defensive structure for New York. One writer described the fort: "A gloomier-looking place than Fort Lafayette, both within and without, it would be hard to find in the whole State of New York, or, indeed, anywhere. On the high bluff on Long Island overlooking Fort Lafayette stood Fort Hamilton, an extensive fortification, whose commanding officer, or commandant, Colonel Martin Burke, had also jurisdiction over Fort Lafayette. Lieutenant Chas. O. Wood, who had, a few months before, received a commission from Mr. Lincoln, was the immediate commanding officer at Fort Lafayette."[1] Lieutenant Wood was called Commander Wood, operating under the authority of Colonel Burke at Fort Hamilton. Prisoners uniformly disliked Burke for his brutality and insensitivity to the needs of both the rebel soldiers and political prisoners of state. The prisoners liked Lieutenant Wood, as he was said to be one of the few men who treated prisoners humanely.

Most prisoners of war and political prisoners would first be registered and searched at Fort Hamilton before being transported the final distance to Fort Lafayette. While inmates at times called all federal prisons "bastilles," Fort Lafayette was the primary institution being called this derogatory name—the "American Bastille." Prisoners were held mostly in the two large gun batteries and in the four brick casemates. Casemates were about 14 feet by 24 feet, poorly lighted, dark, and damp; though fireplaces were present, heating was not successfully accomplished until stoves were installed, close to the end of the incarceration of the Maryland political prisoners. Upon the initial arrival of the first prisoners, the fort had acquired very few articles of furniture. Blankets and pillows were almost nonexistent. Conditions were always crowded, with about 20 men housed in each gun battery and about 10 in each casemate, though at times the numbers were much larger. It was said that the small fort would have been a reasonable jail for about 20 prisoners, but as many as 135–175 were incarcerated there at one time.

Here at Fort Lafayette Kane resided with many of his fellow Marylanders, including William H. Gatchell, George William Brown, Charles Howard, H. M. Warfield, Henry May, John W. Davis, Benjamin Eggleston, S. Teackle Wallis, Lawrence Sangston, Thomas W. Hall, Charles Macgill, F. Key Howard, T. Parkin Scott, and others.[2] Charles Howard, Gatchell, and Davis were transferred from Fort McHenry to Fort Lafayette on July 31, arriving on August 1 via the steamer *Joseph Whitney*. Kane was admitted to Fort Lafayette on September 13, 1861, and transferred to Fort Columbus by order of the Secretary of State on October 11.[3] Many other Maryland prisoners were transferred from Fortress Monroe to Fort Lafayette on the afternoon of September 25, on the steamer *George Peabody*. The *Peabody* arrived the next day, just before dark on September 26. Forty-one of the 175 prisoners held at Fort Lafayette between July and October 1861 were prominent Maryland legislators, judges, and editors.[4]

Prisoners cleaned their own cells, while servants initially washed the laundry at an exorbitant fee (12.5 cents per piece), but later the prisoners learned to do their own laundry when they discovered that it took two to three weeks for an article to be returned. Food was always a complaint of the prisoners; mealtimes were irregular. Breakfast was often cold boiled pork, bread, and coffee (frequently declared undrinkable by the prisoners). Dinner was usually

> a lump of boiled beef, apparently cut with a hatchet; in each tin cup is a greasy looking mixture, which on examination is seen to be intended for rice soup; the piles of good bakers' bread are strewn along the table, with a few plates of salt at intervals; the rice, nine times out of ten, is cooked no softer than it came from its original package, and the whole greasy mess, in its greasy cup, to be eaten with a greasy spoon, seldom fails to turn the stomach of some guests.[5]
>
> Fresh water was scarce and nearly undrinkable: "it was full of animalculæ of quite a respectable growth, and had an odor anything but pleasing."[6]

Letters to and from the prisoners were read and censored, and letters from the prisoners were limited to only one page. Talking at night was not allowed after 9:00 p.m. Guards supervised the exercise of the prisoners twice daily for an hour each time, as long as conditions permitted. As the prison became more crowded, the duration of the exercise sessions decreased, to the point of being canceled. Many of the prisoners who were officers were permitted relatively free access to the grounds of the fort, though soldiers of lower rank were not given such privileges. The political prisoners initially were not afforded the right to walk around the island but were confined to exercise on the parade ground. Later, they had increased access to the premises of the fort. Visitors were not allowed, unless approved by Washington. Inmates could order special items from the stores in New York, but delivery was always quite slow. Newspapers provided were usually the Northern-leaning publications, and prisoners commonly refused to believe what was printed. A few New Yorkers took pity upon the prisoners and sent food and clothing and other necessary articles as gestures of support and friendship. Wine and liquors were allowed at first, though held and controlled by the guards. On Sundays a sermon was usually read or delivered by one of the prisoners, though the garrison guards never participated, in contrast to Fort Warren where Union soldiers and officers—including its commanding officer Colonel Justin Dimick—joined in the services. At Fort Lafayette, only one prisoner ever made an attempt to escape, and his effort was unsuccessful.

In addition to the indignity of being jailed without being charged, prisoners were not allowed to defend themselves in court. They were also deprived of many comforts of life. All had to surrender whatever money they still had in their possession to the military authorities. Their casemates lacked the basics—beds, chairs, and tables. The rooms had "an iron bedstead, a bag of straw, and one shoddy blanket."[7] Space was cramped with beds nearly touching each other.

On September 24, 1861, the *New York Times* described the conditions at Fort Lafayette with a different and highly idealized perspective:

> Fort Lafayette, named by some the American Bastile, is not a Bastile at all, in fact the fort is more like a hotel than anything else, where the proprietor is rather strict and has a wholesome dread of fire, insisting upon all lights being out at 9 o'clock. Beyond that, the fare is excellent, and the view of the ocean extensive....
>
> Upon the arrest of the prisoner, he is delivered to Lieut.-Col. BURKE, commanding Fort Hamilton, ... and carried, by means of a boat, to Fort Lafayette, formerly Fort Diamond, directly opposite Fort Hamilton, and at the distance of one quarter of a mile. On his arrival at Fort Lafayette; he is delivered to the charge of Lieut. WOOD, commanding that post.... If he has means to procure the delicacies of the market, the Ordnance-Sergeant attached to the port is allowed to purchase all that he desires upon a requisition made by the prisoner upon the Commander for the money. There is a mess under the control of the Ordnance Sergeant and his family in which some twenty-eight or thirty prisoners take their meals, paying $1 per day for the privilege. The table is well provided, in fact much better than any second-class hotel at our fashionable watering places....
>
> The prisoners without means or friends, live upon the rations which are distributed to the common soldier, viz.; pork, beef, potatoes, rice, and coffee twice a day; this constitutes the ordinary fare. The facilities for cooking are, however, very bad, and it is not unfrequent [*sic*] that the food is only partially cooked when served upon the table.
>
> The men taken from the privateer vessels are still in shackles, and are confined during the day and night under strict guard. They share the same food as the soldiers of the fort. Their situation has been made comparatively comfortable by the kind liberality of Mrs. GILSEY [likely meaning 'Gelston'], of Fort Hamilton,[8] who furnished them with clothing, aided by the prisoners of the fort, who are in better circumstances.
>
> Two hours each day is allotted for exercise in the open area of the fort. One hour, from

Figure 47. Casemate Prison Cell No. 2, Fort Lafayette, New York, New York Harbor. From *Harper's Weekly*.

six to seven, and one from five to six.... The doors are unlocked at daylight. Shortly after the morning papers arrive, and a free and uninterrupted discussion of the news of the day is canvassed. They amuse themselves during the day by exchanging visits from casemate to casemate, smoking cigars, playing whist, chess, back-gammon, &c., but no gambling. A few of the prisoners are permitted to see their wives and families, and every comfort consistent with the regulations and safety of the prisoners, is always promptly and cheerfully rendered by the commanding officer.[9] (Figure 47).

Harper's Weekly, like the *New York Times*, described the conditions at Fort Lafayette very differently than the prisoners themselves reported:

The prisoners have never at any time been prohibited from getting whatever newspapers they desired.... In all respects the State prisoners are well treated. They are as comfortably lodged as is consistent with safe keeping. They are fed by the Government at its own expense, and with the best material that the market can afford, and any one, or all of them are at liberty to order any luxury in the shape of food they have a mind to from the most fashionable hotel in New York at their own expense.[10]

Another description in the *New York Times* defied belief:

I can conceive of no way in which prisoners in such a place could fare better or enjoy kinder or better treatment. The fare of a government soldier which every one knows to be wholesome and more than can usually be consumed was always at their command. If any however preferred a different diet no matter how luxurious, and were so circumstanced as to be able to procure it, every facility was afforded to carry out their wishes. I have seen as sumptuous dinners gracing the tables of some of Lafayette's prisoners as I could well wish to serve my own epicurean appetite and taste. Luxuries of one sort and another were being constantly received from friends—clothing for those who needed it, bouquets to cheer their supposed semi-dungeons, backgammon boards, cards, chess, &c., &c., so that, in reality, pastime became their occupation, and at times the old fort irresistibly reminded me of the poet's "Castle of Indolence."...All in all, they were as pleasantly situated, as well cared for, and as happy as prisoners could well be.[11]

Prisoners at Fort Lafayette continued to experience constitutional violations, being denied habeas corpus and even legal representation. On December 3, 1861, Seth C. Hawley, chief clerk of the Metropolitan Police Commissioners of New York, relayed an order to the prisoners, promulgated by William H. Seward, Secretary of State: "I am instructed by the Secretary of State to inform you that the Department of State of the United States will not recognize any one as an attorney for political prisoners, and will look with distrust upon all applications for release through such channels; and that such applications will be regarded as additional reasons for declining to release the prisoners."[12] Indeed, Seward had written on November 26, 1861, "You will therefore please inform all the prisoners confined at Fort Warren that this Department will not recognize any person as an attorney in such cases, and that if the fact comes to the knowledge of the Department that any prisoner has agreed to pay any attorney a sum of money or to give to him anything of value as a consideration for interceding for the release of such prisoner that fact will be held as an additional reason for continuing the confinement of such person."[13]

Political prisoners wrote frequently to authorities in the Union government, protesting against their detention and the conditions of the prisons. Often they began by writing directly to President Lincoln himself. John W. Davis, one of the Baltimore Police Commissioners, wrote, referencing a previous letter: "I made an appeal to your Excellency [President Lincoln] on the grounds of humanity, to order my removal to some other place of detention, at which I might have the privilege, which is not denied to condemned felons of the deepest criminality, that of occasionally seeing my wife and children." Lincoln, through his chain of command, had communicated that "the President understands Mr. Davis could at the time of his arrest, could at any time since, and can now be released by taking a full oath of allegiance to the government of the United States, and that Mr. Davis has not been kept in ignorance of this condition of release. If Mr. Davis is still so hostile to the government and so determined to aid its enemies in destroying it, he makes his own choice." Davis objected to this description of what he had been told, and he contended that only a single reference had been made to him about taking an oath of allegiance, and that he thought that it had been a joke. Davis also refused giving an oath because it implied that he had indeed been hostile to, or had intended to destroy, the government of the United States. He believed that the oath he had taken as a Police Commissioner to uphold the Constitution was sufficient and was still binding. He claimed that the grand jury in Baltimore was in session and active at the time he was arrested, and this grand jury had proffered no charges against him.[14]

Mayor George W. Brown wrote about the conditions at Fort Lafayette to Emily Brune, the wife of his law partner Frederick Brune, saying, "I am sitting on my trunk with portfolio on my knee while I write this, because the tables are otherwise occupied and our casemate is full of people.... Frank [Key] Howard and Dr. [J. Hanson] Thomas are now tenants of our room No. 3, two vacancies having occurred which were filled by the vote of the remaining members. Our room is considered the most desirable, having a wood fire, a south exposure and *only* nine inmates. We are, on the whole, rather a cheerful community. There is much kindliness of feeling, the strong being willing to bear the infirmities of the weak, and much unanimity of sentiment about public affairs."[15]

The food at Fort Lafayette was tolerable only if a prisoner had the means to pay for a private supply: "Made arrangements through Mr. Davis to have our meals furnished by Mrs. Graves, the wife of one of the sergeants, at fifty cents per meal, so I shall not suffer on that score; those who have not the means or inclination to make this arrangement, live on the rations furnished by the Government."[16]

Lawrence Sangston described his room, 66 by 22 feet, occupied by 38 men, 23 of them from the Maryland Legislature.[17] Sangston gave a good summary of the housing at Fort Lafayette:

> There are now in the Fort one hundred and seventeen prisoners confined in six rooms. Numbers 1, 2, 3 and 4 are small casemates fourteen by twenty-two feet, arched, five feet high at the spring of the arch, and eight feet in the centre, with two very small slits in the wall for windows and no ventilation when the door is closed, and have respectively, nine, fifteen, ten and nine occupants. The inmates of No. 2 are captured privateersmen and sailors, taken in attempting to run the blockade, and are all kept in chains, not allowed to have beds, or permitted to take any exercise; they sleep on the naked floor with their chains on. Some charitable people offered to furnish them with beds, but the commander refused permission....
>
> Among the prisoners may be found representatives of every grade of society or condition of life, of the highest development of intellect, and of its lowest grade, even to the idiot one of the latter having been sent hither from Kentucky as a "prisoner of State"!!! instead of being sent to a lunatic asylum.[18]

Some days passed well and quickly, though only because of the mercy of friends and the purchase of additional provisions:

> At ten o'clock, Lieutenant Stevens of the Navy read the Episcopal Church Service, and a sermon from Spurgeon, to a large audience, in our room, and in a very effective manner; after service, visited a neighboring room where I found a handsome lunch set out, received partly from kind friends in Baltimore, and partly from New York; cold ducks, pickles, brandy peaches, cheese, biscuits, &c., with some excellent whiskey, enjoyed it very much, regretted it was not in my power to reciprocate, wrote for an hour until dinner; champagne again on the table, the kind gift of Pierce Butler, of Philadelphia, to our mess water to-day undrinkable, each glass would average a dozen tadpoles from one-quarter to one-half inch long without counting the smaller fish; can't use it without straining.[19]

Kane himself suffered during his imprisonment at Fort Lafayette. He was troubled with a fever that he later believed was caused by malaria contracted at Fort McHenry after his arrest.[20] Furthermore, one of his illnesses was characterized primarily by diarrhea. Kane wrote to Lincoln, complaining about the treatment he was receiving at the hands of the military prison officials:

> On the 27th of June last I was taken from my bed at my dwelling in the city of Baltimore about 3 o'clock in the morning by an armed body of about 1,000 or 1,200 men and conveyed to Fort

McHenry. The officers commanding the military referred to had no warrant for and as they informed me did not know the cause of my arrest. General Banks informed my counsel that I was not taken on any specific charge but merely detained as an act of military precaution....

Whilst at that post I contracted the fever resulting from the malaria incident to that locality at certain seasons with which I suffered for upwards of a month, and whilst still laboring under its effects was transferred to this place [Fort Lafayette]. On my arrival here notwithstanding my debilitated condition I was placed in a casemate on the ground floor paved with brick with just space enough for my bed between the gun by my side and the partition of the apartment in which have been incarcerated with me as many as between thirty and forty other prisoners at the same time thus rendering the atmosphere most offensive and pestiferous.

Among other effects of the fever increased by my present confinement I am suffering with prostration of the bowels and required to repair to the only convenience for the purpose by the sea-side outside of the fort ten and twelve times in the twenty-four hours in all kinds of weather. I am locked in my prison room from 6 p.m. till 6 a.m. and only allowed to take with me one tumbler of water for use during that period.

Whilst suffering great agony from the promptings of nature and effects of my debility I am frequently kept for a long time at the door of my cell waiting for permission to go to the water-closet owing to the utter indifference of some of my keepers to the ordinary demands of humanity. I am compelled to obtain at my own expense the mere substantial provisions which I require because the fare prescribed for the State prisoners is not fit for one in full health much less for a person in my present condition.[21]

The collected mass of Maryland citizens incarcerated at Fort Lafayette had similar complaints about the conditions there. The tone and content of the letters from the prisoners themselves were quite different from the description in that *New York Times* article from September 24. The Marylanders wrote a letter to President Lincoln on October 8, 1861:

The undersigned, prisoners confined in Fort Lafayette, are compelled to address you this protest and remonstrance against the inhumanity of their confinement and treatment.

The officers in command at Fort Hamilton and this post [Fort Lafayette] being fully aware of the grievances and privations to which we are obliged to submit we are bound for humanity's sake to presume that they have no authority or means to redress them. They in fact assure us that they have not. Our only resource therefore is to lay this statement before you in order that you may interpose to prevent our being any longer exposed to them.

They continued by describing the cramped conditions wherein about 23 prisoners—two-thirds of them shackled in chains—were confined to casemate cells 14 feet by 24 feet.

Their condition could hardly be worse if they were in a slave ship on the middle passage.... The doors are all fastened from 6 or thereabouts in the evening until the same hour in the morning, and with all the windows (which are small) left open in all weathers it is barely possible to sleep in the foul and unwholesome air....

The undersigned do not hesitate to say that no intelligent inspector of prisons can fail to pronounce their accommodations as wretchedly deficient and altogether incompatible with health....

Many of the prisoners are men advanced in life; many more are of infirm health or delicate constitutions. The greater portion of them have been accustomed to the reasonable comforts of life none of which are accessible to them here and their liability to illness is of course proportionately greater on that account. Many have already suffered seriously from indisposition augmented by the restrictions imposed on them. A contagious cutaneous disease is now spreading in one of the larger apartments and the physicians who are among us are positive that some serious general disorder must be the inevitable result if our situation remains unimproved.

The use of any but salt water except for drinking has been for some time altogether denied to us. The cistern water itself for some days past has been filled with dirt and animalcules and the supply even of this has been so low that yesterday we were almost wholly without drinking water....

The undersigned have entered into these partial details because they cannot believe that it is the purpose of the Government to destroy their health or sacrifice their lives by visiting them with such cruel hardships....

We desire to say nothing here in regard to the justice or injustice of our imprisonment but we respectfully insist upon our right to be treated with decency and common humanity so long as the Government sees fit to confine us.

Commending the matter to your earliest consideration and prompt interference, we are,
Your obedient servants,

> Signed by
> Charles Howard,
> George P. Kane,
> George William Brown,
> William H. Gatchell,
> John W. Davis,
> Henry M. Warfield,
> Thomas W. Hall,
> and seventy-three other State prisoners[22]

Politicians in Washington never replied to this letter.

On October 11, Sangston commented, "Marshal Kane was removed to-day to Fort Columbus, on Governor's Island, five or six miles from here. He has been very unwell for some time, and made such representations of his condition as induced the Government to remove him to Fort Columbus, where he will have much better quarters and larger space to exercise."[23]

Inmates at Fort Lafayette—the political prisoners—reported that the following rules were posted throughout the Fort:

Regulations for the Guidance of Citizen Prisoners confined at this Post.

1st. The rooms of the prisoners will be ready for inspection at 9 o'clock a.m. All cleaning, etc., will be done by the prisoners themselves, unless otherwise directed. All washing will be done in the yard.
2d. No conversation will be allowed with any member of this garrison, and all communication in regard to their wants will be made to the Sergeant of the Guard.
3d. No prisoner will leave his room without the permission of the Sergeant of the Guard
4th. Prisoners will avoid all conversations on the political affairs of this country, within the hearing of any member of this garrison.
5th. Light will be allowed in the prisoners' rooms until 9.15 p.m. After this hour, all talking, or noise of any kind, will cease.
6th. The prisoners will obey implicitly the directions of any member of the guard.
7th. Cases of sickness will be reported at 7 a.m.
8th. Any transgressions of the foregoing rules will be corrected by solitary imprisonment, or such other restrictions as may be required to the strict enforcement thereof.

> (Signed) Charles O. Wood,
> Second Lieutenant, 9th Infantry,
> Commanding Post.
> Fort Lafayette, New York Harbor, August 3, 1861.[24]

Soon after the political prisoners arrived at Fort Lafayette, another rule was added:

No prisoners will be allowed to recognize or have any communication with any persons visiting this Fort, excepting when the visitor brings an order from the proper authority, permitting an interview, which interview will be held in the presence of an officer, and not to exceed one hour; the conversation during the interview will be carried on in a tone of voice loud enough to be distinctly heard by the officer in whose presence the interview is held.[25]

Edward Davis Townsend, Assistant Adjutant-General, wrote of the regulations to be imposed specifically on the Baltimore prisoners: "They will be allowed to receive no visitors, and only to communicate on purely personal or domestic matters by letters to be inspected."[26]

Military officials censored communications of the political prisoners from many of the forts. They feared that contents of the prisoners' letters might influence public opinion about the war, especially comments about the prisoners' arrests and the conditions under which they were incarcerated. Sometimes letters were returned to the prisoners, but often they simply were not delivered. The military used all sorts of reasons to refuse to deliver letters, including being too long. The letters had to use "respectful language," and the subjects addressed were confined to "family and domestic affairs." Letters that contained items reflecting badly upon the government or the conditions in the prisons were returned to the writers. Publication of any of the contents of letters in newspapers was forbidden, and prisoners had to include the following message in all letters: "It is my express desire that the contents of this letter or any part of it will not be put in such a situation as to be published in any newspaper."[27] Thus, all letters were "embargoed" from publication.

Kane himself wrote from Fort Lafayette on September 22, 1861: "I demand a trial and to have an opportunity of confronting the scoundrels who preferred the charges against me before the grand jury." He justified his burning of bridges after the Northern troops passed through Baltimore on April 19, saying, "but for that act there would be scarcely a house standing in Baltimore. The approaching troops from Pennsylvania that arrived twenty-four hours after would have been set upon and slaughtered by an infuriated populace beyond any power of mine to protect them—as efficient as was my force—and the whole North would have retaliated and taken full revenge. …[I]f any portion of that conduct is treason the Government or the Know-Nothing church-burning clubs of Baltimore with their ladies and friends may convict and hang me as high as Haman before I will recant a word uttered or regret a deed done at that time."[28]

Charles Howard of the Police Commissioners, one of the most vocal men in the Baltimore group, was first imprisoned in Fort McHenry, then moved to Fort Lafayette and subsequently to Fort Warren. From Fort Lafayette on August 1 he wrote:

> Yesterday we were landed here [at Fort Lafayette] and are kept in close custody. No provision whatever had been made here for us…. Some of the party by permission brought on our own bedsteads and bedding with which we had been compelled to supply ourselves at Fort McHenry, otherwise we should have been compelled to lie on the bare floor….
>
> We were on our arrival here required to surrender all the money we had and all writing-papers and envelopes, our baggage being all searched for these and other articles that might be shown to be considered as contraband….
>
> I have written this letter on my bed sitting on the floor upon a carpet-bag, there being neither table, chairs, stool nor bench in the room.[29]

Lieutenant Colonel Martin Burke was in charge of Forts Lafayette and Hamilton. The Maryland prisoners were confined mostly to Fort Lafayette. Prisoners complained that while Burke was in charge, he rarely visited Fort Lafayette. In one letter, the Marylanders claimed that even Lieutenant Wood, who was assigned the job of overseeing Fort Lafayette for Burke, was seldom seen. The political prisoners, having little else to do, kept track of the comings and goings of the military officers. They asserted that Burke showed his face at Fort Lafayette only on August 5 and October 26, even though the government claimed that it was demonstrating "unceasing … care and watchfulness" over the prisoners.[30] Charles Howard wrote on October 23, 1861, " I charge and aver, that Lieutenant Wood has not only not devoted all, or even much of his time, to the promoting of our comfort."[31]

The prisoners were purposely denied the writ of habeas corpus while at Fort Lafayette. Lincoln's standing on this matter was clear. On April 27, 1861, Lincoln wrote an order to Lieutenant General Winfield Scott:

> You are engaged in repressing an insurrection against the laws of the United States. If at any point on or in the vicinity of the military line which is now used between the city of Philadelphia via Perryville, Annapolis City and Annapolis Junction you find resistance which renders it necessary to suspend the writ of habeas corpus for the public safety, you personally or through the officer in command at the point where resistance occurs are authorized to suspend that writ.[32]

Scott relayed this order to General Benjamin F. Butler, stating that Lincoln had ordered the suspension of the writ of habeas corpus only "in the extremest necessity."[33] Lincoln would repeatedly confirm this order in future months, removing or changing the geographic limitations set forth in his April 27 declaration. Even as late as December 10, a resolution was offered in the House of Representatives stating that Congress alone had the power to suspend the privilege of the writ of habeas corpus, but it had little effect.[34]

On August 2, 1861, Lieutenant Colonel Burke wrote to Colonel E. D. Townsend: "I have reason to believe that a writ of habeas corpus will be taken out for the Baltimore commissioners and I wish by telegraph an answer to my letter of July 31 [in which he asked for directions about how to respond to such a writ] immediately."[35] On the same day, Lieutenant General Scott wrote to Burke: "Should the writ of habeas corpus come for the production in court of any of your political prisoners you will respond thereto that you deeply regret that pending existing political troubles you cannot comply with the requisition of the honorable judge."[36] On August 8, Secretary of State William H. Seward wrote to General Scott: "This Department having received information to the effect that the late police commissioners of Baltimore now confined at Fort Lafayette, New York Harbor, have taken measures to sue out a writ of habeas corpus I will thank you to direct by telegraph the officer in command there not to obey the writ."[37] Seward reiterated the order in a letter on August 8, written to E. Delafield Smith: "A telegram having been received from Mr. Woodford to the effect that a writ of habeas corpus has been granted in the case of the Baltimore police commissioners I have to direct you to request the military officer having them in custody not to obey the writ."[38] Scott then wrote to Burke on August 12, reemphasizing his previous order: "You will resist any attempt to take your State prisoners. You will resist any attempt to take your person on a writ of attachment."[39] Soon thereafter, Burke at Fort Lafayette wrote that a posse was coming to execute a writ of habeas corpus upon the prisoners—specifically the Baltimore Police Commissioners. He asked General Scott what to do, and Scott replied, "Hold your prisoners to the extent of all your means of defense."[40] Burke was subsequently issued "an attachment issued for my person" for refusing the writ of habeas corpus. In another exchange, Scott wrote again to Burke on August 27, "Allow no writs to be served on you for any of the prisoners under your charge. Give the same answer as heretofore."[41] These messages were unequivocal.

Sick prisoners at Fort Lafayette were not well-attended medically:

> But, if the situation of those who were fortunate enough to enjoy good health was almost insupportable, the condition of the sick was far worse. No provision whatever was made for them. Men suffering from various diseases were compelled to remain in their close and damp quarters, and struggle through as best they could.[42]

There were some bright spots in the treatment of the Maryland prisoners, however. Some local residents aided the detainees:

> I cannot take leave of this portion of my [Frank Key Howard's] narrative without recording the obligations under which the prisoners in Fort Lafayette must ever remain to Mrs. Geo. S. Gelston and Mr. Francis Hopkins, who lived on Long Island just opposite the Fort. They were unwearied in their efforts to alleviate our situation. Day after day, for weeks and months together, they manifested their good will in the most generous and substantial way. Food for those who were too poor to buy a decent meal, delicacies of all kinds for the sick, luxuries for others—all these were supplied by Mrs. Gelston, with a bountiful and untiring hand. To her tender sympathy and generosity, very many of the prisoners were indebted for comforts which were absolutely necessary to enable them to endure the privations to which they were exposed; and I know I but inadequately fulfil [sic] the wishes of every one of the former inmates of Fort Lafayette, in thus giving public expression to thanks which they had no opportunity to return to their good friends in person.[43]

This Mrs. George S. Gelston, a woman dedicated to the relief of the suffering of the inmates at Fort Lafayette by providing food and clothing to them, was prohibited from ministering within the prison, but in a letter to Seward, she insisted upon knowing whether, "after having suspended the Habeas Corpus, the Constitution and the Laws of the country, it was a part of his [William Seward's] policy to suspend the Laws of Humanity."[44] Following the publication of her letter, restrictions on her ministrations were removed.

When referring to their deprivations while in captivity, prisoners jokingly called Fort Lafayette the "United States Hotel," and they referred to themselves as the "Traveling Committee of the Maryland Legislature." They described Mrs. Gelston as "a lady living opposite the Fort, who never lets a day pass without sending something to the prisoners, fruits, flowers, &c., and often more substantial articles…; nor is her kindness confined to the prisoners here, those who have been removed to the jail in New York are equally the recipients of her bounty."[45] The Gelston home overlooked Fort Lafayette, "close to the waters of Narrows," being at the corner of Marine and Fourth Avenues, Fort Hamilton.[46] Her full name was Maria Antoinette (Meinell) Gelston. Her husband George Sears Gelston supported her charity, in part, by farming. They had five children.[47] She was 38–39 years old when she ministered to the soldiers and prisoners, and she died at age 94. As a humble Christian woman who loved attending to the prisoners, as well as bringing them food and supplies, she in her old age refused to let anyone read the letters of thanks written to her from the prisoners, as she considered them to be private and sacred messages.

Prisoners almost uniformly praised Mrs. Gelston as a saintly Christian woman who offered relief to the soldiers and political prisoners at Fort Lafayette, though a few criticized her for supposed Southern-leaning tendencies. The *New York Times* ended an article about conditions at the fort:

> Like every one upon the stage of human action, who would stamp character upon the part they play, at the sacrifice of minor essentials Mrs. GELSTON has her critics and her enemies. She is known throughout the community as a woman of unbounded charity—a charity which looks far back of the time when Fort Lafayette was made a prison, and hence its generous exercise at that institution, which has called down upon her head so much aspersion, cannot be said to have taken its root in and be coeval with rebel sympathy. It was my honored privilege to be her family physician. Scarcely a week passed over my head for eighteen months that I was not sought for to learn of new arrivals at Fort Lafayette, and whether they were in need of anything to make them comfortable and happy. This did not rise in light of REBEL aid or sympathy. I know this from the repeated conversations which I have enjoyed with her directly upon the subject. No one could be a truer unionist than Mrs. G. While she disagrees with many as to the means of reinstating that union yet she never hesitated to openly condemn the act of secession. But her deeds of kindness were in no way connected with a political sentiment. Their origin took root down—far down in the ever living springs of woman's heart—a mother's heart, and she had the foresight to glance along the vista of the future and realize that it was by no means impossible that some near friend—a relative or perhaps her only son—amid the casualties of war might become the inmate of some gloomy prison hold of the enemy. What prayers would then arise to Heaven that some good ministering angel in that enemy's domain might cast the new gleam of her welcome coming across his narrow prison track and mingle with his groans of despair her own kind—cheerful and hopeful words. Should she not then herself embrace the opportunity while yet she had it of exercising this God-born and politic means of humanity? Should we not all be engaged in it?[48]

George William Brown wrote of Mrs. Gelston in a letter to his law partner Frederick W. Brune on September 28, 1861: "On the table where I am writing is a beautiful little bouquet sent by Mrs. Gelston to Mr. Faulkner. This kind lady who lives in the neighborhood of Fort Hamilton is the wife of the brother of Hugh Gelston, + daily manifests her kindness by sending something to the prisoners—sometimes fruit, sometimes flowers, and sometimes provisions for those who are not as well served as we are at our mess."[49]

Indeed, Mrs. Gelston's kindness extended to prisoners even after they had departed from Fort Lafayette. Mayor Brown wrote about Mrs. Gelston on November 26, 1861, to his sister-in-law Emily Brune, after he had been transferred from Fort Lafayette in New York to Fort Warren in Boston: "A few days ago, a box came from kind Mrs. Gelston with 25 turkeys which we at once sent to the Hatteras prisoners, the Common soldiers. And today from the same were a number of bouquets (one for me), some jelly + a large cake. We are getting up a handsome silver pitcher to be made by Kirk[50] to be presented to her by the prisoners. I never knew of a case of such constant kindness to strangers."[51]

Based in part on Kane's and his fellow prisoners' letters, Robert Murray, U.S. Marshal, suggested to Secretary of State William H. Seward by letter that Kane be transferred from Fort Lafayette to Fort Columbus. Not wanting to establish a precedent and realizing that conditions at Fort Lafayette were less than ideal, Murray wrote on October 8, 1861: "You must be aware it is a very difficult matter as a general thing [for] me to advise in these cases as almost every prisoner confined in Fort Lafayette would endeavor upon some pretext to have his quarters changed." Secretary Seward agreed with Murray, and he recommended on October 9 that Kane be transferred to Fort Columbus.[52] But he would not stay there long.

On October 30, 1861, the government transferred a large number of prisoners (military, naval, and political) from Fort Lafayette and Fort Columbus to Fort Warren in the Boston Harbor: George W. Brown, John W. Davis, William H. Gatchell, Charles Howard, Francis Key Howard, Thomas W. Hall, Henry May, Lawrence Sangston, T. Parkin Scott, J. Hanson Thomas, H. M. Warfield, and S. Teackle Wallis.[53] Howard, Gatchell, and Davis were housed together in one of the casemates of the fort; Kane and Brown were roommates in another room nearby. Newspapers reported that the political prisoners "were very loth [*sic*, 'loath'] to leave their comfortable quarters for the uncertainties of their new site of imprisonment."

Fort Columbus was located on the northern side of Governor's Island in the New York Harbor, about one-half mile from what today is Lower Manhattan, just north of Fort Lafayette and Fort Hamilton. Originally called Fort Jay, its name was changed to Fort Columbus in 1806. It served as a hospital and as a temporary prison for Confederate soldiers and political prisoners during the Civil War. In 1904 the name reverted back to Fort Jay.

Kane was only briefly incarcerated at Fort Columbus, but he found it much more agreeable than life at Fort Lafayette. Kane wrote from Fort Columbus on October 26, 1861: "I am in all respects more comfortable than at [Fort] Lafayette at which place my treatment was characterized by an utter and disgraceful disregard of the common dictates of humanity." However, Kane was distressed that he was not received appropriately: "No arrangement has been made for my board on this island and but for the courtesy of some fellow prisoners I should have to live on the rations of the Government in the state in which they are issued." Prisoners had to pay for food if they wanted rations any better than those provided for the common soldier, and Kane objected to his having to pay his own expenses for something approaching the quality of the sustenance to which he had been accustomed as a free man.[54] Kane was also pleading to have his trial conducted because he believed that he was innocent of any imaginable charges; he even asked to have the trial conducted in New York or any other state if the delay was due to attempts to have it conducted in his home territory of Baltimore. He was willing to face charges anywhere. He also sought a parole to conduct his private business, and he expressed his agreement to enter into any arrangement to secure even a brief release to deal with his financial matters. He was willing to report to any specified military officers and give any promises of assurance that he would not engage in subversive or Confederate business while free on parole. Major General John A. Dix spoke on behalf of Kane's parole:

> If Mr. Kane is permitted to visit the city of New York for the purpose of attending to his private business on his parole of honor to surrender himself at a given time and place or whenever and wherever required and in the meantime to have no correspondence and hold no communication with others on political subjects I have no doubt that his engagement will be faithfully kept and that the indulgence may be safely extended to him.

But neither Kane's temporary release nor his trial would be forthcoming any time soon. These delays only exacerbated his medical concerns: "my confinement is destroying my health. I am now under treatment of the garrison surgeon for an affection [sic] of the heart which I attribute to the nature of my confinement at [Fort] Lafayette."[55]

Much to the chagrin of Union officials, Kane also complained of the same conditions at Fort Columbus that he had encountered elsewhere. By October 23, he reported that he was being denied "a requisite supply of air and exercise at Fort Columbus." Once again, high officials dealt with Kane's entreaties. Secretary of State Seward wrote to U.S. Marshal Robert Murray again on October 23, to "have this complaint removed as far as it is possible consistently with the circumstances of his confinement."[56] It seems highly unlikely that all of the thousands of prisoners under Union confinement received such personalized attention from Cabinet members. There was, indeed, a two-tiered prison system, and the prominent political prisoners were treated as gentlemen as far as it was within the powers of the government.

15

Fort Warren

Fort Warren was located on the 43-acre Georges Island in Boston Harbor. Completed in about 1863, its inner parade ground covered four acres. It was large, capable of housing over 800 prisoners, with 200–400 soldiers guarding them. The largest population of inmates was reported to be 394 in February 1865.[1] However, a newspaper article from December 5, 1861, reported "one hundred and twenty political prisoners, between fifty and sixty rebel officers and over six hundred prisoners of war confined in the fort."[2] Regardless of the exact numbers, conditions were crowded. Accommodations were sparse, at best, and during the early days of the Civil War the fort lacked many basic provisions.

The Maryland prisoners actually arrived at Fort Warren on the evening of October 31. Colonel Justin E. Dimick had expected only about 110 prisoners total, but over 400 arrived, 109 political prisoners and 300–600 combatant prisoners of war. Because the fort was unprepared to receive such a large group of prisoners, only a small number were allowed to disembark from their ship that night, so most entered Fort Warren the next day on November 1, 1861.

Colonel Dimick was the Commander at Fort Warren during much of the Civil War, and the prisoners generally respected him. He assumed command of Fort Warren in October 1861, when he was 62, too old for an active combat duty assignment. Running a Confederate prison was less physically demanding.

Frank Key Howard would say of Dimick:

> At Fort Warren, the soldiers of the garrison differed, we were glad to find, from their comrades at Fort Lafayette. While the latter were incapable of delivering a message, or of giving the simplest order, save in a manner at once insolent and brutal, the former were uniformly good-natured and civil. Colonel Dimick, the Commandant of the Post, discharged his disagreeable office in a way to which we could take no exception, and none of us, in any interview with him, ever found him otherwise than courteous and kind. As far as lay in his power, he left nothing undone to promote our comfort.[3]

Lawrence Sangston described Colonel Dimick as one

> who exhibits every disposition to make us as comfortable as possible; this example necessarily influences the behavior of the subordinate officers and soldiers; I have found the old adage "like master, like man," fully exemplified in my experience of military life; we experience none of the rudeness and insolence we had daily to encounter at Fort La Fayette.[4]

Thus, the human character of the prison forts varied widely.

George Kane and many of his friends, including George William Brown,

Charles Howard, Frank Key Howard, John W. Davis, Thomas W. Hall, Charles Macgill, Lawrence Sangston, T. Parkin Scott, J. Hanson Thomas, Henry M. Warfield, S. Teackle Wallis, William H. Gatchell, and others arrived on November 1, 1861. Fort Warren seemed to be the Union's prison of choice for political prisoners from Baltimore, and from Maryland in general. Kane had come from his brief stay at Fort Columbus, while the others came directly from Fort Lafayette. All had been transferred aboard the steamship *State of Maine*. Military officials expected that the winter at Fort Warren would be less harsh than at Fort Lafayette, given the conditions at the two forts, and the military officers were tired of the repeated applications for visitation of the prisoners when they were held at Fort Lafayette. Fort Lafayette was much closer to the population center of New York City and was more accessible to Boston than Fort Warren. Kane expressed reluctance at his transfer because he had found the accommodations at Fort Columbus much better than those at Fort Lafayette, and he did not know what to expect at Fort Warren.[5]

The political prisoners and the prisoners of war generally felt well treated by both the Union soldiers and the citizens of Boston. On rare occasion, some newly arriving prisoners had to march through the streets of Boston on their way to Fort Warren. One such prisoner said, "So we went, making slow but steady progress. Not one rudeness nor insult was offered us during the whole route,—which spoke well for the charity, the refinement and good taste of the Bostonians."[6]

Further, prisoners expressed similar feelings about Colonel Dimick:

> [A] kinder and truer gentleman, a more gallant or chivalrous officer, never lived than Colonel Dimick.... In that large heart of his no bitterness, no malice, no sectional hate could find an abiding place. There was not a prisoner under his charge who did not learn to respect and love him, before a week had rolled over their heads. While doing his duty as a soldier, he did not sacrifice his humanity as a man.[7]

As one group of prisoners was released, they recalled the scene of parting from Colonel Dimick: "[We] serenaded Colonel Dimick and his family, in that sweet farewell song of Schiller's, and afterwards every man of the 'rebel' line went up to the Colonel, and out of a full heart and with dewy eyes thanked him for his undeviating kindness and generous consideration."[8]

Even though the accommodations themselves were better at Fort Warren, the inmates were allowed to (and still had to) spend their own money to furnish their rooms. Lawrence Sangston reported:

> Set to work to-day to fix up my sleeping room; manufactured a very good bedstead out of some pine slats and put up some shelving. My room mates had a cotton sack and fourteen pounds of straw served out to them to-day, which enabled me to get back my under mattress; received some furniture I had ordered from Boston carpet, mat for the side of the bed, chairs, washstand, bowl and pitcher, water bucket and foot bath, writing table with damask cloth cover; stowed all my surplus baggage under the bedstead and tacked a valance of black cambric around the frame, and when all was finished and arranged had about the nicest little prison room that could be found any where; many visitors came in to view and admire it....
>
> NOVEMBER 7 [1861]. Up early this morning to prepare the room and table of our new mess for breakfast, being one of a committee, with Marshal Kane and Captain Berry, to wait on the table for a week; capital breakfast: beefsteaks, mutton-chops, sausage and good coffee; the committee highly complimented on the first result of their labors.[9]

The quality of food is a common complaint in institutional settings—prisons, hospitals, schools, or any facility that must serve food to large numbers of people. Fort Warren was no different. Prisoners complained. The common soldier and the political prisoner without extensive financial means were required to eat the same food as that served to the Union garrison. Fresh beef and potatoes were served three times each week; salted beef, pork, or ham filled out another three days. Sunday was bean day. Twenty-two ounces of bread was the daily allotment. Tea and coffee were available, but it seemed that the prisoners' major complaint was about the quality of the coffee. Alcohol was allowed—though regulated and rationed—as long as the prisoners purchased it themselves.

Political prisoners were allowed to establish "bank" accounts with money they had carried with them from the forts where they had previously been jailed. Colonel Dimick acted as their banker. Meals were the items most often purchased, and some men were able to contract with a private cook to provide meals. Mr. Andrew J. Hall of the Webster House, a Boston hotel, catered the meals for the political prisoners, most of whom were men of high social standing, often wealthy. In most cases, the bank accounts were small. For example, John W. Davis once deposited $50.00; George A. Appleton $5.71; Kane $33.41.[10]

Similar to the regulations at Fort Lafayette, the rules at Fort Warren forbade the use of attorneys for the prisoners, both political and combatant. All were denied legal representation. Secretary of State William H. Seward wrote to the U.S. Marshal in Boston:

> You will therefore please inform all the prisoners confined at Fort Warren that this Department will not recognize any person as an attorney in such cases, and that if the fact comes to the knowledge of the Department that any prisoner has agreed to pay to any attorney a sum of money or to give him anything of value as a consideration for interceding for the release of such prisoner that fact will be held as an additional reason for continuing the confinement of such person.[11]

The political prisoners were given a certain amount of latitude in their choice of accommodations. Kane chose to stay in an upper room overlooking the parade ground; it was one of the larger cells, and he shared it with some army officers. The Police Commissioners were housed in another such room, while Mayor Brown was imprisoned in yet another. In general, the men chose to room with the same person or people who had shared their incarceration at the other forts. Some of the Baltimore prisoners did not fare so well. Frank Key Howard wrote about his housing:

> I thus found myself again among my old room-mates. The other prisoners, generally choosing their own roommates, were quartered in the other rooms and in the casemate before mentioned. The crowded condition of the room I occupied will illustrate the situation of our fellow-prisoners. This room was nineteen and a half by fifteen feet, and one of the little closets of which we had the use was ten by ten and a half feet. Into this room and closet, nine of us were crowded. So close together were our beds, that it would have been impossible to have put another one in the room without blocking up the doors.... [Some inmates] were compelled to sleep in bunks which were arranged one above the other, in three tiers. They had also to cook their meals in the same room.[12]

It was obvious that the officers at Fort Warren had neither expected nor planned for the arrival of so many prisoners. For almost three weeks Howard and the men with him had to sleep on the bare floor. Some prisoners described the food as intolerably bad, and the Baltimoreans arranged with a private provisioner to feed them for one dollar per day. This arrangement yielded hardly any better fare, and after only a week the prisoners established their own mess, ordering food from Boston to be brought over to Fort Warren by boat and cooked at the fort.

Dr. Samuel G. Howe was a physician who inspected the Union prisons, and he suggested that an ideal facility should be sized to allow each prisoner at least 600 cubic feet of air space, based upon calculations done by the British Sanitary Commission. He discovered that Fort Warren had only about 145 cubic feet of air space for each prisoner. This number varied, of course, as the prison population waxed and waned.[13]

The conditions of the privies or outhouses serving the prisons, a subject rarely discussed, were addressed by Dr. Howe:

> For instance, at Fort Warren, the vast trench dug for the common privy could have been constructed so that the tide would cleanse it; or, if this was not desirable, it might have been placed on any side of the fort. But there was *one* side on which it ought not to be placed, because from that come the prevailing wind. But it *is* placed exactly there, in the very eye of the east wind, which sweeps the odor into the interior of the fort. The trench itself, too, when I saw it, was in a very bad state, it did not seem to have been filled over for a long time.[14]

These conditions were imposed upon men of the higher social classes from Maryland, many of them of advanced age, and they were justifiably distressed at their presence in such an environment. No doubt Kane was not accustomed to using an open trench as his restroom, nor to sharing it with about 1,000 other men.

The separation of the classes of prisoners caused the political prisoners to be quartered on the southwest side of the fort, and the officers of the prisoners of war were located on the northwest side. The hospital was placed in the southwest corner of the fort, and the vast majority of the enlisted ranks of the prisoners of war were kept in the north side of the fort.

Despite his intrinsic kindness and respect for humankind, Dimick had been given orders and limitations that constrained his actions. Orders given to Dimick contained seven points.

    1. Prisoners were to be "treated with all kindness," though at the same time "securely held."

    2. Adequate records had to be kept for all prisoners.

    3. Prisoners were to be allowed to purchase items for their own personal use, and they could receive gifts and money in amounts up to $20 at a time that was kept in "bank accounts" run by the officers of the fort.

    4. Newspapers were not forbidden; letters to and from prisoners were allowable, subject to censorship.

    5. Visitors approved by Washington could come to the fort, but always accompanied by a military chaperone.

    6. Upon release from captivity, prisoners were searched to assure that secret messages were not being taken out of the fort.

    7. Officers kept detailed records of the food and clothing provided to each prisoner.

Furthermore, Colonel Dimick, like his fellow officers at other forts, was told not to honor any writ of habeas corpus for the release or trial of any prisoner.[15]

The classes of prisoners did not mix; that is, political prisoners could not mingle with, nor converse with, the officers of the prisoners of war; the enlisted men could not interact with the officers of the prisoners of war, and the enlisted men could not speak with, nor associate with, the political prisoners. However, some newspapers characterized the prisoners' mingling on the parade grounds differently:

> The scene of the parade ground during the day is quite animated and full of interest.—Men of all ranks and professions are here thrown together, all in a greater or less degree connected with the event which has attracted the attention of the whole world, and which has caused the blood of brothers to flow as water.... As a general thing their personal appearance is not at all prepossessing. Seedy apparel is by no means uncommon, and if one did not know the character of the place he would be led to think that it was an asylum for broken down gentlemen. A clean shaven face is rarely to be met with.[16]

Newspapers highlighted the prominence of Marshal Kane as he intermingled with the soldiers and other prisoners:

> One of the most noticeable of these [prisoners] is Marshal Kane, of Baltimore, a fine-looking, well-dressed gentleman, above the middle height. He bustles about, in a Scotch cap, with his pant legs within his boots, and by a stranger might be mistaken for the principal person in the garrison. He converses freely with the officers stationed at the fort and evidently is not much discontented with his position. Mayor Brown, of Baltimore, a quiet, tidy gentleman, evidently does not like his position.[17]

Common soldiers fared more poorly than the richer political prisoners:

> They [the common soldiers] are scantily supplied with clothing, many of them sick and discouraged, and large numbers of them are ignorant.... Many of them cannot read or write. They are remarkably quiet and respectful to the officers of the garrison. There is said to be considerable religious feeling among them at the present time.... There are about fifty now in the hospital. A few have the typhoid fever. Several have consumption [tuberculosis], having been affected before leaving home, with that disease, which is now aggravated by a change of climate. Many have the bronchitis and pneumonia, and upon entering the hospital the visitor will hear so much coughing that he will think it is derision, till informed that it is all the time the same. Many of the men are also having the measles and the mumps.[18]

Medical care followed the pattern of wartime during the Civil War. Often captured doctors tended to the men of their own side of the war, in addition to treating the enemy. In this case, Dr. De Witt Clinton Peters was a Union physician who treated both his own men and the Confederate prisoners at Fort Warren. He had few tools or supplies for his work; the hospital had no bedsteads, and patients slept on mattresses a few inches above the floor. Medicines were in short supply. Nevertheless, survival at Fort Warren was better than at most Civil War prisons, and particularly better than at many Confederate-run prisons, like Andersonville in Georgia. Only 12 deaths were reported among the rebel detainees at Fort Warren during the entire Civil War, out of over 1,000 soldiers who were housed there. Nevertheless, measles, mumps, typhus, and various skin diseases were common.

Spiritual care was likewise delivered poorly, or more commonly not at all. T. Parkin Scott once asked for the ministrations of a Catholic priest, one Reverend A. L. Hitselberger in Boston. Secretary of State William H. Seward intercepted the request and wrote to the priest on November 20, 1861:

> To the Rev. A. L. Hitselberger,
> Boston College, Harrison Avenue, Boston:
>
> Sir: I have to acknowledge the receipt of your note of the 15th instant, with a copy of that which you addressed to Colonel Dimick, on the 15th of November. This Department having adopted a rule which precludes all visits to political prisoners, even from ministers of the Gospel—of any denomination—has hitherto strictly observed it.
>
> If, however, the persons themselves shall, in the event of sickness, or any other reasonable cause, require the services of their spiritual advisers, the rule would be relaxed in favor of any one of undoubted loyalty.
>
> I am, sir, your obedient servant,
> William H. Seward.[19]

By early 1862 these restrictions had been relaxed somewhat, and the officers in charge of Fort Warren allowed at least some church services on the premises.

Josiah Gordon, a Representative of the Maryland House of Delegates from Allegany County, would describe a typical day at Fort Warren in a letter written on March 1, 1862, noting that at least some of the prisoners even had servants:

> We generally wake about 7 in the morning when our servant comes into the room to make the fire. After the room gets warm enough we rise, dress and get ready for breakfast which is ready at ½ past eight. After breakfast we promenade in front of our quarters about an hour then retire to our rooms and read till twelve, when the boat arrives with our mail. We then read the news and letters and converse on them until dinner which is ready at three. After dinner we read a while again then take exercise again till sundown at which time the drum beats retreat and we retire to our rooms for the night. About 7 o'clock we have a cup of tea in our rooms and our neighbors call in and enjoy the tea with us and then we talk for an hour or so. Then we write letters and sometimes play a game of whist ... till 11 o'clock, when we have to put our lights out and go to bed in accordance with the regulations of the garrison. This is the routine to which I have been subjugated day after day and night after night for four long months. While at Fort Lafayette it was still worse for our quarters there were like a pig sty compared with those we have here.

Gordon remained relatively positive into his fourth month:

> Our friends here are all well and in good spirits, hoping ernestly [sic] and believing confidently that the God of Justice and Truth will give success to the cause which is sustained by those principles. And though dark clouds may come and shut out the sunlight of prosperity for a while, we never lose sight of the silver cage which faith governed by reason and enlightened experience always sees.

He even commented upon the more mundane aspects of his imprisonment:

> I am on the committee having charge of our mess this week and you would be surprised I think to see how good a cook and housekeeper I am getting to be. We had for dinner a leg of mutton mildly roasted and a boiled ham with stewed chicken after a dish of tomato soup. We had also potatoes nicely boiled and mashed then put into a pan and cooked till nicely browned. We had also stewed carrots and stewed parsnips also green peas and dried apples also. Then for dessert we had rice boiled in milk and sweetened and a good cup of coffee to finish off with, so my dear you may suppose we did pretty well with the aid of a French cook from Boston.[20]

Needless to say, Gordon was among those more well-to-do prisoners who could pay for their own food and services in prison.

Cooking arrangements varied, sometimes with the inmates doing the duties themselves. Kane fancied himself a good cook, though his compatriots disagreed.[21] Nevertheless, they allowed him to continue trying. On December 23, 1861, Lawrence Sangston reported, "A nice mess of oysters cooked by Marshal Kane, with some Scotch whiskey-punch, closes the day, or rather the night, and to bed at eleven."[22]

In spite of the gloominess of their long imprisonment, the inmates at Fort Warren had time for some fun. On Christmas Day 1861, they held a mock trial and execution of William H. Seward for treason, his having in their opinion abolished the Constitution and the laws of the land.[23]

Baltimore Mayor George William Brown was among the most prominent Marylanders arrested. While Kane was arrested by Union troops on June 27, 1861, for the crime of treason, or at least treasonous thoughts, federal officials delayed arresting Mayor Brown until September 13. Brown was first taken to Fort McHenry, then to Fortress Monroe, Fort Lafayette, and finally to Fort Warren. Brown claimed that he was never given a reason for his arrest.

Mayor Brown wrote of his experience of imprisonment at Fort Warren:

> It is a strange feeling to be deprived of liberty.... At first, I could hardly at times contain my indignation, but I am now calmly resigned to whatever may be in store for me. While I am in the house of bondage, and at all times, I am thankful for the prayers of those whom I love.[24]

Some of Brown's communications suggested that life at Fort Warren, though harsh simply because of the incarceration and lack of freedom, was not as brutal as it might have been for other prisoners: "[W]e have procured servants from Boston and are well served. We have a French cook and the waiter who attends on our room is an Italian named Antonio. Our meals are now good enough in every respect. Formerly with the inexperienced hands, the table was not always inviting."[25] Later, Brown was granted additional privileges in the prison upon his solemn agreement not to try to escape:

> Now that we have, on parole, the liberty of the island we can exercise with pleasure. The harbor is fine, and the view of the water, the picturesque islands, the main land with its villages and towns, and the many passing sails is always pleasing. You would laugh if you could see the game of football which comes off nearly every afternoon. Old and young, tall & short, soldiers and civilians join in the melee and tumble each other & themselves about on the grass in the most unceremonious manner. I have not yet ventured to take part but it is only because the exercise is rather too violent.[26]

Indeed, Brown was not a likely participant in football, given his slight frame and rather delicate features. Brown's final indignity was the smell of his habitation at Fort Warren:

> There is one invading evil which as yet has defied all the efforts to correct it—a very bad smell which comes from the sewer or cesspool.... We suppose that this is the consequence of greater or less proximity to the water-closet. Fortunately my room is on the less nasty side.[27]

In October 1861, Mayor Brown was given the opportunity to secure his release from captivity. He only had to resign his position as Mayor of Baltimore, to remain in New England, to avoid entering Maryland or any state participating in the "insurrection," and to give his word of honor not to commit any act that might be considered treasonous or injurious to the Union government. Brown refused these conditions, explaining that such actions and promises would constitute an admission of guilt of being disloyal to the government. Though Mayor Brown was unwilling to comply with the demands placed upon him for his complete release, his friends and supporters ("prominent citizens of Boston of unquestioned loyalty") petitioned Assistant Secretary of State Frederick W. Seward on November 26, 1861, through lawyer Seth C. Hawley, asking that Brown be released on parole and allowed to live in Boston, where his brother-in-law Dr. George C. Shattuck lived.[28] A 30-day parole was granted, with the conditions that Brown "will not leave the New England States and will not meddle with the public affairs of the State of Maryland or the city of Baltimore but will comport himself as a true and loyal citizen." After this parole he was granted a 90-day extension, but he refused it on the grounds that "it would be consenting to his banishment from his home and duties."[29] During the course of Brown's confinement, many of the Massachusetts soldiers who witnessed his heroic behavior in Baltimore during the April 19 riot wrote on his behalf, but Brown remained imprisoned with the rest of the Baltimore contingent. The sentiments of Union-leaning politicians in Baltimore were not likely to aid the release of Brown, or any other of the Baltimoreans held in federal prisons. The First Branch of the City Council of Baltimore declared on November 15, 1861, "we are confident that the liberation of said prisoners and their return to our midst at this time would be fraught with immense danger to the loyal cause." They opposed the release of their fellow Baltimoreans.[30] Brown persisted in his unwillingness to accept the conditions stipulated for his release, in spite of encouragement from his family members.[31]

While Kane was imprisoned at Fort Warren, his father-in-law John Griffith became ill and was near death. On November 27, 1861, three of Kane's friends wrote to General John A. Dix, who was then stationed in Baltimore, requesting that Kane be granted a brief release to come to his father-in-law's side. The three men—James Hooper, Sr., C. A. Gambrill, and John Clark—all claimed to be "uncompromising Union men."[32] Presumably they would—if anything—have been biased against Kane's temporary release. Dix wrote to Secretary of State Seward asking for brief clemency for Kane. The parole was granted for a three-week leave from the prison at Fort Warren. The parole signed by Kane stated:

> I hereby pledge my word as a gentleman, that if allowed to go to Baltimore to attend the funeral of my father in law, I will report myself in person to the Commanding Officer of Fort Warren, at the end of three weeks from this date, and further that during that time I will do no act of hostility to the Government of the United States, either by word or deed.

This parole, dated November 29 and cosigned by Colonel Justin Dimick, allowed him to stay in Baltimore for three weeks before returning to Boston; he was scheduled to be re-incarcerated at Fort Warren on December 20, 1861.[33] However, Griffith died in Baltimore on November 28 before Kane arrived. Griffith's funeral was held in Baltimore on Saturday, November 30, 1861, with the services beginning at George Kane's home on St. Paul Street. Kane barely arrived in time, hurriedly proceeding from the President Street railroad terminal to his home on that Saturday morning. Kane wrote to Stanton to modify his parole to read, "Not to commit any hostile or injurious act against the Government of the U.S. by word or deed, nor to communicate in any form with any person on the subject of politics in the war."[34] This change was telegraphed to Colonel Dimick. Kane departed Baltimore to return to Boston on Thursday, December 19, 1861.[35] The *Baltimore Sun* proclaimed Kane to be in good general health, in spite of his prolonged incarceration and the illnesses reported that he contracted while in prison.[36] During the Civil War era, such paroles were not uncommon, and the men imprisoned honored their oaths to return to prison as specified. Kane arrived back at Fort Warren on December 20.[37]

Many political prisoners were offered the possibility of release if they would simply sign the oath of allegiance, a document that evolved over the course of the Civil War and thereafter; it took many forms from state to state and from year to year. It usually contained something like:

> I, _____, do solemnly swear, in the presence of the ALMIGHTY GOD, that I will henceforth faithfully support, protect and defend the Constitution of the United States, and the Union of the States thereunder; and that I will in like manner abide by and faithfully support all Acts of Congress passed during the existing rebellion with reference to slaves, so long and so far as not repealed, modified or held void by Congress, or by decision of the Supreme Court; and that I will in like manner abide by and faithfully support all Proclamations of the President made during the existing rebellion, having reference to Slaves, so long and so far as not modified or declared void by decision of the Supreme Court—SO HELP ME GOD.

Such oaths were dated and signed, usually witnessed by one or two persons, specifying where the oath was sworn. Some versions added a physical description of the person taking the oath. Prisoners could thus secure their discharge from prison almost at will, but most refused this route. They believed that signing such an oath was an admission of guilt to some crime, and the "amnesty" offered was offensive to men who believed that they were being imprisoned unjustly. By the fall of 1862, many Marylanders and others refused even a brief parole for the same reasons.[38] Overall, only three or four of the inmates at Fort Warren were willing to take the oath and be released.[39] George Kane also refused to sign any of these documents.

None other than Jefferson Davis himself would later use the same reasoning regarding oaths and pardons. Davis refused to apply for a pardon after the Civil War because he believed that it both was an admission of guilt and required him to repent of his actions. He declared in 1881, "It has been said that I should apply to the United States for a pardon, but repentance must precede the right of pardon, and I have not repented."[40]

Kane's rooming arrangements at Fort Warren changed frequently, as did the accommodations for many of the prisoners as inmates came and went, but in November 1861 Kane shared a room with Lawrence Sangston, Commodore Barron, Colonel Pegram, Colonel Bradford, Captain De Lagnel, Charles Green, Andrew Lowe, and George Appleton. Kane and Appleton shared a passageway "where Marshal Kane has fitted up a very nice room, by running a petition [*sic*, meaning 'partition'] across the lower end, his health not permitting him to sleep in a room with a fire."[41]

President Lincoln eventually appointed a two-man governmental panel to review political prisoners and to determine if they were being held "justly" for crimes against the United States. Secretary of War Edwin M. Stanton issued the order on February 27, 1862, soon after he replaced Simon Cameron as Secretary of War:

> It is ordered,
>
> 1st, That a special commission of two persons, one of military rank, and the other in civil life, be appointed to examine the cases of the State Prisoners remaining in the military custody of the United States, and to determine whether, in view of the public safety and the existing rebellion, they should be discharged or remain in military custody, or be remitted to the civil tribunal for trial.
>
> 2d, That Major General John A. Dix, Commanding in Baltimore, and the Honorable Edwards Pierrepont, of New York, be and they are hereby appointed Commissioners for the purpose above mentioned, and they are authorized to examine, hear and determine the cases aforesaid, *ex-parte*, and in a summary manner, at such times and places as in their discretion they may appoint, and make full report to the War Department.
>
> By order of the President:
> Edwin M. Stanton,
> Secretary of War[42]

Dix and Pierrepont interviewed a large number of the men being held at Fort Warren and declared who deserved to be released and who did not. The panel tried to determine if the charges and evidence were sufficient to continue holding these political prisoners. Some of the imprisoned men refused even such an examination because they believed that the process was similar to a trial, including the calling of witnesses, but without the real authority to declare guilt or innocence. Many wanted a trial by jury for their alleged misdeeds. Nevertheless, the Dix/Pierrepont review disclosed many miscarriages of justice. Dix wrote, "we found persons arrested by military officers who had been overlooked ... lying in prison for months without any just cause.... I must insist that every person arrested shall have a prompt examination." Some witnesses questioned during this review themselves were held in jail to assure that they were available for questioning. Dix, in an attempt at fairness, requested that these witnesses who had to be confined for the hearing be compensated fairly so their families could be supported.[43]

William H. Gatchell was one of the political prisoners examined by this panel:

> As I entered the room in which the Commissioners held their meeting, General Dix advanced with his hand extended, saying, "Good morning, Mr. Gatchell." I declined the proffered hand, remarking, "Excuse me, sir, if you please." In a very short time, Judge Pierrepont observed, "I really forget, Mr. Gatchell, whether you have been offered the parole or not, heretofore." I replied, that "I had been, and that I had declined it, for the reasons stated in my answer to the Secretary of War, which I supposed he had seen." He said he "had not seen that answer." I told him that "I would furnish the Commissioners with a copy, that they might understand the grounds on which I placed my refusal to accept it." I was then asked "whether I continued of the same mind?" I answered, "Certainly." Then, said he, "For the present, we have nothing more to do with your case."[44]

Marshal Kane and Mayor Brown were also present at Fort Warren during the Dix/Pierrepont panel's deliberations, though Kane did not appear before the two-man panel:

> Colonel Kane, against whom the Government had managed to procure an indictment for treason, and who had been carried out of the State immediately afterward, remained

unnoticed also. [He was not examined by the Dix/Pierrepont panel.] He had been removed hundreds of miles away from the place where it was alleged he had committed a crime, and though for nine months the Government had failed to bring him to trial, the Commissioners suffered his case, also, to pass unexamined.[45]

The Civil War era had bred a degree of laudable honesty. Charles Howard had actually been released briefly on parole to visit Baltimore just prior to the time that the Baltimore prisoners at Fort Warren were declared free. Howard had returned to Baltimore to see his sick daughter, who subsequently died. Howard wrote to Colonel Dimick on November 27, 1862:

> I presume that the order [for release from Fort Warren] extends to me. But as I have given to you a pledge that I will return and surrender myself to your custody on Wednesday next the 3rd Dec., I will thank you, if I am right in my supposition, to give me your distinct assurance, that without returning to Ft. Warren, I am absolutely and unconditionally discharged from all the obligations which the parole I gave to you may have imposed upon me. Very respectfully, your obdt. svt., Charles Howard.[46]

Kane objected to his inability to conduct business from the confines of any of the prisons in which he was held, and that his "confinement precluding me from attending to my business has cut off my resources and caused my property to be sacrificed."[47] Kane added that he wanted his trial to be conducted quickly, whether in Baltimore, in New York, or in any other state that the government would choose where he could receive a fair hearing. He concluded by saying "I am now under treatment of the garrison surgeon for an affliction of the heart which I attribute to the nature of my confinement at Lafayette."[48] Perhaps this "affliction of the heart" would be one cause for his inability to join the Confederate Army later during the war.

The Baltimore prisoners, including Kane, Brown, and Wallis, were finally released from Fort Warren on Thanksgiving Day, Thursday, November 27, 1862. They had no conditions placed on their release, and they were free to travel as they wished. The first to arrive in Baltimore were Thomas Parkin Scott, Henry M. Warfield, William G. Harrison, William H. Gatchell, Frank Key Howard, Thomas W. Hall, Jr., and Robert Hull. Hundreds of Baltimoreans met them at the President Street railroad depot, though the mood was quiet without any political overtones. Their reception lacked any noisy demonstrations, and all men retreated calmly to their homes. Colonel Kane, Mayor Brown, S. Teackle Wallis, and Dr. Charles Macgill delayed their arrival in Baltimore, all stopping along the way from Boston for various business reasons.[49] Kane spent the night at the New York Hotel in New York City. Kane, Brown, and Macgill arrived in Baltimore on Saturday, November 29. The crowd meeting them was somewhat more vocal than the reception for the other Fort Warren prisoners, and many Baltimore men jumped on the train cars before they arrived in the depot. The crowd was so thick that the train had to stop before it arrived at the dock. On this day the crowd raised cheers repeatedly, in contrast to the rather solemn reception for the other prisoners two days earlier. The reception was described as "immense and enthusiastic," punctuated by "cheer after cheer."[50] Wallis didn't arrive until November 30.[51]

Mayor Brown reported:

The prisoners have received the warmest reception, many have called to see me and visitors have not yet ceased. A great change has taken place I am told in the state of affairs here. There is a free expression of private opinion, and the press is gradually daring to speak out. Arbitrary arrests are no longer dreaded, tho' the removal of Gen. Wood & the appointment of Gen. Schenck is considered as somewhat threatening, for it is no doubt a concession to the radical & extreme element of the abolition party. I am in danger of being more harmed by feasting than anything else. I have had six invitations to dinner this week, and accepted four.[52]

Federal officials were not so welcoming of Kane to his newfound freedom. They pondered the likelihood that Kane still could be convicted of treason. United States Attorney General Edward Bates wrote to Baltimore United States District Attorney William Price: "Serious doubts are entertained here whether you could at this time safely go to trial in any treason case in Baltimore by reason of the supposed popular feeling and judicial bias."[53] Kane was popular with Baltimoreans. He had plans for the future.

16

Kane's Confederate Activity after Release from Prison

Soon after Kane was released from Fort Warren, he voiced a diatribe about the circumstances of his arrest and the treatment he had received at the hands of his Union captors. He was particularly critical of Secretary of State William H. Seward, whom Kane blamed for his illegal arrest and detainment. Kane immediately began his public invective against Seward, the man (other than Lincoln) Kane thought most responsible for the imprisonment of all of the Marylanders. On November 29, 1862, Kane first sent a letter to the *Baltimore Sun* and to the *Gazette*, but both refused to publish it. Kane alleged that their refusal was not because it was untrue, but because "such truths are not allowed to be published in Baltimore by the despotic censorship to which they are compelled to submit." He subsequently submitted it to the *Baltimore Republican*, also on November 29, which did publish it:

> After an incarceration of seventeen months in four of the forts of the United States now converted by the Government into prisons which have no similitude but in the Bastile of France I avail myself of the first moment of my return to my native State to address a brief word to you.
>
> In this imprisonment I am understood to have been the special victim of Mr. Secretary Seward, who in concert with his hired minions has omitted no occasion to heap upon me accusations which he knew to be false and therefore dared not bring to the ordeal of a public trial.
>
> To these charges the despotic censorship of the prisons in which I have been kept allowed me no reply; and I can only now promise that in due time and upon a proper occasion Mr. Seward shall hear from me in a way which will procure for him if he has not already acquired it the contempt of every honest man and woman in the land.
>
> Without having been held upon any specific charge I am turned out of prison without any reason being assigned for it; and thus in my arbitrary arrest and release I illustrate the most flagrant violation of constitutional liberty.
>
> It would be unbecoming the dignity of the subject to cast abusive epithets upon the author of this gross outrage; but when allowed the opportunity I pledge myself under pain of the forfeiture of the good opinion you have always honored me with to show that all is bad in a man, unpatriotic in a citizen and corrupt in an officer finds itself concentrated in this individual.
>
> Geo. P. Kane[1]

This rather personal attack upon Seward raised the threat of another charge of treason against the former marshal. Northern newspapers challenged Kane's version of the story, claiming that Kane had a "traitorous hostility to the Union and its Government." Kane replied by saying that his actions were intended to thwart the execution of the diabolical purposes expressed toward the City of Baltimore and its inhabitants. *When Northern newspapers were threatening in the most intemperate language that the city should be destroyed by fire, that its streets should be furrowed by cannon balls, and that its women should be given to the pollution of an infuriated mob*, it was not to be expected that its public authorities, especially those charged with the conservation of its peace and the safety of its citizens, should stand listlessly by and await the execution of those base and inhuman threats.[2]

Kane remained embroiled in rumor wars after his release from Fort Warren, his detractors impugning his reputation. One involved the cost of maintaining the Baltimore contingent in the various prisons. The *New York Tribune* in early 1862 had published an article charging that Kane and his friends incurred bills for "various luxuries" provided to them at Fort Warren and elsewhere. Kane was accused of not paying his bill at Fort McHenry before he was transferred to Fort Lafayette. The newspaper article said that

> rebel prisoners confined in Fort McHenry have been in the habit of ordering various luxuries of Mrs. Alice Wilson, the cateress of that establishment, and now refuse to pay for them, leaving their bills to be paid by the Government. Orders have been sent from Washington to pay Mrs. Wilson's bill, amounting to $221. It is to be hoped that all these orders for luxuries by rebel prisoners will hereafter be regarded as personal affairs by those filling them.

The charge continued by naming Kane and others allegedly responsible for ordering the luxuries. These allegedly unpaid accounts covered goods such as food, drink, tobacco, pen and paper, and furniture. In addition, the charges against Kane and his friends were nearly 18 months old—the specific items being those consumed at Fort McHenry where they were imprisoned in the summer of 1861; the newspaper article was written in the winter of 1862. To Kane it seemed that Northern papers were dredging up ancient history. Nevertheless, Kane responded:

> In answer to this infamously false publication, I deem it proper to state, that during the entire period of my confinement at Fort McHenry, up to the 31st of July last, every particle of food of which I partook, and every article of furniture that I required, was furnished to me from Baltimore. At the period mentioned, my fellow political prisoners being ordered to be removed to Fort Lafayette, I was invited by the officers of the United States artillery who lived within the Fort to mess with them, which invitation I accepted, and I continued to mess with them up to the time I was removed to be incarcerated in Fort Lafayette, (the 12th September last). I paid my mess or board bill weekly to the lady referred to in the *Tribune's* article, who resided in the garrison and furnished the officers' mess. On the day on which I was to leave I settled with her in full,—After I had thus paid the bill, the United States Marshal informed me that he himself had authority to settle my bill, and that he had done so in the cases of other political prisoners, and by his direction the money which I had paid was refunded to me. I now hold a certified copy of the Marshal's authority to pay the bill referred to, together with an official certificate that my bill was settled in full to the day I left.[3]

The indignity of being held in prison without a trial was only magnified by these rumors circulating about Kane's behavior.

After his release from Fort Warren, Kane had returned briefly to Baltimore, only to be re-arrested on March 2, 1863.[4] Kane was arrested again because he had been "engaged in getting up a company of seventy or eighty men, to be armed with revolvers, to operate against the authority of the United States. After a thorough investigation, no proof could be adduced against him, and he was released with the understanding that he shall report to the military provost marshal whenever required to do so." This arrest was related to his activities in 1861, not to any new infraction.[5] Kane was then given an April court date, but it was delayed until May. (Even as Kane was embroiled in the specter of a trial for treason, he was active in civic duties in Baltimore.[6]) In early May 1863 the police were still looking for witnesses for this trial, which was to begin on May 4 with Severn Teackle Wallis and George W. Dobbin representing Kane as his attorneys. Here he was again accused, among other offenses, of "organizing a company [of 70–80 men] armed with revolvers, to resist the authority of the United States."[7] Kane appeared before the United States Circuit Court of William Giles on May 4. At that gathering, many of the jurors, lawyers, and even Chief Justice Roger B. Taney were absent. Furthermore, the prosecuting District Attorney William Price was himself detained in Washington, D.C. Since legally Judge Giles could not hold court by himself without Taney, the trial was postponed to May 5. However, the trial did not begin then, either. Kane was finally released on $40,000 bail, with the understanding that he might still need to report to the Provost Marshal, Colonel William Stebbins Fish, upon command. This indictment was finally dropped later in May 1863, presumably to organize even more specific charges against Kane, but by then he had fled to the South and then to Canada.[8]

After Baltimore Police Commissioners Howard, Gatchell, and Davis were finally released from prison in November 1862, they sued Simon Cameron, the Secretary of War, for his role in their arrests in July 1861 (General Winfield Scott had authorized the arrests). Bringing suit in United States Circuit Court, also under Judge William F. Giles, the plaintiffs sought to recover damages related to their arrests and imprisonment. Cameron didn't take lightly being hauled into court. He wrote to President Lincoln on November 1, 1863:

> The Police Commissioners, of Baltimore, have sued me for their arrest—and the trials are expected on this week. My attorney thinks they will be favorably affected by the arrest of all the parties for Treason, and the hope that you will have their arrests ordered immediately has brought me here. The suits need not be prosecuted, unless it is found necessary in the progress of my suits. These of mine are the first suits of the kind and a decision would not only be injurious to the Gov't, but would be injurious to me—and hence my anxiety.[9]

In other words, Cameron was hoping Lincoln would intimidate the plaintiffs by charging them with treason, thereby causing them to drop the lawsuit. Cameron so much as admitted this objective by saying that the treason charges need not be pursued unless the plaintiffs persisted in their suit. Nevertheless, the suit finally went to trial on November 16 after many delays. S. Teackle Wallis was the lawyer for the Police Commissioners, and the case was dropped when all parties agreed to the statement that Cameron himself was not *directly* involved in the arrest of Howard, Gatchell, and Davis, and therefore the lawsuit had no merit and should not be pursued.[10]

Kane at this time was busy aligning himself more tightly with the South by going to work with the so-called Canadian Confederacy (Figure 48). Kane wrote to

Jefferson Davis on July 17, 1863, stating, "I am here [in Canada] to organize an expedition, or expeditions, against the Lake ports of the United States." He wanted

- to liberate the Confederate prisoners on Johnson's Island, and to arm them for battle;
- to capture Chicago, Detroit, and Milwaukee;
- to seize ships on Lake Erie;
- to sink, burn or destroy ships not to be used for Rebel transport;
- to burn Buffalo and Cleveland and their ports and ships;
- to destroy shipping and business in the region, "paralyzing lake commerce," and
- to give "a quickening impetus to the peace feeling" in Wisconsin, Michigan, Iowa, and Illinois.

It was an ambitious undertaking.[11]

Kane offered to lead the raids against Detroit, Buffalo, and Erie, trying to free 1,000 Confederate prisoners held at the Sandusky prison, but he needed money and trained men. Kane told Davis that he needed funds, army soldiers, and navy officers for these expeditions, but that he rejected any means of warfare that were "not sanctioned by the usage of civilized war."[12] Kane then briefly left Canada for an unknown destination.

Figure 48. The Canadian Confederacy. Southern-leaning sympathizers used locations in Canada as a base from which to wage war against the North. From *The Confederate Yellow Fever Conspiracy*.

In an obscure reference, Acting Rear-Admiral Theodorus Bailey, Commander of the Union's Eastern Gulf Blockading Squadron in Key West, Florida, wrote on July 27, 1863, that Marshal Kane was one of 14 men who had been apprehended and from whom Bailey had extracted a parole "not to bear arms against the U.S. Government, nor to give aid, comfort, or information to the enemies of the Government of the United States until regularly exchanged." Kane and the other 13 men were allowed to continue their travels in the fishing sloop *Welcome*, of which one Thomas Blake was the skipper. They were cleared to proceed to Charlotte Harbor, about halfway between Key West and Tampa on the western coast of Florida. It is unknown what Marshal Kane was doing in southern Florida, or even if this report was correct,[13] but the dates mesh with his brief absence from Canada. Kane traveled much after his release from the Fort Warren Prison, and the reasons for his journeys were not always obvious, so this alleged appearance there remains a mystery to this day.

George Kane again returned to Canada in the fall of 1863. The exact dates of his travel are unknown, but we know that he likely arrived in October. It was here that Kane colluded with Patrick Charles Martin to try to free Confederate prisoners held at Johnson's Island, a facility on Lake Erie. This prison was the target of at least three attempts to liberate the Confederate prisoners (in 1862, 1863, and 1864) during the Civil War. It held many Confederate soldiers and officers, the peak being 3,256, and the monthly average being 2,549. It was a structure of 13 two-story wooden buildings located on 300 acres three miles north of Sandusky, Ohio, guarded by 400 Union troops. In the summer it was an island separated from the mainland by about half a mile; in the winter ice often connected the island to the mainland. This prison had a good safety record, both for lack of escapes and for the preservation of good health of the inmates. Reportedly only 12 prisoners ever escaped from this prison; death rates were less than 2 percent per year, a remarkable record for a Civil War prison, either North or South, where a 10–12 percent mortality per year was common. A previous attempt to rescue Confederate soldiers in 1862 had failed, and a later one in 1864 would be equally unsuccessful. In Kane's 1863 plot, one of his friends and a fellow Baltimorean, Isaac R. Trimble, was one of the men imprisoned at Johnson's Island. This conspiracy had multiple facets, all to be accomplished under the leadership of Kane, Martin, James B. Clay, and Clement Vallandigham.

A major player in this plot was Patrick Charles Martin, who has always been rather an enigma. Born in New York in about 1818, he spent his early years there, but received most of his education in Baltimore. He early became a mariner, embarking on a round-the-world job at age 16. Immediately thereafter, he opened a business that sold religious objects in the Wilmington, Delaware, area, and in Philadelphia, his inventory being mostly Bibles, prayer books, pictures, beads, crucifixes, and Catholic artifacts.[14] This business lasted from about 1835 to 1838. Martin and his wife Mary Ann returned to Baltimore to live in 1837 or 1838, where Patrick worked in his father's fruit business, Charles Martin & Son. In this business, Patrick made many trips to various ports of the world as supercargo for the company. The "supercargo" on a merchant ship was the person in charge of the goods being shipped on the boat. He was an accomplished ship's pilot, a merchant, a liquor distiller and distributor, a blockade-runner, and a pirate.[15] In 1841, he was involved in a mutiny on, and plunder of, the brig *Cicero* in Panama. For this crime, Martin was fined $500 and sentenced to two years at hard labor.[16] He was thereafter well known to government officials (in 1862 the Union War Department called him an "uncompromising rebel" and suggested that the Northern government not do any business with him[17]). In 1848 the Martin family moved to Pittsburgh, and Patrick's father Charles died in 1852. Martin again returned to Baltimore, where he became an independent merchant, in 1855–1859, running P.C. Martin & Co., "rectifiers and distillers." In 1860 he was a principal of Martin, Belt & Co., distillers.

Some authors have believed that Martin fled to Canada initially as a result of his involvement in the piracy of a different ship, the *St. Nicholas* in June 1861,[18] made famous by the leader of the group, Richard Thomas, alias "Zarvona," alias the "French Lady."[19] This Zarvona/"French Lady" escapade involved commandeering *St. Nicholas* in the Baltimore harbor on the afternoon of Friday, June 28, 1861, thereafter pirating the additional cargo of three other ships and delivering the goods to the Confederacy. Some historians believe that Patrick Charles Martin was one of the pirates, and that he fled to Canada to escape prosecution. Though initial reports stated that five or six other men were arrested with Zarvona, only two were indicted for the piracy. Martin was not named in the legal proceedings, but he may have been one of the pirateers used by Zarvona for his exploits, though his name does not appear in any of the popular reports of the event.

Because he was identified as a sympathizer with the South, and perhaps as a result of the legal case surrounding the Zarvona piracy of the *St. Nicholas*, Martin took his family to Montreal, where they had established a home by at least the end of the summer of 1862. Mrs. Mary Ann Martin was also thought to be a Confederate agent and courier of Rebel messages. After first arriving in Canada, Martin and his family lodged in Montreal at the Donegana Hotel during approximately 1863–4. There he was co-owner of a business of importing and distilling liquors and wines—Martin & Carroll,[20] partnering with General William Carroll of Tennessee.[21] By 1864–5 Martin was both a distiller and an importer of liquors.[22] While in Montreal, he continued his blockade-running activities and worked to supply materials to the Confederacy,[23] usually through Halifax and the blockade-runners that used the intermediate ports of St. Georges, Bermuda, and Nassau, Bahamas. Wilmington, North Carolina, was a favorite final destination for these goods.

In the fall of 1863 Kane and Martin formalized their conspiracy to free the Confederate prisoners on Johnson's Island. On February 7, 1863, Lieutenant William H. Murdaugh had earlier proposed a similar plan. He wanted to capture the gunboat USS *Michigan* and to use it free the prisoners and to attack various ports and structures on the Great Lakes. Confederate President Jefferson Davis had vetoed this plan because of potential international neutrality issues.

Kane and Martin later resurrected the plan to capture the Union warship USS *Michigan* and then to commandeer other ships in the area to provide transportation for Rebels liberated from the prison on Johnson's Island. Kane at this time was staying in the Martins' home in Montreal.[24] Freeing the prisoners without attacking various nearby ports was their new goal. President Davis and Secretary of the Navy Stephen Russell Mallory both approved this more limited project.[25] The number of

Confederate soldier prisoners (mostly officers) on Johnson's Island at this time was estimated to be 1,500–2,600; Union guards again numbered about 400. The original attacking party organized by Kane and Martin was to be 22, augmented by an estimated 180 liberated and armed Confederates at the prison. When the numbers were finalized, however, the 22 non-incarcerated conspirators had only been able to recruit an additional 32 volunteers at the prison. Nevertheless, they proceeded with their plan. The 22 members of the Confederate naval team left Smithville, North Carolina, on the Cape Fear River on October 7, aboard the blockade steamer *R. E. Lee*. Only three members of the team (Lieutenant John Wilkinson, Lieutenant B. P. Loyal, and Lieutenant Robert D. Minor) actually knew the purpose and logistics of the mission. The other 19 men initially thought that they were headed for England. After running the Union blockade, the *R. E. Lee* first docked at Halifax, Nova Scotia. The 22 men then split into small groups and traveled overland to Montreal, where most of them arrived on October 21. Trying to maintain secrecy, the men sought housing in private lodging homes or boarding houses (including the home of Patrick and Mary Ann Martin).

Mary Ann was to inform the prisoners on Johnson's Island of the plan to liberate them. She visited them personally, but General James J. Archer, a prisoner from Maryland incarcerated there, told her how to communicate with the men in the prison by another technique.[26] The Martins were to use personal notices in the *New York Herald* to relay some of the timing details to the imprisoned Confederates. They used the abbreviation "A.J.L.W." to identify messages in the *Herald* intended for the men involved in the conspiracy, preparing them for their escape.

Robert D. Minor wrote in his report to Confederate officials:

> Finding Marshal Kane and some of our friends in Montreal, we set to work to prepare and perfect our arrangements, the first object of the plan being to communicate with the prisoners on Johnson's Island, informing them that an attempt would be made to release them.[27]

Two Confederate prisoners held on Johnson's Island, General Archer and Major General Isaac R. Trimble, both from Baltimore and both taken captive at the Battle of Gettysburg,[28] were the men looking for those coded messages in the *Herald*. An initial ad read, "a few nights after the 4th of November a carriage would be at the door, when all seeming obstacles would be removed, and to be ready."[29] Ads also appeared in the November 1, 3, 4, 5, and 6 *Herald* that read, "To A.J.L.W.—CANNOT COMPLY WITH YOUR wishes until after Wednesday, the 4th of November. Your solicitude is fully appreciated, and a few nights after that date the carriage will call for you, and the present seeming obstacle will be overcome. Be ready."[30] The identity of the person(s) referenced in the ad is obscure. "A.J.L.W." could represent any number of the Confederate operatives in Canada. Interestingly, another ad appeared only in the November 1 issue: "PATRICK MARTIN, WHO LEFT THE TOWN OF Burr, county Tipperary, Ireland, about two years ago, and arrived here in June inst. is requested to call upon his sister, Ellen Martin, at 34 East Twelfth street."[31] Patrick Martin's daughter was named Ellen, and she would have been about 13–14 years old at the time, living with him in Montreal; he had no recorded sister named Ellen. Furthermore, no one named Martin lived at that particular address. The notice would have made no sense to the average reader. It likely was another coded message.

Captain John Wilkinson and Robert D. Minor were the chief logistic and military directors of this scheme. They achieved tentative funding of $111,000 ($35,000 in direct contributions from the Navy Department and $76,000 to be added from the sale of a cargo of cotton in Halifax).[32] Wilkinson and his team planned to replicate the logistics of the prior 1862 attempt to free the prisoners. They would commandeer one or more civilian boats on the lake nearby the USS *Michigan* (the only Union gunboat on the Great Lakes), which was anchored only about 200 yards from the Johnson's Island Prison. After feigning an accidental collision between their passenger boat and the *Michigan*, then overpowering the sailors on the *Michigan*, they would sail her the short distance to Johnson's Island, point the cannons toward the prison, and demand the release of the Confederate prisoners housed there. The *Michigan* would then be used as one of the ships to transport the freed prisoners.

However, their plan was thwarted when James S. McCuaig, one of their own men, leaked information about the raid, and the entire operation was canceled.[33] The conspirators hastily retreated from Quebec, many of them overland to Halifax and on to Bermuda, arriving on December 17, and ultimately returning to the South on blockade-runners. Wilkinson and the other sailors would eventually submit expense accounts for this audacious adventure. The orders for the members of the Confederate Navy called their assignment a "Special Expedition Abroad," without further specifying the nature or goal of the endeavor.[34] Ledgers listed 73 recipients of reimbursements, including P. C. Martin and George P. Kane. Kane wrote to President Jefferson Davis from Montreal on November 24, 1863, explaining that their scheme to rescue prisoners from Johnson's Island Prison in Sandusky Bay had failed.[35]

The details of Kane's later return to the South have never been well documented. He had first traveled to Bermuda on board the *Alpha*, as did Minor and the others involved in the failed attempt at Johnson's Island. After a brief sojourn in Bermuda, Kane then fled to the Confederacy aboard the steamer *Dare*.[36] The *Dare*, an iron double side-wheel paddle steamer, was cleared to leave Bermuda on January 2, 1864, its first trip as a blockade-runner. It would proceed to Nassau and then to Wilmington, North Carolina, under Captain Thomas B. Skinner. Sailing on Sunday the 3rd, the passengers included Kane and other Southern agents. The *Dare* encountered smooth passage on the first two days of the journey. On the evening of Wednesday the 6th the weather was overcast with a slight rain, making navigation difficult. By this time a Wilmington pilot had taken charge of the vessel, steering toward Lockwood's Folly, and she anchored at 1:00 a.m. on January 7 near Fort Caswell. At daybreak, the Captain discovered three blockading Union ships nearby. After a chase of about one hour, the *Dare* lowered a boat with six passengers, including Kane. They successfully made their way to shore, landing about 45 miles from Wilmington and close to Lockwood's Folly.[37] These six men soon arrived in Wilmington. Meanwhile, the *Dare* continued her run from the Union Navy. It was soon beached and destroyed.[38]

Kane quickly returned to Canada. Newspaper reports incorrectly had him escaping from Johnson's Island with some other prisoners, but he was never imprisoned there.[39] The *Richmond Dispatch* had Kane and these escaped prisoners departing Quebec for Halifax on January 25,[40] and then from Halifax to Bermuda. Indeed, the *Alpha* steamed from Halifax on February 6 to St. Georges, Bermuda, arriving on February 10, the trip usually taking 4–5 days.[41] On board were both Kane and Dr. Luke Pryor Blackburn, of yellow fever fame, in addition to the Confederate officers.[42] They then sailed from Bermuda on February 13, 1864, on the *Advance* (aka the *A. D. Vance*) via Nassau, arriving in Wilmington soon thereafter.[43] Kane then went overland to Petersburg on his way to Richmond, where many friends greeted him.

The *Richmond Dispatch* reported Kane arriving once again in Wilmington on February 21, 1864,[44] traveling through Petersburg, Virginia, and reaching Richmond on the same day by train. This time he was a guest of Mr. William A. Wright, a local lawyer and proprietor of the American Hotel.[45] Newspapers described Kane as "one of the numerous distinguished citizens of that city [Baltimore] committed to a Northern bastile by a tap of Seward's 'bell' and a nod of the despot, Lincoln." Hopes for Kane's influence ran high:

> Marshal Kane ... comes to throw the weight of his influence into the scales of Southern independence. He is one of nature's noblemen, "born to command," and his name is second to none in popularity with the fighting element of his native State, now scattered throughout the South. We trust his mission will be to gather and coagulate this scattered material into a regiment or brigade of invincibles, who shall lead the van when again the Potomac is crossed, and Maryland redeemed from the heel of her oppressor, if she ever is to be.[46]

Richmond received Kane warmly. A group named Smith's Armory Band serenaded him at the American Hotel at about 11:00 p.m. on the evening of his arrival, Monday, February 22. He appeared in a balcony of the hotel with Dr. Charles Macgill, a fellow Marylander from Hagerstown, who said, "Fellow citizens of Maryland and the Confederacy: Allow me to introduce to you Colonel George P. Kane, of Maryland. He has come among you, as you are already aware, to do what he can in aid of the advancement of the Southern cause. His persecutions and sacrifices for Constitutional rights you well know, and he is willing to sacrifice his life, if necessary, in the same cause."

Kane replied:

> Fellow citizens of Maryland and the Confederacy: Public speaking has not been the habit of my life, but I would be unmindful of the warmest impulses of human nature if I neglected to thank you for this spontaneous compliment. All I have to say is, that I have come amongst you at my earliest opportunity, and I do assure you that I intend to remain amongst you until the cause for which we are battling is triumphantly vindicated and acknowledged. My appearance among you is too recent, and my experience of your situation too short, to warrant any dictation from me as to the course my fellow-citizens of Maryland should pursue in this struggle.... Many of you, my fellow-citizens, are veterans in this war, and it would be unbecoming in me to counsel or chide you further at this time. The cause for which we are all fighting is destined to succeed, if we but do our duty to ourselves and the country. Despotism never yet prevailed, over a people determined to be free, and it would be a blot, black as Erebus,[47] on the pages of history, ancient or modern, for the sunlight of Southern independence to be quenched in the night of subjugation.[48]

His audience followed these brief remarks with "uproarious applause," and Dr. Macgill "made a war speech, in which he lashed, without mercy, the hell-hounds of Lincolndom, and applied the scalpel of his sarcasm with a skillful, but unpitying hand." The band played a few numbers, followed by another message from Kane. Finally, Kane said, "There can be no affinity, no community of interest, no companionship with a people who have acted as the fanatics of the North have done towards the South."[49] Kane was then honored with more music, a reception, and later with public dinners. The Virginia House of Delegates awarded Colonel Kane "a privileged seat on the floor of the House during his stay in the city."[50] Kane found it necessary to decline some of the invitations because he was "busily employed preparing for the service of the Confederacy, which he is about to enter, and does not look upon an ovation as well-timed or appropriate just now."[51] Later the *Richmond Examiner* reported that Kane "has come to enter the service, and it is hoped will carry with him the crowd of non-combatant 'exiles' from that State."[52] Two weeks later, on March 16, the same newspaper reported that Kane,

> after a full and satisfactory consultation with the President, General Lee and the Secretary of War, received authority to proceed with the establishment, in the vicinity of Richmond, of a military camp, to be designated "Camp Maryland," for the purpose of gathering into an efficient organization the Marylanders in the Confederacy. The organization is intended to include those not now in the service, as well as the hundreds scattered, without individuality of organization, throughout the various military departments. The latter will be reached by a system of transfer, by companies, where they are full, and it is practicable, and by individuals, where it is otherwise. It is believed that one, or, perhaps, two brigades of excellent troops, including the three arms of the service—infantry, cavalry and artillery—can be raised and equipped in this manner. Upon organization, the right to elect its own commander would derive upon the command. This would secure the three great elements which a Maryland organization has always lacked so far—viz: concentration, harmony, and an *espirit du corps* of purpose and principle.

It lauded Kane by saying, "If there is any one man in the South, calculated by character and example, to unite the fighting element of Maryland under one standard, and fire it with a single and patriotic purpose, that man is Colonel Kane. We trust the response will be commensurate with his zeal, and that all will heartily cooperate with him in his arduous undertaking."[53] Kane intended this camp to become a focal point for the organization of Marylanders to fight for the Confederacy. It was to be both a magnet for soldiers from Maryland already enlisted and a recruiting tool for new soldiers, both the fit and the old and infirm.

Kane then organized a group of men in Richmond that was called the Office of the Maryland Society, including Dr. Charles Macgill, John Calvert, William A. Wright, W. H. S. Taylor, Robert Hough, to raise funds for relief of soldiers of the Maryland Line. Jefferson Davis sanctioned their activity.[54]

George Kane was a man who remembered kindnesses and sought to repay them. In March 1864 he heard of two members of the 11th Regiment of the Massachusetts Volunteers who were imprisoned at Libby Prison in Richmond, one of the most brutal confinements possible for Union soldiers. Union Captain F. R. Josselyn and Lieutenant Jacob Remie had been there for over eight months. Kane wrote to them:

> Whilst confined in Fort Warren, near Boston, for a period of near fourteen months, I was indebted to one of her people, since deceased, and doubtless in Heaven, for acts of kindness, in which my fellow-prisoners participated, and which will never be forgotten. The person to whom I refer had

expressed a deep interest in the personal welware [sic, "welfare"] of yourself and others of your regiment, and I know of no better way of evincing my gratitude for that kindness, which came like a gleam of sunshine to the storm-tossed mariner, than by aiding in a proper mitigation of the sufferings and inconveniences inseparable from your condition as prisoners of war.

At my request, Colonel Ould, Confederate Commissioner of Exchange, has directed that you be released and sent to Fortress Monroe on the first flag-of-truce boat. I would be glad if you would, on your arrival North, make known to _____ _____, [name deleted in the original newspaper publication] to whom I am also indebted for many evidences of humanity and nobleness of heart during my prison life, that I have not forgotten the occurrences of those days, nor the lessons which they taught.

In haste, yours, truly,
GEO. P. KANE

The two soldiers reported that they did not know personally, or know of, this man named George Kane.[55]

So Kane, who for some reason was physically incapable of participating in active military service, occupied his time supporting the Confederate cause by suggesting avenues of service for others who were similarly disqualified from active duty. He sought opportunities for the older Southern male, the disabled, and the men who had already suffered wounds in the war. Furthermore, the reference to "Mr. Kane" in military communications supports the conclusion that Kane was never himself an active duty military officer in the Confederate Army. He was not addressed as "Captain" or "Major" or "Colonel." Nor did he sign his letters with any military title. He was a civilian.

Kane further petitioned Jefferson Davis to organize the Maryland Regiment to fight in the war. The *Richmond Examiner* reported in March 1864 that Kane had already consulted with Davis, General Robert E. Lee, and the Secretary of War James Seddon, and was indeed given permission to establish "Camp Maryland" near Richmond. Kane continued to believe that by concentrating forces from Maryland into one fighting group he would improve both effectiveness and morale.[56]

Newspapers in spring 1864 read, "To Maryland men in the Confederate Service.—It is believed that General Orders No 38, Adjutant and Inspector General's office, just published, obviates all the difficulties which have heretofore interposed to prompt transfers to the Maryland Line."[57] Kane believed that the Maryland troops would coalesce into a Maryland unit if they were only given the opportunity to enlist voluntarily or transfer voluntarily to that Maryland Regiment. He pursued assisting his fellow Marylanders in transferring their service to the Maryland Line. However, he referred to General Lee's "having requested me to suspend my efforts to withdraw Marylanders from his army to the Maryland camps till the present campaign was ended,"[58] meaning that the transfers had to be delayed based on needs elsewhere. Kane further spoke of responding to the "expressed wishes of General Lee," suggesting that Kane was at least in close communication with Lee, or that he was coordinating his efforts with him.

Kane wrote to General Samuel Cooper from Richmond on May 6, 1864, objecting to Confederate guidelines for forced reenlistment of men who had already served their time in the military. General Orders No. 26, issued on March 1, 1864, had specified that all white males between the ages of 17 and 50 were ordered to serve in the military. Furthermore, the orders said that all men between the ages of 18 and 45 currently serving in the military would be retained in service to the South. Kane believed that patriotic Marylanders would be willing to reenlist of their own volition, if allowed, but that those recent orders forcing these men to reenlist would actually cause many to desert their duty. After the fall of Richmond, though most Confederate documents were destroyed, one letter surfaced which had been written from George Kane to William Smith, the Governor of Virginia, on October 7, 1864, from the American Hotel where Kane stayed in February and March 1864. The letter outlined Kane's belief that conscripting Maryland troops after they had already served their time in the military was counterproductive. Kane thought that "the attempt to hold them forcibly will fail to accomplish its object after their term has expired."[59] He believed that many soldiers would reenlist if given the free choice, but that Confederate policy had—in "bad faith"—demanded that they remain in service. James A. Seddon, Secretary of War, replied, saying that he was unwilling to change the policy.

Kane was adamant that Marylanders should be allowed to join their fellow statesmen as a force in the Southern army, both men who had served their term and wanted to reenlist and those who were still on active duty and had not completed their service who wanted to join fellow Marylanders.[60] Kane hastened to observe that he had "embarked in the effort to rally my countrymen, and that I have expended some thousands of dollars, private means, in the effort to accomplish that object."[61] While polite, Kane was at the same time insistent:

> In writing thus plainly I desire you to understand that it is in no spirit of captiousness, still less with purpose of disrespect to the Honorable Secretary or any of the agents of the Department, and I may safely say from no selfish purpose of any kind. I know that I am above any imputation of that sort in the estimation of all high-minded men of Maryland who hold the honor of their State in due estimation, and hence feel that I can afford to speak with frankness on the affairs of that State.[62]

Residents from other states were allowed to join regiments from their own states, but because Maryland evolved from a border state to one supporting the Union, residents from Maryland had fled their state across the Potomac to join forces with other states in the South. As many as 20,000–25,000 men had done exactly that, some combining with Virginians or Carolinians, with others forming what was called the First Maryland Infantry Battalion, Confederate States of America, also referred to as the "Maryland Line." This designation was confusing because there was also a Maryland Line in existence before the Civil War, and the Union Army also had its own Maryland Line. The Maryland Line CSA (Confederate States of America) was first organized in May 1861 and was led by Colonel Arnold Elzey (though first led for a month by Colonel Francis J. Thomas), Lieutenant Colonel George H. "Maryland" Steuart (called "Maryland" Steuart to distinguish him from J. E. B. Steuart), and Major Bradley T. Johnson. These troops drew heavily from preexisting militias in Baltimore, the Maryland Guards, the Baltimore City Guards, the Independent Greys, and the Law Greys.[63]

Kane renewed his insistence that Marylanders be allowed to form their own corps, and he visited the Marylanders who had been arrested for demanding their discharge and reassignment to the Maryland Line, as it were to be allowed to fight "side by side with the men of their own State."[64] Kane expressed dismay that the process was taking so long, and he noted that the appearance of a name in the news other than General Arnold Elzey as the Commander of the Maryland troops was worsening the morale of those expecting to join Elzey's ranks. Next in line to be given the command to form the Maryland Line was Bradley T. Johnson. By this time the troops who had come from Maryland were widely dispersed and difficult to bring together. Nevertheless, on September 22, 1863, Confederate Secretary of War James A. Seddon approved the formal designation as the Maryland Line. Johnson was elected to the command as Colonel on February 6, 1864. Ultimately about 1,500 men from Maryland were organized into the many divisions of the Maryland Line.[65] Kane circulated brochures that encouraged Marylanders to join, and he included the paperwork needed to accomplish this transfer,[66] but many commanders resisted releasing troops from their own state ranks because they needed the men themselves.

Five Maryland soldiers wrote to Kane on June 18, 1864, from Sullivan's Island, South Carolina, asking him to intervene on their behalf to allow them to join the Maryland Line they had been told was forming in Virginia. They claimed that 20–30 Marylanders were on Sullivan's Island wanting to be transferred, but that the officers there refused to allow them that privilege, General Orders No. 38 notwithstanding.[67]

Kane wrote from Richmond on June 24, 1864, to Assistant Adjutant General Colonel H. L. Clay, once again acknowledging the decision of the Secretary of War allowing Marylanders join the Maryland Line and to enlist voluntarily "with companies for the redemption of their state."[68] Kane, however, noted that some Baltimoreans who had gone to defend Charleston as early as 1861 and who had served their terms of enlistment had not yet been allowed to transfer to fight with their Maryland brothers. He cited General Orders No. 38, issued March 23, 1864, which specified the establishment of Camp Maryland in Staunton, Virginia, and a camp near Hanover Junction, Virginia, to be called Camp Howard.[69] The process had been repeatedly delayed.

Kane's precise activities during the summer of 1864 are unknown. Robert E. Lee wrote to Jefferson Davis on June 26, saying that he wanted Davis's judgment about the wisdom of trying to liberate Confederate prisoners from Point Lookout, just north across the Potomac from Virginia. Most Union troops were being deployed to General Ulysses S. Grant's forces elsewhere, making the defense of Point Lookout rather weak. He proposed using Marylanders for the job, saying that they would be "men of excellent material, and much experience." But Lee could not think of an appropriate leader for the raid, knowing that having a Marylander lead the attack would be ideal. Lee considered naming Colonel Bradley Johnson—a Marylander who was an experienced military leader—for the task. In that same letter that Lee wrote to Davis, Lee said, in a new paragraph and without any preamble about the subject, "With relation to the project of Marshal Kane, if the matter can be kept secret, which I fear is impossible, should Genl Early cross the Potomac, he might be sent to join him."[70] The nature of "the project" has been the subject of much speculation, but its purpose is in fact unknown. It could have referenced the liberation of prisoners at Point Lookout or some other venture. Letters around this time from

Kane to Davis do not clarify the matter. It is unlikely that Lee's reference to "the project" related to any of Kane's prior schemes to form a Maryland Regiment by taking former Marylanders from other troops,[71] another attempt to liberate prisoners from Johnson's Island, or Kane's aborted plans to burn Northern cities. The meaning of the word "project" thus still remains elusive.

Kane wrote to Davis on July 15, 1864: "I learn from a person who left Baltimore this day [last] week that all of the steamboats suitable for transports from Baltimore as far north as Portland had been chartered or pressed with orders to report to Fortress Monroe whether this is for point Look out [*sic*, "Point Lookout"] or for purpose of Genl Grant I don't know but send you the information as I get it."[72] This reference may have been to "the project" mentioned in the previous month's letter from Lee to Davis, but it is uncertain.

Later, also from Richmond, on October 8, 1864, Kane wrote to President Jefferson Davis, expressing both his desire to participate actively in the ongoing war and stating his own personal physical limitations: "I do not feel comfortable at being idle in time[s] like these, and yet am not able to shoulder a gun in field service."[73] Still seeking a way to further the Confederate cause, he wrote:

> My attention has frequently been called to the probable intention of the Government to organize a secret-service corps in connection with or to embrace the Signal Corps. If such be the case, and the matter is open, and you feel at liberty to instruct me with the command, I feel confident that I can render efficient service quite commensurate with the expenditure to be incurred. Should I fail to do so, or to come fully up to your expectation, you may rely upon it that I will promptly and voluntarily surrender the trust without waiting to have my commission revoked. My view would be to organize a full regiment of Marylanders not owing service to the Confederacy, not in service, many of whom I feel confident I can bring over to border to organize a corps of heavy artillery to be available on the Potomac, and thus by the activity and energy of the material I should embody I think the navigation of the Potomac by transports could be materially embarrassed at important moments.... My relations with men on the other side, their sons being with me, and my knowledge of men and things up to the Canada line, would very materially facilitate such operations.[74]

Kane was again volunteering to organize a resistance movement that would employ men not currently actively serving in the military—those who had already served, those too old, and those wounded or unfit for service—but who could both man artillery equipment and participate in secret-service activity. They would form a unit to be available for service on the Potomac. Secretary of War Seddon replied that he had not considered organizing such a group for secret service in connection with the Signal Corps, and that he would favorably look upon organizing a group of Marylanders not otherwise liable for military service. However, Seddon didn't think having them support heavy artillery on the Potomac would be wise because he believed that it would be impossible for them to maintain their position at that site, and their presence would likely provoke an attack from Union forces nearby. President Davis then approved raising a regiment of otherwise ineligible Maryland men for additional service as appropriate, perhaps for some kind of special service or support of other troops. He was not at all opposed to adding additional help for his military operations since the war was going badly for the South. On October 19, Davis approved the plan to raise a Maryland Regiment, but rejected the idea that these men—many physically infirm—might operate heavy artillery, the "least of all arms qualified for separate operations."[75] Kane replied on October 28 that he had identified "a number of Marylanders here, most of them old soldiers and exempts (all of them), who wish to render service as far as they are able."[76] He wanted to recruit these men "to work four guns of your permanent fortifications, perhaps a larger number, and thus relieve more active men whom you may require for other service." Kane restated his own disability by saying, "I am not able to march about." On November 12, 1864, Samuel W. Melton, Assistant Adjutant General, replied: "The proposition by Mr. Kane is to form a company for local defense and special service in heavy artillery, with the special provision that it will not be employed elsewhere than in General Pemberton's lines, and then only in emergency, to be composed of Marylanders not liable to service. Respectfully submitted to the Secretary of War, recommended."[77]

The fall of 1864 was a time of intense activity in the Montreal area. On October 18, raiders were attempting to rob banks in St. Albans, Vermont. These Confederates, led by Kentuckian Bennett H. Young, tried to steal money for the Confederate cause, though their real motive was to bring the Civil War to the North, terrorize Northern citizens, and divert Northern resources to defend the Northern border. The perpetrators fled to Canada, only a few miles away, and they were promptly arrested on Canadian soil. A quick trial, with their defense funded by Confederate sources, freed them on a technicality.

Other warfare attempted by the Canadian Confederates working out of Montreal—including Kane—encompassed poisoning of the New York City water supply; an unsuccessful plan to burn New York City; the yellow fever plot of Dr. Luke Pryor Blackburn, whereby he tried to import yellow fever and smallpox to the North; and yet a third scheme to liberate Confederate inmates at Johnson's Island Prison near Sandusky, Ohio.[78] This plan to free the Confederate prisoners once again involved the capture of the Union gunboat *Michigan* that was anchored near the prison. The two similar attempts in 1862 and 1863 had both failed. This attempt in September 1864, led by John Yates Beall, was likewise unsuccessful, and it led to Beall's capture and subsequent execution.

This was the scene encountered by John Wilkes Booth upon his trip to Montreal in October 1864. It was on this trip that Booth made his famous statement about Lincoln: "Abe's contract is near up, and whether re-elected or not he will get his goose cooked."[79] Here, Patrick C. Martin, that successful blockade-runner, had repeated contact with Booth, who arrived in Montreal on October 18, 1864, where he initially registered at room 150 of St. Lawrence Hall. Booth had come to Montreal ostensibly to arrange shipment of his own theatrical wardrobe and props to the South for his continued career on the stage. He had recently been in Boston at the Parker House Hotel on July 26, 1864, allegedly dealing with some Confederates who had connections to the Confederate Secret Service. Cordial Crane was an official at the Boston Customs House who later, at the request of the Union government, examined the hotel register at the Parker House to see who had stayed there at the time. Booth had been registered there along with four other men, one of whom was H. V. Clinton from Hamilton, Canada West, a name also found on the register of the St. Lawrence

Hall in Montreal. Others were Charles R. Hunter from Toronto, Canada West, A. J. Bursted (or Rursted) from Baltimore, and R. A. Leech from Montreal.[80] Likely these names were aliases. Some historians believe that the man from Baltimore was George Kane, though no evidence exists for this identification except for the connection to Baltimore, and Kane was not known for using an alias. Another candidate for this man from Baltimore was Patrick C. Martin, but there is likewise no evidence to identify him as the Bursted (or Rursted) mentioned at this meeting. Confederate agents' paths crossed frequently, and many authors and historians believe that the five men were scheming for either the kidnapping or the assassination of President Lincoln, even at this early date.

During his visit to Montreal, Booth met with Jacob Thompson, chief of the Canadian Confederacy, and George N. Sanders, an ardent secessionist and believer in assassination for political purposes, both residing in Montreal at the time. Sanders's son Major Reid Sanders had died as a prisoner of war at Fort Warren, so the elder Sanders's intensity of hate for the North was understandable. Booth remained in the Montreal area for 10 days, likely longer than necessary simply to pack trunks full of costumes and have them shipped to the South. He also conducted some financial transactions, and while there he allegedly stayed at the home of Patrick Martin after his initial stay at St. Lawrence Hall, as Kane had done in earlier months. Booth apparently had hoped to meet with Kane while in Montreal, but Kane had already left for the South. Kane was reported to be in Richmond on October 9, assisting as a pallbearer in the funeral of a friend, General John Gregg of Texas, who had been killed in fighting near Richmond.[81] While in Montreal, Booth, incidentally, was said to have taken a liking to Martin's daughter, Margaret. On about October 27, after 10 days in Montreal, Booth left for Boston, then to New York, perhaps taking some funding for his future operations from his Confederate sources in Montreal.

Martin also had provided Booth with letters of introduction to Dr. William Queen, an elderly physician who lived at the edge of the Zekiah Swamp on the Potomac River, six miles from Bryantown in Charles County, Maryland; Dr. Samuel Mudd, also in Charles County, Maryland; and reportedly one to George Proctor Kane. Booth likely expected that the two doctors might be able to help him in his plots against Lincoln, or assist him in his escape plans. The letter to Dr. Mudd may have been apocryphal; it was never found, and the only evidence for its existence is a secondhand account of what Lincoln assassination conspirator Samuel Arnold said when he was captured.[82] Arnold's more formal testimony, signed later, did not mention any such letter to Dr. Mudd. The letter to George Proctor Kane is also an enigma. No such letter has ever been found, either, though Kane acknowledged that it existed in a report in the New York *Daily Graphic* in 1876. It is unlikely that Booth needed a letter of introduction to Kane, considering that Booth had previously reacted violently in 1861 upon hearing of Kane's arrest.[83] Either Booth knew Kane well and needed no introduction (in which case the letter may have contained other information—perhaps coded data or instructions for a conspiracy), or Booth was lying or exaggerating in 1861 when describing his friendship with Kane. Years later, Kane described a letter from Martin:

Towards the end of the war, in March or April [1865], I was resting, out of the way, in the Valley of Virginia. While there a letter dated the previous December [1864] was received by me from Martin, in Montreal. It said across the face, after the family and friendly matter in it was complete: "What do you know of John Wilkes Booth? He has been here and stopped at my house. He expressed great disappointment at not finding you, and said he had expected to meet you here. What is his character? He became intimate at my house with my wife and daughter. Has he a good reputation in Baltimore?"

This part of the letter was a mystery to me. I had never known Wilkes Booth, if I had ever heard of him, and I doubt that I had ever heard of him. The host of the house where I was lodging came to me just after I received this letter and said, "Colonel Kane, Stoneman is raiding up the valley. His scouts are close on you and you will be arrested if you stay here." I placed the letter inside of the lining of my traveling bag, mounted a horse with the bag, and rode through the woods and broken country to Danville, where I arrived nearly dead with fever and fatigue. Just after I arrived there Mr. Davis and his party, flying from Richmond to Charlotte, came along and I rode with them in the car to Greensboro, where I had to stop off. While lying there, hardly in my senses, after some days had elapsed, the man of the house said to me: "Colonel Kane, we have a part of a torn New York newspaper here which contains some startling intelligence. A man named Wilkes Booth has assassinated President Lincoln." I endeavored to recall where I had heard that name. I rose up almost delirious and tapped my forehead, muttering "Wilkes Booth. Who is he? How is he connected with me?" Then in a few minutes I cried to the man: "Bring me that sachel [sic]!" I tore out Martin's letter and read it again. Although I never knew Booth, that letter might have cost me my life if it had been found in the sachel at that time.[84]

The statement that Martin did not know Booth's reputation also seems implausible since Martin was writing letters of introduction or reference for Booth, and Booth had supposedly just stayed in Martin's home for over a week. Similarly, if Booth had come to Montreal to meet with Kane, why did Booth need a letter of introduction to him? Furthermore, the letter as related by Kane seems to confirm that Kane and Booth were not friends, though Kane may simply have wanted to distance himself from any association with the assassin and thus denied knowledge of him. Booth had previously claimed that Kane was a good friend of his. Why Kane would hide the letter in the lining of his traveling bag before hearing about the assassination is also perplexing. He would have had no reason to hide it before learning of Booth's deed, unless, of course, the letter contained plans or descriptions of Booth's anticipated murder (or kidnapping) of Lincoln. Or perhaps Kane knew of Booth's assassination plans even before the deed was done.

The story of this letter from Martin to Kane is found only in the article written by George Alfred Townsend, purportedly based on an interview with Kane. Townsend, writing in the New York *Daily Graphic* under the pseudonym of GATH, made assertions about the connections between Martin and Kane that are otherwise unsubstantiated.

After leaving Montreal in October 1864, Booth would then travel to Maryland to meet with Dr. William Queen, known to be a member of the Confederate underground in Charles County, Maryland. Booth arrived in Washington, D.C., on November 9, where he registered at the National Hotel. On November 11 he went to visit Dr. Queen, who lived about six miles south of Bryantown, Maryland. Booth spent the night of November 12 at Dr. Queen's home, but the content of any of their conversations there is unknown. Likely Booth was trying to learn the geography of the area to aid him in his plot against President Lincoln. The next day—a Sunday—Booth and Queen went to St. Mary's Roman Catholic Church, where they met Dr. Samuel Mudd. Dr. Mudd would figure prominently in Booth's escape route after shooting President Lincoln. The actual letter from Martin to Queen has never been found—only a description of it.

As these letters were being written to Queen, Mudd, and Kane, Martin arranged the passage for Booth's theatrical goods on the 73-foot, 90-ton schooner *Marie Victoria*. Martin himself accompanied the items on this particular voyage. The crew had only six men. The items were to go first from Montreal to Nassau, then into the South—likely Richmond—on a blockade-runner. Also on board *Marie Victoria* were 547 barrels of coal oil. Booth's property was packed in trunks labeled "J.W.B."; there were two actual trunks and one long box. The trunks contained his wardrobes, costumes, suits, shoes, and hats, as well as papers, scripts, plays, correspondence, and photographs. The box had his swords, pistols, knives and other stage props. Martin planned to accompany this cargo to the South. However, *Marie Victoria* left Montreal on about October 24, 1864, and it soon encountered bad weather. This region was along the Gulf of St. Lawrence, and it was here that an early winter storm wrecked the boat under mysterious circumstances. A rescue party approached the foundering vessel at about 1:00 p.m. on November 7, but all hands on the deck of the *Marie Victoria* had gone missing. It was a ghost ship with no one on board. The rescue crew salvaged some of the cargo, including Booth's trunks, and stored them, in addition to hauling the ship further on shore to protect it from the coming winter ice. This entire project took over three weeks. It would not be until later in the spring of 1865 that an Admiralty Court would begin its deliberations on the salvage of the vessel itself, which had been valued at $2,280, with the coal oil appraised at $9,656. Because Booth's trunks were to be auctioned after he had assassinated Lincoln, there was great interest in their contents. Secretary of State William H. Seward directed William H. F. Gurley, the new U.S. Consul to Quebec, to examine the contents of the trunks before they were auctioned to see if they contained any useful evidence regarding Lincoln's murder. They didn't.[85] Patrick Martin and the rest of the crew of the *Marie Victoria* were declared lost, and all were assumed to have drowned, though no bodies were ever found.

Kane's activity during this time continued to span many functions. On November 30, 1864, the Confederate Quartermaster General received a letter from him, dated November 29, asking that the Quartermaster Department at Greensboro, North Carolina, be telegraphed "to take charge of 7 bales of goods for Marylanders & send them on gov't trains to this place [Richmond]."[86] Some historians have interpreted this request to help his fellow Marylanders as evidence of his direct involvement in providing uniforms and equipment for Maryland troops in the Army of Northern Virginia.[87]

Kane later visited the Second Maryland Infantry of the Maryland Line in early 1865, close to the end of the war. This Maryland Line had been formed by volunteers from Maryland who had fled to fight for the South, mostly for the Army of Northern Virginia. "He [Kane] was shocked at the condition of the men, and he was moreover surprised at their cheerfulness under such trying circumstances. When he left the boys he promised them each a new uniform and a change of underclothing." William Henry Droste, a Southern sympathizer connected to Kane and a boatbuilder, blockade-runner, and entrepreneur who later became a Baltimore police officer, went to New York City. There he purchased a number of supplies for the Confederate cause, including clothing, and loaded them on a boat headed for the South. A young man—a messenger connected with Kane—accompanied Droste on this mission. This messenger was also holding important Confederate documents addressed to President Jefferson Davis that were to be delivered to Davis in Richmond. Federal agents intercepted the boat in the New York harbor and searched the boat's contents, as well as the documents the messenger was carrying. The messenger was arrested, along with Droste. Droste was held prisoner on the boat for six weeks, and Kane's helper was sent to Boston to be tried as a spy, but he escaped from the train on the passage to Boston.[88] Kane ultimately kept his promise, and on March 4, 1865, the clothing arrived at the Confederate camp. "Many a 'God bless you, Colonel Kane,' went up from those poor boys as they threw aside the miserable rags in which they were clad and donned their comfortable suits."[89]

Kane reportedly returned to Richmond immediately before the end of the war. A correspondent from the *Baltimore American* wrote from Richmond that Kane remained there until about two weeks before the evacuation of the city.[90] Though uncorroborated elsewhere, the *Baltimore Sun* reported that Kane was a "detective" in Richmond around this time, April 1865.[91]

Toward the end of the War, Kane was located near Danville, Virginia, about 150 miles to the south and west of Richmond. Exactly what he was doing there is unknown. That Kane briefly settled in Danville was logical, as it had been an important city along the railroad line that supplied Richmond and the Confederate troops. Though Danville citizens had initially opposed secession, they quickly changed allegiance after the firing upon Fort Sumter. Danville was also an important city in Virginia because of its six prisons, the armory, the businesses, and the schools. After the fall of Petersburg in early April 1865, and as Richmond was about to succumb, Jefferson Davis and his government officials fled on April 2 on the only remaining railroad, the Richmond and Danville Railway, initially to Danville, where it became the "last capital of the confederacy," though surviving only one week, April 3–10, 1865. Kane reported to Davis on April 8, 1865, that he was located 15 miles from Danville, and he detailed troop movements in the area. Kane gave specifics gathered from General Joseph Wheeler's officers, obtained while Kane was looking for General Jubal Early.[92] Kane again expressed his physical limitations, claiming "not being able to ride in myself to night."[93] Davis briefly continued his Confederate presidency at the home of William T. Sutherlin in Danville, though it was obvious to many that Davis could not survive long there. After General Robert E. Lee lost the Battle of Appomattox Courthouse on April 9, Davis and his entourage continued their retreat to the south, initially to Greensboro, North Carolina, with the few Confederate documents that were not destroyed in Richmond and allegedly with portions of the remaining Confederate treasury.

Kane had not yet returned to Baltimore, and the future for Confederate sympathizers there was still uncertain. In Danville, an area rich in Southern history, Kane would become a businessman again.

Kane became the President/Superintendent of the Roanoke Tobacco Company in Danville, advertised as manufacturing "the finest smoking tobacco in the country, ... the Queen of the Southern brands."[94] His company used the "fine Dan River Valley leaf," touted as superior to other varieties.[95] One of his products was named the "Prince of Wales"; another was "Maryland Club,"[96] declared "to be superior to anything of the kind heretofore produced in the United States."[97] Two less elegant-sounding varieties were "Bill Arp" and "Here's Yer Mule."[98] Kane was described as "fitted by nature as the very man for the position—an old smoker and connoisseur of the weed, a gentleman of the highest culture, and of a taste as nice and delicate as a woman's." Further, "It is worthy of remark that this Factory employs wounded Confederates; and many daughters of our gallant dead derive their support from within its walls. We commend this manufactory most heartily to our Southern friends, observing that no devotee of the meerschaum, after once trying its choice brands, considers his larder complete without a good supply in his house."[99] One source claimed that this business employed "nearly one hundred persons, most of them girls and boys in indigent circumstances. It would be a good thing if others would follow in his footsteps—the war having left a large number of this class, who will have to rely upon their daily labor for support."[100] Kane was lauded as "a gentleman of great industry and energy, who, eschewing politics, which he once took great interest, gives all his time and talents to the business of the company whose interests have been committed to his management." He "occupies the same high social position amongst his new acquaintances in Virginia that he did amongst the companions of his youth in his native State."[101] The Roanoke Tobacco Company would subsequently be sold to William Henry Jones who would later run the Jones Leaf Tobacco Warehouse in Richmond. (Coincidentally, this family had provided the name for the Jones Falls in Baltimore.[102]) The company fell upon hard times after Kane left, and it went into bankruptcy in August 1871.[103] Kane's exact dates of residence in Danville during his connection with the tobacco company are unknown. He was listed in Virginia tax records in Virginia as the president of this company, and taxes in his name are recorded at least between the months of July and December 1866.[104]

In the spring of 1867 Kane was listed as one of the organizers and references for a "Gift Concert" to be given for the benefit of the Southern Orphan Association in Baltimore. Colonel George P. Kane was listed as one of the event's "References," though Kane's address was still in Danville.[105] The Southern Orphan Association had its headquarters in Baltimore at No. 13 Holliday Street. The concert, to be held at the Maryland Institute in Baltimore, was scheduled for June 17, though it had been rescheduled from an earlier date for unspecified reasons. Located directly north of Centre Market on Harrison Street between Baltimore and Second Streets, the Maryland Institute (now the Maryland Institute College of Art) had its "Great Hall," at one time the largest meeting hall in Baltimore, said to be capable of seating about 6,000 guests. It was the site of many events, including political conventions and Lincoln's famous "Baltimore Address" or "Liberty Speech," given on April 18, 1864. Ads stated, "The profits of this concert will be given to the Southern Orphans' Association ... for the maintenance and education of the destitute orphans of deceased

Southern soldiers and sailors." The Association was "to erect a home and school for the orphans of the South, both male and female, on an extensive scale, in the city of Richmond, Va." The Legislature of Virginia incorporated the company in January 1867, giving it some degree of respectability and implying that the funds would be used as advertised. Appealing to the sympathies of Southerners, the ads read that it would "attempt to alleviate the sad condition of great numbers of helpless children, rendered thus by the terrible war through which we have passed," and "thus qualifying them for FUTURE USEFULNESS TO SOCIETY AT LARGE" [emphasis in the original]. The Association proposed to sell 500,000 tickets at $1 each, and they guaranteed that each ticket purchased would qualify the buyer for a gift, ranging in value from a 211-acre estate (estimated to cost $30,000) to other real estate, cash prizes up to $2,000, gold, pianos, watches, chains, paintings, Bibles, books, pens, and other items. Everyone who purchased a ticket would receive a gift by random drawing. Kane lent his good name to this enterprise, along with General B. T. Beauregard of New Orleans, William A. Wright, then of Augusta, Georgia, other military dignitaries, and Baltimore businessmen. It is possible that these men sincerely believed in the charity, though it was unclear how 500,000 gifts could be purchased and given on $1 tickets and still turn a profit for the destitute children.[106] Even before the scheme unraveled, the *Baltimore Sun* reported that the "benefit" was really a scam "to benefit alone the speculators." This newspaper said that the "bogus 'agents' of 'memorial associations' and exhibitors of shows for aid ... are going about the country. The public should be on their guard against imposters."[107] As early as February 25, 1867, the authorities in Staunton, Virginia, warned that agents should "discontinue the sale of certificates till further ordered, and to refund the money for those already sold."[108] Tickets were being sold in many states, and one newspaper in North Carolina said, "It should be well enough, however, for the Southern people to beware always of *Gift* enterprises. A great deal of humbug walks around in this world covered with the stolen mantle of Charity, and the unwary are often misled in such things by the evil designing." The Baltimore *Gazette* reported: "certain parties connected with a Grand Charitable Presentation Concert, in aid of the Southern Orphans' Association were arrested upon warrants ... charging them with obtaining money under false pretenses and with conspiracy to defraud the public."[109] Legal battles over the ownership and disposition of the money raised continued through 1869.[110] Kane, however, was not personally scarred by this scandal.

Kane began visiting his native Baltimore again in late 1867. On December 25, he appeared in Baltimore to visit relatives for the Christmas holidays. Friends greeted him warmly at the Camden railroad station, one of the sites made famous by the Baltimore Riot of April 19, 1861.[111] One Northern newspaper predicted "a grand reception and entertainment," though it questioned the propriety of such a reception:

> He will be literally lionized, while numerous poor armless and legless Union soldiers, who fought to save the country, are daily seen ranged on the streets, sitting on their shattered stumps, grinding old organs, and begging pennies for a scanty subsistence from passers-by. Would it not be well to first be generous towards these loyal maimed soldiers, and save them from exposure to the inclement weather and the necessity of begging on the streets?[112]

It wasn't until January 1867 that Kane's arrest in Baltimore in June 1861 on a charge of treason was effectively set aside. Even that action was an equivocation because the charge wasn't rescinded, it was placed on a "stet docket," meaning that it was essentially put into a state of suspended animation. ("Stet" in Latin means "let it stand," meaning that the charge becomes inactive. The defendant must agree to placing his charge in this category since it means that the right to a speedy trial is waived.) The charge could be reinstated or revoked upon further judicial pleas or decisions, but it indefinitely postponed a trial on the issue. It was a hollow victory for Marshal Kane.[113] Newspapers later reported that Kane was finally pardoned by the amnesty declared by President Andrew Johnson and Secretary of State William H. Seward on September 7, 1867.[114] This amnesty, however, required that the person pardoned had to take the oath of allegiance to the United States. There is no record of Kane ever having taken this oath.

Even then, Kane continued his extensive travels (Appendix, Table 8). He visited Atlanta on November 9, 1867,[115] and he was reported to be in Charleston, South Carolina, on November 19, 1868.[116]

17

Return to Baltimore

Kane was loved and honored in Virginia toward the end of the Civil War. On March 4, 1865, an advertisement appeared in the *Richmond Dispatch* announcing the auction of a horse by H. Porterfield Taylor, Auctioneer, No. 63 Main Street, at the Richmond Horse Lot: "I will offer there a DARK-BROWN STALLION, seven years old, real fat, not the least restive with mares, that is unexceptionable [*sic*], both in harness and under the saddle—standing quietly, untied, wherever left; for which the owner was offered last spring $5,000, for presentation to Marshal Kane." It's unclear if the horse was sold or if the money was ever delivered to Kane.[1]

Police from the 1860s also held Marshal Kane in high regard. About one year after the end of the war, when Kane was still living in Danville and struggling financially, he visited Baltimore briefly. The police force that had served under Kane took a collection and presented him with a gift of $5,000. Kane declined the gift, however, saying that even though he was somewhat impoverished, he realized that the men who had served under him were in worse circumstances.[2] This act of humility said much about Kane's character.

In February 1868 his former police officers presented him with an elegant snuffbox created by the George W. Webb & Company Jewelers, a respected firm in Baltimore located at the corner of Baltimore and Light Streets. The gift, valued at $300—a princely sum in 1868—was inscribed with: "Presented to Col. Geo. P. Kane by the police force of 1860, as a testimonial of their esteem for him as a man, and their appreciation of the ability, zeal and unselfish devotion with which he discharged the duties of the office of marshal of police. Baltimore, January, 1868."[3] Clearly Kane's love for the South had not diminished the honor accorded him by his fellow policemen who still lived in Baltimore.

On June 22, 1868, while he was still in Danville, Kane penned the defense of his behavior when Lincoln passed through Baltimore in 1861. In it, he decried the lack of advance communication about Lincoln's passage through town, which would have allowed him to prepare more appropriately. Kane noted that those wanting to welcome Lincoln were "the very scum of the city" and that he (Kane) had immediately asked General John S. Gittings for advice. Gittings, a Democrat himself, agreed to host a Lincoln gathering. The reception was never held for President-Elect Lincoln because Lincoln had been "duped" into making a secret passage through Baltimore. Kane bolstered the story of the confidence that Mrs. Lincoln had shown in his arrangements to protect the presidential party by inviting Kane to meet with her that day, a meeting that was not held because Kane experienced a "sudden and severe indisposition" that prevented her from thanking him.[4]

George Kane would return to Baltimore permanently in late 1868 or early 1869. He was reported to be in Baltimore briefly on February 12, 1869.[5] The *Baltimore Sun* declared on March 6, 1869, that Kane was bound for his native city. The *Danville Register* wrote:

> Whatever in the past may have been the convictions in national politics which led him into a course of action different from that of some of his Maryland fellow-citizens, we have yet to meet with the first gentleman of his own State who hesitated to credit him with a patriotic sincerity, or accord to him the meed of praise as an energetic, upright and impartial officer in all his administrations of public affairs. In common with other citizens we would gladly welcome the colonel, not only as a stranger and sojourner with us, but as a citizen of permanent domicil [sic].[6]

The *Baltimore Sun* detailed Kane's presence at a gathering of the Ninth Regiment, Maryland National Guard, on March 18, 1869.[7]

Sheriff of Baltimore

Kane ran for Sheriff of Baltimore in 1869. Kane or his friends published "cards" (announcements) in the Baltimore newspapers as early as March 1. This run for office had to have been planned while Kane was still in Virginia. By fall 1869 Kane had published—by today's standards—rather mild and understated announcements of his candidacy:

> TO THE VOTERS OF THE CITY OF BALTIMORE: In response to inquiries, and at the instance of friends, the undersigned avails of this medium to announce to his fellow-citizens THAT THE USE OF HIS NAME IN CONNECTION WITH THE SHERIFFALTY, AT THE ENSUING ELECTION, IS MADE WITH HIS FULL SANCTION, and if chosen by the voters for that office, its duties will be discharged with fidelity to the public interests. GEORGE P. KANE[8] [capital letters in original]

Kane's candidacy was not unopposed. There existed a "warm contest" between him and Augustus Albert in the primary of the Democratic Party. Interest in this position was high, and there was "a more than usually large vote for a primary election." Voting on September 15, 1869, was generally quiet, though "several arrests were made for disorderly conduct." In the Ninth Ward a man was seriously stabbed. At the vote count the next day, some men protested "gross frauds" in the Second District. They asserted that some voters known to support Colonel Kane were not allowed to vote and that the ballot box was "stuffed" by one of the judges. Nevertheless, votes were tallied, and Augustus Albert was the winner.[9]

Upon his return to Maryland from Virginia, Kane rapidly became involved in the affairs of the city of Baltimore. His friends quickly recognized him as a leader in the community, one of his first duties being to assist in committees trying to organize and construct a "State Asylum for Inebriates." Kane was appointed from a list of managers to participate in a committee to organize a "fair" to promote the construction of the asylum. The committees were Arrangements, Police, Printing and

Tickets, Decoration, Finance, Transportation, and Music. These civic events were serious business activities of the times.[10] The fair was a ten-day event, held at the Maryland Institute, opening November 23, 1869. On the first day doorkeepers estimated that at least 5,000 people attended. It was events such as these that would eventually propel George P. Kane into the public eye, leading to more serious politics and eventually the Mayor's race in Baltimore.

Kane tried again to win the Sheriff's position in November 1871, running as a Democrat. Kane handily won the Democratic nomination on June 27, with 8,802 votes out of a total 11,399 cast. In the general election Kane faced Republican William B. Johnson. Kane was successful, defeating his opponent 22,470 to 14,839 in a vote taken on November 7.[11] The job was a two-year term. The *Baltimore Sun* said on November 27, 1871: "In consideration of Colonel Kane's experience in local administration, and his well known efficiency and solicitude for the general welfare of the community, it is to be expected that the duties of his new position as sheriff will be well performed."[12]

One might think that the position of Sheriff would be relatively free of political infighting and controversy. Not so. In Baltimore in the 1870s, the Sheriff chose the members of grand juries. On one occasion, *Der Deutsche Correspondent*, the German newspaper of Baltimore, chided Kane for having too few Germans on a grand jury he had picked.[13] Implicit in this attack was the notion that he was ethnically biased. Kane responded by saying that he didn't even know the ethnic background of the people he had chosen for the grand jury. He said that the law didn't distinguish between native-born citizens and naturalized citizens in the composition of a grand jury, and that he had chosen the members from a pool of 750 prospective jurors picked by the judges of the courts strictly on their fitness to serve on the panel.[14] Kane's job required diplomacy, as well as knowledge of the law.

Kane remained Sheriff until 1873. He submitted a letter of resignation on April 21, 1873, to be effective June 20. Resignation from a position before the end of its term was not a new phenomenon for George Kane. He had attempted to resign from his post as Marshal in 1860 after only a few months of service. His rationale then was that the job of cleaning the city of its "Mobtown" reputation had been successfully completed. He would be talked out of that resignation soon after submitting it. Kane would later resign as a member of the Jones Falls Commission because he disagreed with the system under which the Commission operated, and he had been unable to change it. He simply refused to be a part of anything with which he did not agree. Kane's supporters considered this tendency to resign early to be a virtue; his detractors called it a detriment to his effective functioning. Public outcry against his April 1873 resignation as Sheriff was overwhelming. Most Baltimoreans respected Kane, and many pleaded with him to reconsider. He seemed to dislike some aspects of the job that made him responsible for certain issues, but without control over the factors that could make a difference. He was particularly bothered by his inability to bring an end to gambling in the city. Furthermore, he had to listen to complaints about issues over which he had no power. Kane felt that a backlog of cases before the grand jury and in the courts was impeding justice, and that offices outside his control were not functioning appropriately. Court adjournments and continuations seemed to be thwarting the work of the Sheriff's Office. The *Baltimore Sun* reported, "Col. Kane has filled various important offices in this community, and invariably with credit to himself, as well as usefulness to the public."[15] The Governor of Maryland, William P. Whyte, returned Kane's letter of resignation, rejecting it and asking Kane to reconsider:[16]

> Sir: I beg permission to return to you the enclosed letter resigning the office of sheriff of Baltimore city, with the request that it may be withdrawn.
>
> From the moment of its receipt I determined upon this course, which subsequent reflection has satisfied me to be correct.
>
> No reason is assigned by you for the step you have taken, and presuming that none exists which cannot be overcome without sacrifice of principle, I do earnestly request you to reconsider your determination.
>
> The manner in which you have discharged the duties of the office has been highly appreciated by the people of Baltimore city, and their confidence in your integrity and fidelity to their interests is unquestioned.
>
> Your withdrawal from the office to which they so cheerfully elected you would occasion universal regret.
>
> Sincerely yours,
> WM. PINKNEY WHYTE

On May 6, Kane replied to Governor Whyte, saying that he had

> the single object of assuring you that my resignation was not the result of momentary irritation or caprice, much less of any desire to avoid the proper duties and responsibilities of the office, for my election to which I am under so many obligations to my fellow-citizens.
>
> As a lawyer of large experience you do not need to be informed of the hazards and cares which attend the sheriffalty here under the most favorable circumstances, and can know to how much greater responsibility the sheriff is held by the public generally for the execution of the laws than properly attaches to this office.
>
> Under the operation of existing laws, and without any fault of my own, I have so frequently and painfully felt my inability to meet the reasonable public expectations in many particulars, and have met with so many embarrassments that I have more than once before been strongly impelled to request you to put some on in my place.
>
> In presenting my resignation to you at last, I should have desired it to take effect immediately but from the fact, which it may, perhaps, surprise you to be told, that my receipts from the office since the 1st of January have been considerably less than my expenditures, and I could not afford to abandon the place without reimbursing myself for this outlay on public account.
>
> If I were to consult my individual inclination only, I should still respectfully ask your leave to adhere to my purpose of transferring my duties to other hands, but I cannot be insensible to the friendly urgency with which you have done me the honor to press its withdrawal, now to the generally and kindly expressed wishes of the many friends who have insisted that it is my duty to remain at my post until the expiration of my term. I have, therefore, after mature reflection, though with much hesitation, concluded to do so, and have only to tender my thanks to you for your courtesy in the matter. I am, with great respect, your obedient servant.
>
> GEO. P. KANE[17]

Kane remained Sheriff through December 1873. His successor was Augustus Albert, who won the election of November 4, 1873, and who took office in early December.[18]

Jones Falls Commission

Kane became a member of the "Jones Falls Commission" in late 1869.[19] This was a group dedicated to the improvement of the stream called Jones Falls. Named after David Jones, a settler who located in what is now Baltimore in 1661 (an area then called "Jones Town"), the Jones Falls stream enters Baltimore from the north. It ordinarily meandered through the city, finally emptying into the harbor at the City Dock. Customarily a reasonably calm river, and once called "that delectable stream which passes directly through the city," it was prone to catastrophic flooding every few decades. It caused widespread damage in 1817, 1837, and then again in 1868. The 1868 flood, occurring on July 24, was called the "Black Friday Flood of 1868." It killed about 50 people, destroyed over 2,000 homes, trapped many, and caused 2–3 million dollars of damage, including sweeping away bridges at Charles, Madison, Monument, Centre, Bath, Hillen, and Fayette Streets. This ordinarily innocuous stream rose to over 20 feet in depth, at one point rising 5 feet in 10 minutes. The flooding was compounded by an unusually high tide in the bay, and further worsened by winds that pushed water from the bay retrograde into its many tributaries.[20]

Citizens lobbied for improvements to the waterway that would widen, deepen, and straighten its course. Talk of constructing changes to the stream began quickly, and by August 12, 1868, detailed but unofficial plans had emerged. Residents along Jones Falls created an association to improve the stream, and they asked Henry Tyson, a Baltimore civil engineer, to begin planning the construction of improvements along its course. Tyson proposed extensive alterations to the waterway, which had morphed in Baltimoreans' minds from that "delectable stream" to a "loathsome and disease-engendering cess-pool, which winds its filthy way through the midst of our city—a blight as it has always been upon its prosperity, and entirely inadequate for the purpose for which it is maintained."[21] Tyson estimated that the project could be completed in a year and a half at a cost of about $3,250,000. Politicians and engineers wrangled for months, and many plans emerged to solve the problem. Local residents most affected by the flooding, exasperated by the lack of action by city officials, even initially considered attempting portions of this project themselves. It soon became obvious that it had to be a governmental effort, if for no other reason than that by early 1869 the estimated cost for the many solutions to the problem was between $1,000,000 and $6,000,000, huge figures in that era. A detailed plan for the improvement of the Jones Falls was published in the December 15, 1869, *Baltimore Sun*. Debate then transitioned to the tax base to be used for the funding of the project. Some believed that the taxation should have been limited to those along the geographical boundaries of Jones Falls itself; others argued that Jones Falls benefited all Baltimoreans and that the taxation should be applied to the entire city. The latter opinion prevailed.

An early iteration of the Jones Falls Commission in the fall of 1868 had three members: Isaac Ridgeway Trimble, John H. Tegmeyer, and Benjamin J. Latrobe, Jr. Kane soon replaced Tegmeyer. Trimble remained on the final, official Commission, and Henry Tyson replaced Latrobe, though Latrobe would remain active in the process as the chief engineer.

From the beginning, Kane's position on the Jones Falls Commission was a thorn in his side. On the very day that the candidates for membership on the Commission were announced, Kane encountered opposition. Three candidates were proposed to work officially on this project—Kane, Trimble, and Tyson. John D. Stewart, a member of the First Branch of the City Council representing the Tenth Ward, protested Kane's appointment, as did Tyson. Isaac Trimble and Ross Winans had proposed a plan in 1837 to prevent the flooding of this stream, which had been rejected because it was too expensive. Stewart proposed replacing Kane with an unnamed "engineer to be hereafter selected." Stewart claimed that he had nothing against Colonel Kane personally, but that his proposal was made simply for economic reasons—the Commission would be cheaper if one of the members was also an engineer. Tyson was persuaded to withdraw his opposition to Kane, as did Stewart, and the three members were confirmed on April 4, 1870. However, the ensuing months would reveal an antagonism between Tyson and the other two men on the Commission, especially Kane. Each member of the Commission was paid $2,500 per year, and the City Council allowed them to employ a clerk and an engineer to develop the project. Tyson's drawings, approved by the City Council on April 8, 1869, formed the basis for the ongoing development. Benjamin Henry Latrobe, Jr., was chosen as the chief engineer in a split vote, with Tyson voting against him. J. Monroe Heiskell was chosen to be clerk, again by a 2–1 vote.[22]

Many of the disagreements centered around the origin of the plan approved by the Baltimore City Council. Henry Tyson was one of the first to propose a comprehensive renovation of the course and characteristics of Jones Falls. His proposal of August 1868 was the starting point for discussions of the many bridges that needed to be built or rebuilt, which streets needed to be altered, what houses would have to be demolished, etc. Because it was his plan, "his baby," he felt closer to its implementation, and he believed that the City Council had effectively approved him as both the designer and refiner of the program. A revised map dated April 8, 1869, depicting Tyson's proposal was the framework for the beginning of the Commission's deliberations.

Tyson's concept of the duty of the Commission was that he would simply make adjustments to his original plan or expansions of the details as needed, and that many—or most—of the fine points didn't need the deliberations of the entire Commission; he thought some didn't even require further engineering review. Kane and Trimble believed that all refinements needed full review by the Commission and often by the Baltimore City Council. Further, it appeared that Tyson thought it within his purview to initiate the actual implementation of the plans—to negotiate construction contracts. Kane and Trimble disagreed. Tyson often bypassed Chief Engineer Latrobe or at other times worked only with Latrobe and bypassed both Kane and Trimble and the City Council; Kane and Trimble felt that all engineering issues had to pass through Latrobe's hands. Kane and Trimble submitted a resolution (which, of course, passed 2–1) that Tyson's refinements first be presented to the Commission; then, if approved, the ideas would be submitted to the Chief Engineer. Tyson argued that such a process was inefficient and would lead to delay of the project. Basically, the Commission was deadlocked in a power struggle.

Many of the proposals for improvement of the Jones Falls were contentious. Since the project would affect so many streets, railroads, businesses, and homes along its course, it was obvious that one man's "improvement" might be another man's "devaluation."[23]

Trimble and Kane found themselves continuously at odds with Tyson. The *Baltimore Sun* characterized their deliberations as "spicy debate."[24] All parties on the Commission early resorted to publishing their personal interpretations of the Commission's deliberations—as well as their impressions of their own interpersonal actions—in the local newspapers. Kane explained his position in a long article published in the *Baltimore Sun* on July 13, 1870. He began by calling Tyson "overbearing and imperious," decrying his "unnecessary personal questions and suggestions…, rendering harmony impossible." When agreement on many issues seemed to be at an impasse, Tyson suggested that all three members of the Commission resign. Kane responded, objecting to Tyson's belief that Tyson himself was "commissioner, engineer, and contractor." Tyson finally asked for four months for survey work to be completed before any drawings would be available to the Commission. This requirement would seriously delay the start of the work, in addition to allowing one man on the Commission to determine all of the major specifications of the project. By the time the drawings would be available on this timetable, it might be too late for any major changes. Kane said: "I will not allow Mr. Tyson or Mr. Anybodyelse to usurp powers not delegated nor intended to be delegated to him by the mayor and city council."[25]

Trimble published his statement about the functioning of the committee in the same issue of the *Sun*. He began by saying that the Commission was entrusted with "a general plan for the work, without prescribing the mode of its execution by details, working drawings or other particulars." Further:

> Without disparagement to Mr. Tyson, I must say that I could not … commit to him the preparation of working drawings, details, &c., because, so far as I know, he has never had charge of the construction of any railroad, canal or water works, and though he may possess much useful information gleaned from the perusal of engineering works, I do not consider that he possesses a practical knowledge and experience requisite for the successful execution of so important a public work.[26]

Trimble spoke for completion of the entire survey of the project before commencing any condemnation of property, acquisition of right of way, or certainly before any contracts were signed or any construction was begun.

Tyson decried the "evil consequences of our disagreements," and he again proposed that all members of the Commission resign so that "the councils [both Branches of the Baltimore City Council] might at once institute a new commission, so organized as to secure, in any manner their wisdom might suggest, the harmony essential to successful action."[27] Tyson claimed that Kane's and Trimble's statements were "replete with imputations evidently designed to be offensive."

Over the balance of the summer of 1870, the three members of the Commission interacted more "harmoniously," though disputes continued to arise over the surveying of Jones Falls. Various impediments seemed to delay the job, including the presence of obstructions along the course of the waterway (business merchandise, lumber, etc.) that made surveying impossible. Kane complained about the surveyor:

> [H]e makes a general statement that he cannot proceed with his work on account of obstructions. Let us know what these obstructions are. We must have something more specific. I for one am tired of this trifling and prevarication. We must know the names of the persons who refuse to comply with the ordinance, and the character of the obstructions.[28]

Kane was goal-directed; he wanted the project to move forward. Additional surveyors were hired at the end of August, though not without controversy. Initially the Commission requested that all surveyors be Baltimoreans; later even their pay was disputed.

Controversy continued into the fall.[29] In October, the First Branch of the Baltimore City Council entertained a resolution that accurately described the status of the Commission:

> [I]t is beyond all reasonable hope to expect ... [the project] to be carried out effectively and harmoniously by the present members of the board of commissioners.... [T]hese differences and variances, personal and otherwise, seem *irreconcilable*.... [A] new commission is absolutely necessary. We have accordingly herewith reported sections repealing one and two of the original ordinance, which provided for a commission of three persons, at a salary of $2,500 per annum each, and substituting, in lieu thereof, an unpaid commission of five persons.

This proposal even named the five Baltimore citizens who were said to be above reproach and who might bring order to the Jones Falls Commission. The proposal, however, failed to pass, in part because the majority of the City Council members believed that unpaid Commissioners could not devote the amount of time necessary for such a demanding project. Nevertheless, the publication of this proposal simply reinforced the public's view of the disharmony and dysfunctionality of the existing Commission.

Kane was so exasperated with the process that he resigned from the Commission at the end of January 1871. He was principled and refused to remain a part of a system with which he disagreed.[30] Kane felt that the cost would wildly exceed original estimates, and that the final plan "will practically injure the very people whose property it is intended to benefit." He concluded, knowing that the City Council was considering altering the composition of the Commission: "I cannot lend my approval to a matter so much at variance with my judgment, and therefore most respectfully beg leave to withdraw my name from consideration in the proposed reconstruction of the board."[31]

Finally, a month later, the City Council came to the conclusion that regardless of which plan, or which iteration of Tyson's plan, was finally approved, there would always be a large number of persons opposed to it. No plan would please everyone. Controversy continued for years, though it faded somewhat in the mid–1870s. The project began to move forward at a snail's pace. A reduced scope of construction was completed in the 1880s, but a viaduct to manage the waterflow was not completed until 1914.

Kane as Insurance Agent

In 1858 Kane had advertised that he was in the business of real estate auction, real estate sales, and insurance. He was an agent for the sale of buildings, homes, boats, land, stocks, and vessels, mostly at auction. His office opened on April 10, 1858, in the upper part of the Firemen's Insurance Buildings at the corner of South and Second Streets.[32]

After his return to Baltimore in late 1868 or 1869, Kane continued to combine private business and government service. Holding a government job in the 1860s–1870s did not preclude involvement in a private business. Kane ran George P. Kane's Fire Insurance Agency, an arm for the United States Branch of the Imperial Fire Insurance Company of London, England, beginning in 1870.[33] He also ran other insurance businesses at the same office from 1872 to 1877.[34] Thomas C. Harris joined Kane in the insurance business in January 1875 to form a partnership selling policies from Imperial, American Central, St. Louis, and Franklin Insurance Companies.[35]

Kane continued his support of Southern causes for nearly a decade after the Civil War concluded. He maintained involvement with the Southern Relief Fund into 1874.[36] Kane was also active in all things Irish, and St. Patrick's Day was the center of festivities for Baltimore Irishmen. The year 1877, the one in which Kane would ascend to the mayorship of Baltimore, was no exception. It was a snowy St. Patrick's Day, but the chill did not prevent many from assembling along the parade route. The Knights of St. Patrick and the Hibernian Society were both present in great force. Kane, as President of the Hibernian Society, oversaw the awarding of prizes to the students in the Oliver Hibernian Schools at the building on North Street. He addressed the gathering, reminding the young students that they should not let a person's creed, religion, or opinion influence the distribution of any needed charitable aid to them. He implored them to uphold the humanitarian principles of the Society as they grew older. Thereafter, the gathering dismissed to Guy's Hotel for a social event with dinner.[37]

Other Organizations

Kane participated in many other civic affairs of Baltimore. On August 21, 1872, he was inducted as an "Honorary Member" of the Chesapeake Central Greeley Club of Baltimore, a social and political club with many branches and over 100 members in the Chesapeake Central branch. Primarily a political organization, it included many prominent Baltimoreans and many of Kane's close friends.[38]

Kane also became a trustee of the St. Mary's Industrial School in February 1876,[39] and he was the Chairman of the Baltimore Water Board in 1878. Kane continued to be involved in many other charitable causes. He helped to head the collection of funds for yellow fever victims in Savannah and Brunswick, Georgia.[40]

Election to political office was again looming for Kane.

18

A Late Turn as Mayor

George Kane's desire to run for Mayor of Baltimore began as early as 1874. The *Baltimore Sun* reported that Kane "has consented to the use of his name as a Democratic Conservative candidate for the mayoralty."[1] However, this possible run never materialized.

Early support for Kane's next foray into politics as a mayoral candidate emerged in May 1877. He was described as a Democratic Conservative, and he would campaign on the principles of "honest labor and [opposition] against the contract system."[2] In the race for the Democratic nomination, members of his party claimed that "even if [Kane's run for office is] successful by the aid of party machinery at the primaries, it will be but an empty honor," and one candidate even predicted that his candidacy would introduce "the certain downfall of the Democratic party in the near future." His detractors claimed that Kane had opposed the Democratic Party in the recent elections of 1873 and 1876, and that "Kane can never be elected Mayor of Baltimore," calling him a "party disorganizer." Opponents said, "His name must be withdrawn from this contest; even the devotion of a few personal friends must yield to the demand of a large majority of the party. Let us reward with high office only those who have been true to us. We cannot afford to trust those who deserted the party in the hour of its greatest need."[3] Though partisans derided Kane as one of the original Know-Nothings, the public seemed to feel that this accusation was unimportant.

The Democratic primary was held on June 20, 1877, at Raine's Hall in Baltimore. It was so hot that the newspapers reported that some delegates "suffered martyrdom from the heat," and reporters "nearly fainted." Emotions ran high, and "in the lobbies some disorder prevailed, but a considerable show of [policemen's] blue uniforms kept passion within bounds." Some attendees suspected cheating and foul play with stuffing of the ballot boxes used to select the delegates to the primary convention; nevertheless, Kane won the Democratic mayoral nomination on the first ballot, defeating Ferdinand C. Latrobe (the grandson of architect Benjamin Henry Latrobe) by unanimous consent. Kane was said to have won the nomination by the votes of the "working man." The pundits who had predicted Kane's unpopularity had been wrong.

In early October, the Democrats held a meeting at the Masonic Temple in Baltimore. These Democrats denounced the "evils of class legislation." Noting that Baltimore had amassed a $25,000,000 debt, they pushed for the election of Colonel

George Kane, who himself was unable to attend the meeting because of continued "indisposition" from his various health issues, mostly then the result of a dog bite that Kane said was a "temporary but painful injury which has not only disabled me from taking an active part in the mayoralty canvass, but even precluded me, in great measure, from the pleasure of seeing and meeting my fellow citizens."[4] Kane pledged his service, if elected, to all classes of citizens.

Kane won the mayoral vote at the election held on October 24, one that was held under perfect order in the city precincts without disturbances of any kind. Only 25 men were arrested in the entire city throughout voting day. Saloons had been closed, keeping the populace generally sober. Most voting was completed by noon. Newspapers even commented that most men were well dressed and that vagrants and toughs were only infrequently seen.[5] The vote was Kane, 33,188; Joseph Thompson (the "Workingman" and Republican), 17,367; Henry M. Warfield (the "Reformer"), 536.[6] Democrats also won majorities in both Branches of the City Council. Kane received well-wishers at his St. Paul Street residence, though "on account of his lameness remained seated in an arm chair with a pair of crutches at hand."[7] The next day he went to town in a carriage, though newspapers reported that he was expected to be able to walk to his business office.

Kane soon appointed the Reverend Dr. John Poisal as his private secretary.[8] Poisal had recently been serving as the chaplain of the U.S. House of Representatives, and he had been a minister at the Methodist Episcopal Church South and an editor of the *Episcopal Methodist*, a local church paper. He more recently had been appointed by his conference to pastor a church in Martinsburg, West Virginia, but he had kept his home in Baltimore.

Kane assumed duties of Mayor on November 5. A few days before he took office he announced that he would not consider filling positions in the Baltimore government until he had served as Mayor for sufficient time to understand the duties of each appointed office and had acquainted himself with the persons currently filling that position. This move was almost unprecedented in politics. Local Baltimore newspapers thought that it was a welcome departure from the norm of the usual politician who would distribute jobs immediately to friends as election spoils. Kane declared that he would not even consider applications for appointment until at least early January. The *Sun* reported on November 23, a few weeks after Kane had taken over as Mayor:

> It is delightfully refreshing in these evil days of official incapacity and cowardice to be blessed with a public servant like Colonel Kane, who is no respector [sic] of persons or parties, and who discharges his duty without fear, favor or affection.... Most public servants now-a-days, we are sorry to say, are like clay in the hands of the potter, and can be moulded [sic] into any shape by those who secured their nomination and election. But Col. Kane is made of sterner and more honest stuff, and cannot be dictated to or managed by anybody.[9]

Furthermore, Kane—the former Marshal—even believed that the size of the Baltimore police force needed to be reduced back to about 400 men as a cost-cutting measure. He planned to achieve this goal simply by attrition, by not replacing men who died, retired, resigned, or were dismissed for other reasons.[10]

Kane knew that the city government was in disarray, and he recognized that members of his own Democratic Party had contributed to the chaos. He declared that he would not necessarily stick to party allegiances. He was in favor of governmental reform that would see honest men fill important positions in the Baltimore political hierarchy. This stance offended some of his Democratic colleagues; however, most Baltimoreans appreciated Kane's stance. His policies identified him as more of a Reform Party Mayor.

Kane began immediately to overhaul the city government. Feeling that the taxation division had too many employees and that their pay was exorbitant, he sought a cost savings by reducing the size of their office. He determined what "benefits" accrued to the city employees as a result of their work, if newspapers all charged the same for notices of delinquent taxes, and if newspapers or other businesses provided "kickbacks" to government employees for sending jobs to these businesses.[11] These inquiries were bound to offend some businessmen and entrenched government workers. City officials replied quickly that reductions in salaries and expenses were possible, though eliminations of positions would not work well. Bailiffs, who were paid both a salary and a commission, could revert to commissions only.[12]

Furthermore, the Jones Falls project had long been a sore point in city government because of conflicting ideas about which was the best plan to prevent flooding and to protect impacted neighborhoods, including the debate about which construction methods were best. Kane demanded an inspection of the work and materials of this project, including the masonry and the sidewalls of sections. Engineers found deficiencies in the construction methods, one unfortunately being the use of a substandard quality of mortar. Even the alignment of some of the structures was incorrect.[13] Kane's insistence on learning of the progress of the Jones Falls project prompted one assistant committee commissioner official to resign. James A. Bruce alleged that "it is impossible to perform service in any city employment with satisfaction when the mayor is liable to change his mind every few minutes." He proceeded to complain that a disagreement with Kane about a single stone being used in the construction led to his resignation.[14]

Kane's health remained poor. Days before and after the election had been punctuated by waxing and waning of his physical condition. The severe dog bite to his left ankle that he had experienced in the summer of 1877, prior to his election as Mayor, continued to plague him. Kane's physicians had—as a precautionary measure—performed extensive cauterization and debridement of the wound, but his healing was slow, perhaps in part because of his underlying heart and kidney diseases. Newspapers described little of Kane's health, and they even seemed to ignore the fact that he had been frequently absent from the campaign trail because of the injury. At this same time, Kane experienced what he characterized as repeated "indigestion," perhaps a result of either his kidney or heart diseases.

Subtle hints about Kane's health finally began to creep into the news, even as soon as his inauguration:

> Col. George P. Kane, elected Oct. 24, was inducted into the office of mayor at the city hall shortly before noon, at which hour the term of Mayor Latrobe expired. The ceremony was

> characterized by great simplicity. Col. Kane not having entirely recovered from his lameness proceeded to the city hall in a carriage.... After the interchange of greetings Mayor Latrobe read a valedictory address, Col. Kane during the time supporting himself on crutches.[15]

Kane was unable to stand for his acceptance speech, and he was even forced to have his secretary read portions of his remarks. His debility at the outset of his mayoralty would be prophetic for the events ahead during his tenure in office.

Soon after the election, his health further deteriorated. He went to the South for a brief time, trying to recuperate in South Carolina and Georgia. Kane sensed that his illness was serious, and he reported as he left Baltimore that he hoped his disease would "make [its] inroads so slowly that I can live one year as Mayor of Baltimore. I have many reforms to make."[16] Upon his return to Baltimore, his health still waxed and waned, interfering with his ability to discharge his duties as Mayor. The ex officio or acting mayor during Kane's absences and illnesses was Otis Keilholtz, who occasionally reversed some of Mayor Kane's reforms, to Kane's dismay.

Throughout his short tenure as Mayor, Kane missed many governmental functions, and he was unable to participate vigorously in his job. On January 8, 1878, Kane seemed able to address the duties required to begin to prepare the Mayor's annual message.[17] He was still confined to his home, though reporters projected that it would be only a few days before he would be able to return to his office. He repeatedly gave reports suggesting that he would make a quick return to his duties.

Kane's two physicians were both members of the faculty of the University of Maryland School of Medicine, an institution that had been established in 1807. Dr. Francis Turquand Miles was an expert in neurologic diseases. Dr. Alan Pennington Smith was a surgeon; it was said of Smith that he "is better known for his skill with the knife than facility in the use of the pen."[18] Kane could have had any doctors in the city of Baltimore, considering his wealth, social status, and political position. These were the men he chose to care for his health.

On January 10, newspapers described Kane as "decidedly improved," but Dr. Professor Miles was still seeing Kane. Miles was "prescribing for the result of indigestion consequent upon his long confinement from effects of the bite of a dog in the summer, and his recent confinement of nights in his office since his inauguration. The professor objects to his [Kane's] going out till the weather gets somewhat settled." Assistants brought work for Kane to complete at his home, but he declined the work even there because of his inclement health.[19]

January 13 saw reports of Kane's health deteriorating again. He was "considerably indisposed in health during two weeks past. He is still quite ill, confined to his house, and some fear that serious results may ensue. Thus far he has made a most efficient and popular chief magistrate. He acts with marked independence of all mere partisan partialities or political 'rings.'"[20]

Even under the strain of his illness in early February, Kane began work to reorganize the health department of Baltimore City, separating the Department of Health (which included the city vaccination program) from the street cleaning and general sanitary control of the city.[21] He continued to attend to business at his office, though newspapers reported that "he was well worn out with fatigue, consequent on receiving a large number of persons, other than nearly all the members of the city council, in regard to appointments." Planning another retreat in the South to recuperate, newspapers reported that "He does not anticipate, in view of the many and important matters of public business claiming his attention, that he will be able to leave the for the South even as late as Tuesday next."[22] Office seekers continued to hound the Mayor for appointments. Kane discovered that it had been a practice of the secretary of the Mayor to charge fees (from $1–$10) for confirming positions and commissions, enriching the secretary's own pocket. Kane put a stop to this practice, saying that it would not be tolerated under his administration.[23]

Mayor Kane was finally able to retreat again to the South for his health. On March 11, 1878, his party was reported to be at the Purcell House in Wilmington, North Carolina, and he thereafter departed on a special train for points further South.[24] His absence caused him to miss the annual Hibernian Society St. Patrick's Day festivities, one of the highlights of Kane's year, indicating the seriousness of his illness.[25] Nevertheless, the respect his friends held for Kane was manifest by his being elected again that year as President of the Hibernian Society.[26]

His illnesses and absences continued to plague the performance of his duties, and on March 13, 1878, the *Baltimore Sun* reported, "There are now some thirty or more ordinances and resolutions of the city council on the mayor's table on which no action has been taken by the city executive. Twenty-five of the resolutions and ordinances have become laws by lapse of time, Mayor Kane not having acted upon them within the prescribed five days of actual session of the council."[27] These items of business were rather trivial, however, most of them being repair and construction of streets and street lamps and similar minor issues.

Kane was still absent from his mayoral duties on March 20. As the appointment of 40 constables was due by the fourth Monday of March, acting mayor Keilholtz completed these appointments. Mayor Kane at this time was convalescing in Columbia, South Carolina, and on March 20, 1878, it was reported that "his health has very much improved, and he expects to return home the early part of next week."[28] The city was still awaiting Kane's return on March 29, when other contracts for the city's lighting (lamps, lamp repair, gas, cleaning and repair) became due. The City Council and the acting mayor expected Kane's return within about 10 days.[29]

By April 3, Kane was back on duty, visiting projects in the city.[30] His health then again deteriorated dramatically. He went to work at the City Hall on Thursday, April 25, where he seemed improved. Friends visited him in his home that night until about 10:00 p.m. In retrospect, Kane had complained of a cough that evening and in general didn't feel well. At about 2:00 a.m. Friday morning, April 26, he awoke complaining about feeling "very badly," and he sent for his physician. By the time his doctor arrived, complete paralysis in the left leg and partial paralysis in the left arm had developed.[31] Clearly he had suffered a stroke. A report on April 27 said that Kane

> had become suddenly and alarmingly ill…. His mind is clear and he is free from pain…. He was looking unusually well, but said that he did not feel well, though he was cheerful and chatty, and apparently stronger than he had been for some days. The suddenness of his illness before morning was therefore a surprise to those who had been near him the previous evening. The mayor is attended, as heretofore, by Prof. F. T. Miles and Prof. Alan P. Smith. In the

absence of Col. Kane Mr. Otis Keilholtz, president of the first branch city council, discharged the duties of mayor ex officio.[32]

Reporters asking at the door of the Mayor's home were told that he was sick and unable to come talk with them.

The stroke rendered Kane completely unable to perform his official duties. Indeed, it appeared that he was about to die. On April 29, newspapers relayed the report that Kane was in "a very critical condition" and that "His death may occur at any moment."

One report had the paralysis on his left side improving somewhat over a couple of days, with his recovery of much of the use of his left hand and arm. But by April 29, descriptions of the effects of his stroke seemed at odds with each other. "There has been no decided change in the condition of Mayor Kane. On Saturday he was not so well, but since then there has been no noticeable change. He slept well and comfortably on Saturday night, suffers no pain, converses freely with his attendants, and takes food with relish. The paralysis of his left side, however, continues apparently without the slightest relief." In one description, he was "improved"; in another his symptoms continued "without the slightest relief."[33] However, all reports agreed that he never seriously lost mental capacity.

On May 2, Kane was described as "better and stronger," and

> there was some little increase of power in his left arm. He spends much of his time sitting in an arm-chair, and reads the daily papers carefully, taking great interest in city affairs. He has been subsisting principally on what is known as "the milk diet," but the last few days he has desired more substantial food, and has eaten with much relish mutton chops and beef-steaks daily.[34]

On May 3 Kane was reported to be "quite comfortable."[35] By May 9, Dr. Miles "seemed very much encouraged from the condition of his patient." Kane's health was rallying a bit, and on May 9 he was "improving rapidly and in excellent spirits."[36] Kane was again at least partially engaged in his job as Mayor, and he expressed concern over the city's budget. His condition gradually improved further, and on May 22 Kane reported that he was "feeling better than he had since he was taken sick."[37]

But the Mayor's illness would not abate. On June 1, 1878, he was again reported to be "dangerously ill," and newspapers described him as "suffering from a relapse."[38] By June 10, his condition had once again deteriorated. "Kane was in an exceedingly critical state," and "his friends and physicians were not sanguine as to any improvement in his condition."[39]

On June 12, Kane was "very critical," with his breathing greatly impeded by lying in the recumbent position.[40] On Wednesday, June 19, he took an even further dramatic change for the worse. By Saturday, June 22, he was unable to recognize people around him, and he seemed unable to speak. He continued to suffer from breathing difficulty, and he was said to be experiencing "dropsy and heart disease."[41] On June 22, he was "growing weaker every hour." Though city officials sympathized with Kane's family, they noted that "the city and council have thereby been deprived for some months of his valuable aid and counsel in the conduct of public affairs."[42]

Over the week preceding his death, Kane became progressively weaker. His friends and coworkers could detect that the end was near. They authored a resolution:

> Whereas his Honor Mayor Kane has been stricken by disease, and the city and council have thereby been deprived for some months of his valuable aid and counsel in the conduct of public affairs; and whereas it is eminently proper that before adjournment [of the city council] for the summer recess some expression of sympathy with his Honor in his extreme illness, and with his family in the distress occasioned thereby, should be made by members of this body: therefore be it
>
> "*Resolved by both Branches of the City Council*, That we hereby tender to the Hon. George P. Kane, mayor of Baltimore, our heartfelt sympathy in his affliction; and express our earnest hope that a kind Providence may soon restore him to health and his career of usefulness and public labor. And resolved further, that we hereby tender to his afflicted family our heartfelt sympathy in their distress."[43]

Immediately after offering this resolution, members of the City Council received word from Kane's physicians Drs. Miles and Smith that "the mayor is growing weaker every hour. They cannot say how long he may last. He is quiet at this time, and not suffering so much as during the day."[44]

Thereafter, Mayor Kane slipped into a coma, and he never regained consciousness. He died with his wife and a niece at his side, along with a friend, General Charles C. Edgerton, as Catholic prayers for the dying were being said at his bedside. Kane died at 3:42 a.m., June 23, 1878, in Baltimore, Maryland, at his home on St. Paul Street.

Newspapers immediately reported Kane's death, and he was hailed as Baltimore's model citizen. "His death will be regretted by all classes—the loss of no citizen, indeed, could be more deeply deplored. No man was better known in this community than Colonel Kane; none certainly more respected for high courage, rectitude of principle and thorough honesty." Friends described him as "fearless and outspoken" with "the same unyielding devotion to what he believed to be just and right." He found that as he was "entering his office without stain, he should leave it at the end of his term without reproach." His character was "so marked and distinctive, so fearless in expression and so prompt in action, [that he] could never have been a politician of the modern type."[45]

Little of major importance had been accomplished during Kane's short mayoralty. He primarily devoted his energies to municipal projects, such as tunneling of the Jones Falls and widening of various streets in the city. The mundane duties of the city government had consumed what little time and energy Mayor Kane had to devote to his job. He pursued routine taxing and spending bills, and plumbing and drainage issues. He oversaw installation of gas mains and gas lamps at various locations in the city, and many of his ordinances and resolutions dealt with grading, paving, curbing ("kerbing"), widening and opening streets in Baltimore. Kane spearheaded repairs to the old City Hall on Holliday Street, then he assigned this building to the Board of School Commissioners for the use of the Baltimore City Public Schools.[46] The City Council pushed for the construction of a new Post Office, and Kane concurred in this initiative. He even organized a street cleaning bureau during his term as Mayor.⁴⁷ On March 8, 1878, Homewood Park was established.⁴⁸ Dealing with gutters, grates, stepping stones, culverts, and fire plugs was a step down from what Kane had envisioned for the job of restoring integrity to Baltimore's corrupt politics.

After Kane's death, city officials wasted no time in holding an election to replace him. Baltimore had a special election on July 11, 1878, to choose a Mayor to fill the remainder of Kane's term. Democrat Ferdinand C. Latrobe won by a large margin, beating R. Henry Smith, who had run on the Greenback Labor Party ticket, though with a light turnout (16,002 votes, compared to 50,555 in the election in which Kane was the victor). Latrobe beat his opponent 14,608 to 1,394. (Kane had won 33,188 to 17,367.) The election was said to be the quietest in recent years, with no arrests made during the day, even though the ban on the sale of alcoholic beverages was only partially honored.⁴⁹

Kane's physicians Drs. Miles and Smith performed a post-mortem examination. It revealed nothing surprising, but confirmed their previous clinical impressions. Bright's disease had ravaged Kane's kidneys; today it would be called chronic glomerulonephritis. The autopsy also showed "actharomatous [sic] degeneration of the coats of several arteries of the base of the brain, hypertrophy of the heart, and slight fatty degeneration of the liver."⁵⁰ Other organs were normal, and newspapers inexplicably felt the need to report that Kane's brain weighed exactly three pounds. Kane's death certificate listed his age as 58, which would have made his 1820 birth date correct (though the date on his tombstone says August 4, 1817).⁵¹ His primary cause of death was listed as "Bright's Disease," with a duration of this illness being seven months.⁵²

New Mayor Ferdinand C. Latrobe passed Resolution No. 321, "to have painted or purchase for the municipal gallery of the City of Baltimore the portrait of Hon. George P. Kane, late Mayor of Baltimore, and that the sum of three hundred and fifty dollars ($350.00) be, and the same is hereby, appropriated to defray the expense, and to be taken from any money in the treasury not otherwise appropriated. Approved October 23d, 1878. Ferdinand C. Latrobe."⁵³ (Figure 49).

Early eulogies were laudatory of Col. Kane and his life and accomplishments:

> No man was better known in this community than Col. Kane; none certainly more respected for high courage, rectitude of principle and thorough honesty. He was, at all times and in all places, fearless outspoken, and into all the offices with which he was deservedly honored he carried the same unyielding devotion to what he believed to be just and right.... What he did he did openly. What he thought he said, sometimes too strongly and to his own injury, in a political sense. But whatever might be the consequences he would never knowingly do an unworthy act, or compromise the duties of his position. Like many men of strong convictions, he was disposed to be aggressive, and there were times when, in the estimation of his best friends, his impulsiveness would carry him too far. If it were a fault it was a venial one, and the kindliness of his nature and his generosity and openhandedness to the poor and unfortunate more than compensated for it.... With the masses he was popular beyond all other men in the city, yet he never shrunk from telling them what was for their good, or from rebuking them when he believed they contemplated following a course that was wrong.... It is not so much as a politician that his death will be sincerely mourned—for his principles were too rigid for partisans—but as a citizen of Baltimore who by native force of character raised himself to the highest positions in the city of his birth.⁵⁴

And the next day:

> Col. Kane was a man of unswerving integrity and conscientious uprightness of conduct in all the relations and business of life. No man was more esteemed and beloved by his friends. He was frank, open-hearted, generous. A truer friend could nowhere be found.... His faults, indeed, were a mere foil to his virtues, and those who will follow, in long concourse, his remains to their last resting place in 'Bonnie Brae' will attest the hold which his memory has secured in the hearts of the people of his native city.
>
> He had qualities which necessarily made him a leader among men—qualities not often found together in the same individual. He had always possessed a great deal of public spirit united with remarkable firmness of character, and at the same time associated with kindness and gentleness of heart which made him well deserving of his popularity with all classes. Mayor Kane was the possessor of the same quality of moral as physical firmness, and never hesitated to express freely whatever he thought.[55]

Further, Kane was described as "a high-toned, honorable gentleman, bold, fearless and independent in action. No other one man had done more by charitable acts to endear himself to the Irish people of Baltimore, and they all honored him."[56]

Another eulogy said, "As a disciplinarian he was rigid, and his firmness was always tempered by a degree of courtesy which disarmed opposition. As the executive head of the police force he instilled into each individual member something of his own spirit." Yet another: "his strength of character, his unswerving devotion to duty, his never-ceasing fidelity to public trusts will add lustre to his memory." Finally,

> [He had a] kindness and gentleness of heart which made him well deserving of his popularity with all classes. Mayor Kane was the possessor of the same quality of moral as physical firmness, and never hesitated to express freely whatever he thought.[57]

Though Kane had a Presbyterian background, he had joined St. Ignatius Catholic Church, his wife's church, and the Reverend Father Clarke received him in the year before his death. Services were conducted at St. Ignatius at the corner of Calvert Street and Madison Street, very close to Kane's residence on St. Paul Street. The Reverend W. F. Clarke delivered the requiem oration, assisted by the Reverend Father Sourin, the Reverend John Foley of St. Martin's, and the Reverend Bernard J. McManus of St. John's; Archbishop James Gibbons gave the final Catholic absolution. Thousands attended the ceremony, including most of the political dignitaries of Baltimore City. Baltimore Police and Fire Departments were well represented, as was the Hibernian Society, the Fifth Regiment of the military, and the Independent Fire Company, of which Kane had been a founder, organizer, member, and President.

Rev. Clarke gave a profound though rather harsh eulogy, which included a defense of the Catholic Church:

> [T]he mingling here of persons of every creed, and perhaps of no creed, in a Catholic temple and at the foot of a Catholic altar, all indicate that this is not one of those funerals in which a family or a limited circle of relatives and friends are interested, but the funeral of one over whose mortal remains a whole city is mourner....
>
> ... George P. Kane was pre-eminently the champion, especially when, as marshal of police, he tore off the yoke and broke the fetters which had bowed and bound Baltimore in a slavery which was as disgraceful as it was degrading....
>
> Colonel Kane, I am sorry to say, was less a Christian than a patriot. Engrossed in business

or politics, or both, he thought he had not the leisure to examine and decide what he was to believe and what to practice. Not that religion was a matter of total indifference to him, or that he never thought seriously of worshipping God in spirit and in truth, but that he imagined it was impossible to subject to Christian law and discipline a mind and a heart dominated, as his were for the time, by worldly aspirations and aims. Hence unfortunately, he did not become a Christian until his last illness. It was supposed by some that he was a Presbyterian.... Until ... [his baptism], consequently, he was neither Catholic nor Presbyterian, because he was not a Christian....

His determination to become a Catholic he expressed to me five years ago [May 1873], in language the most positive.... He expressed it again to me about eighteen months ago.... His conversion, therefore, was premeditated and planned years before it occurred.... [O]n the evening of his baptism he said to me, "You have been looking for this for twenty years."

Figure 49. George Proctor Kane. Portrait by Oscar Hallwig, 1893, oil on canvas. From the Maryland Center for History and Culture.

Why he became a Catholic I can tell you, for he told me, "I see," he said at one time, "I acknowledge," at another, and, again, "I believe."[58]

The Reverend Clarke thus laid to rest the notion that Kane had become a Catholic simply because his wife insisted. It was his own choice; Clarke also emphasized that though Kane's parents were Presbyterian, Kane himself had never embraced that denomination.

Clark then chided Kane for ignoring faith in his life and compared Kane to the thief on the cross who had ended his life with a confession of faith. He went on to say,

It may be objected to him, and was objected to him, that he squeezed from life's orange its pleasure juice as long as he could, and when there was not a drop more to be extracted, threw the empty peel of diseased old age as a present to God. That he robbed God of nearly all of a life the whole of which belonged to God is, I admit, not only inexcusable, but worthy of strong and unmeasured condemnation. But as all of us are more or less guilty of having stolen from God's altar a portion, perhaps a large portion, of the holocaust of our existence—stolen from Him whenever we sinned by thought, word, deed or omission—I would say, in the language of the Saviour, let him among you who hath no sin cast the first stone at the memory of our deceased friend....

I would ask you, too, while you remember that he gave to ambition the life which belonged to God, to look for a moment with me at the hill of Calvary.... [As Jesus died], the voice of a solitary sinner [the thief on the cross] was heard breaking in, as it were, upon the awful sacredness of the great sacrifice of redemption, to ask something for himself, and Jesus forgot his own pains ... to listen to the prayer and grant the petition of that single individual, though he applied at the last moment, after a life, perhaps, of countless crimes. The dying penitent asked only to be remembered, and Jesus granted him pardon and Paradise. That late but sincere convert had robbed God of his whole life, as Col. Kane did; and had robbed his neighbor too, as Col. Kane never did; for in regard to his fellow-man he was, as you all know, the very soul of honor; not only honest, but generous, noble, culvalrous [sic]. Of the many, very many whose deaths are recorded in the Sacred Scripture there was, then, one who was sincerely converted at the hour of death. There was one, says St. Augustine, that none may despair.

That the mayor found, in the language of St. Paul, one Lord, one faith, one baptism, in his last illness; that then the Good Shepherd, who had sought him so long and so patiently, welcomed him to the one fold..., we are not surprised; not only when we consider that the mercy of God is infinite—and this is the principal motive of our confidence—but also when we remember the moral or merely natural virtues which Col. Kane practiced; not that these could merit for him conversion—for, separated from Christ, he could merit nothing—but that they inclined God to grant and disposed him to receive the grace of conversion. A quarter of a century ago his saintly mother-in-law, speaking to me of him, said, "George would share his last loaf of bread with the poor": and she knew George well.[59]

Catholic Archbishop of Baltimore James Gibbons finished the service with the absolution.

The funeral procession to "Bonnie Brae" Cemetery on Old Frederick Road was huge, numbering over 80 carriages, in addition to the multitude walking. The military numbered 250 muskets; the police force had 192 members; the fire department contributed 130 men to the march. A military salute of three rounds from the large force completed the ceremony. Kane was initially buried in a public vault, but his remains were moved on August 5, 1878, to a family plot in Bonnie Brae (also called the New Cathedral Cemetery). His wife Anna C. (Griffith) Kane would join him in death on June 2, 1882.

Epilogue

George Proctor Kane battled opposing loyalties. On the one hand, his sympathies lay with the Southern cause; on the other hand, his duties often compelled him to behave contrary to his wishes. He generally did a superb balancing act, with a few major exceptions.

Businessman Kane was focused and goal-directed. Honest in his dealings, he established himself as a man to whom Baltimoreans turned when they needed an advocate or a stable force for needed change.

Philanthropist and civic-minded Kane upheld the immigrant and the poor.

Police Chief Kane was firm to the point of being hard-nosed. He enforced the law to the letter. "The book" was everything. He was tough where he needed to be, though some of his law enforcement today would be considered too heavy-handed.

Kane unequivocally backed the South, but he was able to fulfill his Northern duty by the strength of his character and his dedication to justice. When faced with protecting President-Elect Lincoln, Kane initially tried to downplay the risk of Lincoln's travel through Baltimore. When push came to shove, however, he provided a sufficient force to prevent violence against the soon-to-be chief executive. When the Massachusetts troops passed through Baltimore, Kane—though he wanted them to refrain from marching through the city—protected them at the risk of his own life.

Kane's motives must be considered when we analyze the reasons for his arrest and imprisonment. His assent to the burning of bridges near Baltimore was an effort to prevent bloodshed, not an act of defiance against Lincoln. This act was not intrinsically political; it was humanitarian.

Civil War fighter Kane used his influence to attempt to coalesce the Maryland troops, and he helped to provide for the needs of men isolated from family and nearly destitute of supplies and equipment.

Kane unequivocally *knew of* the Booth family, and he likely *knew* both the family and John Wilkes Booth himself. However, even if Kane and Booth were friends, there is no evidence that Kane was a co-conspirator with Booth in Lincoln's assassination.

City improvement planner Kane addressed major environmental issues to protect the citizens of Baltimore.

Sheriff Kane ran his office with integrity.

Mayor Kane answered the call of his supporters, though his health had begun to fail. He began his term with laudable principles and goals, though his advancing poor health and finally his death interrupted the execution of his policies.

George Proctor Kane deserves our respect. We can honor the life of a flawed man for the parts of his life that were laudable, as we decry the philosophies underlying many of his actions. Bravery, devotion to the rule of law, and fidelity also matter.

Appendix

Table 1
Baltimore Militias

Name	Date Founded
Law Grays	1850
First Rifle Regiment	1846
Maryland Cadets	1836
Columbian Riflemen	1846
Baltimore City Guards	1830
Baltimore Independent Blues	1798
Shields Guards	1856
Baltimore City Rifles	1860
Mount Vernon Guards	1854
First Baltimore Light Infantry	1787
Wells and McComas Riflemen	1853
German Guards (First Baltimore German Guards)	1837
American Riflemen	1855
Maryland Guards	1855
Lafayette Guards	1853
Hibernian Corps of Union Greens	1807
Hibernian Infantry	1796
Chesapeake Riflemen	1845
Junior Artillerists (Junior Artillery)	1837
Fifth Regiment	1792
Independent Greys	1833
Fell's Point Eagle Artillery	1789
Monumental Rifles	1853
Montgomery Guards	1853
Jackson Guards	1850
Marion Rifle Corps	1823

Name	Date Founded
Lafayette Light Dragoons	1852*
Taylor Light Dragoons (German Taylor Light Dragoons)	1851*
Eagle Artillery	1807*
Towson Guards (Baltimore County Horse Guards)	1860*
Turner Scheutzen Corps (Turner German Scheutzen Corps)	1859*
Independent Light Dragoons	1834*
Mounted Carabineers	unknown
German Yeagers (German Schwarz Yeagers, Independent German Yeagers)	1839*
National Blues	1845*
National Greys	1838*
First Baltimore Sharp-Shooters	1813*
First Baltimore German Riflemen	1852*
Eutaw Infantry	1835*
Mechanical Volunteers	1763
Washington Light Guard (Washington Guards)	1839*
National Guards	1835*
First Baltimore Invincibles	1838*
Lafayette Volunteers	1824*

* = Exact date of incorporation is unknown. Date listed is the first date recorded in period newspapers.

Table 2
Organization of the Militias

Militias in Baltimore in 1842						
3rd Division, MD Militia		1st Light Division, MD Volunteers				
3rd Brigade	14th Brigade	1st Light Brigade			2nd Light Brigade	
6th Regiment of Infantry	39th Regiment of Infantry	5th Regiment of Infantry	1st Regiment of Cavalry	1st Regiment of Artillery	1st Regiment of Riflemen	53rd Regiment of Infantry***
27th Regiment of Infantry	51st Regiment of Infantry					
55th Regiment of Infantry	52nd Regiment of Infantry					
	56th Regiment of Infantry					
Some Representative Companies						

Militias in Baltimore in 1842						
3rd Division, MD Militia		1st Light Division, MD Volunteers				
3rd Brigade	14th Brigade	1st Light Brigade			2nd Light Brigade	
Eagle Artillerists*		First Baltimore Light Infantry	****	Junior Artillerists	First Baltimore Sharp Shooters	First Baltimore City Guards**
		Independent Blues			Howard Riflemen	Independent Greys
		Mechanical Volunteers			Morgan Volunteers	National Guards
		Eutaw Infantry			++	Maryland Cadets
		Marion Guards				First Baltimore Invincibles
		Baltimore German Guards				Independent German Yeagers
		*****				La Fayette Volunteers
						Eagle Rifle Corps (Baltimore County)
						+

MD = Maryland

Table 3
Categories of Militia ("Citizen Soldiery")

Category		Number
Divisions		
Brigades		
Regiments		
	Infantry	< 10 Companies
	Artillery	< 10 Companies
	Riflemen	< 10 Companies
	Cavalry	< 4 Companies
Companies	Infantry	> 30 men
	Riflemen	> 30 men
	Artillery	> 20 men
	Cavalry	> 20 men

† Established by an Act of the Maryland Assembly of 1835, Chapter 295.
Companies were mostly uniformed, though a few were not.
All able-bodied white men age 21–45 were required to belong to a company; exceptions were made for health and occupation.

After seven years of continuous service, men were released from the requirement to serve in a militia, except during "invasion or insurrection."

The Independent Light Dragoons were attached to the 5th Regiment of Cavalry.

Baltimore was divided into districts for the formation of companies. These districts could be altered as needed, and the boundaries could change, as needed and determined by the military commanding officers. Officers and soldiers could change districts as they moved about, and companies could join whatever regiment they preferred, as long as they were accepted by the regimental commanding staff.

* = attached to the Maryland Militia, 3rd Division; would later be attached to the First Regiment of Artillery, First Light Brigade, First Light Division.

** = The Baltimore City Guards was under the command of the 2nd Light Brigade. It withdrew and became independent in 1851. The Baltimore City Guards in 1858 was officially established as an independent entity, consisting of no less than five Companies of 30–64 men each. It was made separate from all other military organizations, "subject solely to the direct call of the regularly constituted civil authorities, for the suppression of insurrection or riot, the repelling of invasion, or the enforcement of the execution of the laws…."

*** = To this Regiment would later be added the National Blues, the Lafayette Guards, the Montgomery Guards, the National Greys, the Union Guards, the State Guards, and the Mount Vernon Guards, to name a few. In 1855, the 53rd Regiment Infantry comprised the Baltimore City Guards, Independent Greys, National Blues, National Greys, LaFayette Guards, Montgomery Guards, Mount Vernon Guards, Union Guards, and State Guards, with 419 members in this Regiment.

**** = later to include the Independent Light Dragoons, the Mounted Carabiners, the Taylor Light Dragoons, and the Lafayette Dragoons.

***** = later to include the Jackson Guards, the Washington Guards, and the Law Grays

+ = later to include the State Guards

++ = later to include the German Riflemen, the Monumental Riflemen, the Wells and McComas Riflemen, the Marion Rifles, the Baltimore Riflemen, and the American Riflemen

MD = Maryland

Table 4
Baltimore Fire Companies

Baltimore Fire Companies

Name	Location
Union Fire Company	Hanover Street, later moved to Baltimore Street between Light and Charles Streets
Mechanical Fire Company	Belvidere (now North) Street, opposite Lexington, later moved to 29 (or 33) South Calvert Street
Friendship Fire Company	11 Frederick Street
Vigilant Fire Company	High Street between Lombard Street and Granby Street
New Market Fire Company	West side of Eutaw Street near Lexington Street
Liberty Fire Company	Fayette, Liberty and Park Streets
Independent Fire Company	Bridge (now Gay) Street at Harford Street (formerly Federal Fire Company); Ensor at Gay Streets
Deptford Fire Company	NE corner of Market (now Broadway) and Fleet Streets,* Fell's Point, later moved to corner of Strawberry Alley (now Dallas Street) and Gough Street
First Baltimore Hose Company	#10 McClellan's Alley, near Baltimore Street
United Hose and Suction Company	Liberty Street, between Pratt and Lombard Streets; 42 South Howard Street
Washington Hose Company	Lombard Street, near Sharp Street; Conway at Utah Streets
Fell's Point Hose and Suction Company	Over the Fell's Point Market House

Baltimore Fire Companies

Name	Location
Franklin Fire Company	NE corner of Broadway and Fleet Streets, Fells Point*
Columbian Fire Company	NE corner of Market (now Broadway) and Fleet Streets, Fell's Point*
Patapsco Fire Company	Fayette Street at North Street; 121 St. Paul
Howard Fire Company	Paca Street near Fayette Street
Watchman Fire Company	Light Street near York Street; Light at Hill Streets
Lafayette Hose Company	Corner of Caroline and Silver Streets; Caroline at Union Streets
Monumental Hose Company	Corner of North and Lexington Streets
Western Hose Company	West Baltimore Street near Green, later moved to Green Street near Baltimore Street
Pioneer Hook-and-Ladder Company	Harrison Street near Fayette Street
Mount Vernon Hook-and-Ladder Company	In Western Hose Company, later moved to west side of Biddle Street near Ross (Druid Hill Avenue)
United States Hose Company	William Street on Federal Hill

* = sic. Scharf listed the same address for these three companies.

Table 5
Griffith Family Slaves

Name	Age	Value–$
David	29	400
James	17	250
John	14	250
Moses	11	75
Sarah Jane	7	50
Minty	34	300
Ann	18	200
Hester	17	200
Charlotte	35	300
Teresa	10	50

This was the same residence recorded for George and Ann Kane, so some of these slaves were likely the property of the Kanes, or at least were serving the Kanes.

U.S. Census, 1860, accessed at Ancestry.com.

Table 6
Votes For President–1860

Candidate	John C. Breckenridge (SD)	Stephen Douglas (ND)	John Bell (CU)	Abraham Lincoln (R)
Popular Votes				
Baltimore	14,950 (49.6%)	1,502 (5.0%)	12,619 (41.9%)	1,064 (3.5%)

Candidate	Breckenridge	Douglas	Bell	Lincoln
Popular Votes				
Maryland	42,482 (45.9%)	5,966 (6.4%)	41,760 (45.1%)	2,294 (2.5%)
Nationwide	847,953 (18.1%)	1,382,713 (29.5%)	592,906 (12.6%)	1,866,452 (39.9%)

SD = Southern Democrat, ND = Northern Democrat, CU = Constitutional Union, R = Republican. Baltimore County favored Lincoln even less, with him receiving only 0.6% of the vote, a mere 35 of the 5,859 votes.

Table 7
Kane's Baltimore Addresses

Year (Baltimore Directory)	Home Address (dw = dwelling)	Business Title and Address	Comments
1796	dw not listed		
1799	dw not listed		
1800–01	dw not listed	35 Market Space	John M., grocer
1802	dw not listed	35 Market Space	John M.
1803	dw not listed	35 Market Space	John M., grocer
1804	dw not listed	12 Market Space, between 2nd Street and Water Street	John M., grocer
1807	dw not listed		
1808	dw not listed		
1810	72 South Charles Street	NW corner Pratt/Light Streets	John M., grocer
1812	dw not listed		
1814–15	72 S. Charles St.	SW corner Pratt/Light	John M., grocer
1816	10 Pratt Street	cor Light and Pratt Streets	John M., grocer
1817–18	Conway near Hanover	cor Pratt/Light Streets	John M., merchant
1819	Aisquith	cor Pratt/Light	John M., grocer
1822–23	"Aisquith, West side, N of Comet"		John M., gentleman
1824	dw not listed		
1827	dw not listed		
1829	dw not listed		
1831	Aisquith Street near Pitt Street (likely the same as Aisquith at Comet) NOTE: Mrs. Ann Kane, Aisquith Street between Comet and Douglass [sic]	Kane and Polk, grocers and commission merchants, 5 Light Street Wharf	John K.

Appendix

Year (Baltimore Directory)	Home Address (dw = dwelling)	Business Title and Address	Comments
1833	51 Sharp Street (other directory: Sharp Street) NOTE: Mrs. Ann Kane, Aisquith between Comet and Douglass	5 Light Street Wharf	John K., grocer and commission merchant
1835–36	51 S. Sharp Street	No. 5 Light Street Wharf	John K., grocer and commission merchant
1837–38		No. 5 Light Street Wharf 25 Cheapside	John K., grocer and commission merchant
1840–41	dw not listed for George P.	5 Light Street Wharf	George P., wholesale grocer
1840–41 (same as above)	97 Sharp Street	5 Light Street Wharf	John K., commission merchant
1842	dw not listed	5 Light Street Wharf	George P., commission merchant
1845			
1847–48		No. 3, Bowly's Wharf	George P., commission merchant
1849–50	dw Barre	3 Bowly's Wharf	George P., commission merchant
1851	Belvidere Road		Col. George P., Collector, Port of Baltimore
1853–54	Barre, West of Honover [*sic*]		Col. George P.,
1855–56	dw not listed	Exchange Place	Col. George P., Pres., Merchants' Exchange
1856–57	64 Barre	12 Exchange Bldgs.	Col. George P., Pres., Merchants' Exch
1858	64 Barre	12 Exchange Bldgs.	Col. George P., Pres., Merchants' Exch
1858–59	64 Barre	12 Exchange Bldgs.	Col. George P., Pres., Merchants' Exch
		80 Second	Col. George P., Pres., Merchants' Exch
1860	York Road near the first toll gate		President, Merchants' Exchange
1864	163 St. Paul Street		
1865–1866	dw not listed		
1867–1868	dw not listed	At 163 St. Paul Street was Edward Kemp	
1868–1869	dw not listed	At 163 St. Paul Street was Thomas Riggs	

Year (Baltimore Directory)	Home Address (dw = dwelling)	Business Title and Address	Comments
1870	87 North Charles		
1871	143 North Calvert Street	Agent, Imperial Fire Insurance Co., 38 Post Office Avenue	
1872	143 North Calvert	Imperial Fire Insurance Co. of London, SW Corner of South and German; Sheriff, Baltimore City-Basement, Court House	
1873	143 North Calvert		
1874	163 St. Paul Street	Agent, Imperial Fire Insurance	
1875	147 North Calvert	Agent, Imperial Fire Insurance, 8 German near South;	George P. Kanre and Co.
1876	163 St. Paul Street	Kane Insurance, 8 German near South	
1877	163 St. Paul Street	Kane Insurance, 8 German near South	
1878	163 St. Paul Street	Kane Insurance, 8 German near South; Kane and Harris Stockbrokers,	
1879	Mrs. George P. Kane 163 St. Paul Street	Kane Insurance, 33 South Holliday	

Table 8
Kane's Whereabouts

Year	Date	Location	Comments
1817–1861		Baltimore	
1861	June 27	Fort McHenry Baltimore	Initially jailed without charges
	Sept. 13	to Ft. Hamilton	Briefly passed through Ft. Hamilton
	Sept. 13	to Fort Lafayette New York	
	Oct. 11	to Fort Columbus New York	
	Nov. 1	to Fort Warren Boston	
1862	Nov. 26		Released from Fort Warren
	Nov 27	Baltimore	
1863	July 7	Montreal	

Year	Date	Location	Comments
	Unknown date		Left Canada
	July 27	Key West, FL	Brief stay in Key West, then to Charlotte Harbor
	Unknown date	Unknown location	
	October ?	Montreal	Arrived in Montreal
	October 21	Montreal	Near Johnson's Island
	November	Montreal	
	Late December	Halifax	Halifax to Bermuda
1864	January 7	Wilmington	Bermuda via *Dare* to Lockwood's Folly to Wilmington
	January ?	Canada	Returned to Canada from Wilmington
	January 24	Quebec	
	January 25	Halifax	
	February 6	Bermuda	Halifax to Bermuda
	February 13	Nassau	Bermuda to Nassau
	February 21	Richmond	Nassau to Wilmington to Richmond
	March 19	Richmond	Permit to visit prisoners at Libby
	March 30	Richmond	
	April	Charleston	
	May 6–Oct 9	Richmond	
	October 10–16	Montreal	
1865	March	Richmond	
	March or April	Valley of Virginia	
	April 8	15 miles from Danville, VA	
	April 12–13	Greensboro, NC	
1866		Danville	
	~April	Baltimore	
1867	November 9	Atlanta	
	December 25	Baltimore	
		Danville	
1868	~February	Baltimore	
	November 19	Charleston	
		Danville	
1869	~February	Baltimore	
1870–1877		Baltimore	
1877	~November	South Carolina	Recuperation
		Georgia	Recuperation

Year	Date	Location	Comments
	~December	Baltimore	
1878	~March	Wilmington, NC	Recuperation
		"Points further South"	Recuperation
	March 20	Columbia, SC	Recuperation
	~April 3	Baltimore	

Dates noted for Kane's prison movements are arrival dates at the various prisons; departure dates from previous prisons were usually 1–2 days earlier; transportation by ship usually required 1–2 days.

Chapter Notes

Introduction

1. *New York Evening Post*, November 30, 1865.

Chapter 1

1. Richard J. Matchett, *Matchett's Baltimore Director [sic], Corrected up to May 1833* (Baltimore, 1833), p. 106; Richard J. Matchett, *Matchett's Baltimore Director [sic], Corrected up to June 1831* (Baltimore, 1831), p. 209.
Even a few of the basics about Kane's life remain in question. Some sources cite August 21 as his birthday, and some report 1820 as the birth year. The 1860 census listed Kane's age as 41, which would make his birth year 1819. The 1870 census listed his age as 53, rendering the 1817 date correct. His death certificate in 1878 listed his age as 58, which would make 1820 the correct year. However, his tombstone gives 1817 as the year of his birth.
Some sources also report that Kane's father's death occurred on November 28, 1861; however, this was the date of the death of Kane's father-in-law, John Griffith, and it is likely that previous researchers have confused the two men. Major John M. Kane, George Kane's father, had his obituary published in the *Baltimore Patriot* on May 8, 1822, reporting that he had "died at his dwelling in Aisquith Street after a lingering illness." The funeral for the elder Kane was May 9, though the exact date of his death was not reported. [*Baltimore Patriot & Mercantile Advertiser*, May 8, 1822, Maryland Center for History and Culture, Early American Newspapers, microfilm 2497, January 1—June 29, 1822]. In some references George Kane's father is listed as M. John Kane.
One Ann Kane is listed in Baltimore directories as living at the address where George Kane lived, years prior to George's marriage to Ann Griffith; this Ann Kane may have been his mother.

2. *Baltimore Sun*, June 24, 1878.
George's brother was sometimes listed as John J. Kane or James M. Kane.

3. *Baltimore Patriot and Transcript*, December 31, 1840.

4. James E. P. Boulden, *The Presbyterians of Baltimore: Their Churches and Historic Grave-yards* (Baltimore: William K. Boyle & Son, 1875), pp. 78–9.

5. Charles C. Keenan, *Keenan's Baltimore Directory for 1822 & 1823* (Baltimore, 1822), p. 154; Baltimore City Property Tax Records, Field Assessors' Work Books, brg4_bca1608-0035, p. 35, ledger p. 62, Baltimore City Archives, accessed at http://mdhistory.msa.maryland.gov/bca_brg4/bca001608/html/brg4_bca1608-0035.html and http://mdhistory.msa.maryland.gov/bca_brg4/bca001608/pdf/brg4_bca1608-0035.pdf/

6. Matchett, 1831, p. 209.

7. *The Ordinances of the Mayor and City Council of Baltimore* (Baltimore: James Lucas, 1845), p. 21. Pitt Street would later be renamed Fayette Street.

8. Matchett, 1833, p. 106.

9. Richard J. Matchett, *Matchett's Baltimore Director [sic], 1841* (Baltimore, 1841), Directory for 1840–1841, microfilm, Maryland Center for History and Culture.

10. Richard J. Matchett, *Matchett's Baltimore Director [sic], Corrected up to June, 1843* (Baltimore, 1843), p. 228.

11. *Baltimore Sun*, June 24, 1878.

12. Richard J. Matchett, *Matchett's Baltimore Director [sic] for 1847-8* (Baltimore, 1847), p. 181. Note: Bowly's Wharf and Bowly Street were commonly spelled "Bowley" in contemporary publications and in some maps. However, the most common usage in most maps and directories was "Bowly."

13. Richard J. Matchett, *Matchett's Baltimore Director [sic] for 1849–50* (Baltimore, 1849), p. 210; Richard J. Matchett, *Matchett's Baltimore Director [sic] for 1853–4* (Baltimore, 1853), p. 166; John W. Woods, *Woods' Baltimore Directory for 1856-'57* (Baltimore, 1857), p. 140.

14. Richard J. Matchett, *Matchett's Baltimore Director [sic] for 1851* (Baltimore, 1851), p. 145.

15. John W. Woods, *Woods' Baltimore City Directory Ending Year 1860* (Baltimore, 1860), p. 206.

16. Atlas of Baltimore County, Maryland, History and Description 4.tif, p. 38, accessed at https://jscholarship.library.jhu.edu/handle/1774.2/32594.

17. *Baltimore Sun*, August 12, 1859.

Chapter 2

1. *Baltimore Pilot*, April 24, 1840.
2. *Baltimore Commercial Journal*, May 19, 1849.
3. *Baltimore Sun*, August 22 and September 30, 1850, and May 24, 1851, and January 10, 1852.

4. *Baltimore Sun*, April 2, 1852.
5. *Baltimore Sun*, March 2, 1852.
6. *Baltimore Sun*, March 11, 1852.
7. Frank Towers, *The Urban South and the Coming of the Civil War* (Charlottesville: University of Virginia Press, 2004), pp. 81–2.
8. *Baltimore Sun*, April 23, 1853.
9. *Baltimore Sun*, July 11, 1853.
10. *Baltimore Sun*, October 23, 1853.
11. J. Thomas Scharf, *History of Baltimore City and County, from the Earliest Period to the Present Day: Including Biographical Sketches of Their Representative Men* (Philadelphia: Louis H. Everts, J. B. Lippincott, 1881), p. 931.
12. Matthew Ellenberger, "Whigs in the Streets? Baltimore Republicanism in the Spring of 1861," *Maryland Historical Magazine*, 86 (1), Spring 1991, pp. 23–38.
13. *Baltimore Sun*, December 29, 1899 and May 28, 1851; Laws of Maryland, 1852, Session Laws, 1/7/1852–5/31/1852, Volume 615, Chapter 131, pp. 113–115, accessed at aomol.msa.maryland.gov/html/index.html.
14. *Baltimore Sun*, September 25, 1857.
15. *Baltimore Daily Exchange*, March 17, 1858.
16. *Baltimore Sun*, March 13 and 15 and April 22, 1858; Laws of Maryland, 1858, Session Laws, 1/6/1858–3/10/1858, Volume 624, Chapter 415, pp. 623–6, accessed at aomol.msa.maryland.gov/html/index.html.
17. Laws of Maryland, 1860, Session Laws, 1/4/1860–3/10/1860, Volume 588, Chapter 12, pp. 40–43, accessed at aomol.msa.maryland.gov/html/index.html.
18. *Baltimore Sun*, June 17, 1859.
19. *Baltimore Sun*, September 16 and 17, 1858.
20. *Baltimore Sun*, January 1, 2, and 3, 1856.
21. Michael F. Holt, *The Rise and Fall of the American Whig Party: Jacksonian Politics and the Onset of the Civil War* (New York: Oxford University Press, 1999), p. 563.
22. *Baltimore Sun*, April 30, 1856.
23. *Baltimore Sun*, December 24, 1856.
24. *Baltimore Sun*, May 8, 1857.
25. *Baltimore Sun*, October 31, 1857.
26. *Baltimore Sun*, February 1, 1858.
27. *Baltimore Sun*, March 4, 1858.
28. *Baltimore Sun*, March 4 and 13, 1858.
29. *Baltimore Sun*, August 28, 1857.
30. Baltimore Sun, September 2, 1857.
31. *Baltimore Sun*, September 14, 1857.
32. *Baltimore Sun*, October 25 and 26, 1855.
33. *Baltimore Sun*, April 23 and May 11 and 13, 1858.
34. James Slade, *Report Upon a Supply of Water for the City of Baltimore, Made to the Water Commissioners, June 18, 1853* (Baltimore: James Lucas, 1854), p. 15.
35. *Baltimore Sun*, May 13, 1858; *Baltimore Daily Exchange*, May 13, 1858.
36. *Baltimore Sun*, December 20, 1858; *Baltimore Daily Exchange*, December 21, 1858; David A. Gadsby, "'We Had It Hard... but We Enjoyed It': Class, Poverty, and Pride in Baltimore's Hampden," *Historical Archaeology* 45 (3), Archaeologies of Poverty, 2011, pp. 11–25; Oliver Miller (Attorney at Law, and State Reporter), Maryland Reports, Containing Cases Argued and Determined in the Court of Appeals of Maryland, By Maryland Court of Appeals, Volume 15, December Term 1859 (Annapolis: Robert F. Bonsall, 1860), pp. 240–251.
37. *Baltimore Sun*, January 27 and 31 and March 6 and 7, 1860.
38. *Baltimore Daily Exchange*, June 9, 1858.
39. *Baltimore Sun*, February 22 and 23, 1859; *Baltimore Daily Exchange*, February 22, 1859.
40. *Baltimore Sun*, December 7, 1859.
41. *Thirty-Second Annual Report of the Baltimore Association for the Improvement of the Condition of the Poor, October 1881* (Baltimore: Curry, Clay & Co., 1881), p. 18, accessed at https://books.google.com/books?id=WicwAQAAMAAJ&pg=PP14&lpg=PP14&dq=%22Baltimore+Association+for+the+Improvement+of+the+Condition+of+the+Poor%22+1881&source=bl&ots=i-WgYragan_&sig=ACfU3U1_nmWGJt02gsIDzh6RJRW4AG3ncA&hl=en&sa=X&ved=2ahUKEwiTlL_oz5PnAhWCvJ4KHWvjCbUQ6AEwAHoECAUQAQ#v=onepage&q=%22Baltimore%20Association%20for%20the%20Improvement%20of%20the%20Condition%20of%20the%20Poor%22%201881&f=false.

Chapter 3

1. Alternately rendered Joseph K. Randall or John K. Randell; John Thomas Scharf, *The Chronicles of Baltimore, Being a Complete History of "Baltimore Town" and Baltimore City from the Earliest Period to the Present Time* (Baltimore: Turnbull Brothers, 1874), p. 526; *Baltimore Sun*, June 12, 1848; Stephen M. Archer, *Junius Brutus Booth: Theatrical Prometheus* (Carbondale and Edwardsville, Illinois: Southern Illinois University Press, 1992), p. 317.
2. *Baltimore Sun*, June 11 and 19, 1855.
3. J. Thomas Scharf, *History of Baltimore City and County, from the Earliest Period to the Present Day: Including Biographical Sketches of Their Representative Men* (Philadelphia: Louis H. Everts, J. B. Lippincott & Co., 1881), p. 695.
4. This theatre and the street are often misspelled as "Holiday."
5. Alonzo J. May, *May's Dramatic Encyclopedia of Baltimore, 1750-1904*, Maryland Center for History and Culture, MS 995, microfilm roll 3, unpaginated.
6. J. Thomas Scharf, *History of Baltimore City and County from the Earliest Period to the Present Day: Including Biographical Sketches of Their Representative Men* (Philadelphia: Louis H. Everts, J. B. Lippincott & Co., 1881), p. 694.
7. Some references cite the address as 60 Exeter Street, but the 62 Exeter Street address was repeatedly listed in the Baltimore directories in 1850 and 1851; Walter Edgar McCann, "The Booth Family in Maryland," in *Frank Leslie's Popular Monthly* (New

York: Frank Leslie's Publishing House, 1884), Volume 17, Number 4, April 1884, p. 408; Richard J. Matchett, *Matchett's Baltimore Director [sic] for 1851* (Baltimore: Matchett's Publishing, 1851), p. 36; Richard J. Matchett, *Matchett's Baltimore Director [sic] for 1849 '50* (Baltimore: Matchett's Publishing, 1849), p. 44.

    8. May, *Encyclopedia of Baltimore*, unpaginated.

    9. John Rhodehamel and Louise Taper, Eds., *Right or Wrong, God Judge Me: The Writings of John Wilkes Booth* (Urbana and Chicago: University of Illinois Press, 1997), p. 37, citing David Rankin Barbee Papers, Georgetown University Library, Washington, D.C.; Terry Alford, *Fortune's Fool: The Life of John Wilkes Booth* (Oxford and New York: Oxford University Press, 2015), p. 17.

    10. Alford, *Fortune's Fool*, 2015, p. 20; *Baltimore Sun*, October 5, 1905.

    11. *Baltimore Sun*, August 13, 1855.

    12. *Baltimore Sun*, August 14, 1855.

    13. Edwin Forrest might have been a likely alternative "Edwin," but he did not perform anywhere from June 9, 1849, through September 15, 1851, because of a messy divorce that consumed his life and energy during these months. Edwin Booth, on the contrary, did perform during this time frame; Arthur W. Bloom, *Edwin Forrest: A Biography and Performance History* (Jefferson, North Carolina: McFarland, 2019), Chapters 13–14, pp. 98–113.

    14. Playbill, Baltimore Museum and Gallery of the Fine Arts, February 11, 1851. Department of Conservation and Preservation, Brody Learning Commons, The Sheridan Libraries and the Milton S. Eisenhower Library, Johns Hopkins University, Baltimore, Maryland; Arthur W. Bloom, *Edwin Booth: A Biography and Performance History* (Jefferson, North Carolina: McFarland, 2013), p. 15; *Baltimore Sun*, May 28, 1851.

    15. Letter, Cordial Crane to E. M. Stanton, May 30, 1865. NARA. Investigation and Trial Papers Relating to the Assassination of President Lincoln, Record Group 153, M-599, Roll 3.

    16. Otherwise known that year as Wallack's Theatre; this theatre changed ownership and names at least 10 times during its lifespan.

    17. Alford, *Fortune's Fool*, 2015, p. 110.

    18. This quotation has at least two variations. The one listed in *Theatrical and Circus Life* says, "I know George P. Kane *well*; he is my friend, and the man who could drag him from the bosom of his family for no crime whatever, but a mere suspicion that he may commit one some time, deserves a dog's death." Emphasis added; John J. Jennings, *Theatrical and Circus Life; or, Secrets of the Stage, Green-Room and Sawdust Arena* (St. Louis: Dan Linahan & Co., 1882), pp. 479–480.

    19. Alford, *Fortune's Fool*, 2015, p. 110.

Chapter 4

    1. *The American Almanac and Repository of Useful Knowledge, for the Year 1839*. (Boston: Charles Bowen, 1838), p. 168, accessed at https://books.google.com/books?id=H640AAAAMAAJ&pg=PA168&dq=First+Light+Division+Maryland+Volunteer+Militia&hl=en&ei=sm56TJC3Oo7FswbazZWyDQ&sa=X&oi=book_result&ct=result&resnum=3&ved=0CDQQ6AEwAjgK#v=onepage&q=First%20Light%20Division%20Maryland%20Volunteer%20Militia&f=false; "Menonists" were Swiss-German Anabaptists who were later called Mennonites. They opposed military service and were pacifists, like the Quakers; "Tunkers" were a sect of Baptists who also opposed military service.

    2. *The Maryland Code: Public General Laws and Public Local Laws, 1860*, Volume 145, Article 63—Militia, pp. 415–444, accessed at http://aomol.msa.maryland.gov/000001/000145/html/am145--415.html

    3. *American Almanac and Repository*, 1839, p. 168.

    4. Members of the City Council and Officers of the Corporation. *Ordinances of the Mayor and City Council of Baltimore, Passed at the Extra Sessions Held in 1852, and at the January Session 1853: to Which Is Annexed the Acts of the Assembly* (Baltimore: Joseph Robinson, 1853), No. 110, pp. 97–8, accessed at https://books.google.com/books?id=PSQ_AQAAMAAJ&pg=PA98&lpg=PA98&dq=%22be+it+further+provided+that+the+companies+receiving+the+foregoing+sum+shall+be+subject+to+call+for+duty+at+any+time+by+the+Mayor+if,+in+his+wisdom,+he+may+deem+the+same+necessary;+the+same+to+be+performed+without+any+additional+compensation%22&source=bl&ots=ynDuHLYahH&sig=ACfU3U1_iXSu03BOHnCC4ktrVi9U6n5WlQ&hl=en&sa=X&ved=-2ahUKEwiG-I_o_s7lAhUmHzQIHXx5AEoQ6AEwAHoECAAQAQ#v=onepage&q=%22be%20it%20further%20provided%20that%20the%20companies%20receiving%20the%20foregoing%20sum%20shall%20be%20subject%20to%20call%20for%20duty%20at%20any%20time%20by%20the%20Mayor%20if%2C%20in%20his%20wisdom%2C%20he%20may%20deem%20the%20same%20necessary%3B%20the%20same%20to%20be%20performed%20without%20any%20additional%20compensation%22&f=false

    5. J. Thomas Scharf, *History of Baltimore City and County from the Earliest Period to the Present Day: Including Biographical Sketches of Their Representative Men* (Philadelphia: Louis H. Everts, J. B. Lippincott & Co., 1881), pp. 668–9; Robert Reinders, "Militia and Public Order in Nineteenth-Century America," *Journal of American Studies* 11, No. 1 (April 1977): pp. 81–101; *Ordinances of Baltimore, 1853*, pp. 97–8; *Niles' National Register*, Fifth Series, No. 12, Volume 12, Baltimore, May 21, 1842, Volume 62, Whole No. 1599, p. 177, accessed at https://books.googleusercontent.com/books/content?req=-AKW5Qaf4t_l9fMdx6um0y2EQ1frNPpKKAhu-WhhDMuYob4cTUYSGkMvWIrxIbirCxfLmNuX-Jmyj8nArC_dcpggww7-naQRp-D0pyek76Yv0_-MKuKdyYYPu8N0DC2sN8kyr_EQBCcDYdQ9fnyFdspnAR2GG0L4kLZAb

ASrUmzpvFPS5GzZP8tHIEonlR7w3FknKq d5qG1Cc-PGkA6sCA8gMvQ63kxCo_d1I_ o4PftI5cOcsLKKGUbGq-vl0sMB5ItLH_N1lhGgS

6. *Laws Made and Passed by the General Assembly of the State of Maryland* (Annapolis, Maryland: Jeremiah Hughes, 1836), Chapter 295, unpaginated, accessed at https://babel.hathitrust.org/cgi/pt?id=osu.32437123281012;view=1up;seq=405; *Baltimore Sun*, July 16, 1838.

7. *The Maryland Code: Public General Laws and Public Local Laws, 1860*, Volume 145, Article 63—Militia, pp. 415–444, accessed at http://aomol.msa.maryland.gov/000001/000145/html/am145--415.html; Independent Greys Flank Company, 1841–1848, 53rd Regiment, Maryland Volunteers. Maryland Center for History and Culture, MS 479; *Baltimore Sun*, February 16, 1846.

8. *Maryland Session Laws*, 1858, Volume 624, p. 448, accessed at aomol.msa.maryland.gov/00001/000624/html/am624--448.html; *Baltimore Sun*, January 17, 1842.

9. Hanson Hiss, "The Maryland National Guard," First Paper, *Outing*, 20 (2), 1892, pp. 149–154; Maryland Center for History and Culture, MS 364, 53rd Regiment Infantry, Maryland Volunteers; *Baltimore Sun*, October 3, 1854.

10. *The Maryland Code*, 1860, Volume 145, Volume 2, p. 274 ff, accessed at http://aomol.msa.maryland.gov/000001/000145/html/am145b--274.html; *The Maryland Code*, 1860, Volume 145, pp. 415 ff, accessed at http://aomol.msa.maryland.gov/000001/000145/html/am145--415.html; *Craig's Business Directory and Baltimore Almanac for 1842* (Baltimore: Danl. H. Craig, J. Robinson, 1842), p. 930, accessed at https://ia800500.us.archive.org/21/items/craigsbusinessdi1842balt/craigsbusinessdi1842balt.pdf; *Laws of Maryland 1838*, Chapter 393, unpaginated, accessed at babel.hathitrust.org/cgi/pt?id=osu.32437123280964;view=1up;seq=421;size=75; *Laws of Maryland 1835*, Chapter 295, unpaginated, accessed at https://babel.hathitrust.org/cgi/pt?id=osu.32437123280964;view=1up;seq=421; *Laws of Maryland, 1823*, Chapter 188, pp. 128–154, accessed at https://babel.hathitrust.org/cgi/pt?id=osu.32437123280378;view=1up;seq=128; *Baltimore Sun*, January 8, 1847, and May 8, 1855.

11. *Baltimore Sun*, February 23, 1846.

12. *Baltimore Sun*, October 30 and November 6, 1855, and January 7 and 16 and February 19, 1856, and February 14 and December 31, 1857, and February 13, 1858.

13. *Baltimore Sun*, November 17 and December 21, 1842, and January 4, 1843.

14. *Baltimore Sun*, April 6, 1843.

15. *Baltimore Sun*, August 17, 1842; *Baltimore Sun*, October 30, 1843; *Baltimore Sun*, August 19, 1843.

16. *Baltimore Sun*, August 17 and November 17, 1842, and February 16 and April 5 and May 4 and August 19 and October 30, 1843, and July 20, 1844, and February 5, 1845, and January 30 and June 2, 1846; *American Republican and Baltimore Daily Clipper*, March 14, 1846.

17. *Journal of the Proceedings of the First Branch of the City Council of Baltimore* (Baltimore: Joseph Robinson, January Session, 1844), p. 420.

18. *Laws of Maryland, 1845*, Chapter 69, Volume 610, pp. 65–66, accessed at aomol.msa.maryland.gov/000001/000610/html/am610--65.html

19. *Baltimore Sun*, March 18, 1846.

20. *Baltimore Sun*, March 23, 1846.

21. *American Republican and Baltimore Daily Clipper*, March 14, 1846.

22. *American Republican and Baltimore Clipper*, May 19, 1846; *Baltimore Sun*, November 14, 1846, and January 8, 1847; *American Republican and Baltimore Daily Clipper*, June 15 and December 23, 1846.

23. *Baltimore Sun*, March 19, 1850.

24. Richard J. Matchett, *Matchett's Baltimore Director [sic] for 1851* (Baltimore, 1851), p. 145.

25. *Baltimore Sun*, June 18, 1850.

26. *Baltimore Sun*, June 16, 1854, and July 4, 1854, and June 24, 1878.

27. *Baltimore Sun*, June 15, 1855.

28. *Baltimore Daily Exchange*, March 5, 1858.

29. *Baltimore Daily Exchange*, March 18, 1858; *Baltimore Sun*, June 7, 1861.

30. *Baltimore Sun*, March 23, 1858.

31. *Baltimore Sun*, May 8, 1860.

32. *Baltimore Sun*, June 7, 1861.

Chapter 5

1. The Hibernian Society, Boxes 1, 11, and 19. Maryland Center for History and Culture, MS 2029.

2. *American Patriot and Fells Point Advertiser*, August 15, 1803; *Baltimore Federal Gazette*, August 15, 1803; *Baltimore Telegraphe and Daily Advertiser*, August 16, 1803.

3. Harold A. Williams, *History of the Hibernian Society of Baltimore, 1803–1957* (Baltimore: Hibernian Society of Baltimore, 1957), p. 1.

4. *Ibid.*, p. 5.

5. The Hibernian Society, Box 19. Maryland Center for History and Culture, MS 2029.

6. *New York Times*, June 24, 1878.

7. Tracy Matthew Melton, "'We Will All Unite As a Band of Brothers': The Hibernian Society and Sectarian Relations in Baltimore." *Journal of the Maryland Historical Society, Maryland Historical Magazine*, Spring/Summer 2016, 111 (1), pp. 42–85.

8. *Baltimore Sun*, March 19, 1872.

9. *Baltimore Sun*, March 18, 1859.

10. *Baltimore Daily Exchange*, March 1, 1859.

11. *Baltimore Sun*, February 19, 1853, and April 25, 1859.

12. *Baltimore Sun*, March 19, 1851.

13. *Ibid.*

14. *Baltimore Sun*, March 7, 1876.

15. The Hibernian Society, Box 19. Maryland Center for History and Culture, MS 2029.

16. Hibernian Society Minutes. Maryland

Center for History and Culture, unpaginated, entry for June 24, 1878.

Chapter 6

1. J. Thomas Scharf, *History of Baltimore City and County, from the Earliest Period to the Present Day: Including Biographical Sketches of Their Representative Men* (Philadelphia: Louis H. Everts, J. B. Lippincott & Co., 1881); Clarence H. Forrest, *Official History of the Fire Department of the City of Baltimore: Together with Biographies and Portraits of Eminent Citizens of Baltimore* (Baltimore: Williams & Wilkins, 1898), accessed at https://books.google.com/books?id=RhLBWld4_2AC&pg=PP9&lpg=PP9&dq=clarence+h.+forrest+baltimore+fire+department&source=bl&ots=ryHmuz8eNt&sig=ACfU3U0AdWJA4Sd4NhmlxvT6t9Amx3TmmA&hl=en&sa=X&ved=2ahUKEwiA4NeM4tHlAhWFq54KHVR7AdoQ6AEwB3oECAgQAQ#v=onepage&q=clarence%20h.%20forrest%20baltimore%20fire%20department&f=false
2. Scharf, *History of Baltimore City and County*, p. 237.
3. Scharf, *History of Baltimore City and County*, p. 238.
4. Forrest, *Official History*, p. 55.
5. Ibid., p. 59.
6. Ibid., pp. 60–63.
7. Ibid., p. 66; Scharf, *History of Baltimore City and County*, p. 241.
8. *Baltimore Sun,* January 11 and August 19, 1851, and April 15 and October 23, 1854; *American Republican and Baltimore Daily Clipper*, January 29 and February 4 and 11, 1845, and January 8 and 9, 1846; Independent Fire Company, Book II—1838-1847, Maryland Center for History and Culture, MS 478.
9. *Baltimore Sun*, February 7, 1853.
10. *Baltimore Sun*, February 12, 1853.
11. *Baltimore Sun*, September 11, 1854.
12. Forrest, *Official History*, p. 82.
13. *Baltimore Sun*, March 27, 1858.

Chapter 7

1. H. H. Walker Lewis, "The Baltimore Police Case of 1860," *Maryland Law Review* 26, number 3 (1966): p. 215.
2. Ibid., p. 216.
3. United States Census, 1860; Frank Towers, "Violence as a Tool of Party Dominance: Election Riots and the Baltimore Know-Nothings, 1854-1860," *Maryland Historical Magazine*, 93 (1), 1998, pp 5-37.
4. Tracy Matthew Melton, *Hanging Henry Gambrill. The Violent Career of Baltimore's Plug Uglies, 1854-1860* (Baltimore: Maryland Center for History and Culture, 2005), pp. 413-414; Less famous gangs were the Babes, the Blue Dicks, the Cock Robins, the Peelers, the Hunters, the American Rattlers, the Blackguards, the Tormentors, the Rollers, the Gumballs, the Crows, the Will Watchers, the Grizzly Bears, the Will Fights, the Greasy Pigs, the Sandy Bottoms, the Never Sweats, the Screwbolts, the Rangers, the Fountain Rackers, the Tormentors, the Canton Rackers, the Arabs, the Skin Flints, the Blue Bumpers, the Saddle Horses, the Hard Fisters, the Cut Headers, the Single Combatants, the Pollywogs, the Bullfrogs, the Bull Pups, the Stingers, the Tea Towners, the Goat Hillers, the Pine Knots, the Clip Wings, the Swampounders, the Red Rovers, the Walloons, the Rollers, the Cut Wings, the Hell's Delights, the Morning Glories, the Starlights, the Filibusters, the Buccaneers, the Rackers, the Peelers, the Sheep Legs, the Rangers, the Blue Lights, the Lightning Flashers, the Death Dealers, the Sculpnecks, the Corpse Makers, the Grave Diggers, the Whirlwinds, the Hail Storms, the Skull Crackers, the Beelzebubs, the Killers, the Grey Eagles, the Yellow Jackets, the Hornets, the Night Rangers, the Corner Butters, the Squash Neckers, the Adamantines, the Bully Raggers, and the Moon Rangers.
5. Reuben Maury, *The Wars of the Godly* (New York: Robert M. McBride & Company, 1928), p. 161.
6. *Baltimore Sun*, October 27, 1855.
7. Ibid.
8. *Baltimore Sun*, October 27, 1855.
9. Lewis, *Baltimore Police Case*, 1966, pp. 215-28.
10. *Baltimore Sun*, April 11, 1859.
11. Wilbur R. Miller, Ed., "History of Gangs." *The Social History of Crime and Punishment in America: An Encyclopedia.* (Los Angeles: Sage Reference Publications, 2012), Volume 2, p. 672.
12. Towers, *Violence As A Tool*, 1998, p. 15.
13. Lewis, *The Baltimore Police Case*, 1966, p. 219, citing Arthur Hobson Quinn, *Edgar Allan Poe, A Critical Biography* (New York: D. Appleton-Century Company, Inc., 1941), pp. 637-41.
14. Towers, *Violence As A Tool*. p. 15.
15. *Baltimore Sun*, November 7, 1860; Lewis, *The Baltimore Police Case*, 1966, p. 219; Towers, *Violence as a Tool*, 1998, pp. 5-37.
16. Col. J. Thomas Scharf, *The Chronicles of Baltimore; Being A Complete History of "Baltimore Town" and Baltimore City from the Earliest Period to the Present Time* (Baltimore: Turnbull Brothers, 1874), p 769.
17. America Votes. Presidential Campaign Memorabilia from the Duke University Special Collections Library. Know-Nothing Party—1850s, accessed at http://library.duke.edu/rubenstein/scriptorium/americavotes/know-nothing-letter.jpeg
18. Library of Congress, accessed at http://lcweb2.loc.gov/mss/mcc/062/0001.jpg
19. Scharf, *Chronicles of Baltimore*, 1874, p. 548.
20. *Baltimore Sun*, October 9, 1856.
21. Ibid.; J. Thomas Scharf, *History of Baltimore City and County, from the Earliest Period to*

the *Present Day: Including Biographical Sketches of Their Representative Men* (Philadelphia: Louis H. Everts, J. B. Lippincott & Co., 1881), p. 124.

22. *Baltimore Sun*, November 5 and 9, 1856.

23. Scharf, *History of Baltimore City and County*, 1881, p. 124.

24. Scharf, *The Chronicles of Baltimore*, 1874, pp. 549-50.

25. Scharf, *History of Baltimore City and County*, 1881, p. 787.

26. Scharf, *The Chronicles of Baltimore*, 1874, pp. 550-2.

27. Maryland State Archives, Early State Records Online, MSA SC M 3169, pp. 125-34. Letters between Swann and Ligon, accessed at http://msa.maryland.gov/megafile/msa/speccol/sc4800/sc4872/003169/html/m3169-0125.html and http://msa.maryland.gov/megafile/msa/speccol/sc4800/sc4872/003169/html/m3169-0134.html

28. *Baltimore Sun*, October 16, 1857.

29. *Baltimore Daily Exchange*, August 20, 1858.

30. *Baltimore Daily Exchange*, August 16, 1858.

31. Lewis, *The Baltimore Police Case*, 1966, p. 221.

32. *Baltimore Daily Exchange*, November 3, 1858.

33. Scharf, *History of Baltimore City and County*, 1881, p. 125.

34. Lewis, *The Baltimore Police Case*, 1966, p. 222.

35. *Ibid.*, p. 223.

36. Scharf, *History of Baltimore City and County*, 1881, pp. 787-8.

37. Lewis, *The Baltimore Police Case*, 1966, p. 225.

38. Frank Marcotte, *Six Days in April: Lincoln and the Union in Peril* (New York: Algora Publishing, 2005), p. 31.

39. Scharf, *History of Baltimore City and County*, 1881, pp. 125-126.

40. *Ibid.*, p. 788.

41. *Baltimore Sun*, November 7, 1860.

Chapter 8

1. de Francias Folsom, Ed., *Our Police. A History of the Baltimore Force from the First Watchman to the Latest Appointee* (Baltimore, J. D. Ehlers & Co., Guggenheimer, Weil & Co., J. M. Beers, 1888), p. 12.

2. *Ibid.*, p. 21.

3. *Ibid.*, p. 22.

4. *Ibid.*, p. 24.

5. H. H. Walker Lewis, "The Baltimore Police Case of 1860," *Maryland Law Review* 26, issue 3 (1966): p. 218.

6. Folsom, *Our Police*, 1888, p. 29.

7. *Ibid.*, p. 43.

8. *Ibid.*, p. 38.

9. *Baltimore Sun*, January 19, 1860.

10. Baltimore vs. State, 15 Maryland 376, 1860.

11. Lewis, *The Baltimore Police Case*, 1966, pp. 215-28.

12. *Baltimore Sun*, March 30, 1860.

13. Matthew Kent, "'Displaced by a Force to Which They Yielded and Could Not Resist': A Historical and Legal Analysis of Mayor and City Counsel [sic] of Baltimore v. Charles Howard et. al.," undated, Thesis as J. D. Candidate, University of Maryland Francis King Carey School of Law, pp. 6–8, accessed at https://digitalcommons.law.umaryland.edu/cgi/viewcontent.cgi?article=1026&context=mlh_pubs

14. Kent, "Displaced by a Force," pp. 8-9.

15. *Baltimore Sun*, February 23, 1860.

16. *Baltimore Daily Exchange*, February 23, 1860.

17. *Baltimore Sun*, February 23, 1860.

18. Folsom, *Our Police*, 1888, p. 34.

19. "Rules and Regulations for the Government of the Permanent Police Force of the City of Baltimore," *Ordinances and Regulations of the Mayor and City Council of Baltimore*, 1860, p. 30, accessed at https://baltimorecitypolicehistory.com/images/downloads/1861%20BPD%20Rules%20and%20Regulations.pdf

20. "Rules and Regulations," 1860, p. 31.

21. *Ibid.*, p. 33.

22. *Ibid.*, p. 34.

23. *Ibid.*, p. 48.

24. *Baltimore Sun*, May 4, 1860.

25. *Baltimore Sun*, May 8, 1860.

26. Electronic Baltimore City Police Records, Police Department Annual Reports, Baltimore City Archives, MSA SC, BCA BMS33-4-1 bms 33_4_1_4-0002, p. 2, accessed at http://mdhistory.msa.maryland.gov/bca_bms33_4_1/bca_bms33_4_1_4/html/bms33_4_1_4-0002.html

27. Clement Dorsey, "An Act Relating to Vagrants in the City of Baltimore.—1818, Ch. 169," *The General Public Statutory Law and Public Local Law of the State of Maryland from the Year 1692 to 1839 Inclusive: with Annotations Thereto, and a Copious Index*," in Three Volumes, Volume II (Baltimore: John D. Toy, 1840), pp. 1620-1.

28. Jeffrey R. Brackett, "The Negro in Maryland, A Study of the Institution of Slavery." In Herbert B. Adams, Ed., *Johns Hopkins University Studies in Historical and Political Science*, Extra Volume VI (Baltimore: N. Murray, Johns Hopkins University, John Murphy & Co., 1889), p. 221.

29. Katherine A. Harvey, "Practicing Medicine at the Baltimore Almshouse, 1828-1850," *Maryland Historical Magazine*, 74 (3), September 1979, pp. 223-37.

30. Ordinance #46: "An ordinance designating a place for the confinement of Paupers, Beggars, Vagrants, Vagabonds, and disorderly persons in the city of Baltimore." *The Ordinances of the Mayor and City Council of Baltimore, to Which Is Added A Collection of Acts and Parts of Acts of the Assembly, Relating to the Corporation* (Baltimore: George W. Bowen & Co., 1858), p. 202.

31. *Baltimore Sun*, May 22, 1860.

32. *Baltimore Sun*, May 17, 1860.

33. *Baltimore Sun*, May 28, 1860.

34. *Baltimore Sun*, May 30, 1860.
35. *Baltimore Sun*, June 1, 1860.
36. *Baltimore Daily Exchange*, October 10 1860.
37. *Baltimore Sun*, June 20 and 22 and 23 and 25 and 26, and July 3, 1860; *Baltimore Daily Exchange*, June 22 and 23 and 27,1860.
38. *Baltimore Sun*, June 4, 1860.
39. *Baltimore Daily Exchange*, May 30, 1860; The origin of the term "blue law" is obscure. Though some have contended that moralistic regulations, controlling what may be done on the Sabbath, were printed on blue paper by the Puritans in seventeenth-century Connecticut where the laws were first promulgated, there is no evidence for such an origin. The first known use of the term "blue laws" was in 1781 when Reverend Samuel Peters outlined the history of Connecticut. The color blue in the eighteenth century was often associated with something excessively moralistic or Puritanical; *Baltimore Sun*, July 23 and August 25, 1860; *Baltimore Daily Exchange*, August 27, 1860.
40. *Baltimore Sun*, June 4, 1860.
41. *Baltimore Sun*, June 7, 1860.
42. *Baltimore Sun*, June 8, 1860.
43. *Baltimore Sun*, June 11, 1860.
44. *Baltimore Sun*, June 15, 1860.
45. *Baltimore Sun*, June 21, 1860.
46. *Baltimore Sun*, July 7, 1860.
47. *Baltimore Sun*, July 2, 1860; *Baltimore Daily Exchange*, July 3, 1860.
48. *Baltimore Sun*, July 3, 1860.
49. *Baltimore Sun*, July 6, 1860.
50. *Baltimore Sun*, August 3, 1860.
51. *Baltimore Sun*, August 29, 1860.
52. *Baltimore Sun*, October 8, 1860.
53. *Baltimore Sun*, October 2, 1860.
54. *Baltimore Sun*, October 6, 1860.
55. *Baltimore Sun*, October 9, 1860.
56. *Baltimore Sun*, October 10, 1860.
57. *Baltimore Sun*, October 11, 1860.
58. *Baltimore Sun*, October 12, 1860.
59. *Baltimore Sun*, October 13, 1860.
60. *Baltimore Sun*, November 7, 1860.
61. *Baltimore Daily Exchange*, November 12, 1860.
62. *Baltimore Sun*, December 12, 1860.
63. *Baltimore Sun*, November 28, 1860.
64. *New York Times*, September 14, 1861.
65. *Baltimore Sun*, August 22, 1860, emphasis in the original.

Chapter 9

1. *Baltimore Sun*, February 25, 1861.
2. Barbara Jeanne Fields, *Slavery and Freedom on the Middle Ground. Maryland During the Nineteenth Century* (New Haven and London: Yale University Press, 1985), p. 6.
3. The American Civil War. Maryland, Whose Maryland?, accessed at slavenorth.com/cw/maryland.htm
4. Baltimore City Property Tax Records, Field Assessors' Work Books, BCA BRG4-3, 1858, Ward 15, volume 1, brg4_3_bca1613-0195, p. 195, ledger p. 12, Baltimore City Archives, accessed at http://guide.msa.maryland.gov/pages/series.aspx?action=viewdetailedseries&id=brg4-3 and http://mdhistory.msa.maryland.gov/bca_brg4_3/bca_brg4_3_bca1613/pdf/brg4_3_bca1613-0195.pdf; In this entry for the residence at 64 Barre Street, south side, the lot was 23 feet wide by 155 feet deep, improved with a 3-story brick structure with two small houses in the rear; the lot was valued at $1,437, and the main house at $3,500. Each small house was valued at $300. Griffith held slaves, and each had an assessed value (Table 2); U.S. Census, 1860; Ralph Clayton, *Black Baltimore, 1820–1870* (Bowie, Maryland: Heritage Books, Inc., 1987), pp. 63, 65; Ralph Clayton, *Slavery, Slaveholding and the Free Black Population of Antebellum Baltimore* (Bowie, Maryland: Heritage Books, Inc., 1993), pp. 68, 70, 124, 125, and 129.
5. U.S. Census, 1860 and 1870.
6. *The American Presbyterian and Genesee Evangelist* (Philadelphia: September 27, 1860), accessed at https://panewsarchive.psu.edu/lccn/2018264050/1860-09-27/ed-1/seq-3/#date1=01%2F01%2F1860&city=&date2=12%2F31%2F1860&searchType=advanced&language=&sequence=0&lccn=2018264050&index=0&words=Kane&county=&frequency=&ortext=&proxtext=kane&phrasetext=&andtext=&rows=20&dateFilterType=yearRange&page=1
7. Thomas H. Hicks, "To the People of Maryland," Executive Chambers, January 3, 1861, accessed at https://msa.maryland.gov/msa/educ/exhibits/hicks/images/case1/broadside_scaled.pdf

Chapter 10

1. Cleveland Moffett, "How Allan Pinkerton Thwarted the First Plot to Assassinate Lincoln: Stories from the Archives of the Pinkerton Detective Agency," *McClure's Magazine* (New York: S. S. McClure, Limited, 1894), November 1894, p. 523.
2. *Albany Evening Journal*, February 18, 1861.
3. Michael J. Kline, *The Baltimore Plot. The First Conspiracy to Assassinate Abraham Lincoln* (Yardley, Pennsylvania: Westholme Publishing, 2008), p. 88.
4. Kenneth J. Winkle, *Lincoln's Citadel: The Civil War in Washington, D.C.* (New York: W. W. Norton & Company, Inc., 2013), pp. 94–6.
5. Letter, George W. Hazzard to Abraham Lincoln, January 1861, Abraham Lincoln papers, Library of Congress. Underlining emphasis in the original, accessed at www.loc.gov/resource/mal.0698700/?sp=1 and www.loc.gov/resource/mal.0698700/?sp=6
6. *New York Times*, October 20, 1890.
7. Letter, George Stearns to Gov. Thomas H. Hicks, February 7, 1861, Maryland Center for History and Culture, MS.2104.

8. *Baltimore American and Commercial Advertiser*, February 25, 1861.

9. Letter, Gov. Thomas H. Hicks to Lieutenant General Winfield Scott, February 9, 1861, Maryland Center for History and Culture, MS.2104.

10. George William Brown, "Baltimore and the Nineteenth of April 1861. A Study of the War." In Adams, Herbert B., Ed. *Johns Hopkins University Studies in Historical and Political Science, Extra Volume III.* (Baltimore: N. Murray and Isaac Friedenwald, Johns Hopkins University, 1887), p. 15, accessed at https://www.loc.gov/resource/lhbcb.03453/?sp=17

11. William Henry and Jesse William Weik. In: Douglas L. Wilson, Rodney O. Davis, and Terry Wilson, Eds., *Herndon's Informants: Letters, Interviews, and Statements About Abraham Lincoln* (Urbana and Chicago, Illinois: University of Illinois Press, 1998), p. 318.

12. Moffett, *How Allan Pinkerton Thwarted*, 1894, pp. 519–29.

13. Norma B. Cuthbert, Ed., *Lincoln and the Baltimore Plot 1861; From Pinkerton Records and Related Papers* (San Marino, California: Huntington Library Publications; Los Angeles: Pacific Press, 1949), p. 19.

14. William A. Tidwell, James O. Hall, and David Winfred Gaddy, *Come Retribution: The Confederate Secret Service and the Assassination of Lincoln* (Jackson, Mississippi, and London: University Press of Mississippi, 1988), p. 229.

15. Isaac Newton Arnold, "The Baltimore Plot to Assassinate Abraham Lincoln." *Harper's New Monthly Magazine*, 37 (217), June 1868, pp. 123–8; Note that Cipriano Ferrandini is variably spelled "Cypriano." In this work the spelling will be consistent by using "Cipriano."

16. Daniel Stashower, *The Hour of Peril: The Secret Plot to Murder Lincoln Before the Civil War* (New York: Minotaur Books, 2013), pp. 175–6; *The Capital*, Annapolis, Maryland, August 18, 1973; Elihu S. Riley, *"The Ancient City." A History of Annapolis, in Maryland, 1649–1887* (Annapolis, Maryland: Record Printing Office, 1887), pp. 268–72, accessed at https://archive.org/details/ancientcityhisto00rile/page/n4; Elihu S. Riley, "A History of Anne Arundel County in Maryland: Adapted for Use in the Schools of the County" (Annapolis, Maryland: Charles G. Feldmeyer, 1905) pp. 115–6; accessed at https://www.loc.gov/item/06020679/ and https://babel.hathitrust.org/cgi/pt?id=loc.ark:/13960/t70v8qg29&view=1up&seq=5; *Maryland Republican*, Annapolis, Maryland, July 17 and 24 and 31, and August 7, 1847.

17. Allan Pinkerton, *The Spy of the Rebellion; Being a True History of the Spy System of the United States Army During the Late Rebellion* (New York: G. W. Carleton & Co., 1886), p. 59.

18. Pinkerton, *Spy of the Rebellion*, 1886, p. 61.

19. *Ibid.*, p. 50.

20. *Ibid.*, p. 77.

21. Kline, *Baltimore Plot*, 2008, p. 66.

22. Herndon, *Herndon's Informants*, 1998, p. 300.

23. *Ibid.*, p. 319.

24. Find A Grave, accessed at https://www.findagrave.com/memorial/817/allan-pinkerton and https://www.findagrave.com/memorial/6425/kate-warne

25. Kline, *Baltimore Plot*, 2008, pp. 164–165.

26. Cuthbert, *Lincoln and the Baltimore Plot*, 1949, p. xiii.

27. Kline, *Baltimore Plot*, 2008, p. 60; Cuthbert, *Lincoln and the Baltimore Plot*, 1949, p. 36.

28. Edmund Wright, *Narrative of Edmund Wright; His Adventures With and Escape From the Knights of the Golden Circle* (Cincinnati: J. R. Hawley, 1864), pp. 35, 42; John H. Surratt, *The Private Journal and Diary of John H. Surratt, the Conspirator*, Ed. Dion Haco (New York: Frederic A. Brady, 1866), pp. 21–2. Note: This "Diary" is bogus as an accurate reflection of Surratt's life, but might have some validity regarding the description of the Knights' goals and oaths; "A Member of the Order." *Authentic Exposition of the "K. G. C." "Knights of the Golden Circle;" Or, A History of Secession from 1834 to 1861* (Indianapolis: C. O. Perrine, 1861); Anonymous ("A Member of the Order"). *K. G. C. An Authentic Exposition of the Origin, Objects, and Secret Work of the Organization Known as the Knights of the Golden Circle* (Indianapolis: C. O. Perrine, 1861).

29. "Knights of the Golden Circle." *Rules, Regulations and Principles of the K. G. C.: Illustrated, Issued by Order of the Congress of the K. C. S. [Knights of the Columbian Star], and the General President Knights of the Golden Circle* (New York: Benj. Urner, 1859), pp. 1–63, also accessed at Rare Books, Maryland Center for History and Culture, E436.K72.

30. *Baltimore Sun*, June 14 and 23, 1859, and April 5 and 7 and July 19 and 28 and September 5, 1860, and January 7 and May 25, 1861.

31. Moffett, *How Allan Pinkerton Thwarted*, 1894, pp. 520–1.

32. Alan Axelrod, *International Encyclopedia of Secret Societies & Fraternal Orders* (New York: Facts On File, 1997), p. 156.

33. Surratt, *Diary of John H. Surratt*, 1866, pp. 89, 41; William C. Edwards, *The Life and Times of John Wilkes Booth. A Chronology of His Life and the Events Surrounding Him Including New Information and Insights* (Buffalo, New York: NFB Publishing, 2019), pp. 175–9.

34. Anonymous, *K. G. C. Exposition/Origin*, 1861, p. 1; Jay Longley and Colin Eby, "Knights of the Golden Circle," accessed at http://knights-of-the-golden-circle.blogspot.com/2010/06/knights-of-golden-circle-jay-longley.html; Ollinger Crenshaw, "The Knights of the Golden Circle: The Career of George Bickley." *American Historical Review*, 47 (1), October 1941, pp 23–50; *Harrison (Texas) Flag*, November 17, 1860, as cited in Crenshaw, *Knights*, 1941, p. 26.

35. Randolph B. Campbell, "Knights of the

Golden Circle." *Handbook of Texas Online*, Texas State Historical Association, September 19, 2010, accessed at https://tshaonline.org/handbook/online/articles/vbk01

36. Gloria Jahoda, "The Bickleys of Virginia." *Virginia Magazine of History and Biography* 66, No. 4 (October 1958); p. 479; *Cincinnati Daily Commercial*, April 6, 1860.

37. Member of the Order, *Authentic Exposition of the K. G. C.*, 1861, p. ii.
American Cavalier, May 28, 1859, as cited in Crenshaw, *Knights*, 1841, p. 38.

38. Member of the Order, *Authentic Exposition of the K. G. C.*, 1861, p. 34.

39. *Ibid.*, p. 35.

40. *Ibid.*, p. 57.

41. Jack Myers, *Knights' Gold. The Largest Documented KGC Treasure Ever Discovered* (Jack O'Lantern Press and CreateSpace Independent Publishing, 2016), p. 238; David C. Keehn, *Knights of the Golden Circle, Secret Empire, Southern Secession, Civil War* (Baton Rouge: Louisiana State University Press, 2013), pp. 30, 80, 111, 144–5; Duda, Jake. *The Knight's Sword of Baltimore*, p. 4, accessed at https://archive.org/stream/TheKnightsSwordOfBaltimore_20180322/The%20Knight%27s%20Sword%20of%20Baltimore_djvu.txt; Warren Getler, *The Knights of the Golden Circle*, Washington, 2014, accessed at http://mazement53.rssing.com/chan-23655874/all_p4.html

42. *Baltimore Sun*, June 14, 1859.

43. Anonymous. *K. G. C., A Full Exposure of the Southern Traitors; the Knights of the Golden Circle. Their Startling Schemes Frustrated. From Original Documents Never Before Published* (Boston: E. H. Bullard & Co., 1861), accessed at http://lcweb2.loc.gov/service/gdc/scd0001/2002/20021015001kg/20021015001kg.pdf

44. *Baltimore Sun*, July 25, 1884.

45. Members of the various organizations often overlapped. However, just because a person belonged to the Freemasons and the Knights of the Golden Circle does not necessarily mean that the organizations themselves were connected. However, some groups clearly founded others. The "Circle of Honor" spawned the "Order of the Sons of Liberty," which became the "Knights of the Golden Circle," and they were followed by the "Order of the American Knights." Others preceded and followed these societies, but their goals were often quite similar; Felix Grundy Stidger, Ed., *Treason History of the Order of the Sons of Liberty, Formerly Circle of Honor, Succeeded by Knights of the Golden Circle, Afterward Order of the American Knights. The Most Gigantic Treasonable Conspiracy The World Has Ever Known* (Chicago: Felix G. Stidger, 1903, reprinted by Dogwood Press, Hemphill, Texas, 2000), accessed at https://babel.hathitrust.org/cgi/pt?id=wu.89081295123&view=1up&seq=1

46. Kline, *Baltimore Plot*, 2008, pp. 25, 206, citing Tidwell, Hall and Gaddy, *Come Retribution*, 1988, p. 228.

47. Herndon, *Herndon's Informants*, 1998, p. 298.

48. U.S. Election Atlas, 1860, accessed at https://uselectionatlas.org/RESULTS/

49. Herndon, *Herndon's Informants*, 1998, pp. 270, 301.

50. *Ibid.*, p. 303.

51. *Janesville Daily Gazette*, Janesville, Wisconsin, April 3, 1862.

52. John W. Woods, *Woods' Baltimore City Directory Ending Year 1860* (Baltimore, 1860), p. 126.

53. Tidwell, Hall and Gaddy, *Come Retribution*, 1988, p. 228.

54. Arnold, "The Baltimore Plot To Assassinate," 1868, p. 125; Moffett, *How Allan Pinkerton Thwarted*, 1894, p. 522.

55. Kline, *Baltimore Plot*, 2008, p. 112.

56. Brown, *Baltimore and the Nineteenth of April 1861*, 1887, p. 126.

57. Herndon, *Herndon's Informants*, 1998, p. 276.

58. Brown, *Baltimore and the Nineteenth of April 1861*, 1887, p. 125; Ironically, this same Ferrandini was a member of the 1855 53rd Regiment, Maryland Volunteer Infantry, and he would become a member of the Hibernian Society on March 7, 1870, the same day that Kane's name reappeared in the Hibernian records after his arrest in 1861, imprisonment, and Kane's activities in Canada and Virginia; 53rd Regiment Infantry, Maryland Volunteers. Maryland Center for History and Culture, MS 364; Hibernian Society, Box 19, Maryland Center for History and Culture, MS 2029.

59. Kline, *Baltimore Plot*, 2008, p. 125; Arnold, "The Baltimore Plot To Assassinate," 1868, p. 125.

60. *Ibid.*

61. Cuthbert, *Lincoln and the Baltimore Plot*, 1949, p. 53.

62. *Ibid.*, p. 93.

63. Arnold, "The Baltimore Plot To Assassinate," 1868, p. 125.

64. Herndon, *Herndon's Informants*, 1998, p. 281.

65. Kline, *Baltimore Plot*, 2008, pp. 80–1.

66. *Ibid.*, p. 92–3.

67. *Ibid.*, p. 294; Tidwell, Hall and Gaddy, *Come Retribution*, 1988, p. 229.

68. Kline, *Baltimore Plot*, 2008, pp. 61–2.

69. *Ibid.*, p. 93–7.

70. Kline, *Baltimore Plot*, 2008, p. 113.

71. "Alleged Hostile Organization Against the Government Within the District of Columbia," House of Representatives Report No. 79, 36th Congress, 2nd Session, February 14, 1861, p. 2, accessed at http://ia600208.us.archive.org/9/items/allegedhostileor00unit/allegedhostileor00unit.pdf; Tidwell, Hall and Gaddy, *Come Retribution*, 1988, pp. 225–40.

72. Greene, H. Leon. *The Confederate Yellow Fever Conspiracy* (Jefferson, North Carolina: McFarland, 2019); Edward Steers, Jr., *Blood On The Moon: The Assassination of Abraham Lincoln* (Lexington, Kentucky: University of Kentucky Press, 2001), pp. 4, 26, 38–59.

73. Jason Phillips, *Looming Civil War. How Nineteenth-Century Americans Imagined the Future* (New York: Oxford University Press, 2018), pp. 147–8.
74. Arnold, The Baltimore Plot, 1868, p. 125.
75. *Ibid.*
76. Tidwell, Hall and Gaddy, *Come Retribution*, 1988, p. 229–30.
77. *The Baltimore City Code: Comprising the Laws of Maryland Relating to the City of Baltimore, and the Ordinances of the Mayor and City Council, with an Appendix, to the End of the Session of 1877-78.* Compiled by Lewis Mayer, Attorney at Law (Baltimore: John Cox, 1879); Railroads: Article XL.—Ordinances, p. 727, accessed at https://babel.hathitrust.org/cgi/pt?id=uc2.ark:/13960/t8ff3sk4q&view=1up&seq=7
78. The Baltimore and Ohio Railroad also had other terminals: one was the Mount Clare Station, used initially for freight, built in 1830 (and is now the B&O Railroad Museum); the third was the Mount Royal Station, not built until 1896, and currently occupied by the Maryland Institute College of Art. The Susquehanna Terminal (also called the Bolton Hill Station—within blocks of the old Union Station) was located at Cathedral and Hoffman Streets, and it was also used by the B&O Railroad. Others in the central Baltimore area were the old Union Station (also initially a Northern Central Railway Station, built in 1872-1873) further north in the city, located now on Charles Street as the Pennsylvania Station, built in 1911 (an interim name –the New Union Station—was used until 1928). These stations are not to be confused with other smaller stations in Baltimore at the time: the Hillen Street Station, the Oak Street Station (between Howard and North Streets), and the Washington, Baltimore, and Annapolis (WB&A) Station (also called "Terminal Station"—on Liberty Street south of Lexington), the company for which was not incorporated until 1888, and the station not used until the early 1900s. Like theatres in Baltimore, railroad stations frequently changed owners and names; Maryland Center for History and Culture, MD 10438, Box 25.
79. Jacob Friedman, "The History and Construction of the Old Calvert Street Station of the Pennsylvania Railroad at Baltimore, Maryland," dissertation for initiation into Phi Mu, engineering honor society, 1933, p. 5, accessed at https://archive.org/details/TheHistoryAndConstructionOfTheOldCalvertStreetStationOfThe/page/n5
80. Letter, Thos. H. Hicks to Hon. E. H. Webster, November 9, 1860, as cited in Brown, *Baltimore and the Nineteenth of April*, 1887, p. 128.
81. *Baltimore American and Commercial Advertiser*, November 8 and 9, 1860; U.S. Election Atlas, accessed at https://uselectionatlas.org/RESULTS/state.php?fips=24&year=1860&f=0&off=0
82. Herndon, *Herndon's Informants*, 1998, p. 310.
83. *Cincinnati Commercial*, February 25, 1861.
84. Kline, *Baltimore Plot*, 2008, p. 54.
85. *Ibid.*, pp. 29–35.
86. *Ibid.*, p. 143.
87. Letter, Worthington G. Snethen to Abraham Lincoln, January 7, 1861, *Abraham Lincoln Papers*, General Correspondence, 1833–1916, Library of Congress, accessed at https://www.loc.gov/resource/mal.0589600/
88. *Adams Sentinel*, Gettysburg, Pennsylvania, February 27, 1861.
89. *Indianapolis Daily Journal*, February 26, 1861.
90. *Baltimore Sun*, January 21, 1861.
91. Pinkerton, *Spy of the Rebellion*, 1886, p. 61.
92. Kline, *Baltimore Plot*, 2008, p. 86.
93. William Howard Russell and Martin Crawford, Ed., *William Howard Russell's Civil War. Private Diary and Letters, 1861-1862* (Athens, Georgia, and London: University of Georgia Press, 1992), p. 33.
94. *Baltimore Sun*, February 25, 1861.
95. Kline, *Baltimore Plot*, 2008, p. 256; Pinkerton, *Spy of the Rebellion*, 1886, pp. 69, 76, 78–9, 96; Moffett, "Pinkerton Thwarted," 1894, p. 520.
96. Kline, *Baltimore Plot*, 2008, p. 191.
97. Henry Ketcham *The Life of Abraham Lincoln* (New York: A. L. Burt Company, 1901), p. 207. Emphasis in the original.
98. Cuthbert, *Baltimore Plot*, 1949, p. 12.
99. Kline, *Baltimore Plot*, 2008, p 203; Moffett, "Pinkerton Thwarted," 1894, p 524.
100. Tidwell, Hall and Gaddy, *Come Retribution*, 1988, p. 231–2.
101. Bradley R. Hoch, *The Lincoln Trail in Pennsylvania. A History and Guide* (University Park, Pennsylvania: Keystone Books, Penn State University Press, 2013), pp. 6–7.
102. Arnold, "The Baltimore Plot to Assassinate," 1868, p. 127.
103. Hoch, *Lincoln Trail*, 2013, pp. 11, 14.
104. *Ibid.*, p. 14.
105. *Baltimore Daily Exchange*, February 25, 1861.
106. Kline, *Baltimore Plot*, 2008, p. 232.
107. *Ibid.*, p. 233.
108. Kline, *Baltimore Plot*, 2008, p. 209; Cuthbert, *Baltimore Plot*, 1949, p. xvi.
109. Moffett, *How Allan Pinkerton Thwarted*, 1894, pp. 527.
110. *Ibid.*, pp. 527–8.
111. Cuthbert, *Baltimore Plot*, 1949, p. 79; Herndon, *Herndon's Informants*, 1998, p. 290.
112. *Baltimore Daily Exchange*, February 25, 1861.
113. Kline, *Baltimore Plot*, 2008, p. 251.
114. Herndon, *Herndon's Informants*, 1998, p. 286.
115. *Ibid.*, p. 286.
116. *Baltimore Daily Exchange*, February 25, 1861.
117. *Baltimore Sun*, February 25, 1861.
118. Mrs. Lincoln's entourage actually stopped about six blocks short of the Calvert Street Station where the train tracks crossed at North Charles

Street (near Charles between Biddle and John Streets and close to the Bolton Street Station), or Chase at North Avenue where the tracks make a right-angle turn from the East to the South. Some newspaper reports said that it was at the intersection of Bolton and Charles Streets, but there was no such intersection—it probably referred to Charles Street near the Bolton Street Station, which was actually near the intersection of Charles and John or Biddle.

119. Kline, *Baltimore Plot*, 2008, p. 86.
120. Scharf, *History of Maryland*, 1879, Volume 3, p. 395.
121. *Baltimore Sun*, February 25, 1861.
122. *Ibid.*
123. Eutaw House Register, 1861, unpaginated, entry for February 23, 1861, Maryland Center for History and Culture, MS 2089.
124. *Baltimore American and Commercial Advertiser*, February 25, 1861; The total size of the Baltimore police force in 1861 was approximately 400 men. When Federal troops under General Nathaniel Banks took command of the Baltimore police later in 1861, he assigned approximately the same number of men to replace the civilian agency.
125. *Baltimore Daily Exchange*, February 25, 1861.
126. *Baltimore Sun*, February 25, 1861; *Baltimore American and Commercial Advertiser*, February 26, 1861.
127. *Baltimore Sun*, February 25, 1861; Kline, *Baltimore Plot*, 2008, p. 458.
128. *Baltimore American and Commercial Advertiser*, February 25, 1861.
129. Scharf, *History of Maryland*, 1879, Volume 3, p. 386.
130. *Baltimore Sun*, February 25, 1861.
131. *Baltimore American and Commercial Advertiser*, February 25, 1861.
132. Cuthbert, *Baltimore Plot*, 1949, p. xv.
133. Kline, *Baltimore Plot*, 2008, pp. 308–9.
134. *Baltimore Sun*, February 25, 1861.
135. *Gettysburg Compiler*, March 4, 1861.
136. *New York Times*, February 26, 1861.
137. Kline, *Baltimore Plot*, 2008, p. 291.
138. *Baltimore American and Commercial Advertiser*, February 25, 1861.
139. Scharf, J. Thomas. *History of Maryland, from the Earliest Period to the Present Day* (Baltimore: John B. Piet, 1879), Volume 3, p. 387.
140. Scharf, *History of Maryland*, 1879, Volume 3. p. 388; *Baltimore American and Commercial Advertiser*, February 26, 1861.
141. *Baltimore American and Commercial Advertiser*, February 27, 1861.
142. Scharf, *History of Maryland*, 1879, Volume 3, p. 390.
143. *Baltimore American and Commercial Advertiser*, February 25, 1861.
144. Memorandum, Charles P. Stone, February 21, 1861. Abraham Lincoln Papers, Reel 17. American Memory, Library of Congress.
145. Letter, Charles Gould to Henry C. Bowen, February 5, 1861, Abraham Lincoln Papers. American Memory, Library of Congress, accessed at https://www.loc.gov/item/mal0716600
146. *Baltimore American and Commercial Advertiser*, February 25, 1861.
147. Brown, *Baltimore and the 19th of April*, 1887, p. 9.
148. *Ibid.*, pp. 11–12.
149. Scharf, *History of Maryland*, 1887, Volume 3, p. 393.
150. Cuthbert, *Baltimore Plot*, 1949, p. xvii.
151. *Ibid.*, pp. xix–xx.
152. *Baltimore Sun*, June 22, 1868.
153. *Baltimore Sunday Telegram*, June 21, 1868, as cited in John Thomas Scharf, *History of Maryland from the Earliest Period to the Present Day*, 1879, Volume 3, J. B. Piet, Baltimore, "Marshal Kane and the Assassination Plot," pp. 395–6.

Chapter 11

1. Abraham Lincoln. Proclamation 80—Calling Forth the Militia and Convening an Extra Session of Congress, April 15, 1861, accessed at http://www.presidency.ucsb.edu/ws/index.php?pid=70077; Abraham Lincoln Papers: Series 1. General Correspondence. 1833–1916: Abraham Lincoln, Monday, April 15, 1861 (Proclamation on State Militia). Manuscript/Mixed Material. Library of Congress, accessed at https://www.loc.gov/item/mal0907400/; U.S. War Department. *The War of the Rebellion: A Compilation of the Official Records of the Union and Confederate Armies* (hereinafter designated as "OR"). Government Printing Office, Washington, 1899, index accessed at Cornell University Library, "Making of America," http://collections.library.cornell.edu/moa_new/waro.html; OR, Series 1, Volume 3, pp. 67–69.
2. Letter, Tho. H. Hicks to Abraham Lincoln, April 17, 1861, OR, Series 3, Volume 1, pp. 79–80; Papers of Abraham Lincoln, accessed at https://s3.us-east-2.amazonaws.com/papersofabrahamlincoln/PAL_Images/PAL_PubMan/1861/04/270113.pdf; Letter, Simon Cameron to Thomas H. Hicks, April 17, 1861, OR, Series 3, Volume 1, p. 80.
3. Charles Camper and J. W. Kirkley, Eds., *Historical Record of the First Regiment Maryland Infantry* (Washington: Gibson Brothers, 1871), pp. 2–6.
4. Richard F. Miller, Ed., *States at War, Volume 4: A Reference Guide for Delaware, Maryland and New Jersey in the Civil War* (Hanover, New Hampshire, and London: University Press of New England, 2015), p. 290.
5. John G. Nicolay and John Hay. *Abraham Lincoln. A History* (New York: The Century Co., 1890), Volume 4, p. 93.
6. Frank Moore, Ed., *The Rebellion Record: A Diary of American Events* (New York, G. P. Putnam, 1862), Volume 1, pp. 76–7.
7. *Ibid.*, p. 77; *Baltimore Sun*, April 19, 1861.

8. *Ibid.*
9. Michael G. Williams, "Bullets Vs. Bricks In Baltimore," *Civil War Times*, October 2011, 50 (5), pp. 34–41.
10. Edward G. Everett, "The Baltimore Riots, April, 1861," *Pennsylvania History: A Journal of Mid-Atlantic Studies*, 24 (4), October 1957, pp. 332–3.
11. OR, Series 1, Volume 2, p. 577.
12. *Baltimore Sun*, April 19, 1861.
13. *Baltimore Daily Exchange*, April 19, 1861.
14. OR, Series 2, Volume 1, p. 629.
15. *Baltimore Sun*, April 19, 1861.
16. Clayton Coleman Hall, Ed., *Baltimore: Its History and Its People, Volume 1—History* (New York and Chicago: Lewis Historical Publishing Company, 1912), p. 710; *Baltimore Daily Exchange*, April 19, 1861.
17. *Baltimore Sun*, April 22, 1861.
18. *Baltimore Daily Exchange*, April 19, 1861.
19. At this time the Confederate Flag or Secession Flag was called the "Stars and Bars" and had three horizontal bars, red on the top and bottom, white in the middle, with a blue corner square having seven white stars in a circle.
20. *Baltimore American and Commercial Advertiser*, April 19, 1861; *Baltimore Sun*, April 19, 1861.
21. OR, Series 1, Volume 2, p. 577.
22. *Baltimore American and Commercial Advertiser*, May 3, 1861.
23. John W. Hanson, Chaplain, *Historical Sketch of the Old Sixth Regiment of Massachusetts Volunteers, During Its Three Campaigns In 1861, 1862, 1863, and* 1864 (Boston: Lee and Shepard, 1866), p. 23.
24. *Ibid.*, p. 37; Sixth Regiment Massachusetts Volunteer Militia (Infantry) Three Months, accessed at http://www.civilwardata.com/active/hdsquery.dll?RegimentHistory?981&U%3E; The Baltimore Riot of 1861 and the First Combat Deaths of the Civil War, accessed at http://www.rumormillnews.com/cgi-bin/archive2.cgi?noframes;read=16841
25. OR, Series 1, Volume 2, p. 16.
26. *Baltimore Sun*, July 19, 1861; J. L. Harrison, "The Baltimore Riot," accessed at userpages.umbc.edu/~jamie/html/the_baltimore_riot.html
27. *Baltimore Daily Exchange*, April 20, 1861.
28. *Baltimore South*, April 23, 1861.
29. Hanson, *Historical Sketch*, 1866, p, 25.
30. Michael G. Williams, "Baltimore Riot of 1861," accessed at https://www.historynet.com/-baltimore-riot-of-1861.htm
31. OR, Series 1, Volume 2, p. 7.
32. *Baltimore Daily Exchange*, April 20, 1861.
33. Robert Underwood Johnson and Clarence Clough Buel, Eds., "The Century War Series" in *The Century Magazine. Battles and Leaders of the Civil War* (New York, The Century Co., De Vinne Press, 1884–1887), Volume 1, p. 150.
34. *Ibid.*, p. 151; Williams, "Baltimore Riot."
35. Miller, *States at War*, 2015, pp. 293–306
36. Robert F. Bailey, III, "Pratt Street Riots Reconsidered: A Case of Overstated Significance?" *Maryland Historical Magazine*, 98 (2), Summer 2003, p. 170.
37. Letter, George P. Kane to Chas. Howard, May 3, 1861, "Report of Marshal Kane to the Board of Police Commissioners. An Official Narrative of the Facts in Relation to the Occurrences Which Took Place in this City on Friday, April 19, 1861." OR, Series 2, Volume 1, p. 630, accessed at https://en.wikisource.org/w/index.php?title=File:Kane_george_defense.pdf&page=1
38. OR, Series 1, Volume 2, p. 10.
39. *Baltimore American and Commercial Advertiser*, April 20, 1861.
40. Bailey, "Pratt Street Riots," 2003, p. 155.
41. Charles W. Mitchell, Ed., *Maryland Voices of the Civil War* (Baltimore: Johns Hopkins University Press, 2007), p. 56.
42. Hanson, *Historical Sketch*, 1866, p, 25.
43. *Ibid.*, p, 27.
44. OR, Series 1, Volume 2, p. 7.
45. "Baltimore Police History, 1861 Riots. The Civil War's First Dead. 19 April 1861," accessed at https://baltimorecitypolicehistory.com/our-police/riots-1861.html
46. *New York Times*, July 12, 1861; Jonathan W. White, "Forty-seven Eyewitness Accounts of the Pratt Street Riot and Its Aftermath," Research Notes & Maryland Miscellany, *Maryland Historical Magazine*, Volume 106, Issue 1, Spring 2011, pp. 70–93. These depositions were taken from Record Group 21, U.S. Circuit Court for the District of Maryland, National Archives, Philadelphia.
47. *Ibid.*
48. National Archives and Records Administration (NARA), Record Group (RG) 21, Records of the U.S. Circuit Court for the District of Maryland, Baltimore Division, Criminal Docket, 1864–1903, Volume 1 and Case Files Boxes.
49. Some of those additional men indicted were: Joseph Cook, Joseph Hood, Frederick Uhlhorn, George Peters, Richard Thomas, Joseph Wilhelm, Thomas Skinner, John Merryman, Charles Cockey, B. Welch Owens, Isaac R. Trimble, George P. Kane, George M. Hollins, George W. Alexander, Samuel Tatum, Richard Gilmor, John Henderson, Jr., Edward Costello, Samuel Thompson, William Phelps, John Bosley, George W. Jones, James Whiteford, James McGirvin (or James M. Girvin), Richard Price, George Konig, Sr., Joseph Bonnetti, Washington Goodrich, Jerome Pendergast, Clifford Anderson, George McGowan, Thomas Gifford, William Henry Hiss, George R. McGee, William Konig, Samuel Maccubbin, John Myers, Daniel Steever, Fountain Morgan, Thomas Goodrich, George Pearsall, H. S. Eckels (aka Tim Eckels), James Hudgins, General George H. Steuart, J. Sidney Hall, B. Rush Dallam, William Michael, William Wilson, James Halloway, Elbridge Gallup, Augustus Hoffman, John Quinn, Robert Smith, Clinton James, Josiah J. Grindall, George W. Goodrich, Philip Cashmyer (or Cashmeyer), Daniel Steeyer, and a Mr. Cosgrove (first name not listed).

50. *Baltimore Sun*, November 7, 1861.

51. "Baltimore Police History, 1861 Riots. The Civil War's First Dead. 19 April 1861," accessed at https://baltimorecitypolicehistory.com/our-police/riots-1861.html

52. J. Thomas Scharf, *The Chronicles of Baltimore; Being A Complete History of "Baltimore Town" and Baltimore City from the Earliest Period to the Present Time* (Baltimore, Turnbull Brothers, 1874), p. 592; "Baltimore Police History, 1861 Riots. The Civil War's First Dead. 19 April 1861," accessed at https://baltimorecitypolicehistory.com/our-police/riots-1861.html

53. Hanson, *Historical Sketch*, 1866, p. 29, emphasis added.

54. *Ibid.*, p. 42.

55. *Baltimore Daily Exchange*, April 20, 1861.

56. OR, Series 1, volume 2, pp. 7–8; Everett, *Baltimore Riots*, 1957, pp. 334–5.

57. "Baltimore Police History, 1861 Riots. The Civil War's First Dead. 19 April 1861," accessed at https://baltimorecitypolicehistory.com/our-police/riots-1861.html; Edward Ayrault Robinson, "Some Recollections of April 19, 1861," *Maryland Historical Magazine*, Volume 27, 1932, p. 275; Stephen M. Klugewicz, "The First Martyrs: The Sixth Massachusetts and the Baltimore Riot of 1861," *Southern Historian*, Volume 20, 1999, pp. 6–8.

58. Surgeon General Joseph K. Barnes, Joseph Janvier Woodward, Charles Smart, George Alexander Otis, and David Lowe Huntington, *The Medical and Surgical History of the War of the Rebellion. (1861–65)* (Washington, D.C.: Government Printing Office, 1870), 2 (1), p. 58; *New York Times*, April 27, 1861. This article incorrectly called Needham a Private. He was a Corporal.

59. *Hudson North Star*, Hudson, Wisconsin, April 24, 1861.

60. "Baltimore Police History, 1861 Riots. The Civil War's First Dead. 19 April 1861," accessed at https://baltimorecitypolicehistory.com/our-police/riots-1861.html

61. *Baltimore Sun*, November 26, 1878.

62. OR, Series 1, Volume 2, p. 17.

63. de Francias Folsom, Ed., *Our Police. A History of the Baltimore Force from the First Watchman to the Latest Appointee* (Baltimore: J. D. Ehlers & Co., Guggenheimer, Weil & Co., and J. M. Beers, 1888), p. 58.

64. OR, Series 2, Volume 1, pp. 631, 658-9.

65. OR, Series 2, Volume 1, p. 661.

66. George William Brown, "Baltimore and the Nineteenth of April, 1861. A Study of the War." In Herbert B. Adams, Ed., *Johns Hopkins University Studies in Historical and Political Science, Herbert B. Adams, Ed., Extra Volume III* (Baltimore: N. Murray and Isaac Friedenwald, Johns Hopkins University, 1887), p. 54.

67. *Ibid.*, p. 37.

68. Tracy Matthew Melton, "The Lost Lives of George Konig, Sr. & Jr., A Father-Son Tale of Old Fell's Point," *Maryland Historical Magazine*, 101 (3), Fall 2006, pp. 332–61.

69. White, *Forty-Seven Eyewitness Accounts*, 2011, p. 78.

70. *Ibid.*, p. 79.

71. *Ibid.*, p. 80.

72. *Ibid.*, p. 81.

73. The quotations from White are copied as the original handwritten documents were recorded. Spelling, grammar, sentence structure, and punctuation are unchanged from the originals, at times making interpretation difficult.

74. Geoffrey W. Fielding, "Gilmor's Field Report of His Raid in Baltimore County," *Maryland Historical Magazine*, 47 (3), September 1952, p. 234.

75. *Baltimore American and Commercial Advertiser*, May 3, 1861.

76. *Daily National Republican*, Washington, D.C., January 9, 1863; *Civilian and Telegraph*, Cumberland, Maryland, June 20, 1861.

77. *Baltimore South*, July 19, 1861.

78. Matthew Kent, "'Displaced by a Force to Which They Yielded and Could Not Resist': A Historical and Legal Analysis of Mayor and City Counsel [sic] of Baltimore v. Charles Howard et. al." Thesis as J. D. Candidate, University of Maryland Francis King Carey School of Law, accessed at https://digitalcommons.law.umaryland.edu/cgi/viewcontent.cgi?article=1026&context=mlh_pubs

79. John G. Nicolay and John Hay, *Abraham Lincoln. A History*, Volume 4, New York, The Century Co., 1890, pp. 121–122, emphasis added.

80. *Baltimore South*, April 23, 1861.

81. *Baltimore Daily Exchange*, April 20, 1861.

82. John G. Nicolay and John Hay, "Abraham Lincoln: A History. The National Uprising," *Century Illustrated Monthly Magazine* (New York: The Century Company, 1888),Volume 35, New Series 13, November 1887-April 1888, p. 910.

83. OR, Series 2, Volume 2, p. 305.

84. *Baltimore South*, April 23, 1861.

85. *Ibid.*

86. *Baltimore Daily Exchange*, April 20, 1861.

87. Henry Elliot Shepherd, *History of Baltimore, Maryland, from Its Founding as a Town to the Current Year, 1729–1898* (Uniontown, Pennsylvania: S. B. Nelson, 1898), p. 142.

88. *Baltimore South*, April 23, 1861.

89. *Ibid.*

90. Letter, George P. Kane to Chas. Howard, May 3, 1861, "Report of Marshal Kane to the Board of Police Commissioners. An Official Narrative of the Facts in Relation to the Occurrences Which Took Place in this City on Friday, April 19, 1861." OR, Series 2, Volume 1, p. 630, accessed at en.wikisource.org/w/index.php?title=File:Kane_george_defense.pdf&page=3

91. J. Thomas Scharf, *History of Baltimore City and County, from the Earliest Period to the Present Day: Including Biographical Sketches of Their Representative Men* (Philadelphia: Louis H. Everts, J. B. Lippincott & Co., 1881), p. 499.

92. *Baltimore American*, April 20, 1861; *Baltimore South*, April 23, 1861; This original message to Lincoln had multiple iterations. The first,

handwritten from Brown and Hicks, was dated—apparently incorrectly—on April 18. This note was sent by telegraph (correctly dated April 19, but with no time recorded), and a copy was also given to William Prescott Smith and hand-delivered to Washington by the Honorable Reverdy Johnson. Another copy was also carried by Bond, Brune, and Dobbin who met personally with Lincoln and pled the case for the Baltimore and Maryland officials. Handwritten copy accessed at https://s3.us-east-2.amazonaws.com/papersofabrahamlincoln/PAL_Images/PAL_PubMan/1861/04/214554.pdf

93. Telegram, William P. Smith to Abraham Lincoln, April 19, 1861 (time of day not specified), Library of Congress, accessed at www.loc.gov/resource/mal.0924100/?sp=1 and http://hdl.loc.gov/loc.mss/ms000001.mss30189a0924100]]

94. *Baltimore Daily Exchange*, April 22, 1861, accessed at https://s3.us-east-2.amazonaws.com/papersofabrahamlincoln/PAL_Images/PAL_PubMan/1861/04/214545.pdf

95. *Baltimore Sun*, April 22, 1861.

96. Charles W. Mitchell, Ed., *Maryland Voices of the Civil War* (Baltimore: Johns Hopkins University Press, 2007), p. 70, citing reference 59; William Bruce Catton, "John W. Garrett of the Baltimore and Ohio: A Study in Seaport and Railroad Competition, 1820–74," Ph.D. Dissertation, Northwestern University, 1959, p.278.

97. *Baltimore Sun*, April 22, 1861; *Baltimore South*, April 23, 1861.

98. Isaac R. Trimble, Trimble Papers, Introduction by Charles McHenry Howard, "Baltimore and the Crisis of 1861," *Maryland Historical Magazine*, December 1946, 41 (4), pp. 280–281.

99. *Ibid.*, pp. 257–281; Trimble would later volunteer with the Confederate Army where he would attain the rank of Major General and suffer a wound at Gettysburg, resulting in the loss of a leg. Trimble's command would be very short-lived, as he was instructed on May 2 that the immediate danger had passed and that he was to disband the volunteer troops. Furthermore, Charles Howard ordered Trimble on May 2 to retrieve all weapons distributed to the troops and store them safely under guard, later to be returned to the police. Mayor George William Brown followed Howard's letter with his own on May 6, requesting the disbandment of the volunteer forces. Trimble's troops later surprised both the Board of Police Commissioners and the Mayor's Office by requesting payment for their services. Though both Howard and Brown were initially opposed to paying the volunteers, they finally relented, mostly to keep morale high and relationships good with men who obviously could organize against them to become a hostile force in the future. The Mayor and Board agreed to allocate $3,200 for payment to be divided among the many volunteer companies.

100. Trimble, *Baltimore Crisis*, 1946, pp. 268–9; Thomas would be successful, shipping his weaponry toward Baltimore from the South by rail, since the port blockade—the naval part of Lincoln's and Scott's "Anaconda Plan"—had already been put into effect. The initial destination of the weapons was Winchester, Virginia, with subsequent details of shipment to be determined. Thomas estimated that he had been able to procure from Virginia, North Carolina, and South Carolina inventories some 20 32-pound cannons, 24 24-pound cannons, 5 68-pound cannons, and 10,000–15,000 small arms.

101. John C. Robinson, "Baltimore In 1861," *Magazine of American History*, Volume 14, 1885, pp. 257–68.

102. OR, Series 2, Volume 1, p. 630.

103. *Ibid.*

104. George Lovic Pierce Radcliffe, "Governor Thomas H. Hicks of Maryland and the Civil War," Ed. J. M. Vincent. *Johns Hopkins University Studies in Historical and Political Science* (Baltimore: Johns Hopkins Press, November-December 1901), Series 19, Numbers 11–12, p. 57.

105. OR, Series 2, Volume 1, p. 583.

106. *Ex parte Merryman*, 17 F. Cas. 144, 148 (C.C.D. Md. 1861), accessed at https://ipfs.io/ipfs/QmXoypizjW3WknFiJnKLwHCnL72vedxjQkDDP1mXWo6uco/wiki/Ex_parte_Merryman.html

107. Edward G. Everett, "The Baltimore Riots, April, 1861," *Pennsylvania History: A Journal of Mid-Atlantic States*, 24 (4), October 1957, pp. 341–2.

108. OR, Series 1, Volume 2, p. 12.

109. OR, Series 1, Volume 2, p. 13; *Baltimore Sun*, June 11, 1861.

110. OR, Series 1, Volume 2, p. 14.

111. *Ibid.*

112. *Ibid.*, p. 15; Though reference is made here to "written orders," none have survived.

113. Hicks, Thomas H., to the Maryland Senate. Letter, May 4, 1861, accessed at https://msa.maryland.gov/msa/educ/exhibits/hicks/images/case4/hicks_message.pdf

114. *Baltimore Sun*, June 11, 1861.

115. *Cumberland Civilian & Telegraph*, Cumberland, Maryland, June 20, 1861; *Baltimore Sun*, June 22, 1861.

116. *Ibid.*

117. Telegram, Geo. Wm. Brown to President Lincoln, April 20, 1861, accessed at https://s3.us-east-2.amazonaws.com/papersofabrahamlincoln/PAL_Images/PAL_PubMan/1861/04/288804b.pdf

118. OR, Series 1, Volume 2, p. 581.

119. OR, Series 1, Volume 2, pp. 588–9, accessed at https://s3.us-east-2.amazonaws.com/papersofabrahamlincoln/PAL_Images/PAL_PubMan/1861/04/214615.pdf

120. Seward, William H., to Thomas H. Hicks. Letter, April 22, 1861, accessed at https://msa.maryland.gov/msa/educ/exhibits/hicks/images/case1/seward_letter.pdf

121. *Cumberland Civilian & Telegraph*, Cumberland, Maryland, June 20, 1861; *Baltimore Sun*, June 22, 1861.

122. *Baltimore Daily Exchange*, April 22, 1861.

123. Lincoln, *Collected Works*, 1953, Volume 4, pp. 340–1.

124. *Baltimore Sun*, April 22, 1861.
125. *Baltimore Sun*, April 27, 1861.
126. Lincoln, *Collected Works*, 1953, Volume 4, p. 342.
127. Telegram, Geo. Wm. Brown, to President Lincoln, April 21, 1861, accessed at https://s3.us-east-2.amazonaws.com/papersofabrahamlincoln/PAL_Images/PAL_PubMan/1861/04/214595.pdf
128. Mitchell, *Maryland Voices*, 2007, p. 66.
129. *Baltimore South*, April 23, 1861.
130. *Baltimore Sun*, April 22, 1861; Though the general tone and meaning of this communication is not changed by the ambiguities, the original handwritten note says, "Three thousand ~~troops~~ (3000) Northern troops are reported to be at Cockeysville. Intense excitement prevails. Churches have been dismissed, and the people are arriving (arising?) in mass. To prevent terrific bloodshed, the results of your interview and arrangements with President Lincoln are awaited. When do you expect to return to Baltimore." The slightly different interpretations center around the word "arming" or "arriving" or "arising." The handwritten note has "arriving," with an editor's insertion above the word saying "(arising?)." The newspaper article uses "arming." In all cases, the gist of the note is the same, accessed at https://s3.us-east-2.amazonaws.com/papersofabrahamlincoln/PAL_Images/PAL_PubMan/1861/05/228551.pdf
131. Everett, *Baltimore Riots*, 1957, p. 340.
132. The Northern Central Railroad was originally the Baltimore and Susquehanna Railroad. It was created as a financial entity by the combination of four other railroads: the Baltimore & Susquehanna, the York & Maryland, the York & Cumberland, and the Susquehanna; Maryland Center for History and Culture Library Department. "Traveling through History: Stories of the Northern Central Railroad during the Civil War," accessed at http://www.mdhs.org/underbelly/2016/12/01/-travelling-through-history-stories-of-the-northern-central-railroad-during-the-civil-war/
133. *Baltimore South*, April 22, 1861.
134. Franklin Ellis and Samuel Evans. *History of Lancaster County, Pennsylvania: With Biographical Sketches of Many of Its Pioneers and Prominent Men* (Philadelphia: Everts & Peck, 1883), Volume 1, pp. 89–90.
135. *Baltimore Sun*, April 22, 1861; The General was incorrectly identified in this *Baltimore Sun* article as "General Wikoff," rather than the correct "General Wynkoop;" "Quincey" was otherwise spelled "Quincy."
136. *Baltimore South*, April 23, 1861.
137. *Ibid.*
138. *Baltimore South*, April 23, 1861.
139. *Baltimore Sun*, April 23, 1861.
140. *Ibid.*
141. *Philadelphia Press*, April 25, 1861.
142. OR, Series 1, Volume 2, p. 28.
143. Letter, George P. Kane to Chas. Howard, President of the Board of Police, "Report of Marshal Kane to the Board of Police Commissioners, May 3, 1861." In Kane, George P. (1820–1878) Archives of Maryland (Biographical Series). MSA SC 3520–12478, accessed at http://www.msa.md.gov/megafile/msa/speccol/sc3500/sc3520/012400/012478/html/12478bio.html
144. *New York Daily Tribune*, May 7, 1861.
145. *Baltimore Sun*, April 23, 1861.
146. Trimble, "Baltimore and the Crisis of 1861," 1946, p. 261.
147. *Baltimore Sun*, April 24, 1861.
148. *Baltimore Sun*, April 24, 1861.
149. Militia organization in Baltimore in 1861 was complex. Newspapers reported the following Baltimore militias initially responding to the crisis:
First Regiment of Light Artillery—Eagle Artillery, Junior Artillery, City Guards.
Fifth Regiment of Infantry—Law Greys, Zouave Law Greys, Shields Guards, Jackson Guards
First Rifle Regiment—Wells and McComas Rifles
Fifty-third Regiment—Maryland Guards, Independent Greys, The Maryland Line
Other local militias included the Home Guards, the "Bummers Club" (Hook and Ladder Company #1), and uniformed volunteers, otherwise unspecified.
In addition, militias from nearby Maryland counties also participated; *Baltimore Sun*, April 22, 1861; *Baltimore South*, April 23, 1861.
150. *Baltimore Sun*, April 27, 1861.
151. Letter, A. to Lieutenant-General Scott, April 25, 1861, In John G. Nicolay and John Hay, Eds., *Abraham Lincoln: Complete Works, Comprising His Speeches, Letters, State Papers, and Miscellaneous Writings* (New York: The Century Co., 1894), Volume 2, p. 38.
152. Nicolay, *Abraham Lincoln: Complete Works*, 1894, pp. 39, 45–46, 54, 85.
153. Henry J. Raymond, *Abraham Lincoln, His Life and Times, Volume 1* (Chicago: Thompson and Thomas, 1891), .p. 389.
154. *Baltimore Sun*, May 10, 1861.
155. *Baltimore Daily Exchange*, May 7–15, 1861.
156. Butler, Benj. F. *Autobiography and Personal Reminiscences of Major-General Benj. F. Butler. Butler's Book. A Review of His Legal, Political, and Military Career* (Boston: A. M Thayer & Co., 1892), p. 227.
157. OR, Series 1, Volume 2, pp. 30–2.
158. OR, Series 1, Volume 2, p. 28.
159. *Ibid.*
160. John R. Kenly, Kenly Papers, 1861–1872. Maryland Center for History and Culture, MS 1696.
161. OR, Series 1, Volume 2, p. 29.
162. Morgan Dix, *Memoirs of John Adams Dix Compiled By His Son Morgan Dix* (New York, Harper & Brothers, Franklin Square, 1883), Volume 2, p. 36.
163. Semmes, Raphael. "Vignettes of Maryland History," *Maryland Historical Magazine*, 40 (1), March 1945, pp. 51–2.

164. *Baltimore Sun*, May 22, 1861.
165. *Baltimore Sun*, June 3, 1861.
166. OR, Series 2, Volume 1, p, 706.
167. *Raftsman's Journal*, Clearfield, Pennsylvania, October 21, 1863.
168. Lederman, Martin S. "The Law (?) of the Lincoln Assassination," *Columbia Law Review*, 118 (2), March 2018, pp. 323–490.

Chapter 12

1. Terry Alford, *Fortune's Fool: The Life of John Wilkes Booth* (Oxford and New York: Oxford University Press, 2015), p. 110.
2. *New York Tribune*, June 28, 1861.
3. Elliot G. Storke and L. P. Brockett. *A Complete History of the Great American Rebellion, Embracing Its Causes, Events and Consequences, with Biographical Sketches and Portraits* (Auburn, New York: Auburn Publishing Company, 1865), Volume 1, p. 275.
4. Storke and Brockett, *Complete History*, 1865, p. 276.
5. Anonymous, "The Arrest of Marshal Kane, Or, How It Took Eighteen Hundred Men To Capture One Man." In *The Grayjackets: and How They Lived, Fought and Died, For Dixie. With Incidents & Sketches of Life in the Confederacy, By A Confederate* (Richmond: Jones Brothers & Co., 1867), pp. 489–90.
6. *Frank Leslie's Illustrated Newspaper*, July 13, 1861, p. 129, accessed at https://archive.org/details/franklesliesilluv1112lesl/page/128
7. *Baltimore Sun*, June 28, 1861.
8. *Baltimore American and Commercial Advertiser*, June 28, 1861; Baltimore *South*, June 27, 1861; OR, Series 1, Volume 2, pp. 140–1; OR, Series 2, Volume 1, pp. 623–5; General Banks' Proclamation of June 27th, Baltimore City Archives, BCA BMS33-4-1, bms33_4_1_6-0017, accessed at mdhistory.msa.maryland.gov/bca_bms33_4_1/bca_bms33_4_1_6/html/bms33_4_1_6-0017.html
9. OR, Series 1, Volume 2, p. 141.
10. *Baltimore South*, June 27, 1861.
11. Ezra J. Warner, *Generals In Blue, Lives of Union Commanders* (Baton Rouge: Louisiana State University Press, 1992), pp. 261–22, accessed at http://ranger95.com/civil_war_us/generals_of_the_union/john_reese_kenly.htm and https://fr.wikipedia.org/wiki/John_Reese_Kenly
12. OR, Series 1, Volume 2, p. 139.
13. OR, Series 2, Volume 1, p. 622.
14. *Ibid.*, pp. 621–2.
15. *Ibid.*, p. 627.
16. *Baltimore American and Commercial Advertiser*, June 28, 1861.
17. *Baltimore South*, June 27, 1861.
18. OR, Series 2, Volume 1, pp. 586.
19. OR, Series 1, Volume 2, p. 145.
20. *Ibid.*, p. 147.
21. OR, Series 1, Volume 2, p. 148.
22. *Ibid.*, p. 155.
23. *Ibid.*, p. 156.
24. OR, Series 2, Volume 1, pp. 619–21.
25. Mark E. Neely, Jr., "The Lincoln Administration and Arbitrary Arrests: A Reconsideration," *Journal of the Abraham Lincoln Association*, 5 (1), 1983, p. 8, accessed at https://quod.lib.umich.edu/j/jala/2629860.0005.103/--lincoln-administration-and-arbitrary-arrests?rgn=main;view=fulltext
26. David Detzer, *Dissonance: The Turbulent Days Between Fort Sumpter and Bull Run* (New York: Harvest Book, Harcourt, Inc., 2006), p. 276.
27. Neely, *Lincoln Administration*, 1983, p. 10.
28. Neely, *Lincoln Administration*, 1983, pp. 6–24.
29. OR, Series 2, Volume 1, p. 609, emphasis added.
30. *Ibid.*, pp. 609–10.
31. *Ibid.*, p. 618.
32. *Ibid.*, p. 617.
33. *Baltimore South*, May 17, 1861.
34. Charles B. Clark, "Suppression and Control of Maryland, 1861–1865; A Study of Federal-State Relations During Civil Conflict," *Maryland Historical Magazine*, 54 (3), Sept 1959, pp. 268–70.
35. Report of the Police Commissioners of Baltimore City, with Accompanying Documents, Document L, House of Delegates, Baltimore City Archives, Electronic Baltimore City Police Records, Police Department Annual Reports, 1861, BCA BMS33-4-1, bms33_4_1_6-0003, ccessed at mdhistory.msa.maryland.gov/bca_bms33_4_1/bca_bms33_4_1_6/html/bms33_4_1_6-0003.html
36. *Baltimore American and Commercial Advertiser*, June 28, 1861; *Baltimore South*, June 27, 1861; *Baltimore Sun*, June 28, 1861; Appendix, Preamble and Resolutions Adopted by the Board of Police, on June 27th, Baltimore City Archives, BCA BMS33-4-1 bms33_4_1_6-0019, accessed at mdhistory.msa.maryland.gov/bca_bms33_4_1/bca_bms33_4_1_6/html/bms33_4_1_6-0019.html
37. Appendix, General Banks' Proclamation of July 1st, Baltimore City Archives, BCA BMS33-4-1 bms33_4_1_6-0021, accessed at mdhistory.msa.maryland.gov/bca_bms33_4_1/bca_bms33_4_1_6/html/bms33_4_1_6-0021.html; OR, Series 1, Volume 2, pp. 141–142.
38. *Ibid.* p. 142.
39. *Baltimore American and Commercial Advertiser*, June 28, 1861.
40. *New York Daily Tribune*, June 28, 1861.
41. *Baltimore American and Commercial Advertiser*, June 28, 1861.
42. OR, Series 2, Volume 1, pp. 591–592.
43. *Frank Leslie's Illustrated Newspaper*, July 13, 1861, p. 130.
44. *Baltimore American and Commercial Advertiser*, June 29, 1861.
45. *Frank Leslie's Illustrated Newspaper*, July 13, 1861, p. 130.

46. *Frank Leslie's Illustrated Newspaper*, July 20, 1861, p. 147.

47. The Baltimore Police Bill, Laws of Maryland, Chapter 7, Acts of 1860.

48. The debate concerning the payment of police salaries to the force relieved of its duties but allegedly still on the payroll would continue for years. In 1867 the First Branch of the City Council voted to pay the claims of the furloughed police of 1861, with interest. The principal was $83,176.15, and with interest, court costs, Commissioners' salaries, and lawyers' fees ballooned to $115,475, to be covered by the tax levy of 1868. Northern newspapers found this payment to be an outrage because it would, in effect, be rewarding men who ostensibly were plotting against federal forces. These police were said to have "protected unlawful combinations of traitors, organized for resistance to the laws of the United States; concealed the existence of hidden deposits of arms and ammunition; encouraged contraband trade with the Rebels in open arms, and, while in this way giving aid and comfort to public enemies, stealthily awaited an opportunity to join the armies of the slaveholders' Rebellion;" *Baltimore Sun*, November 21, 1867; *Philadelphia Inquirer*, November 22, 1867.

49. OR, Series 1, Volume 2, p. 140.

50. OR, Series 2, Volume 1, p. 626.

51. *Pennsylvania Daily Telegraph*, Harrisburg, Pennsylvania, June 29, 1861; *Baltimore Sun*, June 29, 1861.

52. *Baltimore American and Commercial Advertiser*, June 29, 1861.

53. Snethen, Worthington G., to Winfield Scott. Letter, June 29, 1861. Abraham Lincoln Papers, Library of Congress, accessed at https://www.loc.gov/resource/mal.1044600/?sp=2 and https://www.loc.gov/resource/mal.1044600/?sp=1 and https://s3.us-east-2.amazonaws.com/papersofabrahamlincoln/PAL_Images/PAL_PubMan/1861/09/230308.pdf

54. *Baltimore Daily Exchange*, June 29, 1861; *Baltimore South*, June 28, 1861.

55. Letter, Nathaniel P. Banks to William H. Seward, July 9, 1861, Abraham Lincoln Papers, Library of Congress, accessed at https://www.loc.gov/resource/mal.1070100/?sp=1 and https://s3.us-east-2.amazonaws.com/papersofabrahamlincoln/PAL_Images/PAL_PubMan/1861/07/215163.pdf

56. OR, Series 1, Volume 2, pp. 18–9.

57. OR, Series 2, Volume 2, p. 796.

58. *Baltimore American and Commercial Advertiser*, as quoted in the *Pennsylvania Daily Telegraph*, Harrisburg, Pennsylvania, July 20, 1861, and *The Press*, Philadelphia, Pennsylvania, July 18, 1861.

59. *Ibid.*

60. *Baltimore Sun*, November 12, 1861.

61. *Baltimore Exchange*, July 16, 1861.

62. *The Times*, Philadelphia, Pennsylvania, June 24, 1878.

63. OR, Series 2, Volume 1, pp. 631–3.

64. Frank Key Howard in John A. Marshall, *American Bastille. A History of the Illegal Arrests and Imprisonment of American Citizens During the Late Civil War* (Philadelphia: Thomas W. Hartley, 1871), Eighth Edition, p. 643, emphasis in the original.

65. OR, Series 2, Volume 1, p. 567.

66. OR, Series 1, Volume 5, p. 193.

67. Letter, Major General George B. McClellen to General Nathaniel Banks, September 12, 1861, in Edward McPherson, *The Political History of the United States of America During the Great Rebellion* (Washington: Philp [sic] & Solomons, 1865), Second Edition, p. 153.

68. OR, Series 2, Volume 2, p. 793.

69. Charles W. Mitchell, Ed., *Maryland Voices of the Civil War* Baltimore: Johns Hopkins University Press, 2007), p. 235, citing Frederick W. Seward *Reminiscences of A War-Time Statesman and Diplomat: 1830-1915* (New York and London: G. P. Putnam's Sons, The Knickerbocker Press, 1916), p. 177.

70. Christopher Dell, *Lincoln and the War Democrats: The Grand Erosion of Conservative Tradition* (Rutherford, New Jersey: Fairleigh Dickinson University Press, 1975), p. 88.

71. Severn Teackle Wallis, *Writings of Severn Teackle Wallis, Memorial Edition, Vol. II, Critical and Political* (Baltimore: John Murphy & Co., 1896), pp. 250-2, accessed at https://play.google.com/books/reader?id=nOVcAAAAcAAJ&printsec=frontcover&output=reader&hl=en&pg=GBS.PA252

72. OR, Series 2, Volume 1, pp. 676–677.

73. *Ibid.*, p. 682.

74. *Ibid.*, p. 684.

75. *Ibid.*, p. 685.

76. *Ibid.*, p. 688.

77. The following men were arrested as part of this broad roundup of legislators: William G. Harrison, Legislature, Baltimore County; J. Lawrence Jones, House, Talbot County; Dr. J. Hanson Thomas, Legislature, Baltimore County; Ross Winans, Legislature; Thomas J. Claggett, House, Frederick County; Lawrence Sangston, Legislature, Baltimore County; Dr. Andrew A. Lynch, Senate, Baltimore County; Leonard G. Quinlan, House of Delegates, Baltimore County; Robert W. Denison, House of Delegates, Baltimore County; William R. Miller, Legislature; Thomas J. McKaig, Maryland Senate; Henry M. Warfield, Legislature, Baltimore City; Josiah H. Gordon, Allegany County, Legislature; E. G. Kilbourne, Speaker of the House; Dr. Richard C. Mackubin, Allegany County, Legislature; William E. Salmon, House, Frederick County; S. Teackle Wallis, Legislature; T. Parkin Scott, House, Baltimore City; Clarke J. Durant, House, St. Mary's County; Andrew Kessler, Jr., House, Frederick County; Henry M. Morfit, Baltimore City; Charles H. Pitts, Legislature, Baltimore; James U. Dennis, Legislature, Somerset County; John J. Heckart, Legislature, Cecil County; James W. Maxwell, Legislature, Elkton; George W. Landing, House, Worcester County; Philip F. Rasin,

Legislature, Kent County; Bernard Mills, Legislature, Carroll County; Oscar Miles, Senate, St. Mary's County; John M. Brewer, Chief Reading Clerk of the Senate; S. P. Carmack, Assistant Clerk of the Senate; F. Key Howard, Editor, *Exchange*, not Legislature; Thomas W. Hall, Jr., Editor, Baltimore *South*, not Legislature; John C. Brune, Baltimore City; Henry May, U.S. Congress, not Maryland Legislature; E. A. Hanson; Thomas E. Schleigh, Doorkeeper of the House; Charles Macgill, Senate, Hagerstown; Milton Y. Kidd, Clerk of the House, Cecil County; Thomas H. Moore, Assistant Clerk of the House, Baltimore County; William Kilgour, Reading Clerk and Secretary of the Senate; Robert W. Rasin, not in the Legislature, but he recruited soldiers to Confederate Army;

Also, Mr. Elkins, Mr. Riley, John Hagan, hotel-keepers, Frederick City; *Maryland Times*, Baltimore, September 19, 1861; OR, Series 2, Volume 1, pp. 619–21; OR, Series 2, Volume 1, pp. 667–75; *Ibid.*, pp. 649–50; OR, Series 2, Volume 2, pp. 226–8; *New York Times*, September 17 and 19, 1861; *Cincinnati Daily Press*, September 14, 1861; *Baltimore Sun*, September 14, 1861; Letter, Major General John A. Dix to Simon Cameron, Secretary of War, September 13, 1861, The Abraham Lincoln Papers at the Library of Congress, General Correspondence, 1833–1916, accessed at https://memory.loc.gov/cgi-bin/ampage?collI d=mal&fileName=mal1/116/1163000/malpage. db&recNum=0&tempFile=./temp/~ammem_cQx Z&filecode=mal&itemnum=1&ndocs=1; General Assembly, Special Session, July 30-August 7, 1861, Maryland Archives, Historical List, accessed at msa.maryland.gov/msa/speccol/sc2600/sc2685/ genassem/html/ga1861july.html

78. Mitchell, *Maryland Voices*, 2007, p. 141.
79. Mitchell, *Maryland Voices*, 2007, p. 291.
80. Roy P. Basler, Ed., *Collected Works of Abraham Lincoln* (Ann Arbor, Michigan: University of Michigan Digital Library Production Services, 2001), Volume 4, p. 523.
81. OR, Series 2, Volume 2, pp. 113, 225–6, 230, 285.

Chapter 13

1. Roll of Prisoners of War at Fort McHenry, Baltimore, Maryland, Selected Records of the War Department Relating to Confederate Prisoners of War, 1861–1865, National Archives Microfilm Publications, Microcopy No. 598. Roll 145, Volumes 425–427, Registers of Prisoners at Various Military Prisons, 1861–65, Washington, The National Archives, National Archives and Records Service, General Services Administration, 1965, p. 54, accessed at archive.org/stream/ selectedrecordso0145unit#page/n92/mode/1up
2. Charles W. Mitchell, Ed., *Maryland Voices of the Civil War* (Baltimore: Johns Hopkins University Press, 2007), p. 274.
3. OR, Series 2, Volume 1, pp. 592–3.

4. Parole and General Order No. 52, Col. George P. Kane, August 12, 1861, ccessed at www. fold3.com/image/252335654
5. Rev. Dr. T. D. Witherspoon, "Prison Life at Fort McHenry," *Southern Historical Society*, Richmond, Volume 8, January-December 1880, pp. 111–5.
6. Frank Key Howard in John A. Marshall, *American Bastille. A History of the Illegal Arrests and Imprisonment of American Citizens During the Late Civil War* (Philadelphia: Thomas W. Hartley, 1871), Eighth Edition, pp. 645–6.
7. Member of the Maryland Legislature, Lawrence Sangston, *The Bastilles of the North* (Baltimore: Kelly, Hedian & Piet, 1863).
8. For a complete description of the members of the Maryland Legislature who were arrested and imprisoned, along with the charges filed against them and the locations of their imprisonment, see OR, Series 2, Volume 1, pp. 667–75.
9. OR, Series 2, Volume 1, p. 593.
10. *Baltimore Sun*, September 12, 1861.

Chapter 14

1. John A. Marshall, *American Bastille. A History of the Illegal Arrests and Imprisonment of American Citizens During the Late Civil War* (Philadelphia, Thomas W. Hartley, 1871), 22nd edition, p. 653.
2. Selected records of the War Department Relating to Confederate Prisoners of War, 1861–1865, List of Prisoners Received and Accounts of Prisoners, 1861–1862, Fort Lafayette, NYH, General Register No. 1, National Archives and Records Administration.
3. Anonymous, but attributed to William W. Gilchrist, "A Prisoner," *Two Months In Fort Lafayette* (New York, publisher not listed, 1862) p. 5.
4. Charles B. Clark, "Suppression and Control of Maryland, 1861–1865; A Study of Federal-State Relations During Civil Conflict," *Maryland Historical Magazine*, 54 (3), September 1959, p. 243.
5. Gilchrist, *Two Months*, 1862, p. 20.
6. *Ibid.*, p. 25.
7. Marshall, *American Bastille*, 1871, p. 654.
8. Likely referring to Mrs. George S. Gelston, a resident of Fort Hamilton famed for her charitable efforts to soothe the plight of prisoners held at Fort Lafayette.
9. *New York Times*, September 24, 1861.
10. *Harper's Weekly*, Volume 5, Number 245, September 7, 1861, p.571.
11. New York Times, October 2, 1864.
12. OR, Series 2, Volume 2, p. 156.
13. OR, Series 2, Volume 1, p. 614.
14. Letter, John W. Davis to President Abraham Lincoln, September 20, 1861, Library of Congress, accessed at https://s3.us-east-2.amazonaws. com/papersofabrahamlincoln/PAL_Images/PAL_ PubMan/1861/09/215707.pdf and https://s3.us-east-2.amazonaws.com/papersofabrahamlincoln/ PAL_Images/PAL_PubMan/1861/09/202269.pdf

15. OR, Series 2, Volume 2, p. 830.
16. Anonymous, "Personal Journal of a 'Prisoner of State' in Forts McHenry, Monroe, La Fayette, and Warren," in: Member of the Maryland Legislature. *The Bastilles of the North* (Baltimore: Kelly, Hedian & Piet, 1862), pp. 22–23.
17. *Ibid.*, pp. 23–4.
18. *Ibid.*, pp. 26–7.
19. *Ibid.*, pp. 39–40.
20. *Baltimore Sun*, July 23, 1861.
21. Mitchell, *Maryland Voices*, 2007, pp. 272–3; Letter, George P. Kane to His Excellency the President, September 30, 1861, OR, Series 2, Volume 1, p. 648.
22. OR, Series 2, Volume 1, pp. 649–50.
23. Anonymous, "Personal Journal," 1862, p. 45.
24. Marshall, *American Bastille*, 1871, p. 668.
25. *Ibid.*, p. 668–9.
26. OR, Series 2, Volume 1, p. 597.
27. OR, Series 2, Volume 1, p. 639.
28. *Ibid.*, pp. 644–5.
29. *Ibid.*, pp. 634–5.
30. Letter, Lieutenant-Colonel Martin Burke to United States Marshal Robert Murray, October 24, 1861, cited by Frank Key Howard, in Marshall, *American Bastille*, 1871, p. 671.
31. Letter, Charles Howard to Secretary of War Simon Cameron, October 23, 1861, cited by Frank Key Howard, in Marshall, *American Bastille*, 1871, p. 676.
32. OR, Series 2, Volume 1, p. 567.
33. *Ibid.*, p. 675.
34. *Ibid.*, p. 664.
35. *Ibid.*, p. 635.
36. *Ibid.*, p. 636.
37. *Ibid.*, p. 637.
38. *Ibid.*, p. 638.
39. *Ibid.*, p. 641.
40. *Ibid.*, p. 640.
41. *Ibid.*, p. 643.
42. Frank Key Howard, in Marshall, *American Bastille*, 1871, p. 679.
43. *Ibid.*, pp. 680–81.
44. Anonymous, "Personal Journal," 1862, p. 46.
45. Frank Key Howard, *Fourteen Months in American Bastilles* (Baltimore: Kelly, Hedian & Piet, 1863), p. 46.
46. Charlotte Rebecca Woglom Bangs (Mrs. Bleecker Bangs), *Reminiscences of Old New Utrecht and Gowanus* (Brooklyn: Brooklyn Eagle Press, 1912), p. 162.
47. U.S. Selected Federal Census Nonpopulation Schedules, New York, Kings, New Utrecht, 1850; U.S. Census, 1850; Find-A-Grave Index.
48. *New York Times*, October 2, 1864.
49. Letter, George Brown to Frederick Brune, September 28, 1861, Maryland Center for History and Culture, Brune-Randall Family Papers, 1782–1972, MS 2004, Box 6.
50. Samuel Kirk and Son were goldsmiths, silversmiths, and jewelers in Baltimore, located at 172 West Baltimore Street. Samuel Kirk was also a Director of the Mechanics Savings Bank of Baltimore.
51. Letter, George Brown to Emily (Barton) Brune, November 26, 1861, Incoming Letters, Emily [Barton] Brune, Maryland Center for History and Culture, Brune-Randall Family Papers, 1782–1972, MS 2004, Box 15.
52. OR, Series 2, Volume 1, p. 651.
53. *New York Daily Tribune*, October 31, 1861.
54. OR, Series 2, Volume 1, p. 656.
55. *Ibid.*, p. 657.
56. *Ibid.*, p. 653.

Chapter 15

1. Lonnie Speer, *Portals To Hell, Military Prisons of the Civil War* (Mechanicsburg, Pennsylvania: Stackpole Books, 1997), p. 195.
2. *Richmond Dispatch*, December 5, 1861.
3. Frank Key Howard in John A. Marshall, *American Bastille. A History of the Illegal Arrests and Imprisonment of American Citizens During the Late Civil War* (Philadelphia: Thomas W. Hartley, 1871), Eighth Edition, p. 703.
4. Member of the Maryland Legislature, Lawrence Sangston, *The Bastilles of the North* (Baltimore: Kelly, Hedian & Piet, 1863), p. 72.
5. Selected Records of the War Department Relating to Confederate Prisoners of War, 1861–1865, accessed at archive.org/stream/selectedrecordso0137unit#page/n285/mode/1up and archive.org/stream/selectedrecordso0137unit#page/n286/mode/1up and archive.org/stream/selectedrecordso0137unit#page/n293/mode/1up; *Baltimore Sun*, November 1, 1861.
6. Alexander Hunter, "Confederate Prisoners In Boston," *New England Magazine* (Boston: Warren F. Kellogg, September 1900-February 1901), New Series, Volume 23, p. 693.
7. *Ibid.*, p. 695.
8. *Ibid.*, p. 697.
9. Sangston, *Bastilles of the North*, 1863, pp. 73–4.
10. Selected Records of the War Department Relating to Confederate Prisoners of War, 1861–1865, accessed at archive.org/stream/selectedrecordso0137unit#page/n342/mode/1up; NARA, M598, Roll #137, Selected Records of the War, Department Relating to Confederate Prisoners of War, 1861–1865, Volume 409–413, Records Relating to Individual Prisons or Stations, Fort Warren, Mass., Military Prison, Letters Sent and Registers of Prisoners, 1861–1865; NARA, M598, Roll #85, Selected Records of the War, Department Relating to Confederate Prisoners of War, 1861–1865, Volume 284–286, Records Relating to Individual Prisons or Stations, Fort Lafayette, New York, Military Prison, General Register of Prisoners and Accounts of Money and Effects of Prisoners, 1861–1865.
11. OR, Series 2, Volume 1, p. 614.

12. Howard in Marshall, *American Bastille*, 1871, p. 688.

13. Samuel Gridley Howe, "A Letter of the Sanitary Condition of the Troops in the Neighborhood of Boston" (Washington: Government Printing Office, 1861), p. 8, accessed at https://books.google.com/books?id=Wt1JAQAAMAAJ&pg=PA3&dq=%22troops+in+the+neighborhood+of+boston%22&hl=en&sa=X&ved=0ahUKEwjzpcWXwePaAhUR5GMKHQx7BDEQ6AEILTAB#v=onepage&q=%22troops%20in%20the%20neighborhood%20of%20boston%22&f=false, as cited in Minor H. McLain, "The Military Prison at Fort Warren," in William Best Hesseltine, Ed., *Civil War Prisons* (Kent, Ohio: Kent State University Press, 1962), p. 33.

14. Howe, "Sanitary Condition," 1861, p. 12.

15. McLain, "Military Prison," 1962, p. 34.

16. *Richmond Dispatch*, December 5, 1861.

17. *Baltimore Sun*, November 7, 1861.

18. *Baltimore Sun*, November 7, 1861.

19. Howard in Marshall, *American Bastille*, 1871, p. 704.

20. Letter, Josiah Gordon to Kate Gordon, November 1, 1861, Josiah H. Gordon Papers (M-2886.3), William L. Clements Library, University of Michigan, Ann Arbor, Michigan.

21. Sangston, *Bastilles of the North*, 1863, p. 96.

22. *Ibid.*, p. 119.

23. Sangston, *Bastilles of the North*, 1863, pp. 120–1.

24. Charles W. Mitchell, Ed., *Maryland Voices of the Civil War* (Baltimore: Johns Hopkins University Press, 2007), p. 269.

25. Letter, George William Brown to Dr. George Shattuck, February 9, 1862, George William Brown Collection, Maryland Center for History and Culture, MS 2398.

26. Letter, George William Brown to Eleanor Shattuck, June 18, 1862, George William Brown Collection, Maryland Center for History and Culture, MS 2398.

27. Letter, George William Brown to Dr. George Shattuck, November 19, 1862, George William Brown Collection, Maryland Center for History and Culture, MS 2398.

28. OR, Series 2, Volume 1, pp. 661–2.

29. *Ibid.*, p. 665.

30. *Ibid.*, p. 660.

31. Letter, George William Brown to Dr. George Shattuck, February 21, 1862, George William Brown Collection, Maryland Center for History and Culture, MS 2398.

32. OR, Series 2, Volume 1, p. 660.

33. *Baltimore South*, November 30, 1861; Geo. P. Kane Parole Letter, November 29, 1861, Letters Received by the Adjutant General, 1861–1870, year 1861, File K443, Civil War—Union, NARA M619, Archives #300368, RG 94, Roll 34, accessed at https://www.fold3.com/image/299770702 and https://www.fold3.com/image/299770697

34. Geo. P. Kane Parole Modification, 1861 (otherwise undated), Letters Received by the Adjutant General, 1861–1870, year 1861, File K443, Civil War—Union, NARA M619, Archives #300368, RG 94, Roll 34; accessed at https://www.fold3.com/image/299770694

35. *Baltimore South*, December 14, 1861.

36. *Baltimore Sun*, December 2, 1861.

37. Sangston, *Bastilles of the North*, 1863, p. 117.

38. Mitchell, *Maryland Voices*, 2007, p. 281.

39. Sangston, *Bastilles of the North*, 1863, p. 87.

40. John William Jones, *The Davis Memorial Volume; Or, Our Dead President, Jefferson Davis and the World's Tribute to His Memory* (Richmond: B. F. Johnson & Co., 1890), p. 451.

41. Sangston, *Bastilles of the North*, 1863, pp. 82–3.

42. Order of the President of the United States, by Edwin M. Stanton, Secretary of War, February 27, 1862, accessed at https://s3.us-east-2.amazonaws.com/papersofabrahamlincoln/PAL_Images/PAL_PubMan/1862/02/293491.pdf

43. OR, Series 2, Volume 4, pp. 398–9.

44. Howard in Marshall, *American Bastille*, 1871, p. 705.

45. Howard in Marshall, *American Bastille*, 1871, p. 706.

46. John Eager Howard Papers, 1662–1919, Maryland Center for History and Culture, MS 469, Box 27, Folder 6.

47. OR, Series 2, Volume 1, p. 656.

48. *Ibid.*, p 657.

49. *Baltimore Sun*, November 29, 1862.

50. *Semi-Weekly Observer*, Fayetteville, North Carolina, December 15, 1862.

51. *Baltimore Sun*, December 1, 1862.

52. Mitchell, *Maryland Voices*, 2007, pp. 291–2; George William Brown Collection, Maryland Center for History and Culture, January–December 1862, MS 2398.

53. OR, Series 2, Volume 1, p. 667. After Release from Prison.

Chapter 16

1. OR, Series 2, Volume 1, pp. 666–667; Charles W. Mitchell, Ed., *Maryland Voices of the Civil War* (Baltimore: Johns Hopkins University Press, 2007), p. 291.

2. *New York Daily Tribune*, December 18, 1862, italics in the original.

3. *Baltimore South*, January 25, 1862; *Baltimore Sun*, January 27, 1862.

4. *Richmond Dispatch*, February 22, 1864; *Alexandria Gazette*, Alexandria, Virginia, March 3, 1863; *Richmond Whig*, March 10, 1863; *Baltimore Sun*, May 5, 1863.

5. *Baltimore Sun*, March 3, 1863; *Richmond Dispatch*, March 9, 1863.

6. *Baltimore Sun*, April 25, 1863.

7. *Richmond Whig*, March 10, 1863; *Alexandria Gazette*, Alexandria, Virginia, March 3, 1863; *Richmond Dispatch*, March 9, 1863.

8. *Baltimore Sun*, May 5, 1863; *Philadelphia Inquirer*, June 22, 1863.

9. Letter, Simon Cameron to Abraham Lincoln, November 1, 1863, Abraham Lincoln Papers, Library of Congress, accessed at https://www.loc.gov/resource/mal.2773900/?sp=1 https://s3.us-east-2.amazonaws.com/papersofabrahamlincoln/PAL_Images/PAL_PubMan/1863/11/222113.pdf

10. *Baltimore Sun*, November 17, 1863.

11. *Pittsburgh Daily Commercial*, November 16, 1863; *Cincinnati Enquirer*, November 18, 1863; *Buffalo Commercial*, November 20, 1863.

12. Jefferson Davis, in Lynda L. Crist, Mary S. Dix, and Kenneth H. Williams, Eds., *Papers of Jefferson Davis* (Baton Rouge, Louisiana: Louisiana State University Press, 1997), January-September 1863, Volume 9, pp. 285-6.

13. OR Navies, Series 1, Volume 17, pp. 515-6.

14. *Catholic Herald* (Philadelphia), at least 30 entries between December 18, 1834, and June 28, 1838; Martin ran the business selling religious books and merchandise from early 1835 to 1838. He was connected to the Fielding Lucas, Jr., Company in Baltimore, supplier of Bibles, books and religious products, located at 138 Baltimore Street, accessed at https://thecatholicnewsarchive.org/?a=cl&cl=CL1&sp=cst&e=-------en-20-cst-1-byDA-txt-txIN-%22election+day%22------, archived as the *Catholic Standard and Times*, in The Catholic News Archive.

15. *New York Herald*, March 12, 1842; Patrick Charles Martin is not to be confused with Colonel Robert Martin, another Confederate who attempted to burn New York City.

16. *Army and Navy Chronicle*, Washington, D.C., Volume 13, January 22, 1842, p. 13; *New York Herald*, March 12, 1842.

17. Adam Mayers, *Dixie and the Dominion: Canada, the Confederacy, and the War for the Union* (Toronto: Dundern Press, 2003), p 159; William A. Tidwell, James O. Hall, and David Winfred Gaddy, *Come Retribution: The Confederate Secret Service and the Assassination of Lincoln* (Jackson, Mississippi: University Press of Mississippi, 1988), pp. 329-30.

18. Mayers, *Dixie and the Dominion*, 2003, p.159; George Alfred Townsend, alias GATH, "Thomassen. The Dynamite Fiend Amongst the Assassins of President Lincoln," *New York Daily Graphic*, March 22, 1876; The same report of Kane's response to questions about his association with John Wilkes Booth, as reported by GATH, was also published in the *St. Albans Daily Messenger*, March 27, 1876.

19. OR Navies, Series 1, Volume 4, pp. 553-6; J. Thomas Scharf, *History of the Confederate Navy From Its Organization to the Surrender of Its Last Vessel* (New York: Rogers & Sherwood, 1887), p. 112; George Nicholas Hollins, "Autobiography of Commodore George Nicholas Hollins, CSA," *Maryland Historical Magazine*, September 1939, 34 (3), pp. 228-43.

20. *Mackay's Montreal Directory for 1863-64 (corrected to July 1, 1863)* (Montreal: John Lovell, 1863), p. 202.

21. Barry Sheehy, *Montreal. City of Secrets* (Montreal: Baraka Books of Montreal, 2017), p. 44.

22. *Mackay's Montreal Directory for 1864-65 (corrected to July 1, 1864)* (Montreal: John Lovell, 1864), p. 285.

23. OR Navies, Series 2, Volume 2, p. 714.

24. John Wilkinson, *Narrative of a Blockade Runner* (New York: Sheldon & Company, 1877), p. 182.

25. OR Navies, Series 1, Volume 2, pp. 822-828; Jefferson Davis, in Lynda L. Crist, Kenneth H. Williams, and Peggy L. Dillard, Eds., *Papers of Jefferson Davis* (Baton Rouge: Louisiana, Louisiana State University Press, 1999), Volume 10, October 1863-August 1864, p. 86.

26. OR Navies, Series 1, Volume 2, pp. 824-6.

27. *Ibid.*, p. 824.

28. Selected Records of the War Department Relating to Confederate Prisoners of War, 1861-1865, NARA, Microcopy 598, Volume 1, Roll 80, Johnson's Island, Ohio, Military Prison, pp. 4 and 158 (note: Trimble is misspelled "Trimball."), accessed at https://archive.org/stream/selectedrecords00080unit#page/n124/mode/1up

29. John Bell, *Rebels on the Great Lakes: Confederate Naval Commando Operations Launched from Canada, 1863-1864* (Toronto: Dundurn, 2011), p. 31; Captain Robert Dabney Minor, "The Plan To Rescue Johnson's Island Prisoners," Southern Historical Society Papers, Volume 23, 1895, p. 286.

30. *New York Herald*, November 1 and 3 and 4 and 5 and 6, 1863.

31. *New York Herald*, November 1, 1863, emphasis in the original.

32. OR Navies, Series 1, Volume 2, p. 824.

33. OR Navies, Series 1, Volume 2, pp. 822-28; *Bermuda Royal Gazette*, December 22, 1863.

34. Subject File of the Confederate States Navy, 1861-1865, NARA, RG 45, Roll 24, M1091, accessed at www.fold3.com/image/282414830 through www.fold3.com/image/282415558

35. Davis, *Papers of Jefferson Davis*, 1999, p. 86.

36. *Bermuda Royal Gazette*, January 5, 1864; *Baltimore Sun*, February 5, 1864; *Hartford Courant*, Hartford, Connecticut, January 26, 1864; *Evening Star*, Washington, D.C., January 26, 1864.

37. *The Daily Progress*, Raleigh, North Carolina, January 16, 1864, quoting the *Richmond Dispatch*.

38. *Ibid.*, January 16, 1864; OR Navies, Series 1, Volume 9, pp 388-93, 683-4.

39. *Yorkville Enquirer*, Yorkville, South Carolina, February 17, 1864.

40. *Richmond Dispatch*, January 30, 1864.

41. *Daily Missouri Republican*, St. Louis, Missouri, February 8, 1864.

42. *Richmond Dispatch*, February 22, 1864; Greene, *Confederate Yellow Fever Conspiracy*, 2019, pp. 95-6; *Bermuda Royal Gazette*, February 16, 1864.

43. *Raleigh Progress*, Raleigh, North Carolina, as cited in the *Charlotte Democrat*, Charlotte, North Carolina, March 1, 1864.

44. *Richmond Dispatch*, February 22, 1864.

45. *Cleveland Morning Leader*, February 29, 1864; *Nashville Daily Union*, March 1, 1864; *Abingdon Virginian*, Abington, Virginia, March 4, 1864; *Richmond Enquirer*, February 22, 1864; *Harrisburg Evening Telegraph*, Harrisburg, Pennsylvania, February 27, 1864, and February 29, 1864; *Petersburg Express*, Petersburg, Virginia, as quoted in the *Iredell Express*, Statesville, North Carolina, March 3, 1864; *Richmond Examiner*, February 21, 1864, and February 22, 1864.
46. *Richmond Examiner*, February 22, 1864.
47. In Greek mythology, Erebus was the personification of evil, or a region through which the dead pass where it is devoid of light.
48. *Richmond Examiner*, February 24, 1864; *Baltimore Sun*, April 4, 1864.
49. *Richmond Enquirer*, February 24, 1864.
50. *Richmond Whig*, March 4, 1864.
51. *Richmond Examiner*, February 27, 1864; *Baltimore Sun*, March 4, 1864.
52. *Richmond Examiner*, March 1, 1864.
53. *Richmond Examiner*, March 16, 1864.
54. *Richmond Dispatch*, March 30, 1864.
55. *Baltimore Sun*, April 13, 1864.
56. *Richmond Examiner*, March 16, 1864.
57. *Richmond Dispatch*, May 4, 1864.
58. OR, Series 4, Volume 3, p. 510.
59. OR, Series 4, Volume 3, p. 387.
60. *Ibid.*, pp. 387–8.
61. *Ibid.*, p. 511.
62. *Ibid.*, p. 512.
63. For a detailed review of Maryland troops in the Civil War and their rather confusing alliances with similarities of the names of their various regiments, see:
Kevin Conley Ruffner, "Lost in the Lost Cause: The 1st Maryland Infantry Regiment (C.S.)," *Maryland Historical Magazine*, 90 (4), Winter 1995, pp. 425–45.
64. OR, Series 4, Volume 3, p. 512.
65. Daniel D. Hartzler, *Marylanders in the Confederacy* (Silver Spring, Maryland: Family Line Publications, 1986), Chapter 9—The Maryland Line, pp. 39–40.
66. Library of Congress, accessed at https://www.loc.gov/resource/rbpe.03101700/?st=gallery and https://www.loc.gov/resource/rbpe.03101700/?sp=1&st=text
67. OR, Series 4, Volume 3, pp. 512–3.
68. *Ibid.*, pp. 510–12.
69. Library of Congress, accessed at https://www.loc.gov/resource/rbpe.03101700/?sp=1&st=text and https://www.loc.gov/resource/rbpe.03101700/?sp=2&st=text and https://www.loc.gov/resource/rbpe.03101700/?sp=3&st=text
70. Clifford Dowdey and Louis H. Manarin, Eds., *The Wartime Papers of Robert E. Lee* (New York: Da Capo Press, Inc., 1961), letter #816, pp. 806–8.
71. Davis, *Papers Of Jefferson Davis, Volume 10*, 1999, p. 86.
72. *Ibid.*, p. 530.
73. OR, Series 4, Volume 3, p. 717.
74. *Ibid.*; Jefferson Davis, in Lynda L. Crist, Barbara J. Rozek, and Kenneth H. Williams, Eds., *Papers of Jefferson Davis. Volume 11* (Baton Rouge: Louisiana State University Press, 2003), September 1864-May 1865, p. 98.
75. Davis, *Papers of Jefferson Davis*, Volume 11, p. 98.
76. OR, Series 4, Volume 3, p. 747.
77. OR, Series 4, Volume 3, p. 747.
78. NARA, Selected Records of the War Department Relating to Confederate Prisoners of War, 1861–1865, Microcopy 598, Volume 1, Roll 80, Johnson's Island, Ohio, Military Prison, Archer, p. 4, and Trimble (misspelled "Trimball"), p. 158, accessed at https://archive.org/stream/selectedrecordso0080unit#page/n124/mode/1up
79. Clayton Gray, *Conspiracy In Canada* (Montreal: L'Atelier Press, 1957), p. 51; Adam Mayers, *Dixie and the Dominion. Canada, the Confederacy, and the War for the Union* (Toronto: Dundern Press, 2003), p. 155.
80. Letter, Cordial Crane to E. M. Stanton, May 30, 1865, NARA, Investigation and Trial Papers Relating to the Assassination of President Lincoln, Record Group 153, M-599, Roll 3.
81. *Richmond Dispatch*, October 10, 1864.
82. Eaton G. Horner, for the Prosecution—May 18. Testimony Concerning Samuel Arnold, accessed at http://media.virbcdn.com/files/60/-248659ad3eace3bd-Bplact11.pdf; Benn Pitman, Complier, *The Assassination of President Lincoln and the Trial of the Conspirators* (New York: Moore, Wilstach & Baldwin, 1865), pp. 234–5.
83. Stanley Preston Kimmel, *The Mad Booths of Maryland* (New York: Dover, 1970), pp. 167–8; John J. Jennings, *Theatrical and Circus Life; or, Secrets of the Stage, Green-Room and Sawdust Arena* (St. Louis: Dan Linahan & Co., 1882), pp. 479–80.
84. *New York Daily Graphic*, March 22, 1876; Kane's memory of dates may have been faulty, or the entire story about a letter of introduction to Booth written from Martin to Kane may have been a fabrication. Martin would have written the letter in October 1864 (or, at the latest, mid-November 1864), not December, since Martin apparently drowned in mid-November. It also seems unlikely that the letter only reached Kane in March or April of 1865, a time when Kane was in Virginia when and where it would have been implausible that the letter would have ever reached Kane. On the other hand, Kane would seem to have had no reason to invent the existence of such a letter since no one of that era wanted to admit any association with Booth, whatsoever.
85. *Quebec Morning Chronicle*, July 19, 1865; David Beasley, *McKee Rankin and the Heyday of the American Theater* (Waterloo, Ontario: Wilfred Laurier University Press, 2002), pp. 46, 53, 68, 448, 452; Stuart, *Case of the Marie Victoria*, 1875, pp. 109–13.
86. Register of Letters Received by the Office of the Confederate Quartermaster, NARA, RG

109, Volume 12, "K-25," as cited in HistoryNet, "America's Civil War," accessed at https://www.historynet.com/americas-civil-war-may-2001-letters.htm

87. Ibid.; America's Civil War: May 2001 Letters, referring to the letter written by George Kane on November 29, 1864, accessed at http://www.historynet.com/americas-civil-war-may-2001-letters.htm

88. de Francias Folsom, *Our Police* (Baltimore: J. Ehlers & Co., 1888), pp. 279–8.

89. Goldsborough, *Maryland Line*, 1900, p. 144.

90. *Daily National Intelligencer*, Washington, D.C., May 9, 1865.

91. *Baltimore Sun*, April 1, 1865.

92. Davis, *Papers of Jefferson Davis*, Volume 11, p. 525.

93. OR, Series 1, Volume 47, p. 772.

94. *Wilmington Morning Star*, Wilmington, North Carolina, October 3, 1867.

95. *Richmond Daily Dispatch*, August 13, 1866.

96. *Norfolk Journal*, Norfolk, Virginia, June 10, 1867.

97. *Richmond Whig*, October 20, 1868.

98. Bill Arp was the pen name of Charles Henry Smith, a Southern lawyer who wrote humorous letters during the Civil War, frequently published in Southern newspapers sympathizing with the plight of the South.

99. *Wilmington Morning Star*, Wilmington, North Carolina, October 3, 1867.

100. *Daily Express*, Petersburg, Virginia, April 15, 1869.

101. *Richmond Whig*, October 20,1868.

102. Dr. Robert A. Brock and Prof. Virgil A. Lewis, *Virginia and Virginians. Eminent Virginians* (Richmond and Toledo: H. H. Hardesty, 1888), Volume 2, pp. 790–1.

103. *Richmond Daily Dispatch*, August 29, 1871.

104. U. S. IRS Tax Assessment Lists, 1862–1918, Virginia, District 5, accessed at Ancestry.com.

105. *Wilmington Daily Dispatch*, Wilmington, North Carolina, April 25, 1867; *Atlanta Daily Intelligencer*, June 8, 1867.

106. *The Indicator*, Warrenton, North Carolina, January 26, 1867; *Wilmington Daily Dispatch*, Wilmington, North Carolina, June 13, 1867.

107. *Baltimore Sun*, February 13, 1867.

108. *Staunton Vindicator*, Staunton, Virginia, as cited in the *Baltimore Sun*, February 25, 1867.

109. *The Old North State*, Salisbury, North Carolina, April 26, 1867, citing the *Baltimore Gazette*.

110. *Baltimore Sun*, December 16, 1868.

111. *Baltimore Sun*, December 25, 1867.

112. *Philadelphia Inquirer*, December 25, 1867.

113. *Wilmington Daily Dispatch*, Wilmington, North Carolina, January 22, 1867; *The Evening Telegraph*, Philadelphia, Pennsylvania, January 18, 1867.

114. *Keowee Courier*, Pickens, South Carolina, October 12, 1867.

115. *Charleston Daily News*, November 9, 1867.

116. *Charleston Daily News*, November 20, 1868.

Chapter 17

1. *Richmond Dispatch*, March 4, 1865.

2. *Baltimore American and Commercial Advertiser*, June 24, 1878.

3. *Baltimore Sun*, February 5, 1868.

4. J. Thomas Scharf, *History of Maryland, From the Earliest Period to the Present Day* (Baltimore: J. B. Piet, 1879), Volume 3, pp. 395–6.

5. *Harrisburg Telegraph*, Harrisburg, Pennsylvania, February 13, 1869.

6. *Baltimore Sun*, March 6, 1869, citing the *Danville Register*.

7. *Baltimore Sun*, March 18, 1869.

8. *Baltimore Sun*, August 31, 1869.

9. *Baltimore Sun*, September 16, 1869; *Richmond Whig*, September 17, 1869.

10. *Baltimore Sun*, October 22, 1869.

11. *Baltimore Sun*, November 7, 1871; *Baltimore Sun*, November 8, 1871.

12. *Baltimore Sun*, November 27, 1871.

13. *Der Deutsche Correspondent*, Baltimore, Maryland, September 6, 1872.

14. *Baltimore Sun*, September 7, 1872.

15. *Baltimore Sun*, April 23, 1873.

16. *Staunton Spectator*, Staunton, Virginia, April 29, 1873; *Baltimore Sun*, April 24 and 25, 1873.

17. *Baltimore Sun*, May 8, 1873.

18. *Richmond Whig*, July 18, 1873; *Baltimore Sun*, November 4 and 5, and December 5 and 10, 1873.

19. Now called "Jones Falls," it was initially referred to as "Jones's Falls" in the 1800s, then "Jones' Falls," and finally—including today—"Jones Falls."

20. Baltimore Flood 1868. Baltimore Police History, accessed at https://baltimorecitypolicehistory.com/our-police/baltimore-flood-1868.html

21. *Baltimore Sun*, August 12, 1868.

22. Aunaleah Gelles, "Public Opinion of the Jones Falls after the Flood of 1868. From 'the pride of Baltimore City' to 'a nuisance, an expense, and an eyesore.' " Chapter 6: Creating the Tyson Plan, accessed at http://scalar.usc.edu/works/jonesfallsflood/creating-the-tyson-plan

23. The Baltimore City Council was restructured in 1922 when the voters petitioned to change the bicameral system to a unicameral system; larger districts replaced the smaller wards.

24. *Baltimore Sun*, July 7, 1870.

25. *Baltimore Sun*, July 13, 1870.

26. *Baltimore Sun*, July 13, 1870.

27. *Baltimore Sun*, July 20, 1870.

28. *Baltimore Sun*, July 27, 1870.

29. *Baltimore Sun*, October 19, 1870.

30. *Baltimore Sun*, February 1, 1871.

31. *Baltimore Sun*, February 1, 1871.

32. *Baltimore Sun*, April 14, 1858; *Baltimore Daily Exchange*, March 31, 1858.

33. *Baltimore Sun*, January 1, 1870.

34. *Baltimore Sun*, January 3 and 5, 1870, April

2 and December 12, 1872, March 10 and October 10, 1877; *Baltimore Underwriter*, February 24 and March 2 and April 20, 1876, and April 26, 1877.
35. *Baltimore Sun*, January 5, 1875.
36. *Baltimore Sun*, May 19, 1874.
37. *Baltimore Sun*, March 19, 1877.
38. *Baltimore Sun*, August 21, 1872.
39. *Baltimore Sun*, February 29, 1876.
40. *Baltimore Sun*, October 2 and 4, 1876;

Chapter 18

1. *Baltimore Sun*, June 19, 1874.
2. *Baltimore Sun*, May 22, 1877.
3. *Baltimore Sun*, June 2, 1877.
4. *Baltimore Sun*, October 11, 1877.
5. *Baltimore Sun*, October 25, 1877.
6. *Baltimore Sun*, December 29, 1899; *Chestertown Transcript*, Chestertown, Pennsylvania, November 2, 1877; J. Thomas Scharf, *History of Baltimore City and County, From the Earliest Period to the Present Day* (Philadelphia: Louis H. Everts, 1881), p. 166.
7. *Baltimore Sun*, October 25, 1877.
8. *Baltimore Sun*, November 2, 1877.
9. *Baltimore Sun*, November 23, 1877, quoting the *Cumberland Times*, Cumberland, Maryland.
10. *Baltimore Sun*, November 3, 1877.
11. *Baltimore Sun*, November 21, 1877.
12. *Baltimore Sun*, November 23, 1877.
13. *Baltimore Sun*, November 22, 1877.
14. *Baltimore Sun*, December 11, 1877.
15. *Baltimore Sun*, November 6, 1877.
16. *The Times*, Philadelphia, Pennsylvania, June 24, 1878.
17. *Baltimore Sun*, January 8, 1878.
18. *Baltimore Sun*, January 10, 1878; Eugene Fauntleroy Cordell, M.D., *Historical Sketch of the University of Maryland School of Medicine (1807–1890)* (Baltimore: Isaac Friedenwald, 1891), p. 136, accessed at https://babel.hathitrust.org/cgi/pt?id=uc2.ark:/13960/t9f47mk9r;view=1up;seq=184
19. *Baltimore Sun*, January 10, 1878.
20. *The Times-Picayune*, New Orleans, January 13, 1878.
21. *Baltimore Sun*, February 15, 1878.
22. *Baltimore Sun*, February 21, 1878.
23. *Baltimore Sun*, February 26, 1878.
24. *Baltimore Sun*, March 11, 1878.
25. *Baltimore Sun*, March 16, 1878.
26. *Baltimore Sun*, March 19, 1878.
27. *Baltimore Sun*, March 13, 1878.
28. *Baltimore Sun*, March 20, 1878.
29. *Baltimore Sun*, March 29, 1878.
30. *Baltimore Sun*, March 3, 1878.
31. *Herald Torch and Light*, Hagerstown, Maryland, May 1, 1878.
32. *Baltimore Sun*, March 27, 1878; *Baltimore Sun*, April 27, 1878.
33. *Baltimore Sun*, April 29, 1878.
34. *Baltimore Sun*, May 2, 1878.
35. *Baltimore Sun*, May 3, 1878.
36. *Baltimore Sun*, May 9, 1878.
37. *Baltimore Sun*, May 22, 1878.
38. *Denton Journal*, Denton, Maryland, June 1, 1878.
39. *Baltimore Sun*, June 10, 1878.
40. *Baltimore Sun*, June 12, 1878.
41. *Baltimore American and Commercial Advertiser*, June 24, 1878; "Dropsy" was a term used in that era that denoted congestive heart failure.
42. *Baltimore Sun*, June 22, 1878.
43. *Baltimore Sun*, June 22, 1878.
44. *Baltimore Sun*, June 22, 1878.
45. *Baltimore Sun*, June 24, 1878.
46. *The Ordinances and Resolutions of the Mayor and City Council of Baltimore, Passed at the Annual Session of 1878* (Baltimore: John Cox, City Printer, 1878), pp. 15–6.
47. Baltimore American and Commercial Adverser, June 24, 1878.
48. *Baltimore Ordinances and Resolutions, 1878*, pp. 16–8.
49. *Baltimore Sun*, July 12, 1878.
50. *Baltimore Sun*, June 25, 1878.
51. Even in death, George Kane's life remained partially a mystery. His tombstone says that he was born in 1817; most news reports and his death certificate gave 1820 as his birth year.
52. Board of Health, City of Baltimore, Certificate #25919, filed June 24, 1878.
53. *Baltimore Ordinances and Resolutions, 1878*, p. 163.
54. *Baltimore Sun*, June 24, 1878.
55. *Baltimore Sun*, June 25, 1878.
56. *Baltimore Sun*, June 25, 1878.
57. *Baltimore Sun*, June 24, 1878.
58. *Baltimore Sun*, June 26, 1878.
59. *Baltimore Sun*, June 26, 1878.

Bibliography

Alford, Terry. *Fortune's Fool: The Life of John Wilkes Booth*. Oxford and New York: Oxford University Press, 2015.

Anonymous. "Personal Journal of a 'Prisoner of State' in Forts McHenry, Monroe, La Fayette, and Warren," in: Member of the Maryland Legislature. *The Bastilles of the North*. Baltimore: Kelly, Hedian & Piet, 1862.

Anonymous ("A Member of the Order"). *K.G.C. An Authentic Exposition of the Origin, Objects, and Secret Work of the Organization Known as the Knights of the Golden Circle*. Indianapolis: C.O. Perrine, 1861.

Archer, Stephen M. *Junius Brutus Booth: Theatrical Prometheus*. Carbondale and Edwardsville, Illinois: Southern Illinois University Press, 1992.

Barnes, Surgeon General Joseph K., Joseph Janvier Woodward, Charles Smart, George Alexander Otis, and David Lowe Huntington, *The Medical and Surgical History of the War of the Rebellion. (1861-65)*. Washington, D.C.: Government Printing Office, 1870.

Basler, Roy P., Ed. *Collected Works of Abraham Lincoln*. Ann Arbor, Michigan: University of Michigan Digital Library Production Services, 2001.

Bell, John. *Rebels on the Great Lakes: Confederate Naval Commando Operations Launched from Canada, 1863-1864*. Toronto: Dundurn, 2011.

Bloom, Arthur W. *Edwin Booth: A Biography and Performance History*. Jefferson, North Carolina: McFarland, 2013.

Bloom, Arthur W. *Edwin Forrest: A Biography and Performance History*. Jefferson, North Carolina: McFarland, 2019.

Boulden, James E.P. *The Presbyterians of Baltimore: Their Churches and Historic Grave-yards*. Baltimore: William K. Boyle & Son, 1875.

Brown, George William. "Baltimore and the Nineteenth of April 1861. A Study of the War." In Adams, Herbert B., Ed. *Johns Hopkins University Studies in Historical and Political Science, Extra Volume III*. Baltimore: N. Murray and Isaac Friedenwald, Johns Hopkins University, 1887.

Butler, Benj. F. *Autobiography and Personal Reminiscences of Major-General Benj. F. Butler. Butler's Book. A Review of His Legal, Political, and Military Career*. Boston: A. M Thayer & Co., 1892.

Clayton, Ralph. *Black Baltimore, 1820-1870*. Bowie, Maryland: Heritage Books, Inc., 1987.

Clayton, Ralph. *Slavery, Slaveholding and the Free Black Population of Antebellum Baltimore*. Bowie, Maryland: Heritage Books, Inc., 1993.

Craig's Business Directory and Baltimore Almanac for 1842. Baltimore: Danl. H. Craig, J. Robinson, 1842.

Cuthbert, Norma B., Ed. *Lincoln and the Baltimore Plot 1861; From Pinkerton Records and Related Papers*. San Marino, California: Huntington Library Publications; Los Angeles: Pacific Press, 1949.

Davis, Jefferson, in Lynda L. Crist, Barbara J. Rozek, and Kenneth H. Williams, Eds. *Papers of Jefferson Davis, Volume 11*. Baton Rouge: Louisiana State University Press, 2003.

Davis, Jefferson, in Lynda L. Crist, Kenneth H. Williams, and Peggy L. Dillard, Eds. *Papers of Jefferson Davis, Volume 10*. Baton Rouge: Louisiana, Louisiana State University Press, 1999.

Davis, Jefferson, in Lynda L. Crist, Mary S. Dix, and Kenneth H. Williams, Eds. *Papers of Jefferson Davis, Volume 9*. Baton Rouge, Louisiana: Louisiana State University Press, 1997.

Dix, Morgan. *Memoirs of John Adams Dix Compiled By His Son Morgan Dix*. New York, Harper & Brothers, Franklin Square, 1883.

Dowdey, Clifford, and Louis H. Manarin, Eds. *The Wartime Papers of Robert E. Lee*. New York: Da Capo Press, Inc., 1961.

Edwards, William C. *The Life and Times of John Wilkes Booth. A Chronology of His Life and the Events Surrounding Him Including New Information and Insights*. Buffalo, New York: NFB Publishing, 2019.

Ellis, Franklin, and Samuel Evans. *History of Lancaster County, Pennsylvania: With Biographical Sketches of Many of Its Pioneers and Prominent Men*. Philadelphia: Everts & Peck, 1883.

Fields, Barbara Jeanne. *Slavery and Freedom on the Middle Ground. Maryland During the Nineteenth Century*. New Haven and London: Yale University Press, 1985.

Folsom, de Francias, Ed. *Our Police. A History of the Baltimore Force from the First Watchman to the Latest Appointee*. Baltimore, J.D. Ehlers & Co., Guggenheimer, Weil & Co., J.M. Beers, 1888.

Forrest, Clarence H. *Official History of the Fire Department of the City of Baltimore: Together with Biographies and Portraits of Eminent Citizens of Baltimore.* Baltimore: Williams & Wilkins, 1898.

Gray, Clayton. *Conspiracy In Canada.* Montreal: L'Atelier Press, 1957.

Greene, H. Leon. *The Confederate Yellow Fever Conspiracy.* Jefferson, North Carolina: McFarland, 2019.

Hall, Clayton Coleman, Ed. *Baltimore: Its History and Its People, Volume 1—History.* New York and Chicago: Lewis Historical Publishing Company, 1912.

Hanson, John W., Chaplain. *Historical Sketch of the Old Sixth Regiment of Massachusetts Volunteers, During Its Three Campaigns In 1861, 1862, 1863, and 1864.* Boston: Lee and Shepard, 1866.

Hartzler, Daniel D. *Marylanders in the Confederacy.* Silver Spring, Maryland: Family Line Publications, 1986.

Henry, William, and Jesse William Weik. In: Douglas L. Wilson, Rodney O. Davis, and Terry Wilson, Eds., *Herndon's Informants: Letters, Interviews, and Statements About Abraham Lincoln.* Urbana and Chicago, Illinois: University of Illinois Press, 1998.

Hibernian Society, Maryland Center for History and Culture, MS 2029.

Hoch, Bradley R. *The Lincoln Trail in Pennsylvania. A History and Guide.* University Park, Pennsylvania: Keystone Books, Penn State University Press, 2013.

Holt, Michael F. *The Rise and Fall of the American Whig Party: Jacksonian Politics and the Onset of the Civil War.* New York: Oxford University Press, 1999.

Howard, Frank Key. *Fourteen Months in American Bastiles.* Baltimore: Kelly, Hedian & Piet, 1863.

Howard, Frank Key, in John A. Marshall. *American Bastille. A History of the Illegal Arrests and Imprisonment of American Citizens During the Late Civil War.* Philadelphia: Thomas W. Hartley, 1871, Eighth Edition.

Jennings, John J. *Theatrical and Circus Life; or, Secrets of the Stage, Green-Room and Sawdust Arena.* St. Louis: Dan Linahan & Co., 1882.

Jones, John William. *The Davis Memorial Volume; Or, Our Dead President, Jefferson Davis and the World's Tribute to His Memory.* Richmond: B.F. Johnson & Co., 1890.

Keehn, David C. *Knights of the Golden Circle, Secret Empire, Southern Secession, Civil War.* Baton Rouge: Louisiana State University Press, 2013.

Keenan, Charles C. *Keenan's Baltimore Directory for 1822 & 1823.* Baltimore, 1822.

Ketcham, Henry. *The Life of Abraham Lincoln.* New York: A.L. Burt Company, 1901.

Kimmel, Stanley Preston. *The Mad Booths of Maryland.* New York: Dover, 1970.

Kline, Michael J. *The Baltimore Plot. The First Conspiracy to Assassinate Abraham Lincoln.* Yardley, Pennsylvania: Westholme Publishing, 2008.

"Knights of the Golden Circle." *Rules, Regulations and Principles of the K.G.C.: Illustrated, Issued by Order of the Congress of the K.C.S. [Knights of the Columbian Star], and the General President Knights of the Golden Circle.* New York: Benj. Urner, 1859.

Mackay, Christina. *Mackay's Montreal Directory for 1863–64 (corrected to July 1, 1863).* Montreal: John Lovell, 1863.

Mackay, Christina. *Mackay's Montreal Directory for 1864–65 (corrected to July 1, 1864).* Montreal: John Lovell, 1864.

Marcotte, Frank. *Six Days in April: Lincoln and the Union in Peril.* New York: Algora Publishing, 2005.

Marshall, John A. *American Bastille. A History of the Illegal Arrests and Imprisonment of American Citizens During the Late Civil War.* Philadelphia: Thomas W. Hartley, 1871.

Matchett, Richard J. *Matchett's Baltimore Director [sic] for 1847–8.* Baltimore, 1847.

Matchett, Richard J. *Matchett's Baltimore Director [sic] for 1849–50.* Baltimore, 1849.

Matchett, Richard J. *Matchett's Baltimore Director [sic] for 1851.* Baltimore, 1851.

Matchett, Richard J. *Matchett's Baltimore Director [sic] for 1853–4.* Baltimore, 1853.

Matchett, Richard J. *Matchett's Baltimore Director [sic], 1841.* Baltimore, 1841.

Matchett, Richard J. *Matchett's Baltimore Director [sic], Corrected up to June 1831.* Baltimore, 1831.

Matchett, Richard J. *Matchett's Baltimore Director [sic], Corrected up to June, 1843.* Baltimore, 1843.

Matchett, Richard J. *Matchett's Baltimore Director [sic], Corrected up to May 1833.* Baltimore, 1833.

May, Alonzo J. *May's Dramatic Encyclopedia of Baltimore, 1750–1904,* Maryland Center for History and Culture, MS 995.

Mayers, Adam. *Dixie and the Dominion: Canada, the Confederacy, and the War for the Union.* Toronto: Dundern Press, 2003.

Melton, Tracy Matthew. *Hanging Henry Gambrill. The Violent Career of Baltimore's Plug Uglies, 1854–1860.* Baltimore: Maryland Center for History and Culture, 2005.

"A Member of the Order." *Authentic Exposition of the "K. G. C." "Knights of the Golden Circle"; Or, A History of Secession from 1834 to 1861.* Indianapolis: C.O. Perrine, 1861.

Miller, Wilbur R., Ed. "History of Gangs." *The Social History of Crime and Punishment in America: An Encyclopedia.* Los Angeles: Sage Reference Publications, 2012.

Mitchell, Charles W., Ed. *Maryland Voices of the Civil War* Baltimore: Johns Hopkins University Press, 2007.

Moore, Frank, Ed. *The Rebellion Record: A Diary of American Events.* New York, G.P. Putnam, 1862.

Myers, Jack. *Knights' Gold. The Largest Documented KGC Treasure Ever Discovered.* Jack O'Lantern Press and CreateSpace Independent Publishing, 2016.

National Archives and Records Administration (NARA), Record Groups (RG) 51 and 153.
Nicolay, John G., and John Hay, *Abraham Lincoln. A History*. New York: The Century Co., 1890.
Nicolay, John G., and John Hay, Eds. *Abraham Lincoln: Complete Works, Comprising His Speeches, Letters, State Papers, and Miscellaneous Writings*. New York: The Century Co., 1894.
Phillips, Jason. *Looming Civil War. How Nineteenth-Century Americans Imagined the Future*. New York: Oxford University Press, 2018.
Pinkerton, Allan. *The Spy of the Rebellion; Being a True History of the Spy System of the United States Army During the Late Rebellion*. New York: G.W. Carleton & Co., 1886.
Pitman, Benn, Complier. *The Assassination of President Lincoln and the Trial of the Conspirators*. New York: Moore, Wilstach & Baldwin, 1865.
Raymond, Henry J. *Abraham Lincoln, His Life and Times, Volume 1*. Chicago: Thompson and Thomas, 1891.
Rhodehamel, John, and Louise Taper, Eds., *Right or Wrong, God Judge Me: The Writings of John Wilkes Booth*. Urbana and Chicago: University of Illinois Press, 1997.
Riley, Elihu S. *"The Ancient City." A History of Annapolis, in Maryland, 1649–1887*. Annapolis, Maryland: Record Printing Office, 1887.
Sangston, Lawrence, Member of the Maryland Legislature. *The Bastilles of the North*. Baltimore: Kelly, Hedian & Piet, 1863.
Scharf, Col. J. Thomas. *The Chronicles of Baltimore; Being A Complete History of "Baltimore Town" and Baltimore City from the Earliest Period to the Present Time*. Baltimore: Turnbull Brothers, 1874.
Scharf, J. Thomas. *History of Baltimore City and County, from the Earliest Period to the Present Day: Including Biographical Sketches of Their Representative Men*. Philadelphia: Louis H. Everts, J.B. Lippincott & Co., 1881.
Scharf, J. Thomas. *History of Maryland, from the Earliest Period to the Present Day*. Baltimore: John B. Piet, 1879.
Scharf, J. Thomas. *History of the Confederate Navy From Its Organization to the Surrender of Its Last Vessel*. New York: Rogers & Sherwood, 1887.
Sheehy, Barry. *Montreal. City of Secrets*. Montreal: Baraka Books of Montreal, 2017.
Shepherd, Henry Elliot. *History of Baltimore, Maryland, from Its Founding as a Town to the Current Year, 1729–1898*. Uniontown, Pennsylvania: S.B. Nelson, 1898.
Speer, Lonnie. *Portals To Hell, Military Prisons of the Civil War*. Mechanicsburg, Pennsylvania: Stackpole Books, 1997.
Stashower, Daniel. *The Hour of Peril: The Secret Plot to Murder Lincoln Before the Civil War*. New York: Minotaur Books, 2013.
Steers, Edward, Jr. *Blood On The Moon: The Assassination of Abraham Lincoln*. Lexington, Kentucky: University of Kentucky Press, 2001.
Storke, Elliot G., and L.P. Brockett. *A Complete History of the Great American Rebellion, Embracing Its Causes, Events and Consequences, with Biographical Sketches and Portraits*. Auburn, New York: Auburn Publishing Company, 1865.
Surratt, John H., in Jennings, John J. *The Private Journal and Diary of John H. Surratt, the Conspirator*, Ed. Dion Haco. New York: Frederic A. Brady, 1866.
Tidwell, William A., James O. Hall, and David Winfred Gaddy. *Come Retribution: The Confederate Secret Service and the Assassination of Lincoln*. Jackson, Mississippi, and London: University Press of Mississippi, 1988.
Towers, Frank. *The Urban South and the Coming of the Civil War*. Charlottesville: University of Virginia Press, 2004.
U.S. Naval War Records Office. *Official Records of the Union and Confederate Navies in the War of the Rebellion*. Washington, D.C.: Government Printing Office, 1894.
U.S. War Department. *The War of the Rebellion: A Compilation of the Official Records of the Union and Confederate Armies*. Washington, D.C.: Government Printing Office, 1880.
Wallis, Severn Teackle. *Writings of Severn Teackle Wallis, Memorial Edition, Vol. II, Critical and Political*. Baltimore: John Murphy & Co., 1896.
Warner, Ezra J. *Generals in Blue, Lives of Union Commanders*. Baton Rouge: Louisiana State University Press, 1992.
Wilkinson, John. *Narrative of a Blockade Runner*. New York: Sheldon & Company, 1877.
Williams, Harold A. *History of the Hibernian Society of Baltimore, 1803–1957*. Baltimore: Hibernian Society of Baltimore, 1957.
Winkle, Kenneth J. *Lincoln's Citadel: The Civil War in Washington, D.C.* New York: W.W. Norton & Company, Inc., 2013.
Woods, John W. *Woods' Baltimore City Directory Ending Year 1860*. Baltimore, 1860.
Woods, John W. *Woods' Baltimore Directory for 1856–'57*. Baltimore, 1857.
Wright, Edmund. *Narrative of Edmund Wright; His Adventures With and Escape From the Knights of the Golden Circle*. Cincinnati: J.R. Hawley, 1864.

Newspapers

Abingdon Virginian, Abington, Virginia
Adams Sentinel, Gettysburg, Pennsylvania
Albany Evening Journal
Alexandria Gazette, Alexandria, Virginia
American Patriot and Fells Point Advertiser, Fells Point, Maryland
American Republican, Baltimore, Maryland
Atlanta Daily Intelligencer
Baltimore American and Commercial Advertiser
Baltimore Commercial Journal
Baltimore Daily Clipper
Baltimore Daily Exchange

Baltimore Federal Gazette
Baltimore Patriot & Mercantile Advertiser
Baltimore Patriot and Transcript
Baltimore Pilot
Baltimore Sun
Baltimore Sunday Telegram
Baltimore Telegraphe and Daily Advertiser
Baltimore Underwriter
Bermuda Royal Gazette, Hamilton, Bermuda
Buffalo Commercial
Capital, Annapolis, Maryland
Catholic Herald
Catholic Standard and Times
Charleston Daily News
Charlotte Democrat, Charlotte, North Carolina
Chestertown Transcript, Chestertown, Pennsylvania
Cincinnati Commercial
Cincinnati Daily Press. Cincinnati Enquirer
Civilian and Telegraph, Cumberland, Maryland
Cleveland Morning Leader
Cumberland Civilian & Telegraph, Cumberland, Maryland
Cumberland Times, Cumberland, Maryland
Daily Express, Petersburg, Virginia
Daily Missouri Republican, St. Louis, Missouri
Daily National Intelligencer, Washington, D.C
Daily National Republican, Washington, D.C
Daily Progress, Raleigh, North Carolina
Danville Register, Danville, Virginia
Denton Journal, Denton, Maryland
Der Deutsche Correspondent, Baltimore, Maryland
Evening Star, Washington, D.C
Evening Telegraph, Philadelphia, Pennsylvania
Frank Leslie's Illustrated Newspaper
Gettysburg Compiler
Harper's Weekly
Harrisburg Telegraph, Harrisburg, Pennsylvania
Hartford Courant, Hartford, Connecticut
Herald Torch and Light, Hagerstown, Maryland
Hudson North Star, Hudson, Wisconsin
Indianapolis Daily Journal
Indicator, Warrenton, North Carolina
Janesville Daily Gazette, Janesville, Wisconsin
Keowee Courier, Pickens, South Carolina
Maryland Republican, Annapolis, Maryland
Maryland Times, Baltimore, Maryland
Nashville Daily Union
New York Daily Graphic. New York Daily Tribune
New York Evening Post
New York Herald
New York Times
Norfolk Journal, Norfolk, Virginia
Old North State, Salisbury, North Carolina
Pennsylvania Daily Telegraph, Harrisburg, Pennsylvania
Petersburg Express, Petersburg, Virginia
Philadelphia Inquirer
Philadelphia Press
Pittsburgh Daily Commercial
Quebec Morning Chronicle
Raleigh Progress, Raleigh, North Carolina
Richmond Dispatch
Richmond Whig
St. Albans Daily Messenger, St. Albans, Vermont
Semi-Weekly Observer, Fayetteville, North Carolina
Staunton Spectator, Staunton, Virginia
Staunton Vindicator, Staunton, Virginia
Times, Philadelphia, Pennsylvania
Times-Picayune, New Orleans, Louisiana
Wilmington Daily Dispatch, Wilmington, North Carolina
Wilmington Morning Star, Wilmington, North Carolina
Yorkville Enquirer, Yorkville, South Carolina

Index

abolitionist 82–85, 87, 105
Academy of Music Theatre 16
account 12, 34, 37, 62, 79, 85, 88, 94, 105, 107, 119–121, 126, 155, 157, 170, 176, 186–187, 197, 203, 211, 224, 228, 262n46, 263n69, 268n2, 269n10
accusation 196, 227
Acton, Massachusetts 112
A.D. Vance (ship) 204
Adams, Emilius 30
Adelaide 168
Adelphi Theatre 16, 18, 24
adjutant-general 126, 178, 208, 210, 270n33, 270n34; assistant 178, 208, 210
Adjutant-General of the Volunteer Forces 126
Admiralty Court 213
Advance (ship) 204
advocate 75, 82, 150, 238
"AFC" 85
affliction of the heart 194
agriculture 71
aide-de-camp 130
Airey, Edward 121
Aisquith Street 3, 19, 21, 246–247, 251ch1n1
"A.J.L.W." 202
alarm 14, 40–41, 43, 49, 65, 157; fire 40–41, 43
Albany 72–74, 257n2, 277
Albert, Augustus 219, 221
Allegany County (Maryland) 69, 189, 267n77
Allen, E.I. 80
Allen, E.J. 80
Alliance, Ohio 72
alm-giving 15
almshouse 62–63, 256n29
Alpha (ship) 203–204
American Bastille 171, 267n64, 268ch13n6, 268ch14n1, 268ch14n7, 269n24, 269n30, 269n31, 269n42, 269n45, 269ch15n3, 270n12, 270n19, 270n19, 270n44, 270n45, 276
American Central Fire Insurance Company 226
American Hotel 204, 207
American Party 44–45, 69, 114, 160

American Patriot and Fells Point Advertiser 33, 254n2, 277
American Riflemen 241, 244
ammunition 11, 28, 112, 118, 123, 131, 134, 137–138, 140, 146–147, 154–157, 267n48
amnesty 192, 217
Anabaptist 253n1
Anaconda Plan 264n100
anarchy 52, 157
anchor 113, 203, 210
Anderson, James M. 31
Andersonville 188
angel 181
animalcule 171, 177
ankle 229
Annapolis 87, 128, 131, 133, 135, 139–142, 160, 179, 254ch4n6, 258n16, 260n78, 277, 278
Annapolis and Elk Ridge Railroad 132
Annapolis Junction 179
Anne Arundel County 69, 258n16
Antonio 190
anxiety 198
Anybodyelse, Mr. 224
Apostate 74
apple 189
Appleton, George A. 186, 192, 255ch7n13
April 19 Riot 108, 118–119, 137, 146, 160, 191, 216
Archer, Gen. James J. 202
armory 28–29, 125, 128, 204, 214
Arnold, Samuel 211
Arnold's Olympic Theatre 16–18
arsenal 99, 147, 149, 152, 155, 160
arson, arsonist 2, 11, 14, 86, 88
artillery 28–32, 109, 140, 146, 148, 197, 205, 209–210, 241–244, 265n149
Ashland, Maryland 128
Ashland Station 134
assassination 26, 71, 74, 76, 78, 82–85, 87–89, 92, 95–98, 102–107, 157, 165, 211–213, 238, 253n15, 257n1, 257n3, 258n14, 258n15, 259n54, 259n59, 259n63, 259n63, 259n72, 260n102, 261n153, 266n168, 271n17, 271n18, 272n80, 272n82, 276–277
asylum 33, 175, 188, 219

Atlanta 217, 249, 273n105, 277
attorney 9, 15, 64, 93, 121, 174, 186, 195, 198, 252n36, 260n77
attrition 228
auction 13, 14, 213, 218, 225
Augusta, Georgia 216
awl 44, 49–50, 53–55
axe 50, 127

B&O 75, 90, 92, 96, 98, 101, 104, 110, 112–115, 125, 129, 132, 140, 260n78
Babbidge, Chap. Charles 119
Back River 77–78, 128
backgammon 173–174
badge 40–41, 58, 110–111, 153
Bahamas 201
Bailey, Theodorus 200
bailiff 229
balancing act 238
ballot box 47–50, 85, 88, 96, 151, 219, 227
Baltimore American 105, 137, 214
Baltimore American and Commercial Advertiser 104, 277
Baltimore and Ohio (B&O) Railroad Station 75, 135, 260n78, 264n96
Baltimore Association for the Improvement of the Condition of the Poor 15, 252n41
Baltimore Association of Firemen 40
Baltimore Bastille 143; *see also* bastille
Baltimore City Board of Trade 124
Baltimore City Council 5, 10, 30, 42, 59, 125, 131, 157, 223–225, 273n23
Baltimore City Guards 30, 127, 135, 207, 241, 243–244
Baltimore City Hall 15, 59
Baltimore City Public Schools 233
Baltimore City Rifles 241
Baltimore Clipper 36, 105
Baltimore Commercial Journal 277
Baltimore County 57, 69, 134, 168, 242–243, 246, 251n16, 263n74, 267n77, 268n77

279

Baltimore County Horse Guard 128, 242
Baltimore Criminal Court 124
Baltimore Exchange, Baltimore Daily Exchange (newspaper) 60, 162, 167
Baltimore Exchange Company, Exchange Company (building) 6, 9, 14
Baltimore Federal Gazette 33, 278
Baltimore Gazette 216
Baltimore Independent Blues 30, 241, 243
Baltimore Invincibles 30, 241–243
Baltimore National Blues 29–30, 242, 244
Baltimore Patriot 251, 278
Baltimore Patriot & Mercantile Advertiser 251, 278
Baltimore Patriot and Transcript 278
Baltimore Pilot 278
Baltimore Regiment 27, 153
Baltimore Republican 93, 105, 196
Baltimore Republican Committee 93, 104–105
Baltimore South 162
Baltimore Street 68, 111, 125, 244–245, 269n50
Baltimore Sunpapers Building 92
Baltimore Telegraphe and Daily Advertiser 278
Baltimore United Fire Department 38, 40–43
Baltimore United States District Attorney 195
Baltimore Water Board 226
"Baltimore's Own" 148
band 32–33, 65, 82, 85, 96, 106, 115, 118, 125, 138, 151, 204–205
Bangs, George H. 86
bank 3, 7, 9, 131, 150, 155, 186–187, 210, 215
Banks, Gen. Nathaniel P. 121, 142, 146–149, 152–155, 157, 161–162, 164, 176, 261n124
banner 12, 44, 55, 141–142, 166, 168
bar 35, 47, 61, 66, 68, 79, 86, 88, 139, 148, 151, 153
barber 82, 92, 143; pole 143
Barley, Mrs. M. 80
Barnum's City Hotel 17, 35–36, 78–81, 83, 86, 94, 97–98, 101–103, 105, 120, 123, 138, 164, 172–173, 180, 186, 194, 201, 204, 207, 210, 212, 226
Barre Street 4, 247, 257ch9n4
Barron, Commodore 192
Barton, T.J. 24
basin 3, 79, 167
bastille 171, 275–277
Bates, Atty. Gen. Edward 195
Bath Street 222
baton 50, 58, 153
battalion 27, 32, 117, 128, 207
battery, gun 171

Battle of Baltimore 12, 79
Battle of Gettysburg 202
Battle of North Point 3, 12
battoon 58
Baumonbough, F. 42
bay 164, 203, 222
bayonet 156
bead 200
Beale, William E. 98
Beall, John Yates 210
"beat cops" 58, 61
Beatty, E.W. 116
Beauregard, Gen. B.T. 216
bed-chamber 126
bedding 166, 168, 178
begging 15, 57, 110, 216, 256ch8n30
Belair, Maryland 19–20
Belair Academy 20
Belger, Maj. James 135–136
bell 40–41, 135, 150, 204
Bell, John 55–56, 68, 245
belt 58, 62
Belvidere Road 4, 244, 247
benefit 5, 18, 20, 22, 24–25, 29, 150, 167, 215–216, 222, 225, 229
Benton, Benjamin 45
Berglund, Richard 10
Bermuda 201, 203–204, 249, 278
Berret, James Gabriel 87, 94
Berry, Captain 185
Bible 200, 216, 271n14
Bickley, George William Lamb 82–84
Biddle Street 245, 261n118
"Bill Arp" 215, 273n98
"billy club" 58
birth 3, 13, 29, 44, 71, 166, 234, 251n1, 274n51
Bishop, James E. 98
"black flag warfare" 88
Black Friday Flood of 1868 222
"black republican president" 75
Black Snakes 44, 46
Blackburn, Dr. Luke Pryor 204, 210
blackjack 50
blacksmith 49
Blake, Thomas 200
blanket 138, 171–172
blight 222
Bloats 44
blockade-runner 200–201, 203, 210, 213–214
Blood on the Moon 88, 277
blood, Maryland 121, 158
Blood Tubs 44, 46, 49, 53
Bloody Eights 44
blue law 257n39
Blumenberg, Leopold 98
Board of Police 59, 62, 64, 67, 105, 119, 123, 127, 137, 139, 141, 144, 148–149, 152, 155, 157, 162, 264n99
Board of School Commissioners 233
board of surgeons, military 126
Board of Trade 9, 124

boatbuilder 214
Bolton Street Railroad Station 75, 89, 102, 110–111, 260n78, 261n118
bomb 73, 139, 144, 168
Bond, Hugh Lennox 124, 130, 132–133, 264n92
Bonifant, Washington 143
Bonnie Brae Cemetery 235, 237
Bookstaver, David S. 97
Booth, Asia 20
Booth, Edwin 18, 22, 24, 253n13, 275
Booth, George W. 116
Booth, John Wilkes 16, 18–26 73–74, 82–83, 119–120, 210–213, 238, 271n18, 272n84, 275–277
Booth, Junius Brutus 18–20, 22, 23–25
Boston 24–25, 33, 112, 119–120, 140, 155, 158, 165, 181–182, 184–187, 189–192, 194, 205, 210–211, 214, 248, 275–276
Boston College 189
Boston Customs House 210
Boston Harbor 182, 184
Boston Light Artillery 140
Bowen, Henry 106
bowler 44
Bowly's (Bowley's) Wharf 4, 9, 247, 251n12
Boyd, Captain 128
Boyle, Dr. Cornelius 84, 87
Boyle, Edward C. 35
Boyle's Tavern 35
Bradey, Barney 53
Bradford, Colonel 192
brain 234
brainchild 53
brainless 107
brandy 175
bravery 53, 79, 119, 122, 239
Breckinridge, John C. 11, 65, 68–69, 83
Breckinridge and Lane Club 84
bridge 2, 77–78, 85–86, 89, 102, 113, 118, 125–130, 133–134, 137, 158, 170, 178, 222–223, 238, 244
Bridge Street 244
brigade 27, 29, 31, 38, 88, 111–112, 141, 204–205, 242–244
Bright's disease 234
British Sanitary Commission 187
Broad Street 100, 118
Broadway Street 25, 39, 244–245
bronchitis 188
Brooklyn 69, 170
brothel 86
Brown, George William 5, 6, 53, 55, 60, 62, 67, 83, 93, 106, 109–112, 114–116, 119–120, 122–127, 129–133, 135, 137, 139–140, 149–150, 152, 157, 165, 168, 171, 174, 177, 181–182, 184, 186, 188, 190–191, 193–194, 264n92, 264n99, 275
Brown, John Cumming 123, 126, 129

Index

Bruce, James A. 229
Brune, Emily 174, 181
Brune, Frederick 174, 181
Brune, John C. 9, 124, 130, 132–133, 135, 264n92, 268n77
Brunswick, Georgia 226
Brutus 88, 157
Bryantown, Maryland 211–212
Bryden's Tavern 33
Buchanan, James 11, 50, 51, 86, 92
budget 232
"B.U.F.D." 40
Buffalo 72–73, 88, 199
buffoon 107
bullet 11–12, 113, 116–117, 130, 156
Burke, Col. Martin 170, 172, 179, 180
Burr 202
Bursted, A.J. 24–25, 211
Bush River 77, 128
businessman 2, 24, 57, 83, 95, 214, 238
Butler, Gen. Benjamin 140–141, 146, 160, 179
Butler, Pierce 175
Buttenders 44
Byrne, William 83–84

Cadwalader, Brevet Maj. Gen. George 141–143
Calithumpians 44
Calvary 236
Calvert, John 205
Calvert County 69
Calvert Street 12, 75, 79–81, 89–90, 92, 95–96, 102–103, 111, 125–126, 135, 235, 244, 248, 260n79, 260n118
Calvert Street Railroad Station 80, 89, 90, 92, 95–96, 102, 126, 260n118
Calverton Road 63
Camden Street 75, 89–92, 96, 101, 101, 110, 112–118, 122, 124–125, 158, 216
Camden Street Railroad Station 75, 89–92, 96, 101, 104, 110, 112–118, 122, 124–125, 158, 216
Cameron, Simon 109, 111, 131, 149–150, 161–162, 165, 193, 198
Camp Carroll 134, 146
Camp Curtin 134
Camp Douglas 199
Camp Howard 208
Camp Maryland 205–206, 208
camphene 127
Canada 26, 163, 198–203, 209–211, 248–249, 259n58, 275–276
Canadian Confederacy 198–199, 211
canal 34, 163, 224
cannister 156
cannon 45, 51, 65, 126, 134, 153–156, 197, 203, 264n100
Canon, Patty 13
Canton 5, 118, 157, 255ch7n4
Canton Bridge 128
cap 62, 99, 123, 146, 153, 156, 188

cap, secession 151
cape 41
Cape Fear River 202
capital 71, 108–109, 111, 122, 130, 214
capitol 75, 77, 87, 98–99, 104, 108, 158, 161
caprice 221
captain 10, 29–30, 42, 58, 61, 74, 78, 82, 103, 115–116, 120, 126–128, 148, 153, 185, 192, 203, 205–206
carbine 156
card 174, 219
cargo 201, 203, 213
Caribbean 82–83
Carlisle, Pennsylvania 64
Caroline County 69
Caroline Street 245
Carolinians 207
carpenter 121
Carpenter, William H. 165
carriage 41, 45, 91, 96, 100, 102, 104, 146, 155, 202, 228, 230, 237
Carroll, Gen. William 201
Carroll County 69, 268n77
carrot 189
carter 121
cartridge 11, 156
casemate 171–173, 175–176, 182, 186
"Castle of Indolence" 174
Catholic Church 33–35, 44–45, 49, 69, 189, 200, 213, 233, 235–237, 271n14
cauterization 229
cavalry 28, 30, 205, 242–244
Cecil County 69, 267n77, 268n77
cell 46, 155, 168, 171, 173, 176, 186
censorship 144, 171, 178, 187, 196
Central America 82–83
Central Police Station 149
Centre Market 63, 215
Centre Street 63, 92, 215, 222
cess-pool 190, 222
chair 167–168, 170, 172, 178, 185, 228, 232
chairman 6, 9, 42, 99, 162, 226
champagne 175
champion 35, 75, 235
chaperone 187
chaplain 119, 228
character 1, 37, 55, 69, 70, 75, 105, 137, 150, 158, 181, 184, 188, 205, 212, 218, 224, 233–235, 238, 278
charity 15, 37, 64, 180–181, 185, 216
Charles County 69, 211–212
Charles Martin & Son 200
Charles Street 4, 222
Charleston 79, 208, 217, 249
Charlotte 212, 245
Charlotte Harbor 200, 249
Cheapside 247
cheer 108, 110, 113–115, 118, 122–123, 173–175, 181, 194, 213, 221, 231
Cherry, Mrs. 80

Chesapeake Central Greeley Club 226
Chesapeake Riflemen 29–30, 241
chess 173–174
Chester, Charlotte 70
Chester, Sarrah 70
Chicago 80, 199
chimney 38
chivalry 1, 83
Christian 120, 181, 235–236
Church Home and Hospital 47
Cibber, Colley 20
Cicero 201
cigar 65, 168, 173
Cincinnati 72
cistern 177
citizen 1, 2, 6, 27–28, 30, 35–36, 38–39, 41, 43, 48, 51–54, 57–58, 60, 63, 66, 69–71, 83, 86, 94, 105, 108–109, 111–112, 115–118, 120–125, 128, 130–131, 133–136, 138–140, 142–145, 150–151, 153, 162, 164–165, 167, 176–177, 185, 191, 196–197, 204, 210, 214, 219, 221–222, 225, 228, 233–234, 238, 243; Native-born 49, 220; naturalized 220
City Council 5, 6, 9–10, 30, 42, 45, 54–55, 59–60, 67, 93, 123, 125, 131, 155, 157, 191, 223–225, 228, 231–233, 267n48, 273n23
city dock 90, 222
City Guard Battalion 30, 117, 127, 135, 207, 241, 243–244, 265n149
City Hall 9, 12, 15, 18, 59, 134, 154, 229–231, 233
civil rights 53, 151
Civil War 1, 30–32, 34, 68–71, 82, 87, 106, 108–109, 112, 118, 128, 145, 150, 155, 157, 163, 165, 170, 182, 184, 188, 192, 194, 200, 207, 210, 218, 226, 238, 276–277
Clark, Asia Booth 20
Clark, James C. 95, 99, 102
Clarke, John 20, 22, 191
Clarke, John Sleeper 20, 22, 191
Clarke, J.S. Clarke 20, 22, 191
Clarke, the Rev. Father W.F. 235–236
clay 228
Clay, Henry 5
Clay, Col. H.L. 208
Clay, James B. 200
Cleveland 72–73, 199
Clinton, H.V. 210
cloak 75, 99; military 99
Cloud, Charles F. 10
club 27, 29, 31, 44–45, 47, 50–51, 55, 58, 61, 82, 84, 178, 215, 226
coal 138, 154, 213
coat 62, 75, 86, 99, 110, 156, 234
cockade 151
Cockey, Peter 134
Cockey's Fields 134
Cockeysville 127–128, 133–137, 262n49, 265n130
cockfighting 45
co-conspirator 26, 106, 238

code 48, 63, 83, 101, 202–203, 211
Code of Maryland 63
coffee 82, 167, 171–172, 185–186, 189
Cold Spring Lane 128
Coleman, Robert B. 94, 102–103, 119
collector of customs 5
collector, port 2, 5, 6, 9
collision 68, 110, 114, 124, 129, 132, 203
colonel 30–31, 35–36, 42, 70, 74, 85, 87, 96–97, 102, 104, 112, 116, 120, 126–127, 130, 142, 144, 147–149, 152–155, 157, 166, 170, 172, 179, 184–186, 188–189, 191–194, 198, 204–208, 212, 214–215, 219–220, 223, 227–228, 233, 235, 271n15
Columbia, South Carolina 231, 250
Columbian Fire Company 39, 43, 245
Columbian Riflemen 241
Columbus 72, 86
column 68, 112, 114, 116, 137
coma 233
Comet Street 2, 19, 21, 246–247
Commerce Street 113, 116
commission 30, 59, 62, 84, 141, 157, 170, 193, 209, 220–225, 229, 231, 233
commission merchant 3–4, 6–7, 246–247
commissioner 9, 55, 59, 60–62, 64–65, 68, 112–115, 125, 137–138, 147–155, 157, 162, 167, 174, 178–180, 186, 193–194, 198, 206, 264n99, 267n48
Committee on Federal Relations 162
Company C 115, 118, 120
Company D 118
Company I 118
Company L 118
condemnation 121, 224, 236
conduct, Christian 120
Confederate Army 30, 144–145, 157, 194, 206, 264n99, 268n77
Confederate Commissioner of Exchange 206
Confederate quartermaster general 213
Confederate Secret Service 210
Confederate States 141, 161, 207
Confederate Yellow Fever Conspiracy 199, 276
Connecticut 257n39
conspiracy 87, 106, 122, 199–202, 211, 216, 276
constable 57, 231
constitution 12, 15, 55, 59–60, 71, 83, 87, 109, 139, 146, 151–152, 160–162, 174, 176, 180, 190, 192, 196, 204
Constitutional Union Party 55, 245
consumption 148, 188

contraband 147, 153, 178, 267n48
contract 186, 210, 223–224, 227, 231
convention 5, 6, 11, 30, 55, 61, 65, 110, 161, 215
Conway Street 3, 4, 244, 246
cook 171–172, 186–187, 189–190, 210
Cooper, Gen. Samuel 206
cooping 46–47, 63, 66
Corkran, Francis S. 98
Corn and Flour Exchange 9
Corsican 82, 84
cortège 45, 105
cosh 50
costume 211, 213
cotton 13–14, 82, 185, 203
coup d'etat 85
court martial 28
Court of Common Pleas 64
courtesy 182, 221, 235
courthouse 9, 11, 15, 214, 248
Courtland Street 103
cracker 66, 255ch7n4
Crane, Cordial 210
Crawford, William 109
crib 63–64
criminal 10, 63, 65–66, 124, 162, 167, 174
crowbar 127
crucifix 200
crutch 228, 230
culvert 234
curbing 233
curfew 138, 151
Curtin, Andrew Gregg 98–99, 101
customs 5, 7, 9–10, 14, 60, 210
Customs House 10, 79, 210

Daily Exchange 68, 110, 113, 131, 165–166
Daily Exchange and Gazette 110
Dallas Street 244
Dan River Valley 215
Danville, Virginia 107, 212, 214–215, 218–219, 249
Dare 203, 249
Davies, Harry W. 85–86, 96
Davis, Judge David 102
Davis, Jefferson 83, 87, 110, 113, 192, 199, 201, 203, 205–206, 208–209, 212, 214, 275–276
Davis, John W. 59–60, 112, 114–115, 148–152, 155, 160, 162, 171, 174–175, 177, 182, 185–186, 198
Davis Street 86
death 2, 3, 10, 26, 34, 37, 47, 49, 72, 80, 82, 106, 110, 117, 123, 126, 133, 150, 188, 191, 200, 232–235, 237, 239, 251ch1n1, 253n18, 274n51
debridement 229
Declaration of Independence 97
Defenders' Day 12
De Lagnel, Captain 192
Delaware 200
Democrat 5–6, 10–11, 45, 49–50, 53, 55, 60, 65, 69, 79, 95–96
Democratic Conservative 227

Democratic National Convention 65
Department of Annapolis 141–142
Department of Health 230
Department of Maryland 142
Department of State 145, 150, 174
Department of War 145
depot 63, 75, 85, 88–90, 94, 102–103, 105, 110, 114, 117, 121, 133, 156, 194
Deptford Fire Company 29, 39, 244
deputy marshal 61, 148
derail 78, 113
derby 44
despot 168, 196, 204
detective 78–80, 84, 86, 88, 97, 100, 106–107, 156, 165, 214
detriment 134, 220
Detroit 199
Der Deutsche Correspondent 220
devaluation 223
Devine Being 73
DeVoe, Eli 97
devotion 1, 70, 218, 227, 233–235, 239
diarrhea 175
diatribe 196
Dimick, Col. Justin E. 172, 184–189, 191–192, 194
disability 101, 206, 210, 228
discipline 28–29, 43, 58, 62, 66–68, 142, 235, 236
disease 34, 167, 180, 188, 222, 229–230, 232–234, 236; cutaneous 176, 188; neurologic 230
disorganizer 227
distiller 200–201
distributor 200
district 4, 7, 12, 38–42, 45, 58, 63, 79, 103, 108–109, 116, 132, 140, 143, 149, 156–158, 195, 198, 219, 244, 273n23
Dix, Dorothea 75–78, 97, 107
Dix, Maj. Gen. John Adams 142–143, 150–151, 153, 161–162, 165–168, 182, 191, 193–194
"Dixie's Land" 110
Dobbin, George W. 64, 124, 130, 132–133, 135, 157, 169, 198, 264n92
Dobbin, Robert A. 9
docket 153, 217
Dodge, George R. 154
dog bite 228–230
dog's death 26, 253n18
Donegana Hotel 201
Dorchester County 12, 69–70
double file 114
Double Pumps 44, 46
double time 114
Douglas, Stephen 55, 68, 245
Douglas (Douglass) Street 3, 21, 246–247
Draper, Simeon 94
Driscoll, Kenny 10
dropsy 232, 274n41

Droste, William Henry 214
Druid Hill Avenue 245
drum 110, 138, 156, 189
Drury, Old 18
Duke Pescara 74
Dunn, George R. 100–101
Dutchman 38

Eagle Artillery 29, 30, 32, 148, 241–242, 265n149
Earl of Richmond 20
Early, Gen. Jubal 214
Eastern Gulf Blockading Squadron 200
Eastern Shore 12, 49, 69–70, 112
economy 2, 45, 69, 71
Edgerton, Gen. Charles C. 233
editor 60, 110, 121, 144, 150, 157, 162, 164–167, 171, 228, 265n130, 268n77
Egerton, Philip A. 31
Eggleston, Benjamin 171
Ehrman, John 121
Eighth New York 140
Election Day 46–47, 52, 56, 66
Electoral College 86
Eleventh Regiment of the Massachusetts Volunteers 205
Ellsworth, Col. Elmer Ephraim 74
Elzey, Col. Arnold 207–208
Emancipation Proclamation 71
embargo 178
embarrassment 104, 221
emblem 55, 151
engine, engineer 13–14, 38, 40–43, 89, 99, 113, 124, 151, 222–224, 229
England 33, 150, 190–191, 202, 226
enigma 1, 200–211
ensign 29, 141
Ensor Street 244
envelope 135, 151, 178
epidemic 5, 61
Episcopal 175, 228
Episcopal Methodist 228
epithet 196
equipment 28, 40–43, 58, 62, 153, 209, 213, 238
Erebus 204, 272n47
escort 1, 75, 85, 94–95, 98–99, 102, 104–105, 114, 137
espantoon 50, 58
espirit du corps 205
Essex County, Massachusetts 111
Establishment Act 155
ethnic 29, 44, 220
Eutaw House Hotel 17, 35–36, 94, 102–104, 119–120
Eutaw Infantry 242–243
Eutaw Street 90, 92, 94, 96, 102, 244
ex officio 59, 60, 62, 152, 230, 232
ex-parte 128, 193
Ex parte Merryman 128
Exchange Hotel 7, 17
Exchange Place 7, 14, 247

execution 67, 190, 197, 210, 221, 224, 239, 244
exercise 54, 152, 161, 171–172, 175, 177, 181, 183, 189–190
Exeter Street 19–21, 23, 252ch3n7
expedition 199, 203

faint 227
Fair Daughters of Erin 34
farewell 20, 22, 73, 185
Farmers and Planters Bank of Baltimore 155
fatigue 65, 212, 230
Faulkner, Mr. 181
fault 1, 64, 221, 234–235, 272n84
Fawn Street 114
Fayette Street 14, 18, 80–81, 109, 222, 245, 251n7
Federal Hill 139–141, 146, 245
Fells Point 241, 244–245
Fells Point Eagle Artillery 241
Fells Point Hose & Suction Company Fire Company 244
felon, felony 41, 67, 174
Felton, Samuel Morse 75–79, 85–86, 97–98, 100–101, 122
Fernandina 79
Ferrandini, Cipriano 79, 82, 84, 87, 106, 258n15, 259n58
ferry 27, 77, 89, 128
ferrymen 27
fever 5, 167, 175–176, 188, 199, 204, 210, 212, 226, 276; ship 5
fidelity 219, 221, 235, 239
Fifteenth Ward 10–11
Fifth Cavalry Regiment 30
Fifth Regiment 235, 241, 265n149
Fifty-third Infantry 32
Fifty-third Maryland Militia 32
Fifty-third Regiment 30, 32, 242, 244, 254ch4n7, 254ch4n9, 259n58
fighting 11, 13, 32, 38, 40, 42–43, 45, 50, 116–117, 123, 135, 160, 204–206, 211, 220
Fillmore, Millard 5, 6, 11, 50–51
firefighter 2, 40–41
Firemen's Insurance Buildings 225
fireplug 40
firework 66
First Baltimore German Guards 30, 241, 243
First Baltimore German Riflemen 242, 244
First Baltimore Hose Company Fire Company 39, 42, 244
First Baltimore Invincibles 30, 242, 243
First Baltimore Light Infantry 241, 243
First Baltimore Sharp-Shooters 242
First Branch 5, 6, 10, 42, 131, 191, 223, 225, 232, 267n48
First Light Brigade 31, 244
First Light Division 30–31, 244

First Maryland Infantry Battalion 154, 207
First Maryland Regiment of Light Artillery 31
First Regiment of Pennsylvania 112
First Rifle Regiment 31, 241
first Southern soil 95
Fish, William S. 143
Fish, Col. William Stebbins (Provost Marshal) 198
Fisher, Lieutenant 128
flag 88, 97–98, 110–111, 114, 122–123, 138–139, 141–142, 151, 168, 206, 262n19
Flannegan, Andrew 36
flask 156
Fleet Street 39, 244–245
flint 156, 255n4
flooding 222–223, 229
Florida 200
flour 9, 13–14, 60, 138
flower 180–181
Foley, the Rev. John 235
Follansbee, Capt. Albert S. 115–116, 120
Folsom, de Francias 59, 275
football 190
Ford's Theatre 16
Forrest, Edwin 24, 275, 253n13
Fort Caswell 203
Fort Columbus 163–165, 171, 177, 182–183, 185, 248
Fort Diamond 172
Fort Hamilton 163–165, 170–172, 176, 180–182, 268n8
Fort Jay 164–165, 182
Fort Lafayette 163–166, 168–186, 189–190, 197, 248, 268n8
Fort McHenry 5, 68, 119, 126, 128, 140–142, 144, 146, 148–149, 152, 157, 162–163, 165–169, 171, 175, 178, 190, 197, 248
Fort Sumter 88, 214
Fort Warren 25, 155, 158–159, 163, 165, 168, 172, 174, 178, 181–182, 184–197, 200, 205, 211, 248
Fortress Monroe 162, 168, 171, 190, 206, 209
fortune-teller 62
fountain 9–10, 33, 255n4
Fountain Inn 17, 33
Fourth Avenue 180
Fourth Regiment of Pennsylvania 112
Franciscus, George Charles 98–100
Frank Leslie's Illustrated Newspaper 146–147, 154
Frank Leslie's Popular Monthly 21, 252ch3n7
Franklin Fire Company 39, 245
Franklin Fire Insurance Company 226
Franklin Street 92, 103
Frederick, Maryland 121, 132, 141, 158, 160–161, 164, 268n77
Frederick County 69, 121, 267n77

Frederick Street 244
freedom of the press 165
Freemason 259*n*45
Fremont, John C. 50–51
French 32, 62, 189–190
French Lady 150, 201
Frick, William 18
Friendship Fire Company 38–39, 43, 244
Front Street 18
Front Street Theatre 16, 18
fruit 164, 180–181, 200
funeral 29, 45, 191, 211, 235, 237, 251*ch1n*1

Gallant Fire Company 42
Gallows Hill 154
gambling 11, 45, 62, 64, 83–84, 173, 220
Gambrill, C.A. 191
Gambrill, Henry Clay 45–46
gang 35, 38–41, 44–51, 53–55, 58–60, 62, 67, 80, 91, 255*ch7n*4
Garrett, John Work 6, 9, 125, 133, 135
Garrett, T.E. 100
Gatchell, William H. 59–60, 114, 148–152, 155, 160, 162, 171, 177, 182, 185, 193–194
GATH 212, 271*n*18
Gay Street 7, 9, 19, 53, 113, 244
Gelston, Mrs. George S. 172, 180–181, 268*n*8
Gelston, George Sears 180
Gelston, Hugh 181
Gelston, Maria Antoinette (Meinell) 180
General Assembly 30, 98, 139, 161–162
General Orders 141, 167, 206, 208
George P. Kane's Fire Insurance Agency 226
George Peabody 171
George W. Webb & Company Jewelers 218
Georges Island 184
Georgia 188, 216, 226, 230, 249
germ warfare 88
German 27, 30, 35, 44–45, 49, 69, 118, 220, 241–244, 248, 253*n*1
German Guards (First Baltimore German Guards) 30, 241, 243
German Street 4, 248
German Yeagers (German Schwarz Yeagers, Independent German Yeagers) 30, 242–243
Gettysburg Compiler 104
Gibbons, James, Archbishop 235, 237
Gifford, Thomas 61, 148–149, 262*n*49
"Gift Concert" 215
Giles, William F. 117, 159, 198
Gill, John 3
Gilsey, Mrs. 172
Gittings, Gen. John Sterrett 6, 95–96, 99, 102, 104, 218
Gittings Mansion 96, 99, 102–104

Gleeson, William E. 98
Glenn, William Wilkins 165–166
glomerulonephritis 234
glove 62
goats 162
Godefroy, John Maximilian Maurice 7
Good Shepherd 237
goose 210
Gordon, Josiah 189–190, 267*n*77
Gough Street 244
Gould, Charles 106
Governor of Maryland 2, 31, 70, 87, 108–109, 124, 221
Governor of Virginia 71, 207
Governor's Island 177, 182
Graceland Cemetery 80
grading 233
Grafton 125
Granby Street 244
Grand Charitable Presentation Concert 216
grand jury 64, 116, 121, 158–159, 162, 174, 178, 220
grand marshall 5
Grant, Gen. Ulysses S. 208–209
grate 234
Graves, Mrs. 175
Great Hall 215
Great Lakes 201, 203
Greeley, Horace 104
Greeley Club 226
Green, Charles 192
Green Street 74, 245
Greenback Labor Party 234
Greenmount Avenue 4, 13, 111, 143
Greensboro 212–214, 249
Gregg, Gen. John 211
grenade 66, 78
Griffith, Anna (Ann, Annie) 12, 237, 251*ch1n*1
Griffith, John 70, 191, 245, 251*ch1n*1, 257*n*4
Griffith, Mary 12, 70
gristmills 14
grocery, grocer 3, 4, 6–7, 246–247
groggery 63
Guilford Avenue 34
Gulf of St. Lawrence 213
gunboat 201, 203, 210
gunpowder 77, 118–119, 128, 138, 157
Gunpowder River 77, 128
Gurley, William H.F. 213
gutter 114, 234
Guy, William 35, 79–80, 226
Guy's Monument House Hotel 17, 35, 79–81, 226

habeas corpus 2, 128, 139, 145, 150–151, 161, 174, 179–180, 188
hack 45
Hagerstown, Maryland 204, 268*n*77
hairdresser 82
Halifax 199, 201–204, 249
Hall, Andrew J. 186

Hall, Thomas W., Jr. 77, 110, 162, 165, 168, 171, 177, 182, 185, 194, 268*n*77
Hall's House Hotel 17
Hallwig, Oscar 236
Haman 178
Hamilton, Canada West 199, 210
Hampden 13
Hance, James 10
handshake 83
"hangers-on" 40
Hanover Junction, Virginia 208
Hanover Street 3–4, 11, 35, 83, 244, 246
Harbor Basin 79
Harford County 19–20, 69, 89
Harford County Academy 20
Harford Turnpike 6
Harkersville 6
Harper's Weekly 52, 117, 143–144, 173
Harris, J. Morrison 14, 132
Harris, Thomas C. 226
Harris Creek 128
Harrisburg, Pennsylvania 72, 74–75, 86, 89, 92, 95–103, 105, 109, 128, 130, 134–135, 137
Harrison, William G. 168, 194
Harrison, William Henry 5
Harrison Avenue 189
Harrison Street 215, 245
hats: brown felt 99; plug 44; Scottish plaid 99; slouched 75; stovepipe 99; top 99
Hatteras 181
Havana, Cuba 83
Havre de Grace 77, 86, 89, 112, 115
Hawley, Seth C. 174 191
Hay, John 109, 122, 277
Hazzard, Capt. George Washington Whitfield 74–75, 78
health 5, 33, 61, 148–149, 167, 176–177, 180, 183, 192, 200, 228–233, 239, 243
Heaven 181, 205
Heiskell, J. Monroe 223
helmet 44
"Here's Yer Mule" 215
Herndon, William Henry 78
Herring, Benjamin W. 58–59, 62
Hewitt, John Hill 16, 18
Hibernian Corps of Union Greens 34, 241
Hibernian Free School 34, 36
Hibernian Infantry 34, 241
Hibernian Society (Hibernian Society of Baltimore, Benevolent Hibernian Society) 24, 33–37, 41, 226, 231, 235, 241, 259*n*58, 276
Hicks, Thomas Holliday 55, 70–71, 78, 87, 92, 108–113, 122–127, 129–133, 139, 141, 144, 155, 160–161, 164, 264*n*92
High Street 19, 244
Hill, Mr. 88
Hill Street 245

Index

Hillen Street 222, 260n78
Hilliard, Otis K. 84, 86–87
Hinds, Samuel 58, 155
Hinks, Charles Dent 54, 59, 60, 112, 148–149, 152, 155
Hinks, Samuel 50
Hitselberger, the Rev. A.L. 189
Holiday 252ch3n4
Holliday Street 18–19, 22, 24, 111, 132, 154, 215, 233, 248
Holliday Street Theatre 16, 18–19, 22, 24–25, 252ch3n4
Holt, Joseph 150
Home Guard 138, 265n149
homeless 45, 57
Homewood Park 234
honesty 54, 57, 61–62, 78, 194, 233–234
Hooper, James 191
Hopkins, Francis 180
Hopkins, Johns 6, 9, 13, 18, 22, 91
horse 4, 91, 101, 113–114, 128, 138, 156, 167, 212, 218, 242, 255ch7n4
hose 38–41, 43, 244–245
hospital 47, 68, 82, 182, 186–188
"Hospital for Sick Patriotism" 68
hotel 7, 16–17, 35–36, 78–79
Hough, Robert 205
house, gaming 64
House of Refuge 63
Howard, Charles 16, 18, 59–60, 64, 67, 114, 137–138, 148–149, 150–152, 155, 157, 160, 162, 165, 171, 177–179, 182, 185, 194, 198, 264n99
Howard, Frank Key 150, 162, 164–165, 167–168, 171, 175, 180, 182, 184–187, 194, 268n77, 276
Howard, Joseph 85, 88, 96
Howard, William Key 18
Howard Athenaeum and Gallery of Arts Theatre 23–24
Howard Fire Company 39, 245
Howard House Hotel 17
Howard of New Orleans 88
Howard Street 78–79, 90, 92, 244, 260n78
Howe, Dr. Samuel G. 187
Hughes, Anna 86
Hughes, John 31
Hull, Robert 194
Hunter, Charles R. 211
Hunter, Maj. David 74
Hutcheson 79–80
Hutchinson, John H. 79–80

Illinois 1, 72, 199
immigration 1–2, 27, 29, 33–36, 44–45, 49, 57, 69, 238
Imperial Fire Insurance Company 226, 248
imprisonment 35, 64, 146, 150, 160, 167, 175, 177, 182, 189–190, 196, 198, 238, 259n58
improvement 9, 15, 58, 221–223, 232
impulsiveness 234

inauguration 1, 11, 68, 71, 76, 78, 82–83, 85, 94, 104, 106, 119, 229–230
incendiary 14
incognito 75, 89, 105
income 6, 57, 63, 153
Independence Hall 97–98
Independent (political party) 10–11
Independent Blues 30, 241, 243
Independent Fire Company 29, 39, 41–42, 235, 244
Independent German Yeagers 242
Independent Greys (Independent Grays) 29, 31, 116, 135, 207, 241, 243–244, 265n149
Independent Light Dragoons 29, 242, 244
Indianapolis 72
indictment 116–117, 158, 193, 198
indigestion 229–230
indigo 82
indisposition 107, 176, 219, 228
industry 71, 215
infantry 28, 32, 34, 88, 118, 131, 140, 154, 177, 205, 207, 213, 241–244, 259n58, 265n149
infirm 138, 175–176, 205, 210
inmate 167–168, 171–172, 175, 177, 180–181, 184–186, 190, 192, 200, 210
Inner Harbor 3, 6, 70, 79, 166
inspector general 87, 206
insurance 14, 38, 225–226, 248
insurrection 79, 117, 139–141, 150, 158, 161, 179, 191, 244
invasion 28, 139–140, 244
Iowa 199
Ireland 3, 27, 33–36, 44–45, 69, 118, 202, 226, 235
Irish Social and Benevolent Society 35
irritation 221
Italy 82, 84, 190
itinerary 73–74, 86

Jackson, Stonewall 1
Jackson Guards 241, 244, 265n149
Jackson Hall 156
James, Jesse 83
James McCormick's Saloon 35
Jeffers, James 63–64
Jeffers, Madison 63–64
Jenkins, Hugh 9, 34
Jesuit 88
Jesus 236–237
Johannes, Capt. John G. 128
Johnson, Andrew 217
Johnson, Bradley T. 121, 132, 142, 144, 158, 207–208
Johnson, Reverdy 18, 264n92
Johnson, William B. 220
Johnson's Island 199–203, 209–210, 249
Johnston, Dr. John M. 42
Jones, David 222

Jones, Col. Edward F. 112, 116, 120, 148
Jones, William Henry 215
Jones Falls 13–14, 215, 221–224, 233, 273n19, 273n22
Jones Falls Commission 220–222, 225, 229
Jones House Hotel 98
Jones Leaf Tobacco Warehouse 215
Jones Town 222
Joseph Whitney 171
Josselyn, Capt. F.R. 205
Judd, Norman B. 86, 88, 96–97, 102
Judge Advocate General 150
juggler 62
Junior Artillerists (Junior Artillery) 30, 241, 243, 265n149
jury 64, 116, 121, 158–159, 162, 174, 178, 193, 220
"J.W.B." 213

Kane, Ann C. (Anna, Annie) 12–13, 245–247, 251ch1n1
Kane, Clara 145
Kane, Elizabeth 145
Kane, James M. 251ch1n2
Kane, John J. 251ch1n2
Kane, John K. 3, 246–247, 251ch1n1
Kane, Maj. John M. 3
Kane, M. John 251ch1n1
Kane and Polk 3, 246
Kansas 12
Keilholtz, Otis 230–232
Kemble Company 18
Kemp, Edward 247
Kenly, Brig. Gen. John Reese 30, 141, 147–149, 152–155
Kennedy, Anthony 132, 160
Kennedy, John A. 97, 105–107
Kenney, Henry F. 100–101
Kensington Street Station 97
Kent County 268n77
Kentucky 71, 175
kerbing 233
Key, Francis Scott 12, 166
Key West 200, 249
kickback 229
kidney 229, 234
Kirk, [Samuel] 42, 181, 269n50
knife 55, 74, 88, 97, 99, 101, 107, 230; Bowie 83, 101; dirk 50, 156
Knights of St. Patrick 226
Knights of the Golden Circle 79–80, 82–84, 275–277, 258n28, 259n45
Know-Nothing Party 10–11, 45, 47, 49–51, 53–55, 58–60, 69, 178, 227
knuckles, brass 50, 99, 107
Konig, George 114, 262n49

labor 57, 63–64, 69, 82, 131, 176, 185, 201, 215, 227, 233–234
ladder 38, 42, 44, 50, 245, 265n149

Lafayette Guards 241, 244
Lafayette Hose Fire Company 245
Lafayette Light Dragoons 242, 244
Lafayette Volunteers 242
Lake Erie 199–200
Lake Roland 128
lameness 228, 230
Lamon, Ward Hill 74, 84, 98–101, 104, 106–107
lamp 57, 231, 233
Lane, Joseph 65, 84
Latrobe, Benjamin Henry 7, 223, 227
Latrobe, Benjamin J., Jr. 222
Latrobe, Ferdinand Claiborne 227, 229–230, 234
Lavender Hill 6
Law Grays (Law Greys) 135, 207, 241, 244, 265n149
Lawrence, Massachusetts 118
Laws of Humanity 180
lawyer 2, 14, 51–53, 97, 117, 121, 123, 150, 156–157, 159, 169, 191, 198, 204, 221, 267n48, 273n98
Lazaretto Point 5
Lecompton Constitution 12
Lee, Gen. Robert E. 205–206, 208–209, 214, 275
Leech, R.A. 211
Legislature of Virginia 216
letter 14, 26, 51, 53, 88, 105–107, 119, 122–124, 131–132, 141, 144–145, 148–149, 151, 153, 157, 160, 171, 174, 176–182, 187, 189, 196, 206–209, 211–213, 220–221, 238, 264n99, 272n84, 273n98
Lewis, Enoch 99–100, 126
Lexington Street 244–245, 260n78
Libby Prison 205, 249
liberty 35, 149, 158, 173, 190, 196, 209, 259n45
Liberty Fire Company 39, 244
Liberty Party 49
"Liberty Speech" 215
Liberty Street 35, 244, 260n78
lieutenant 29–30, 58, 61, 78, 128, 147–148, 155, 170, 175, 177, 179, 201–202, 205, 207
Light Street 3, 4, 33, 115, 245–247
Light Street Wharf 246–247
Ligon, Thomas Watkins 11–12, 31, 50–52
limber 155–156
Lincoln, Mary 98, 102–104, 107, 218, 260n118
Lincoln, Robert 102, 104
Lincoln, Thomas ("Tad") 102, 104
Lincoln, William ("Willie") 102, 104
liquor 64–66, 83, 139, 153, 166, 172, 200–201
litmus test 162
Litzenburg, John 101
Lockwood's Folly 203, 249
locomotive 89, 91

Locust Point 140, 144
loiterer 63
Lombard Street 7, 9, 35, 47, 79, 83, 244
Long Island 170, 180
lottery 96
Low Street 18
Lowe, Andrew 192
Lowe, Enoch Louis 87, 123, 126
Lowell, Massachusetts 112
Lower Manhatten 182
Loyal, Lt. B.P. 202
Luckett, James H. 84, 105
Luckitt 84
lumber 224
lunatic 175
luxury 145, 173–174, 180, 197
Lyons, Lord Richard B.P. 131, 150

Macgill, Dr. Charles 171, 185, 194, 204–205, 268n77
Mactier, Samuel 116–117
Madison Street 222, 235
magistrate 59, 64, 230
mail 27, 165, 189
malaria 167, 175–176
Mallory, Stephen Russell 201
Maltby Hotel (Maltby House) 17, 83
Mann's Hotel 17
Mansfield, Brig. Gen. J.K.F. 149
march 27, 29–30, 32, 85, 108, 110–116, 118, 123–124, 131–135, 138, 140, 151, 185, 210, 237–238
mare 218
Marie Victoria 213
Marine Avenue 180
Marion Rifle Corps 241, 244
Market House 244
Market Space 246
Market Street 30, 39, 98, 100, 244–245
marksmanship 27, 29
Marriott, William H. 5
Marshall, Judge William L. 98–99
martial law 118, 143, 145, 151–152
Martin, Ellen 202
Martin, Margaret 211
Martin, Mary Ann 201–202
Martin, Patrick Charles 25–26, 83, 200–203, 210–213, 271n14, 271n15, 272n84
Martin & Carroll 201
Martin, Belt & Co. 201
Martinsburg, West Virginia 228
martyrdom 227
Mary Provost's Theatre 25
Maryland (ferry) 77, 89, 128
Maryland Cadets 241, 243
"Maryland Club" 215
Maryland General Assembly 139, 161
Maryland Guard Battalion Company 32, 128
Maryland Guards 31–32, 125, 135, 207, 241, 265n149

Maryland House of Delegates 124, 189
Maryland Institute 215, 220
Maryland Institute College of Art 78, 215, 260n78
Maryland Legislature 9, 55, 109, 139, 150, 160–161, 164, 168, 175, 180, 268n77, 268ch13n7, 275, 277
Maryland Line 107, 205–208, 213, 265n149
Maryland Line CSA 207
Maryland Militia 11, 27, 30–32, 141, 244
Maryland Penitentiary 154
Maryland Regiment 31, 206, 209
Maryland Senate 130, 161, 267n77
Maryland State Constitution 60
Maryland Volunteers 31, 146, 259n58
Mason-Dixon line 69
Masonic Temple 227
Massachusetts Regimental Marching Band 115, 118
Massachusetts Sixth Infantry 140
Massachusetts Sixth Regiment 1, 111–112, 119–120
Master of Transportation 124
"masterly inactivity" 70
match 59, 156
Matchett Baltimore Directory 30
mattress 168, 185, 188
May, Henry 157, 162, 168, 171, 182, 268n77
Mayor Latrobe 229–230, 234
mayoralty 53, 68, 227–228, 230, 233
McAllister, Robert A. 31
McCahn, Daniel 30
McClellan, Maj. Gen. George B. 153, 161–162, 165–166, 169
McClellan's Alley 244
McCuaig, James S. 203
McGonnigan 54
McKim House 143
McManus, Bernard J., Reverend 235
measles 188
Mechanical Fire Company 10, 29, 38–39, 244
Mechanical Volunteers 242–243
meerschaum 215
Melton, Samuel W. 210
Melville Bridge 128
memorial 31, 79, 151, 216
Mennonite 253n1
Menonist 27, 253n1
Mercer, Col. R.S. 130
Merchants' Exchange, Merchants' Exchange Building 6–10, 14–15, 247
Merchants' National Bank 7–9
Merrill & Thomas Manufactory 157
Merryman, Lt. John 128, 262n49
Methodist Episcopal Church South 228
Metropolitan Police

Commissioners of New York 174
Mexican War 30, 148
Michigan 199
Michigan (ship) 201, 203, 210
Middle District Police Station 156
Middlesex County, Massachusetts 111
Miles, Dr. Francis Turquand (professor) 230–234
"milk diet" 232
mill 13–14
Milwaukee 199
Minié 156
minister 27, 34, 150, 180–181, 189, 228
Minor, Lt. Robert D. 202–203
"Minute Men" 111
Missouri 71
Mitchell, John 10
mobtown 56–57, 62, 89, 220
mold, bullet 156
money 12, 15, 36, 111, 126, 155, 170, 172, 174, 178, 185–187, 197, 199, 210, 216, 218, 234
Montgomery, Alabama 82
Montgomery County 69, 135
Montgomery Guards 29, 31, 241, 244
Montreal 199, 201–203, 210–213, 248–249, 277
Monument House 35, 79–81
Monument Square 54–55, 65, 79, 85, 122
Monument Street 11, 79, 222
Monumental Hose Fire Company 39, 245
Monumental Rifles 241
Morris, Col. William W. 166
mortar 229
"most loyal rebel" 121
motive 71, 139, 210, 237–238
Mount Clare Railroad Station 89, 110, 260*n*78
Mount Royal Station 260*n*78
Mount Vernon Guards 241, 244
Mount Vernon Hook-and-Ladder Company 39, 44, 50, 245
Mount Vernon Railroad Station 89
Mount Vernon Square 96
Mounted Carabiners 242
Mud Theatre 18
Mudd, Dr. Samuel 211, 213
mumps 188
Munroe, James 112
Murdaugh, Lt. William H. 201
murder 26, 45, 50, 54, 57, 59, 74, 84, 87–88, 105–106, 157, 212–213, 277
Murray, U.S. Marshal Robert 182–183
music 138, 151, 205, 220; martial 138
musket 50–51, 115–116, 144, 153–157, 237

Napoleon III 84
Nassau, Bahamas 201, 203–204, 213, 249
National Blues 29–30, 242, 244
National Greys 242, 244
National Guard 219
National Guards 242–243
National Hotel 212
National Theatre 18
National Volunteers 80, 83–85, 87, 109
Navy Department 203
Needham, Corp. Sumner Henry 118, 263*n*58
New Cathedral Cemetery 237
New Gayety Theater 74
New Market (gang) 46
New Market Fire Company 29, 39, 42, 50, 244
New Orleans 6, 79, 88, 216
New York City 25, 65, 69, 72–73, 88, 97, 99, 105–106, 138–139, 150, 170, 172–175, 180, 182–183, 185, 194, 200, 210–212, 214, 248, 271*n*15
New York Daily Graphic 211–212, 272*n*84
New York Harbor 169–170, 173, 177, 179, 182, 214
New York Herald 202
New York Hotel 194
New York Seventh Regiment 126
New York Times 68, 172–173, 176, 181
New York *Tribune* 137, 197
Nicolay, John G. 102, 109, 122, 277
"nine days' wonder" 86
Ninth Regiment, Maryland National Guard 219
noblemen 204
nolo contendere 64
Norris, Richard, Jr. 119
North Carolina 201–203, 213–214, 216, 231, 264*n*100
North Street 34, 226, 244–245, 260*n*78
Northern Abolitionists 82
Northern Central Railroad 75–76, 86, 90, 92, 95–96, 99, 102, 110, 122, 125, 127–129, 130, 132, 134, 158, 260*n*78, 265*n*132
Northern Democrat 55, 245
Northern Maryland 69
"notorious traitor" 121
Nova Scotia 202
nuts 101

oath 48, 54, 62, 83–84, 125, 144, 150–153, 162, 166, 174, 182, 192, 217, 258*n*28
oath of allegiance 144, 150–151, 153, 166, 174, 192, 217
O'Brien, William Smith 35
O'Connell, P.J. 31
O'Donnell, John 33
Office of the Maryland Society 205

Ohio 72–76, 135, 150, 200, 210, 260*n*78
oil 213, 236
O'Laughlen, Michael 83
Old Frederick Road 237
Old Maryland Guard 32
Oliver, John 33–34
Oliver Hibernian School 34, 36, 226
orange 236
ordinance 41, 89, 224–225, 231, 233
ordnance .126, 172
organ 234
orphan 29, 215–216
Orsini, Felice 84
Ottawa 199
Ould, Colonel 206
overcoat 75, 99; bobtail 99
Owens' Charles Street Theatre 16–18, 20, 22–24
oyster 35, 190

Paca Street 245
paddle steamer 203
pallbearer 211
Palmer, Judge Joseph M. 98
Palmetto Guard 79, 88
Panama 201
pants 62, 118
parade 5, 27–29, 82, 94, 151, 169, 172, 184, 186, 188, 226
Paradise 237
paralysis 231–232
pardon 166, 192, 217, 237
Park Street 244
Parker House Hotel 24, 210
Parkville 6
parole 150, 182–183, 1900–194, 200
parsnip 189
passage, middle 176
password 83
Patapsco Fire Company 39, 245
Patch, William 114
Patterson, William 6
pauper 15
paving 45, 113, 116, 233
P.C. Martin & Co. 201, 203
Pegram, Colonel 192
Pemberton, General 210
Pennsylvania Railroad 98–99
Pennsylvania Regiment 146
Pennsylvania State Capitol Building 98
Pennsylvania Station 260*n*78
Pennsylvania Volunteers 134
Perryville 77, 111, 130, 132, 135, 140, 179
personality 2, 69, 84
Peters, Dr. De Witt Clinton 188
Petersburg, Virginia 204, 214
Petherbridge, Col. Edward 144
Philadelphia 20, 23, 65, 69, 72–73, 75, 77, 88–89, 93, 96–98, 100, 101, 107, 111–112, 115, 118, 125, 130, 135, 137–139, 175, 179, 200
Philadelphia, Wilmington, and

Baltimore (PW&B) Railway 75, 77, 91, 129–130
philanthropist 2, 60, 75, 238
Phillips, C.C. 30
physician 5, 27, 34, 53, 84, 102, 176, 181, 187–188, 211, 229–234
pick 50, 55, 127
pickpocket 64
Pierce, Franklin 6
Pierrepont, Edwards 193–194
pike 49, 144
pillow 171
pilot 28, 200, 203
Pinkerton, Allan 78–80, 82, 84–86, 88, 95–101, 104–105, 107, 165, 277
Pioneer Hook and Ladder Company 39, 43, 245
pirate 200–201
pistol 45, 50–51, 67, 83, 116, 155–156, 213
Pitcairn, John, Jr. 100
Pitt Street 3, 246, 251n7
Pittsburgh 3, 72, 86, 201
"places of amusement" 138
play 16, 18, 20, 22, 24, 106, 181, 189, 213, 227
Plug Uglies 44–46, 47–48, 50, 83, 92
plugs, fire 40, 234
plums 101
pneumonia 188
Poe, Edgar Allan 46–47
Point Lookout 208–209
"Points Further South" 231, 250
Poisal, Dr. John (Reverend) 228
poison 88, 210
Police Board 64–65, 148, 152, 155–156, 160
police chief 65, 95, 100, 119, 238
politician 5, 19, 28, 43, 53–54, 57, 60, 62, 98, 150, 177, 191, 222, 228, 233–234
poll-watcher 48
polling station 46–47, 50
Pope, Capt. John 74
Port of Baltimore 5, 11, 60, 247
Portland, Maine 209
posse 180
post office 8–9, 14–15, 19, 28, 233, 248
potato 172, 186, 189
Potomac River 108, 204, 207–209, 211
potter 228
Poughkeepsie 72
Pratt, Thomas George 30
Pratt Street 1, 3–4, 90, 101, 112–114, 116, 118, 244, 246
Pratt Street Bridge 113, 118
Pratt Street Riot 1, 118
prayer book 200
precaution 149–150, 176, 229
precinct 47, 56, 228
Presbyterian 3, 14, 33–34, 235–236
presentment 158, 162
president-elect 1, 65, 73–74, 76, 78–79, 85, 88, 92–104, 119, 160, 218, 238
President Street 89–92, 101, 110, 112–116, 118, 120–121, 158, 191, 194
President Street Railroad Station 89–92, 101, 110, 112–115, 118, 120–121, 158, 191, 194
Preston, William P. 123
prevarication 224
"preventive arrest" 65
Price, William 195, 198
Prime Street Station 100
Prince George's County 69
"Prince of Wales" 215
principle 6, 9, 11–12, 54, 60, 67, 97, 130, 144, 151, 189, 205, 221, 225–227, 233–234, 239
prisoner: citizen 177; combatant 184; political 150, 166–167, 170–172, 174, 177–179, 181–189, 192–193, 197; state 166, 173, 176–177, 193
privateer 172, 175
privy 187
proclamation 52, 71, 108–109, 125, 140–141, 147–148, 151, 192
professor 27–28, 230
prop 210, 213
prostitution 45, 62
prostration 176
Protestants 34, 49
Providence 122, 233
provost-marshal (provost marshal) 143, 145, 148–149, 152–154, 168, 198
publication 12, 83, 172, 178, 180197, 206, 225
publishing 73, 99, 105–106, 143, 157–158, 178, 196–197, 206, 219, 222, 224
pump 38
Purcell House 231
Puritan 257n39
PW&B 75, 86, 89–90, 98, 100–101, 109–110, 122, 125, 127, 130

Quaker 27, 253n1
quartermaster 29, 112, 135, 213
Quebec 203–204, 213, 249
Queen, Dr. William 211–213
Queen Anne's County 69
Quincey, William H. 134–135

rafter 154
Raine's Hall 227
Randall, John K. 18
Randall, Joseph K. 18
rattle 58, 153
R.E. Lee (ship) 202
real estate 14, 216, 225
rebel 53, 78–79, 84, 94, 121, 140, 146, 149, 157, 168, 170, 181, 184–185, 188, 197, 199, 201, 267n48, 275
recuperation 249–250
reenlistment 157, 206–207
Reform Acts 32
Reform Association 53–54
Reform Central Committee 54
Reform Party 49, 54–55, 229
Reformer 52–55, 228
Regimental Marching Band 115, 118
regulation 38, 58, 61, 68, 123, 173, 177–178, 186, 189, 257n39
Regulators 44, 46, 54
relapse 232
Relay House 113, 125, 128, 132, 140–141
Remie, Lt. Jacob 205
Rennert House Hotel 81
Republican 50–51, 55, 75, 85, 92–96, 98, 102, 104–105, 156, 196, 220, 228, 245
reputation 12, 40, 57, 78, 104, 197, 212, 220
resignation 30–31, 67–68, 190, 220–221, 224–225, 228–229
resolution 37, 42, 109, 148–149, 152–153, 160–162, 179, 223, 225, 231, 233–234
Revocation Act 155
Revolutionary War 27
revolver 50, 99, 101, 153, 156, 198
ribbon 153
rice 82, 171–172, 189
Richard III 20, 22, 24
Richmond 20, 22–24, 46, 84, 170, 204–209, 211–216, 218, 249
Richmond and Danville Railway 214
Richmond Dispatch 204, 218
Richmond Horse Lot 218
rifle 28–31, 45, 50, 121, 155–158, 241–244, 265n149
Rigdon, Robert 45
Riggs, Thomas 247
Rip-Raps 44, 46, 50, 54
ritual 83
Roanoke Tobacco Company 215
Robert E. Lee (ship) 202
Robinson, Dr. Alexander C. 122
Robinson, Capt. John C. 126
Rochester 72–73
Rockdale Factory, Rockdale Mill 13–14
rocket 66
Ross Street 245
Rough Skins 44, 46, 53
rowdies 80, 94–95, 143
Ruffin, Edmund 88
rule 2, 10, 14, 27–28, 40–41, 43, 45, 48, 54, 58, 63–64, 67–68, 80, 83, 88, 112, 138, 148, 150–151, 155, 177, 186, 189, 239
"rules of engagement" 87, 112
runners 40, 201, 203
Rursted, A.J. 24, 211
Ruscelli 84

sachel 212
Sacred Scripture 237
safekeeping 160
sailor's pea jacket 99
St. Alban's, Vermont 21, 199

Index

St. Augustine 237
St. Clair Hotel 17, 81
St. Georges, Bermuda 201, 204
St. Ignatius Catholic Church 235
St. John's 235
St. Lawrence Hall 210–211
St. Louis Fire Insurance Company 226
St. Louis Hotel 97
St. Martin 235
St. Mary's County 69
St. Mary's Industrial School 226
St. Mary's Roman Catholic Church 213
St. Nicholas (ship) 201
St. Patrick's Day 34–35, 226, 231
St. Paul 237
St. Paul Street 4, 35, 146, 191, 228, 233, 235, 245, 247–248
salary 155, 225, 229
salvage 14, 213
Sampson, Thomas 97
sand 113
Sanders, George N. 83, 211
Sanders, Maj. Reid 211
Sandusky 199–200, 203, 210
Sandusky Bay 203
Sanford, Edward S. 100
sarcasm 205
sausage 185
Savannah, Georgia 226
Saviour 236
scam 216
Scharf, John Thomas 39, 41, 51, 245, 277
schedule 27, 73–75, 82, 86–87, 89, 92–95, 98, 102, 117, 191, 215
Schenck, Gen. Robert C. 143, 151, 195
schoolmaster 27
schooner 213
Scott, Thomas Parkin 109, 150, 162, 165, 168, 171, 185, 189, 194
Scott, William H. 86
Scott, Gen. Winfield 77–78, 87, 97, 107, 124, 131–133, 135, 139–141, 148, 155, 161, 179–180, 182, 198, 264n100
script 213
scum 218
secession 69–71, 75, 78–80, 82–83, 85, 88, 93, 109–111, 114, 122, 138–145, 149, 151, 153–154, 157–158, 160–162, 164, 168, 181, 211, 214, 262n19
Second Branch 6, 131
Second Street 7, 14, 53, 98, 215, 225, 246
Secret Service 73, 209–210
secretary 87, 108, 111, 117, 131, 135, 147, 149, 161, 165, 167, 171, 174, 179, 182–183, 186, 189, 191, 193, 196, 198, 201, 205–210, 213, 217; private 228, 230–231
Secretary of State 131, 161, 167, 171, 174, 179, 182–183, 186, 189, 191, 196, 213, 217
Secretary of the Interior 87

Secretary of the Navy 201
Secretary of War 108, 111, 117, 131, 135, 149, 161, 165, 193, 198, 205–210
security 54, 57–58, 62, 67, 73–74, 150
Seddon, James A. 206–209
Select Committee of Five 86–87
sergeant 58, 61, 103, 172, 175, 177
sergeant of the guard 177
servant 57, 64, 70, 171, 177, 189–190, 221, 228; public 57, 228
Seward, Frederick W. 97, 161, 191
Seward, Sen. William H. 97–98, 107, 131, 145, 150, 157, 167, 174, 179–180, 182–183, 189–190, 196, 204 213, 217
sewer 190
Sharp Street 3, 4, 244, 247
Shattuck, Dr. George C. 191
shawl 99
sheep 162
Shelow, Augustus 42
sheriff 2, 18, 219–221, 238, 248
Sherwood Hotel 17
Shields Guards 29, 241, 265n149
ships: ghost 213; slave 176
shipwrights 36
shoemaker 44, 49, 55
shot 26, 45, 50, 55, 84, 88, 106, 115–117, 121, 138, 156
Shot Tower 19, 138
shotgun 45, 50, 121, 156
shovel 127
Shutt, A.P. 10
side-wheel 203
sign 30, 34, 53–54, 83, 143–144, 152, 177, 191–192, 206, 211, 224
signal 106, 125–126, 209
Signal Corps 209
Silver Street 245
Simms, Joseph 10
single file 114
Sixth Regiment of Massachusetts Volunteers 1, 111–112, 119–120
Skinner, Capt. Thomas B. 203, 262n49
slavery 1, 12–13, 49, 60, 64, 69–71, 75–76, 79, 82–83, 96, 104, 176, 192, 235, 245, 257n4, 267n48
slugshot 50, 99, 107
slungshot 50
Small, Gen. William F. 111–112
smallpox 210
Smith, Dr. Alan Pennington (professor) 230–231, 233–234
Smith, Charles Henry 234, 273n98
Smith, E. Delafield 179
Smith, John Spear 31
Smith, R. Henry 234
Smith, Samuel W. 53
Smith, William Prescott 92, 121, 124, 207, 264n92
Smith's Armory Band 204
Smith's Wharf 115
Smithville 202
snail 225

Snethen, Worthington Garrettson 93, 98–99, 156
snuffbox 218
sober 228
Somerset County 69
Sons of the Old Defenders of Baltimore 12
Sourin, Reverend Father 235
South Carolina 70, 88, 208, 217, 230–231, 249, 264n100
South Carolina Infantry Regiment 88
South Street 7, 56, 78, 84, 116
Southern Confederacy 77, 111, 113
Southern Democrat 55, 65, 69, 245
Southern Maryland 69
Southern Orphan Association 215–216
Southern Rights Club 82
Southern Rights Convention 110
"Southern soil" 69, 85, 95
Southern Volunteers 106
spantoon 58
spear 157
Special Expedition Abroad 203
specter 198
speculators 216
Sperry, William 18
"spicy debate" 224
spike 44, 157
spittoon 56
spoils 6, 228
Springfield, Illinois 1, 72–73
Spurgeon, [Charles Haddon] 175
squadron 27, 200
squib 66
stable, horse 6, 167
Stack, John 31
stage 16, 18, 20, 22, 24, 27–28, 74, 181, 210, 213
stallion 218
Stanton, Edwin M. 117, 150, 191, 193
star 12, 114, 152, 166, 168, 262n19
"Star-Spangled Banner" 12, 166, 168
State Asylum for Inebriates 219
State Board of Commissioners 55
State of Maine (ship) 185
Staten Island 170
states rights 1, 123
Staunton, Virginia 208, 216
steamer 138, 168, 171, 202–203
Stearns, George 78
Steers, Edward 87, 277
stet docket 217
Steuart, Lt. Col. George H. "Maryland" 27, 31, 126, 207, 262n49
Steuart, J.E.B. 207
Steuart, William 39
Steubenville 72
Stewart, Dr. James A. 110
Stewart, John D. 222–223
Stevens, Lieutenant 175
Stewart, Michael 4
stick 153, 229

stone 14, 45, 50, 108, 112–116, 121, 229, 234, 236, 251ch1n1, 274n51
Stone, Col. Charles P. 87, 97, 106
Stoneman 212
stool 167, 178
Stowell, William J. 121
Strawberry Alley 244
street cleaning 230, 233
stroke 231–232
stump 216
Suffolk County, Massachusetts 111
Sullivan's Island 208
Sumner, Col. Edwin V. 74, 102
supercargo 200
superintendent of arrangements 93
Superior Court of Baltimore City 60
supper 140
surgeon 126, 183, 194, 230
Surratt, John 83, 258n28, 277
Susquehanna River 75, 77, 85, 89, 106, 112, 115, 128, 132, 135
Susquehanna Terminal 260n78
Suter, James S. 14
Sutherlin, William T. 214
Swann, Thomas 42, 50–53, 58, 60, 62
sword 146, 156, 213
sympathizer 1, 82, 88, 114, 121–122, 125, 140, 142, 146, 156, 166, 199, 201, 214
sympathy 79, 94, 149, 165, 180–181, 233
Syracuse 72

Talbot County 69
"Tam o'Shanter woolen cap" 99
Tampa 200
Taney, Supreme Court Justice Roger Brooke 117, 128, 159, 198
target practice 27, 29
Tarr, Lt. Frederick 147
tavern 33, 35, 47, 132, 151
tax 2, 3, 53, 65, 70, 215, 222, 229, 233, 267n48
"TAX PAYER" 53
Taylor, H. Porterfield 218
Taylor, Levi 10
Taylor, W.H.S. 205
Taylor, Zachary 5
Taylor Building 109–110
Taylor Light Dragoons (German Taylor Light Dragoons) 242, 244
tea 186, 189, 255ch7n4
Tegmeyer, John H. 222
telegraph 33, 65, 77, 100–101, 106, 124, 128, 131, 133–135, 158, 179, 192, 213, 264n92
Tennessee 71, 201
terror 45, 55, 67, 83, 210
Thanksgiving Day 194
theatre 16–25, 51, 252ch3n4, 253n16, 260n78
thespian 16, 18
Thespian Association 18

thief on the cross 236
Third Brigade, Maryland Militia 141
Third Wisconsin Regiment 164
Thirtieth Street 4
Thirty-first Street 4
Thirty-second Street 4, 100
Thomas, Col. Francis J. 126, 207, 264n100
Thomas, Dr. J. Hanson 175, 182, 185, 267n77
Thomas, Phillip Francis 6
Thomas, Richard 150, 201, 262n49
Thompson, J. Edgar 125
Thompson, Jacob 87, 211
Thompson, Joseph 228
Tick-Tack 38
Tigers 44, 46
Tippecanoe, Old 5
Tipperary, Ireland 202
tobacco 69, 82, 168, 197, 215
Tonge, Samuel D. 13–14
Tootles 20
Toronto, Canada West 199, 211
torpedo 66
towel 167
Townsend, Col. Edward Davis 178–179
Townsend, George Alfred 212, 271n18
Towson Guards (Baltimore County Horse Guards) 128, 242
tragedian 19, 22
train, inaugural 72–73, 86, 102
traitor 84, 117, 121, 138, 140, 150–151, 154, 157, 165, 196, 267n48
"Traveling Committee of the Maryland Legislature" 180
Travers, William R. 18
Travis, Annette, Madame 86
treason 110, 117, 140, 145, 147, 149–151, 158–159, 164, 178, 190–191, 193, 195–196, 198, 217
trench 99, 187
Trenton 72
trial 2, 54, 64, 117, 128, 144, 150, 154, 159–160, 167, 178, 182–183, 188, 190, 193–198, 210, 217
trifling 224
Trimble, Maj. Gen. Isaac Ridgeway 126–128, 135, 200, 202, 222–224, 262n49, 264n99, 271n28
Trist, Nicholas Philip 77
Troy, New York 72–73
trunk 126, 174, 211, 213
tuberculosis 148, 188
Tubman, Charlotte 70
Tubman, Harriet 13
Tudor Hall 19
tugboat 119
Tunker 27, 253n1
turkey 181
Turner, William H.H. 84
Turner German Scheutzen Corps 242

turnkey 58
turpentine 127
tutor 27
typhoid fever 167, 188
typhus 5, 188
tyranny 87
Tyson, Henry 222–225

underclothing 214
Underground Railroad 13
unfit 209
uniform 227–30, 32, 41, 43, 58, 61, 63, 68, 110–111, 117, 126, 134, 153, 170, 181, 184, 213–214, 227, 243, 265n149
Union Fire Company 38–39, 244
Union Station 260n78
Union Street 245
United Hose and Suction Company 39, 42, 50, 244
United States Army 29, 97
United States Branch 226
United States Circuit Court 117, 198
U.S. Consul to Quebec 213
United States District Court 116, 158
United States Hose Company 245
United States Hotel 180
U.S. House of Representatives 228
United States Supreme Court 128, 192
"unscrupulous political knaves" 94
Utah Street 244
Utica, New York 72

vaccination 230
vagabond 62, 256n30
vagrancy 62–64, 228
Vallandigham, Clement 200
Valley of Virginia 212, 249
valuables 1709
Vermont 210
Verrazano-Narrows Bridge 170
vestibule 92, 102
Vigilant Fire Company 39, 42, 244
Virginia 23, 71, 76, 108, 121–122, 126, 138, 158, 204–205, 207–208, 212–216, 218–219, 228, 249, 259n58, 264n100, 272n84
Virginia House of Delegates 205
Virginians 207
virtue 1, 37, 220, 235, 237

Waggner, Francis 30
wagon 136, 144, 157
waiter 190
Wallace, Dr. W.S. 102
Wallack's Theatre 253n16
Wallis, Severn Teackle 18, 53–54, 123, 133, 135, 150, 162, 164–165, 168, 171, 182, 185, 194, 198, 267n71, 277
Wampanoags 44, 51
War of 1812 3, 12, 27, 79, 166

Ward, Francis X. 117
wardrobe 210, 213
warehouse 5, 126, 146, 157, 215
Warfield, Henry M. 9, 150, 162, 165, 168, 171, 177, 182, 185, 194, 228, 267n77
Warne (Waren), Kate (Kay) 80, 88, 100–101
warrant 51, 62, 153, 158, 160, 162, 166–168, 176, 204, 216
Warren, Kittie 82
Washburne, Elihu B. 101
Washington, George 34, 74
Washington Brigade of Philadelphia 111–112
Washington College Hospital 47
Washington, D.C. 1, 65, 72–74, 76–78, 84, 87–88, 93–95, 97, 99, 101, 108, 111, 128, 133, 161, 198, 212
Washington Fire Company 42, 244
Washington Guards 242, 244
Washington Hose Company 244
Washington Monument 79, 102
Washington Station 90
Watchman Fire Company 39, 245
watchmen 128
water 9, 13–14, 38, 40, 88–89, 118–119, 171–172, 175–177, 180, 185, 188, 190, 210, 222, 224, 226, 246
water-closet 190
water works 224
waterflow 225
waterfront 89, 91
Waters, James B. 42
waterway 89, 222, 224

Watson, Maj. Benjamin F. 116
Watson, William H. 148
Waverly Avenue 4
weapon 28, 30, 58, 74, 99, 109, 111, 116, 123, 125–126, 138, 143–144, 146, 152, 155–157, 160, 170, 244n100, 264n99
Webster, Timothy 85, 96
Webster House 186
Welcome (ship) 200
Wells and McComas Riflemen 29, 241, 244, 265n149
West Indies 83
West Philadelphia 98, 100–101
Western Hose Company 39, 43, 245
Western Maryland 49, 69, 144, 161
Westfield 72
wheat 14, 69, 134
Wheeler, Gen. Joseph 214
Whig 5, 6, 10–11, 47, 49–50, 55, 60, 276
whiskey 175, 190
whist 173, 189
White, John Campbell 33
whitewash 86
Whyte, William Pinkney 221
Wilkinson, Lt. John 202–203, 277
Willard Hotel 101
William Street 245
Williams, Nathaniel 18
Wilmington, Delaware 75, 77, 91, 129–130, 200
Wilmington, North Carolina 201, 203–204, 231, 249–250
Wilson, Alice 197

Winans, Ross 168, 223, 267n77
wine 143, 172, 201
Wisconsin 164, 199
witness 39, 48, 56, 62, 84, 87, 103, 119–121, 159, 168, 191–193
Wood, Lt. Charles O. 170, 172, 177, 179
Wood, General 195
Wood, Mr. 106
Wood, William S. 74, 93
Woodford, Mr. 179
Woods, Nicholas L. 155
Wool, Gen. John E. 143
Worcester County, Maryland 69
Worcester County, Massachusetts 111
working man 227
Workingman 228
wounded 3, 50–51, 115–118, 209, 215
Wright, Edmund 258n28, 277
Wright, Robert Clinton 50
Wright, William A. 204–205, 216
writ 128, 139, 161, 179–180, 188
Wynkoop, Brig. Gen. George G. 134–136, 265n135

yellow fever 199, 204, 210, 226, 276
York, Pennsylvania 76, 135, 137
York Road 4, 44, 247
York Roaders 44
Young, Bennett H. 210

Zarvona 150, 201
Zekiah Swamp 211
Zouaves 32

www.ingramcontent.com/pod-product-compliance
Lightning Source LLC
Chambersburg PA
CBHW080801300426
44114CB00020B/2783